Information Hiding

For a complete listing of titles in the
Artech House Computer Security Series,
turn to the back of this book.

Information Hiding

Stefan Katzenbeisser

Fabien Petitcolas

ARTECH
HOUSE

BOSTON | LONDON
artechhouse.com

Library of Congress Cataloging-in-Publication Data
A catalog record for this book is available from the U.S. Library of Congress.

British Library Cataloguing in Publication Data
A catalogue record for this book is available from the British Library.

Cover design by John Gomes

ISBN 13: 978-1-60807-928-5

© 2016 ARTECH HOUSE
685 Canton Street
Norwood, MA 02062

10 9 8 7 6 5 4 3 2 1

Contents

Preface

Fifteen years ago we published the book *Information Hiding Techniques for Steganography and Digital Watermarking*, which turned out to be one of first scientific books on the topic. Back then, the field was in its infancy; the scientific community had just started to explore how information could be embedded invisibly or inaudibly in multimedia data. One of the main driving forces at that time was the desire to mark images, videos, or audio files with metadata that identified either the owner or recipient of the document. Steganography also turned out to be a key technology to counter surveillance or censorship. In the early days, many designs were ad-hoc, not based on a solid mathematical theory and repeatedly broken. Furthermore, methods to detect invisible communication, commonly referred to as *steganalysis*, were in their infancy.

Today, fifteen years later, it is time again to reflect the state-of-the-art in the field of information hiding. Our community now has a solid understanding of the performance and security of information hiding techniques; we have developed a mathematical theory of steganalysis and have explored new promising application domains. The present book aims to capture the state-of-the-art in various domains that are commonly subsumed under the term *information hiding*. Each chapter is written by renowned experts in the field and aims to give a good introduction to on specific topic. We therefore hope that the book will motivate students to consider studying this field and, of course, professors to consider adding it to their curriculum.

It is our great pleasure to thank all contributors of the book. Despite their busy schedules, they managed to provide a comprehensive state-of-the-art review of their research areas. For us, it has been a pleasure to work with them. We also want to thank Aileen Storry and Helen Pain from Artech House, who convinced us to pursue this project.

Stefan Katzenbeisser and Fabien A. P. Petitcolas
December, 2015

Foreword

Most of us are familiar with cryptography as an efficient means of obscuring information: encryption scrambles (digital) messages into meaningless sequences of zeroes and ones, and only those that are in possession of the proper *key* are able to unscramble. Unauthorized users may not be able to unscramble, but they can deduce that information is exchanged between parties: in many cases the knowledge of occurrence of information exchange may be harmful (or useful, depending on your point of view), even if the content of the exchange is not known. A recent example is provided by the alleged activities of the NSA, only recording elementary metadata related to phone calls, but not the content of the calls themselves.

Information Hiding in its purest form goes one step beyond classical cryptography, and is concerned with the art and science of obscuring the fact of information exchange from unintended observers, either in transit and stored. In terms of popular cryptographic characters, Alice is sending a message to Bob, and Eve is not even aware of the information exchange. Chapter 1 of this book provides an example that goes back to antiquity, describing how Demeratus warned the city of Sparta of an imminent attack by Xerxes by hiding a message under the wax layer of a tablet. It is important to note that information hiding and classical message security are orthogonal concepts: the fact of message exchange is independent of the message being scrambled or not. In the example above, Demeratus could have chosen to scramble his message hidden under the wax layer (he did not). It follows that the notions of security are different for classical message security and information hiding: the former is concerned with the complexity of unscrambling a given cipher text in absence of a decryption key, whereas the latter is concerned with the complexity of guessing the existence of any message exchange in the first place.

This book provides the reader with an excellent overview of the state-of-the-art in Information Hiding and related technologies. It is a composed of a collection of articles by authors who are preeminent experts in their fields. In the first chapter, the editors of this book provide an introduction to the field of Information Hiding, emphasizing its key characteristics as well as differences with cryptography. This chapter also introduces the notion of watermarking as a form of information hiding with the additional constraint of robustness: the ability to withstand passive or active attacks. The authors of this book are to be lauded for clearly stating the similarities and differences of watermarking with pure Information Hiding: more often than not, these two concepts are confused in the relevant literature. What is also to be lauded is that watermarking is not immediatedly equated to copyright/copy protection.

The second chapter of this book is concerned with one of the most common methods of information hiding, viz. using multimedia (audio, images, video) as a carrier for hidden messages. In particular this chapter focusses on methods that modify the cover data for carrying messages while minimizing the statistical and perceptual impact of the modifications. The fourth chapter is concerned with hiding information in various layers of common network protocols, similarly aiming to minimize statistical impact on network traffic.

The third chapter discusses the other side of the coin. Whereas Chapters 2 and 4 take the point of view of Alice, the sender of the message, Chapter 3 focuses on Eve, and discusses steganalysis: the science of and methods for detecting (the likelihood of) the presence of hidden messages, and beyond that, (partially) reading message content. This is a fascinating expose on the continuing cat and mouse game between methods to improve secret communication and methods for detecting and breaking secret communication.

The book changes gear in Chapter 5, focusing on *robust watermarking*, the subfield of information hiding that has created the resurgence of information hiding techniques in the early 90's. Whereas Chapter 5 provides a general overview of robust watermarking, the subsequent chapters go into detail on some of the aspects that are relevant for practical applications. Chapter 6 discusses *watermarking security*, which, as noted earlier, is different from classical message security. This chapter does an excellent job in defining the notion of watermarking security, as well as stating some of the fundamental results. Chapter 7 addresses *fingerprinting*, an application of watermarking that is in active use and to which most of us have been exposed to: forensically marking of audio-visual content as rendered in a movie theater, with the purpose of tracing the source of pirated content as captured with camera and microphone. The particular challenge for fingerprinting is the possibility of many colluding (well-funded) attackers, imposing severe limits on what can practically be achieved. Chapter 8 covers *fragile watermarking* and authentication watermarking, a topic that has, undeservedly so, obtained relatively little attention in recent literature.

The last two chapters of this book cover topics that are somewhat different but still strongly related to the main topic. In Chapter 9 the authors discuss weak signatures left behind by source devices and/or processing. These weak signatures act like watermarks and, when retrieved, allow the *identification* of (classes of) source devices and/or processing steps. The final chapter of this book considers watermarking in a secure encrypted environment. This is a relatively new topic and is relevant in cases where content may not be converted to cleartext until it has been appropriately marked. Forensic marking of encrypted Blu Ray audio/video would be a primary example of such an application.

As should be evident from the description above, this book provides a comprehensive and up-to-date overview of information hiding and related techniques. The editors have done an excellent job of guaranteeing coherence between the various chapters. The authors of the various chapters, experts in their fields, have provided both breadth and depth in their well-written exposes. The end result is book that provides at the same time an holistic overview of the field, as well in depth information on the various subtopics. This book is highly recommended for both novices and experts in the field of information hiding and watermarking.

Ton Kalker
December, 2015

List of Contributors

Mauro Barni
Università degli Studi di Siena, Italy

Tiziano Bianchi
Politecnico di Torino, Italy

Rainer Böhme
Universität Innsbruck, Austria

Luca Caviglione
National Research Council of Italy, Italy

Gwenaël Doërr
Technicolor R&D France, France

Jessica Fridrich
University of Binghamton, USA

Teddy Furon
INRIA, France

Stefan Katzenbeisser
Technische Universität Darmstadt, Germany

Matthias Kirchner
University of Binghamton, USA

Huajian Liu
Fraunhofer SIT, Germany

Wojciech Mazurczyk
Warsaw University of Technology, Poland

Fabien A.P. Petitcolas
Vasco Data Security, Belgium

Alessandro Piva
Università degli Studi di Firenze, Italy

Boris Škorić
Technische Universiteit Eindhoven, The Netherlands

Martin Steinebach
Fraunhofer SIT, Germany

Andreas Westfeld
HTW Dresden, Germany

Chapter 1

Introduction to Information Hiding

Stefan Katzenbeisser and Fabien A. P. Petitcolas

In this chapter, we first give an overview of the different subdisciplines of information hiding which will be treated in more details in the subsequent chapters of this book. Subsequently, we will take a closer look at the different types of steganographic systems as well as their security properties.

1.1 A BRIEF HISTORY OF INFORMATION HIDING

The desire to send messages unbeknownst to a third party can be traced back several centuries. For example in war times, messages of strategic importance needed to be transmitted through the enemy lines; diplomatic messages needed to reach their recipient without raising suspicion of a customs agent; and messages by dissidents had to get spread without being noticed by the authorities. In recent years, steganography and related techniques were utilized for invisibly marking documents, for disguising traces of digital communication or for exfiltrating secret data out of high-security computing environments.

The most famous examples of steganography go back to antiquity. In his *Histories* [1], Herodotus (c. 486–425 B.C.) tells, for instance, how Demeratus, a Greek at the Persian court, warned Sparta of an imminent invasion by Xerxes, King of Persia: he removed the wax from a writing tablet, wrote his message on the wood underneath and then covered the message with wax. The tablet looked exactly like a blank one (it almost fooled the recipient as well as the customs men).

In 1857, Sir David Brewster, inventor of the kaleidoscope already suggested hiding secret messages "in spaces not larger than a full stop or small dot of ink" [2]. By 1860 the basic problems of making tiny images had been solved by René Dragon, a French photographer: during the Franco-Prussian War of 1870–1871, while Paris was besieged, messages on microfilm were sent out by pigeon post [3, 4]. During the Russo-Japanese war of 1905, microscopic images were hidden in ears, nostrils, and under fingernails [5]. Finally, Brewster's idea became real by World War I when messages to and from spies were reduced to *microdots* by several stages of photographic reduction and then stuck on top of printed periods or commas in innocuous cover material such as magazines [6, 7].

Invisible inks have been used extensively. They were originally made of available organic substances (such as milk or urine) and developed with heat; progress in chemistry helped to create more sophisticated combinations of ink and developer by the first World War, but the technology fell into disuse with the invention of "universal developers" which could determine which parts of a piece of paper had been wetted from the effects on the surfaces of the fibers [8, pp. 523–525]. This led to the more familiar application-specific information hiding and marking technologies found in the world of secure printing. Watermarks in paper are a very old anti-counterfeiting technique (see Figure 1.1); more recent innovations include special ultraviolet fluorescent inks used in printing traveler's checks. A comprehensive survey of optical document security can be found in [9].

A widely used method of linguistic steganography is the acrostic. The most famous example is probably Giovanni Boccaccio's (1313–1375) *Amorosa visione* which is said to be the "world's hugest acrostic" [11, pp. 105–106]. Boccaccio first wrote three sonnets—containing about 1,500 letters all together—and then wrote other poems such that the initial of the successive tercets correspond exactly to the letters of the sonnets. Another famous example of acrostic comes from the *Hypnerotomachia Poliphili* [12],[1] published in 1499. This puzzling and enigmatic book, written anonymously, reveals the guilty love between a monk and a woman: the first letter of the thirty eight chapters spelled out "Poliam frater Franciscus Columna peramavit."[2]

Expanding on the simple idea of the acrostic, monks and other literate people found ways to better conceal messages mainly into text. By the 16th and 17th centuries, there had arisen a large amount of literature on steganography and many of the methods depended on novel means of encoding information. In his 400 page

---

1   The English version of 1592 was published under title "The Strife of Love in a Dreame" in London.
2   Translated as: "Brother Francesco Colonna passionately loves Polia." Colonna was a monk, still alive when the book was published.

Figure 1.1 Monograms figuring TGE RG (Thomas Goodrich Eliensis—Bishop of Ely, England—and Remy/Remigius Guedon, the papermaker). One of the oldest watermarks found in the Cambridge area (c. 1550). At that time, watermarks were mainly used to identify the mill producing the paper; a means of guaranteeing quality. Courtesy of E. Leedham-Green, Cambridge University Archives, England. Reproduction technique: beta radiography. Reprinted from [10].

book *Schola Steganographica* [13], Gaspar Schott (1608–1666) expands the "Ave Maria" code proposed by Trithemius in *Polygraphiæ*, together with *Steganographia* (see Figure 1.3) two of the first known books in the field of cryptography and steganography. Schott also explains how to hide messages in music scores; each note corresponds to a letter (Figure 1.2). Another method, based on the number of occurrences of notes used by J. S. Bach, is mentioned by Bauer [14].

An improvement is made when the message is hidden at random locations in the cover-text. This idea is the core of many current steganographic systems. In a security protocol developed in ancient China, the sender and the receiver had copies of a paper mask with a number of holes cut at random locations. The sender would place his mask over a sheet of paper, write the secret message into the holes, remove the mask, and then compose a cover message incorporating the code ideograms. The receiver could read the secret message at once by placing his mask over the resulting letter. In the early 16th century Gerolamo Cardan (1501–1576), an Italian mathematician, reinvented this method which is now known as the Cardan grille.

Further examples come from the world of mathematical tables. Publishers of logarithm tables and astronomical ephemerides in the 17th and 18th century used

Figure 1.2   Hiding information in music scores: Gaspar Schott simply maps the letters of the alphabet to notes [13, p. 322]. Courtesy of the Whipple Science Museum, Cambridge, England.

to introduce errors deliberately in the least significant digits (e.g., [15]). To this day, database and mailing list vendors insert bogus entries in order to identify customers who try to resell their products.

Since the early 1990's, steganography mainly focused on embedding data in digital objects. Though some of the novel steganographic techniques are loosely based the above mentioned ancient ideas, the digital world forms a perfect domain for steganographic communication: for example, pixels of images can be altered, the frequency spectrum of audio signals can be changed or network transmissions can be deliberately altered. Some of these techniques will be treated in depth in Chapters 2 and 4.

1.2   DISCIPLINES OF INFORMATION HIDING

Techniques generally subsumed under the term "information hiding" serve different purposes. An important subdiscipline of information hiding is *steganography*, explored in depth in Chapter 2. While cryptography is about protecting the content of a transmitted message, steganography is about concealing the very fact that a secret communication exists at all. For this purpose, a secret message is typically

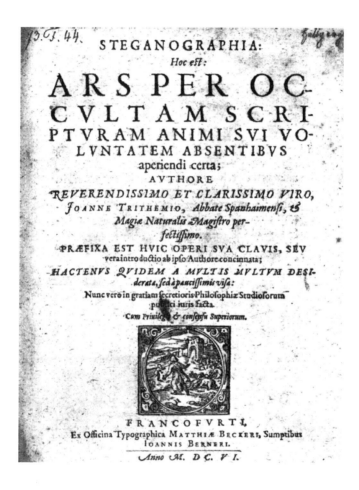

Figure 1.3   Title page of Trithemius' *Steganographia* (printed 1606 in Frankfurt, Germany). Many of Trithemius' works—including the *Steganographia*—are obscured by his strong belief in occult powers. Courtesy of H. Frodl, Austrian National Library, Vienna, Austria.

embedded in an innocuous looking one. Examples include sending a message to a spy by marking certain letters in a newspaper using invisible ink, invisibly changing the color of certain pixels in an image or adding sub-perceptible echo in an audio recording.

On the contrary, *covert channels* refer to communication paths that were neither designed nor intended to transfer information; they use entities not normally viewed as data objects to transfer information from one subject to another [16]. Covert channels have first been studied by Lampson [17], in the context of multi-level secure systems, as a means to leak information from a highly classified portion of the system to a low one. For example, one process could signal sensitive information in the timestamp attached to a file indicating its last access to a process of a lower level who has access to the same file. Some of the techniques will be discussed in the context of network steganography in Chapter 4. The central security requirement of steganography is the undetectability of the communication for a party that is not involved in the communication itself. The task of breaking a steganographic communication this way is called *steganalysis* and discussed further in Chapter 3.

In contrast to steganography, *watermarking* has the additional requirement of being robust against attackers that try to remove the hidden data (called the watermark) or make its presence undetectable. Watermarks do not always need to be hidden inside a document, as there exist proposals for visible digital watermarks [18] which overlay some sort of logo over the document itself. Nevertheless most of the literature over the last two decades has focused on *imperceptible* (invisible, transparent or inaudible) designs. In contrast to steganography, the data embedded in a document as watermark often refers to the document itself and can, for example, encode annotations, author or purchasing information. Watermarking is the main topic of Chapters 5, 6 and 10. Watermarks can also be used to provide a proof of document integrity, as discussed in Chapter 8.

Fingerprinting refers to the attempt to distinguish an individual copy of an object. In general fingerprinting can be active and passive. In the active case, a unique data item (such as a serial number) is embedded into a digital object by means of a watermarking scheme; in the passive case some features which are already present in the object are utilized for unique identification. The predominant application of active fingerprinting is tracing the distribution of digital content, which requires fingerprints to be collusion-secure: even in case an attacker has access to multiple fingerprints, he should not be able to remove marks completely. We will deal with this problem further in Chapter 7.

A topic that is narrowly related to information hiding is *information forensics*, which aims at identifying the source (such as the camera or a scanner) of a digital document or uncovering traces of modifications that were applied to the document during its lifetime. A survey of forensic techniques can be found in Chapter 9.

1.3 APPLICATIONS OF INFORMATION HIDING

Techniques of information hiding have been used in the past to solve a number of different problems. In the following we briefly mention a couple of them.

- **Hidden and unobtrusive communication** is enabled by steganographic techniques. Even if content is encrypted, traditional communication means allow to collect metadata by an attacker (e.g., who contacts whom). This metadata is valuable on its own and often utilized by the intelligence community. Steganography allows to hide the very existence of a communication, limiting the amount of available metadata. Furthermore, the hidden communication can be made hard to remove and jam.

- **Covert channels.** Information hiding techniques also form the basis of different attacks on *multilevel secure* systems, where processes and resources are assigned different security levels ranging from "low" to "high". Processes in high regions may signal classified information to low regions by means of covert channels. For example, suppose that a process acting at a high security level is able to write data onto a disk; another process, operating at a lower security level, can access the file table (i.e., the names and sizes of all files created by the other process), although it has no access to the data itself. Such a situation can lead to a covert channel: the high process can send information to the low process by choosing appropriate file names and sizes. In case data is intentionally declassified, sensitive information may be directly hidden in declassified data. For example, in *image downgrading* the most significant bits of a sensitive image can be hidden in the least-significant bits of a public image. While the public image looks innocuous, an approximation of the secret image can be reconstructed from inspecting its least-significant bits [19].

- **Subliminal channels in cryptographic schemes.** Cryptographic primitives such as digital signatures, which were never designed to transmit secret information, can be used to hide messages as well. Simmons [20] first showed that two people can communicate invisibly by exploiting randomness present in a digital signature: instead of selecting random portions truly at random, a sender can, for instance, encrypt a secret message under a shared key and use the resulting ciphertext as randomness. In case the primitive allows to reconstruct the randomness, the recipient can decode the secret message, while any adversary will be unable to distinguish between an ordinarily computed signature and one with an additional embedded message. The detection of such subliminal channels stressed the need for *subliminal free* cryptographic primitives [21], schemes which are provably free of subliminal channels. Subliminal channels are surveyed in [22, ch. 10].

- **Censorship circumvention, plausible deniability.** Information hiding techniques have been used to circumvent censorship. For example, traffic of widely used anonymization tools shows very special timing characteristics, which enables blocking of anonymized content by simple filters based on packet characteristics and timing [23]. Steganographic techniques can be utilized to evade such traffic filtering. Information hiding techniques can be also used in situations where plausible deniability is required, i.e., where a sender should be able to falsely deny that he sent or possessed a message. For example, data can be hidden in a steganographic file system [24] so that its existence is not obvious if a disk is inspected through forensic means.

- **Data infiltration.** Critical data or code can be embedded in or transformed to innocuous data or code so that it can bypass virus scanners or intrusion detection tools. For the case of executable code, obfuscation techniques, primarily developed to protect re-engineering of software products, can be used to store additional information in executable files [25]. Furthermore, the statistics of code can be altered so that it does not look suspicious [26].

- **Copyright marking.** Robust digital watermarks can help to encode the owner or originator directly into a digital object. This information can potentially be used to trace back the author or resolve ownership disputes. In order not to interfere with the visual quality, mainly invisible watermarks are utilized for this purpose. Watermarking techniques have mainly been developed for images, audio and video material. Nevertheless, marking techniques have even been proposed for formatted text: data can be stored in the size of interline or inter-word spaces [27–29]. In contrast, linguistic steganography hides data directly in text by modifying its semantics [30].

- **Automatic monitoring of copyrighted material.** Marked content can facilitate automatic tracing of copyrighted material. For example, web robots can search for watermarked content and identify its spread. Furthermore, a computer can record broadcasts of radio stations and look for marked content indicating that a particular piece of music, or advertisement, has been broadcast (broadcast monitoring). As an alternative to watermarks, robust digests (hashes) of content may be computed and compared to a database of known pieces of content; the same technique can also be used to prevent re-uploading of blocked content to a web archive.

- **Data augmentation.** Information can be added in the form of a watermark in order to annotate a digital work. The annotation can refer to work details (like the interpreter of a song) or purchasing information (nearest shop, price, producer, etc.). This enables new business models, e.g., someone listening to the radio in a car could simply press a button to order the music which is currently aired. Hidden data can also be used to index pictures or music tracks in order to provide more efficient retrieval.

- **Tamper proofing.** The information hidden in a digital object can be a signed digest of the document itself. In case a document is modified, the hidden data can be extracted to verify document integrity. In some constructions, the hidden data even provides information at which position the tampering occurred. This application will be detailed in Chapter 8.

1.4 TYPES OF STEGANOGRAPHY

In 1984 Simmons [31] introduced a model for invisible communication, called the "prisoners' problem": Alice[3] and Bob are arrested and are thrown in two different cells. Both want to develop an escape plan, but unfortunately all communication between them is intercepted by a warden named Wendy, who *passively* monitors messages sent by all prisoners. If she notices any suspicious behavior (including the use of encryption techniques), she will place Alice and Bob in solitary confinement and thus suppress the exchange of any further messages. Therefore, to successfully devise an escape plan, Alice and Bob must communicate invisibly in order not to arouse Wendy's suspicion.

A practical way to do so is to hide a meaningful secret message in some harmless piece of data, called *cover*. The resulting data object, which has both an

---

3   In the field of cryptography, communication protocols usually involve two fictional characters named Alice and Bob. The standard convention is to name the participants in the protocol alphabetically (Carol and Dave often succeed Alice and Bob in a multiperson protocol), or with a name whose first character matches the first letter of their role (e.g., Wendy the warden). We will follow this convention in this book.

overt and a covert semantic, is called *stego-object*. The recipient can finally extract the secret message from the stego-object; this can typically be done without having access to the original unmodified cover—we speak of a *blind* extraction process. (Some authors proposed *non-blind* techniques as well, where the recipient indeed has to have access to the original cover or some data derived from it; but these techniques are less favorable in practice, as either both parties need to share access to a pool of covers or the covers in use need to be transmitted securely).

To fool Wendy, stego-objects need to "look identical" to covers both for a human and a computer that is looking for suspicious statistical patterns. In other words, Wendy should not be able to decide whether the sender is actively embedding secret messages in covers or whether he only transmits ordinary covers — she should be unable to distinguish cover-objects from stego-objects. In a more advanced setting, Wendy may even change the information that is transmitted between Alice and Bob; in this case we call the attacker *active*. We discuss security issues in Section 1.5.

The model described above is generally applicable to many situations in which invisible communication takes place. Alice and Bob represent two communication parties who want to exchange secret information invisibly. The warden, Wendy, represents an eavesdropper who is able to read and probably alter messages sent between the communication partners.

In the literature, three types of steganographic protocols are discussed: *pure steganography*, *secret key steganography*, and *public key steganography*. We briefly describe all three types in the following sections.

1.4.1 Pure Steganography

We call a steganographic system that does *not* require the prior exchange of some secret information (like a stego-key) *pure steganography*. Formally, the embedding process can be described as a mapping $E : C \times M \rightarrow C$, where C is the set of possible covers and M is the set of possible messages. The extraction process consists of a mapping $D : C \rightarrow M$, extracting the secret message out of a cover. We furthermore require that $E(m, c)$ is perceptually similar to c. Both sender and receiver have access to a "custom" embedding and extraction algorithm, that is assumed not to be known by the attacker.

Theoretically, the cover set C could consist of any computer-readable data type— such as image files, digital sound, or written text, — that two communication partners would be able to exchange without raising suspicion. In practice, however, not all data can be used as cover for secret communication, since the modifications employed in the embedding process should not be visible to anyone not involved in the communication process. This requires the cover to contain sufficient redundant data, that can be replaced by secret information. due to measuring errors, any data, that is the result of some physical scanning process will contain a stochastic component called *noise*. Such random artifacts can be used for the transmission of secret information. In fact, it turns out that noisy data has advantageous properties in most steganographic applications; if it is possible to code the secret information in such a way that it is indistinguishable from true random noise, and if the noise component in a cover can be replaced by such an encoded message, it will be difficult for an attacker to detect the modification.

The simplest way of hiding information in a sequence of binary numbers (such as pixels of a digital image or samples of an audio file) is to replace the least significant bit (LSB) of every element with one bit of the secret message m. Because the size of the hidden message is typically much smaller than the number of available bits, the rest of the LSB can be left unchanged. Since flipping the LSB of a byte (or a word) only means the addition or subtraction of a small quantity, the sender may assume that the difference will lie within the noise range and that it will therefore not be generally noticed. We now know that this reasoning is flawed (see Chapter 3), as the embedding does not respect statistical dependencies between cover bytes. Indeed, LSB embedding is known to be secure only for low embedding rates (i.e., stego systems that replace a small fraction of all available LSBs).

In contrast to the embedding approach mentioned above, stego-objects may also be directly generated for the sole purpose of using them in a steganographic setting. Such approaches have predominantly been used in the context of data hiding in natural language texts. For example, Wayner [32, 33] uses context-free grammars (CFG) to create cover-texts and chooses the CFG productions according to the secret message that is to be transmitted. Thus, the secret information is not embedded in the cover, the cover itself (actually, the way it has been produced by a CFG) represents the secret message. If the grammar is unambiguous, the receiver can extract the information by applying standard parsing techniques. For example, the SpamMimic [34] application uses this approach to disguise a secret message as spam mail.

Although steganography is different from cryptography, we can borrow some wisdom from the latter. In 1883, Auguste Kerckhoffs enunciated the first principles of cryptographic engineering, in which he advised that, during the design of a cipher, one must assume that the encryption algorithm itself is known to the opponent and that security should only rest on the choice of a (secret) key [35].

Since then, the history of cryptology has repeatedly shown the folly of "security-by-obscurity"—the assumption that the enemy will remain ignorant of the system in use. Applying this wisdom to the case of steganography entails that we should analyze the security of a stego-system under the assumption that the interceptor, Wendy, knows the embedding and extraction functions E and D. Clearly, pure steganography, which, by definition, does not rely on keys, is insecure under this assumption; Wendy may apply D to every intercepted cover and check for suspicious messages. To counter this threat, some steganographic methods combine cryptography with steganography; the sender encrypts the secret message prior to embedding with a pure stego-system. However, this does not necessarily yield to a secure stego-system; encryption of the secret message just makes its decoding hard, while it does not necessarily have an influence on Wendy's ability to distinguish covers from stego-objects.

1.4.2 Secret Key Steganography

With pure steganography, no information (apart from the functions E and D) is required to start the communication process; the security of the system thus depends entirely on its secrecy, which clearly violates Kerckhoffs' principle. Secret key steganography attempts to remove this problem by assuming that Wendy knows the algorithm Alice and Bob use for information transfer, but parameterizes them with a secret (called a stego-key) that was previously shared between the communication partners. The security of a secret key steganographic system thus entirely rests on the secrecy of the stego-key.

The secret-key steganographic channel is illustrated in Figure 1.4. Alice, who wants to share a secret message m with Bob, randomly chooses (using a private random source r) a harmless cover c which can be transmitted to Bob without raising suspicion, and embeds the secret message into c by using a stego-key k. This way, Alice obtains a stego-object s. This must be done in a very careful way, so that a third party — knowing only the apparently harmless message s — cannot detect the existence of the secret. After transmission over the channel, Bob can reconstruct m because he knows the embedding method used by Alice and has access to the stego-key k used in the embedding process. Anyone who does not have access to the stego-key k should not be able to obtain evidence of the embedded information. Again, the cover c and the stego-object s need to be perceptually and statistically similar.

Returning to the example mentioned before (LSB embedding), one can easily turn LSB embedding into a secret-key steganographic system; instead of using

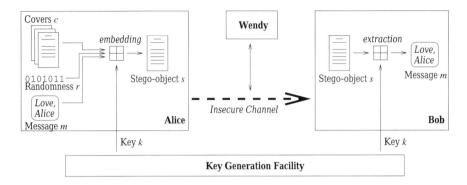

Figure 1.4 Secret-key steganographic channel: Alice randomly chooses a cover c using her private random source r and embeds the message m in c using a stego-key k that she shares with Bob, creating the stego-object s, which she then passes on to Bob. Bob reconstructs m with the stego-key k.

every cover-element for information transfer, one can select only some elements in a pseudo-random manner according to the stego-key for embedding and leave the others unchanged. Alternatively, all cover-elements can be permuted pseudorandomly before embedding [36]. During detection, the key is used to determine the embedding locations or the embedding permutation.

Note that in the previous simple construction, the embedder did not pay attention to the statistical properties of the cover (such as the distribution of LSBs in the cover). If the embedder dramatically changes these characteristics, a passive attacker may exploit this fact and break the system. To avoid such an attack, some researchers proposed to first *model* the cover-characteristics and subsequently use the model to selectively change the cover so that the differences are least pronounced [37]. Such steganographic systems are called *adaptive*; in general, adaptive steganography is hard to achieve, as setting up a realistic model is not an easy undertaking, and the whole strategy has the inherent danger that an attacker with greater resources and a willingness to spend more time on the problem is able to deduce a better model, which he can use to detect patterns encoded in the cover by the unsophisticated model the sender used.

1.4.3 Public Key Steganography

As in public key cryptography, public key steganography does not rely on the exchange of a secret stego-key. Public key steganography systems enable the use of two stego-keys, one private and one public. Whereas the public stego-key is used in the embedding process, the private stego-key is used to reconstruct the secret message.

The construction of practical public key steganographic systems seems to be challenging. Historically, [38, 39] proposed the first construction that is based on the fact that the decoding function D in a pure steganography system can be applied to any cover c, whether or not it already contains a secret message (recall that D is a function on the entire set C). In the latter case, a random element of M will be the result, which we will call "natural randomness" of the cover. To construct the scheme, Alice encrypts her message using the Bob's public key in order to transform it into a seemingly random stream of bits. Subsequently, she chooses a random cover and embeds the message using a pure steganographic system, thereby replacing some of the "natural randomness" in the cover. Bob, who cannot decide a priori if secret information is transmitted in a specific cover, will suspect the arrival of a message and will simply try to extract the randomness from the cover and decrypt it using his private key. If the cover actually contains information, the decrypted information is Alice's message. If the encrypted embedded message is indistinguishable from the natural randomness, Wendy will be unable to detect the steganographic communication.

Another construction principle in public key steganography systems is rejection sampling, which is at the core of [40]. Instead of taking a cover and embedding a message, covers are repeatedly sampled from a set of possible covers; the sampling procedure is continued until a cover that already contains the desired message is found. That is, a cover c is randomly chosen by Alice so that $D(c) = m$ holds without any active embedding process. Again, if $D(c)$ follows the same distribution as a transmitted message, the scheme can be considered secure.

The two proposed approaches were shown to work in theoretical settings. Up to now, it is an open research question as to how to construct practical and secure public key steganographic systems.

1.5   SECURITY OF STEGANOGRAPHIC SYSTEMS

The security of steganographic systems can be defined in terms of different attacker models that describe the influence of an attacker on ongoing steganographic communication. As seen above, passive attackers simply observe the communication and do not interfere with transmission of messages, while active attackers alter covers sent over communication links or impersonate a communication partner. Typically, steganographic systems are designed with passive attackers in mind.

1.5.1 Passive Attackers

A passive attacker simply observes the communication between two parties and faces the problem of deciding whether one particular cover contains a hidden message or not (in mathematical terms, he either has to support or reject the hypothesis that a given cover carries a secret message). Note that a steganographic systems must already be considered broken if an attacker can correctly make this choice with a large probability, even if he cannot decode the hidden message itself. We stress that detecting the presence of a hidden message and its decoding are two completely orthogonal problems; it may be possible that detection is easy (due to the use of an improper steganographic embedding algorithm), while decoding is hard (due to the use of state-of-the-art encryption).

For example, in the field of network steganograpy it is common practice to change the content of optional fields in order to transmit information. Neverthelss, as shown by Murdoch and Lewis [41], the content of these fields may follow certain non-uniform distributions; simply replacing them with random data makes the steganographic transmission highly detectable. Thus, the distribution of cover messages plays a very important role in judging the success rate of an attacker.

Security of steganographic systems against passive attackers can be evaluated in two different ways. First, practical steganalysis tools were developed in the last few years; these tools can provide some statistical evidence (mainly through machine learning techniques) that a secret message has been embedded in a certain cover. This research field is surveyed in Chapter 3. If a novel steganographic system resists the state-of-the-art steganalysis tools, we can claim that it is steganographically secure in practice. Secondly, one can attempt to define a mathematical model of steganographic security, and can subsequently formally prove that a certain scheme provides this security property; this approach follows the common trend in cryptography towards provable security. Such security models can either be formulated in terms of information theory, where they provide security independent on the computional power of an attacker (unconditional security) or in terms of complexity theory. A common example of the former is the definition of steganographic security given in [42], which requires the distribution of covers to be identical to the distribution of stego objects (thus, the Kullback-Leibler divergence between the two distributions must be zero, see Section 2.5). Examples of the latter are [43] and [40], which build on the framework of provable security in cryptography. The main drawback of these formal definitions is that (up to now) none of the practical steganographic systems can be proven secure; this is in stark contrast to cryptography, where provably secure and practical encryption schemes are known. Most constructions that can be proven steganographically-secure follow the general approach of rejection sampling mentioned above; covers are repeatedly sampled until they intrinsically contain the steganographic message. Due to these insufficiencies, in practice, the first approach to empirically evaluate steganographic security is typically chosen.

1.5.2   Active Attackers

Active attackers are able to change a cover during the communication process; Wendy could capture one stego-object sent from Alice to Bob, modify it and forward the result to Bob. Typically, one assumes that an active attacker is not able to change the cover and its semantics entirely, but only makes minor changes so that the original and the modified stego-object stay perceptually or semantically similar.

Most of the current steganographic systems are not designed with active attackers in mind. For example, for simple schemes, an attacker may simply add random noise to the transmitted cover, change its format, or apply other signal processing operations to destroy the embedded information.

Schemes that provide security against active attackers need to be *robust* so that the embedded information cannot be altered without making drastic changes to the stego-object. Typically, there is a trade-off between robustness and security: the more robust a system will be against modifications of the cover, the less secure it can be, because robustness is typically achieved by redundant information encoding that will degrade the cover heavily and possibly provide a steganalyst hint towards embedded data. Thus, many practical steganographic systems are designed to be robust only against a specific class of distortion (e.g., JPEG compression/decompression, filtering, addition of white noise, etc.).

Generally, there are two approaches in making steganography robust. First, by foreseeing possible cover modifications, the embedding process itself can be made robust so that modifications will not entirely destroy secret information. A second approach tries to reverse the modifications that have been applied by the attacker to the cover, so that the original stego-object can be restored. Both methods will be explored in the context of digital watermarks in Chapter 5.

The holy grail of steganographic systems that are secure against active attackers is supraliminal channels, first proposed by Craver [44]. If we assume that an active attacker can only make minor changes to a stego-object, then every cover contains some sort of perceptually significant information that cannot be removed without entirely changing the semantics of the cover. By encoding a secret message in a way that it forms such perceptually significant parts of a cover, information can be transmitted between two communication partners with high integrity. Implementing such a supraliminal channel thus requires one to be able to generate "perceptually significant" cover components from a secret message through a special generation function; subsequently, once extracted from the cover, these components need to be decoded to the secret message again. Implementing supraliminal channels is an active field of research (e.g. see [45] or [46]).

References

[1] Herodotus, *The Histories*, London, England: J. M. Dent & Sons, Ltd, 1992.

[2] Brewster, D., "Microscope," in *Encyclopædia Britannica or the Dictionary of Arts, Sciences, and General Literature*, Vol. XIV, Edinburgh, IX—Application of photography to the microscope, pp. 801–802, 8th ed., 1857.

[3] Hayhurst, J., "The Pigeon Post into Paris 1870–1871," 1970. `http://www.cix.co.uk/~mhayhurst/jdhayhurst/pigeon/pigeon.html`.

[4] Tissandier, G., *Les merveilles de la photographie*, Boulevard Saint Germain, Paris, France: Librairie Hachette & Cie, VI—Les dépêches microscopiques du siège de Paris, pp. 233–248, Bibliothèque des merveilles, 1874.

[5] Stevens, G. W. W., *Microphotography—Photography and Photofabrication at Extreme Resolutions*, London: Chapman & Hall, 1968.

[6] Hoover, J. E., "The Enemy's Masterpiece of Espionage," *The Reader's Digest*, Vol. 48, May 1946, pp. 49–53. London edition.

[7] Newman, B., *Secrets of German Espionage*, London: Robert Hale Ltd, 1940.

[8] Kahn, D., *The Codebreakers—The Story of Secret Writing*, Scribner, 1996.

[9] van Renesse, R., *Optical Document Security*, Artech House, 2004.

[10] Petitcolas, F. A. P., R. J. Anderson, and M. G. Kuhn, "Information Hiding—A Survey," *Proceedings of the IEEE*, Vol. 87, No. 7, 1999, pp. 1062–1078.

[11] Wilkins, E. H., *A History of Italian Literature*, London: Geoffrey Cumberlege, Oxford University Press, 1954.

[12] Anonymous, *Hypnerotomachia Poliphili: The Dream Battles of Polia's Lover*, 1st ed., 1499.

[13] Schott, G., *Schola Steganographica*, Jobus Hertz, printer, 1680.

[14] Bauer, F. L., *Decrypted Secrets—Methods and Maxims of Cryptology*, Berlin, Heidelberg: Springer-Verlag, 1997.

[15] Wagner, N. R., "Fingerprinting," in *Symposium on Security and Privacy*, IEEE Computer Society, 1983, pp. 18–22.

[16] Kemmerer, R. A., "Shared Resource Matrix Methodology: An Approach to Identifying Storage and Timing Channels," *ACM Transactions on Computer Systems*, Vol. 1, No. 3, 1983, pp. 256–277.

[17] Lampson, B. W., "A Note on the Confinement Problem," *Communications of the ACM*, Vol. 16, No. 10, 1973, pp. 613–615.

[18] Braudaway, G. W., K. A. Magerlein, and F. Mintzer, "Protecting publicly-available images with a visible image watermark," in *Proceedings of the SPIE Vol. 2659, Optical Security and Counterfeit Deterrence Techniques*, 1996, pp. 126–133.

[19] Kurak, C., and J. McHugh, "A Cautionary Note on Image Downgrading," in *Computer Security Applications Conference*, San Antonio, Texas, USA, Dec. 1992, pp. 153–159.

[20] Simmons, G. J., "The Subliminal Channel and Digital Signatures," in *Advances in Cryptology, Proceedings of EUROCRYPT '84*, Vol. 209 of *Lecture Notes in Computer Science*, Springer, 1985, pp. 364–378.

[21] Desmedt, Y., "Subliminal-Free Authentication and Signature," in *Advances in Cryptology, Proceedings of EUROCRYPT '88*, Vol. 330 of *Lecture Notes in Computer Science*, Springer, 1988, pp. 22–33.

[22] Young, A. L., and M. Yung, *Malicious Cryptography. Exposing Cryptovirology*, Wiley, 2004.

[23] Weinberg, Z., et al., "StegoTorus: a camouflage proxy for the Tor anonymity system," in *Proceedings of the 2012 ACM Conference on Computer and Communications Security (CCS'12)*, ACM Press, 2012, pp. 109–120.

[24] Anderson, R. J., R. M. Needham, and A. Shamir, "The Steganographic File System," in *Proceedings of the Second International Workshop on Information Hiding (IH'98)*, Vol. 1525 of *Lecture Notes in Computer Science*, Springer, 1998, pp. 73–82.

[25] Schrittwieser, S., et al., "Covert Computation — Hiding Code in Code Through Compile-time Obfuscation," *Computers & Security*, Vol. 42, 2014, pp. 13–26.

[26] Wu, Z., et al., "Mimimorphism: A New Approach to Binary Code Obfuscation," in *Proceedings of the 17th ACM Conference on Computer and Communications Security (CCS'10)*, ACM Press, 2010, pp. 536–546.

[27] Brassil, J., N. F. Maxemchuk, and L. O'Gorman, "Electronic Marking and Identification Techniques to Discourage Document Copying," in *Proceedings of INFOCOM'94*, 1994, pp. 1278–1287.

[28] Low, S. H., N. F. Maxemchuk, and A. M. Lapone, "Document Identification for Copyright Protection Using Centroid Detection," *IEEE Transactions on Communications*, Vol. 46, No. 3, 1998, pp. 372–383.

[29] Maxemchuk, N. F., "Electronic Document Distribution," *AT&T Technical Journal*, September/October 1994, pp. 73–80.

[30] Bennett, K., "Linguistic Steganography: Survey, Analysis and Robustness Concerns for Hiding Information in Text," Technical Report CERIAS Tech Report 2004-13, Center for Education and Research in Information Assurance and Security, Purdue University, 2004.

[31] Simmons, G. J., "The Prisoners' Problem and the Subliminal Channel," in *Advances in Cryptology, Proceedings of CRYPTO '83*, Plenum Press, 1984, pp. 51–67.

[32] Wayner, P., "Mimic Functions," *Cryptologia*, Vol. XVI/3, 1992, pp. 193–214.

[33] Wayner, P., "Strong Theoretical Steganography," *Cryptologia*, Vol. XIX/3, 1995, pp. 285–299.

[34] "SpamMimic," http://www.spammimic.com.

[35] Kerckhoffs, A., "La Cryptographie Militaire," *Journal des Sciences Militaires*, Vol. 9, Jan. 1883, pp. 5–38.

[36] Aura, T., "Practical Invisibility in Digital Communication," in *Information Hiding: First International Workshop, Proceedings*, Vol. 1174 of *Lecture Notes in Computer Science*, Springer, 1996, pp. 265–278.

[37] Sallee, P., "Model-Based Steganography," in *Digital Watermarking, Second International Workshop (IWDW 2003)*, Vol. 2939 of *Lecture Notes in Computer Science*, Springer, 2004, pp. 154–167.

[38] Anderson, R. J., "Stretching the Limits of Steganography," in *Information Hiding: First International Workshop, Proceedings*, Vol. 1174 of *Lecture Notes in Computer Science*, Springer, 1996, pp. 39–48.

[39] Anderson, R. J., and F. A. P. Petitcolas, "On The Limits of Steganography," *IEEE Journal of Selected Areas in Communications*, Vol. 16, No. 4, 1998, pp. 474–481.

[40] Ahn, L. V., and N. J. Hopper, "Public-Key Steganography," in *Advances in Cryptology-EUROCRYPT 2004*, Vol. 3027 of *Lecture Notes in Computer Science*, Springer, Springer, 2004, pp. 323–341.

[41] Murdoch, S., and S. Lewis, "Embedding Covert Channels into TCP/IP," in *Information Hiding — 7th International Workshop, Proceedings (IH'05)*, Vol. 3727 of *Lecture Notes in Computer Science*, Springer, 2005, pp. 247–261.

[42] Cachin, C., "An Information-Theoretic Model for Steganography," in *Information Hiding — Second International Workshop, Proceedings (IH'98)*, Vol. 1525 of *Lecture Notes in Computer Science*, Springer, 1998, pp. 306–318.

[43] Katzenbeisser, S., and F. A. P. Petitcolas, "Defining Security in Steganographic Systems," in *Proceedings of the SPIE Vol. 4675, Security and Watermarking of Multimedia Contents IV*, 2002, pp. 50–56.

[44] Craver, S., "On Public-Key Steganography in the Presence of an Active Warden," in *Information Hiding: Second International Workshop*, Vol. 1525 of *Lecture Notes in Computer Science*, Springer-Verlag, Berlin, Germany, 1998, pp. 355–368.

[45] Li, E., and S. Craver, "A Supraliminal Channel in a Wireless Phone Application," in *Multimedia and Security Workshop (MM&Sec'09), Proceedings*, ACM Press, 2009, pp. 151–154.

[46] Crawford, H., and J. Aycock, "Supraliminal Audio Steganography: Audio Files Tricking Audiophiles," in *Information Hiding: 11th International Workshop (IH 2009), Proceedings*, Vol. 5806 of *Lecture Notes in Computer Science*, Springer, 2009, pp. 1–14.

Chapter 2

Multimedia Steganography

Andreas Westfeld

The idea behind multimedia steganography is to have a part of the cover that is practically indistinguishable from randomness. This part is replaced by an encrypted, hence random-looking message. From the resulting stego-data, the intended recipient can extract the secret message correctly.

Which elements are indistinguishable from randomness, depends on the measures taken.

1. At first glance, the seemingly random part can be replaced by a random-looking message. The random part of a cover, however, is hard to find. Virtually all steganalytic results (see Chapter 3) stem from the fact that the attacker can easily find a deviant model that was not taken into account while embedding. If this irrelevant data were easily determined, engineers would have removed it already in order to save bandwidth, and, if necessary, would replace it by randomness after transmission (like, for instance, the film grain in high-definition television, which is filtered out before transmission and artificially generated at the receiver again). So, the part that is easily determined as randomness or irrelevance is rarely available for steganography because it is not transmitted.

2. Most multimedia data is quantized. Every quantization entails quantization distortion, even if the irrelevance was filtered out beforehand. The steganographer can try to model this quantization distortion and exploit it for embedding. On the other hand, the adversary has an opportunity to wait for the steganographer's choice of model and to select their own model afterwards. Hence,

steganography succeeds only if the steganographer can foresee the model of possible adversaries or work with sufficient minimum distance for security reasons.

2.1 MULTIMEDIA COVERS

Steganography needs a plausible cover. Most multimedia data (digital audio, video, text) is addressed to humans. The aim of steganography is the transmission of secret information embedded undetectably into cover data. A third party should not be able to tell whether a covert communication is present at all aside from the plausible, overt one.

The expression of reality is too complex to be observed exactly. Hence, most multimedia data consists of samples (e.g., pixels in spatial domain, audio samples in time domain). For example, digital images are restricted in several ways. The luminance (brightness) is a continuous function of light emitted from a surface per unit area in a given direction. It is:

- Discretized—measured at an equidistant grid;

- Quantized—mapped from a continuous set of values to a countable set I; with

- Limited amplitude;

- The color, which is a continuous function of wavelength, is either ignored (grayscale images) or mapped to distinct components of intensities (red, green, and blue in true color images) or even further quantized to a limited set in a predetermined color table (index color images).

So, we have approximate samples (quantization noise), a limited range of values, and restricted resolution. The human eye permits a further reduction of color resolution. In color JPEG images, the intensities are separate for chrominance, the difference between luminance and selected color components (red, blue).

Digital audio data is sampled by similarly restricting a continuous function, which is usually converted by a microphone and defined as the difference between the instantaneous pressure at a point in the presence of a sound wave and the static pressure of the medium.

2.1.1 Notation of Covers

Covers $\mathbf{x}$ consist of n elements $x_i \in I$ (e.g., the intensity or a color component of a pixel in spatial domain or quantized audio samples in time domain). If spatial

Figure 2.1 An image, cut to blocks of 8×8 pixels (left), and DCT basis images (right).

location matters (e.g., to address the local surrounding of pixels in 2D images with n_1 lines and n_2 columns), we denote the image by an $n_1 \times n_2$ matrix $\mathbf{X} = (x_{u,v})$. For the sake of brevity, we assume that n_1 and n_2 are multiples of 8.

2.1.2 Side Information of Covers

Side information is information about the cover that is not part of the cover itself. It is available to the sender only, who gains it by using an information-reducing preprocessing function between the cover source [1] (or precover [2]) $\mathbf{S}$ and the cover $\mathbf{X}$. Examples for such preprocessing functions include the quantization after reducing the sampling rate in the time domain, the image size in the spatial domain, or the information loss during JPEG compression to the frequency domain.

2.1.3 JPEG Covers

JPEG is a format for lossy compressed images that is used by most digital cameras. It is based on the discrete cosine transform (DCT), which represents a number of pixels by the same number of frequency coefficients. The DCT has excellent compaction for highly correlated pixels. It concentrates the information on a few coefficients. The remaining coefficients are very small and quantized to zero, with insignificant visual effect. JPEG has a typical compression ratio of $10 : 1$, which is controllable by a quality factor.

Figure 2.1 shows an example image of an old traffic sign with a smiling car and a biker above. For JPEG compression, the source image $\mathbf{S}$ is split to blocks $\mathbf{S}^{(b)}$ of 8×8 pixels. The block no. 56 with the biker's head is framed. Each block consists of 64 pixels, which are processed by the DCT.

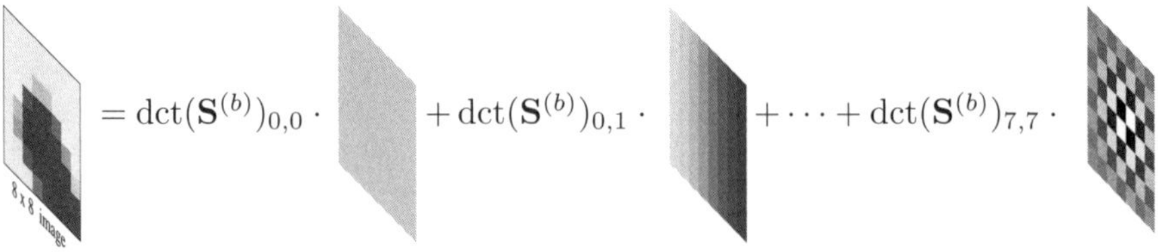

$$= \text{dct}(\mathbf{S}^{(b)})_{0,0} \cdot \quad + \text{dct}(\mathbf{S}^{(b)})_{0,1} \cdot \quad + \cdots + \text{dct}(\mathbf{S}^{(b)})_{7,7} \cdot$$

Figure 2.2   Block with the head of the biker ($b = 56$), represented by a series of DCT basis images.

$$\text{dct}(\mathbf{S}^{(b)})_{u,v} = \frac{1}{4} w_u w_v \sum_{i=0}^{7} \sum_{j=0}^{7} \cos \frac{(2i+1)u\pi}{16} \cos \frac{(2j+1)v\pi}{16} s_{i,j}^{(b)} \qquad (2.1)$$

where

$$w_k = \left\{ \begin{array}{ll} \frac{1}{2}\sqrt{2} & \text{for } k = 0 \\ 1 & \text{for } k > 0 \end{array} \right.$$

The DCT subbands $(0,0), \ldots, (7,7)$ are indexed by u and v. The resulting 64 raw DCT coefficients $\text{dct}(\mathbf{S}^{(56)})$ are real numbers and represent the biker's head by a linear combination (Figure 2.2) with the 64 DCT basis images. There are basis images (Figure 2.1, right) for all DCT subbands with raising horizontal and vertical frequencies together with their combinations. The subband $(0,0)$ is called the DC subband; while all others are AC subbands because they have signs of contribution in common with a direct or alternating current (flowing in one direction only or reversing its direction at regular intervals, respectively).

A great deal of information is lost during the quantization step. Given an 8×8 quantization matrix $\mathbf{Q}$, the 64 DCT coefficients of each block are first divided by a DCT subband specific value

$$\dot{x}_{u,v}^{(b)} = \frac{\text{dct}(\mathbf{S}^{(b)})_{u,v}}{q_{u,v}} \qquad (2.2)$$

and then rounded and limited to 11 bit integers in $I_{i11} = \{-1024, \cdots, 1023\}$: $\mathbf{X}^{(b)} = [\dot{\mathbf{X}}^{(b)}]$. All blocks of DCT coefficients can be arranged to correspond to the spatial image $\mathbf{S}$ in a rectangular matrix $\mathbf{X}$, respectively $\dot{\mathbf{X}}$. The (nonrounding) function j maps the whole image $\mathbf{S} \mapsto \dot{\mathbf{X}}$. Its counterpart j^{-1} does the inverse (using the inverse blockwise DCT) *without* rounding and limiting to unsigned bytes $I_{u8} = \{0, \cdots, 255\}$.

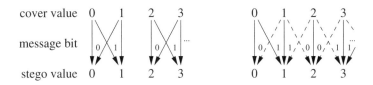

Figure 2.3 Binary embedding by LSB replacement (left) and LSB matching (right).

2.2 POPULAR EMBEDDING OPERATIONS AND BUILDING BLOCKS

Embedding operations change an element x_i of the cover to represent a message symbol m_j. Let emb be the embedding operator, producing a stego value, and ext its corresponding extraction operator, interpreting a cover or stego value as a message symbol:

$$y_i = \text{emb}(x_i, m_j) \tag{2.3}$$
$$m_j = \text{ext}(y_i) \tag{2.4}$$

In the binary case, these message symbols are bit values $\{0, 1\}$, which seems to be natural for digital operations (see Section 2.2.1). Sometimes q-ary symbols $m_j \in \{0, 1, \cdots, q - 1\}$ are embedded (see Section 2.2.3). Prior to embedding, the message may be optimally coded (compressed) or encrypted in order to provide an extra level of security. Note that the cover elements are not necessarily consulted in the order in which they appear in the file or stream. Permutative straddling permits an even distribution of the embedding changes over the cover independent from the capacity consumed by the message. Without the straddling key, the actual steganographically used places are indistinguishable from those that are unused.

2.2.1 LSB Replacement

In the simplest case, the least significant bit (LSB) of a cover element x_i is replaced by a message bit m_j (Figure 2.3). To achieve this, x_i is first rounded down to a multiple of 2 and then incremented by m_j, yielding the corresponding stego element y_i. This is probably the oldest and most widespread digital embedding operation.

$$\text{lsb}(x_i) = x_i \bmod 2 := \begin{cases} 0 & \text{if } x_i \text{ is even} \\ 1 & \text{if } x_i \text{ is odd} \end{cases} \tag{2.5}$$
$$y_i = x_i - \text{lsb}(x_i) + m_j \tag{2.6}$$

The message is extracted by concatenation of $\text{lsb}(y_i)$.

Because of its least significance, the bit replacement operation has almost no influence on the fidelity of **y** to **x**. Nevertheless, this operation has a clear effect on the histogram shape. Assuming encrypted, independent, and identically distributed message bits, pairs of values (even values and their successors) have a tendency to equalize their frequency.

2.2.2   LSB Matching

As with LSB replacement, LSB matching modifies a cover element x_i so that its least significant bit is equal to the current message bit m_j. Hence, there is no difference in the way of message extraction. However, the LSB is not simply replaced. Note that $\text{lsb}(x_i + 1) = \text{lsb}(x_i - 1)$. In case $\text{lsb}(x_i)$ differs from m_j, a coin is flipped. Depending on the outcome of the coin toss, x_i is incremented or decremented by 1, respectively. This avoids the aforementioned tendency to equalize frequencies [3].

We have to take care with saturated values. For example, the cover used in Figure 2.3 (right) has nonnegative values only. A zero value cannot be decremented. The only option to change $\text{lsb}(0)$ is to increment it. Compared with LSB embedding, this operation is only slightly more complicated.

2.2.3   Ternary Embedding and Beyond

There are three options to change x_i by at most 1 (incrementing, decrementing, and leaving it unchanged). If we interpret the *least significant ternary digit* of a cover or stego value—using the function $\text{lstd}(\cdot)$—as message symbol (using a base of three), we can substitute the coin flipping with extra information that is carried to the recipient:

$$\text{lstd}(x_i) \quad = \quad x_i \bmod 3 \tag{2.7}$$
$$y_i \quad = \quad x_i + 1 - \text{lstd}(x_i + 1 - m_j) \tag{2.8}$$

For example, if we want to embed $m_j = 0$ into a mid-gray pixel value $x_i = 128_{10} = 11202_3$ we increment, yielding $y_i = 129_{10} = 1121\underline{0}_3$. For $m_j = 1$, we yielded $y_i = 127_{10} = 1120\underline{1}_3$, while we left the pixel unchanged for $m_j = 2$. Thus, we can embed $\log_2 3$ bits per pixel, which is an increase of 58.5%, but also a rise in the change density of 33.3% (2/3 changes per pixel instead of 1/2 on average) compared to binary embedding.

The message is extracted by concatenation of $\text{lstd}(y_i)$. However, we have to once again use caution with saturated values. Some options are (1) to allow a change distance larger than ± 1; (2) to ignore saturated cover elements during extraction at the receiver side and embed the message symbol that was lost before (shrinkage), repeatedly until a nonsaturated value is produced (e.g., F5 [4]); or ideally (3) to foresightedly encode the message to render repetitions of message bits unnecessary [5] (e.g., nsF5 [6]).

LSB replacement, LSB matching, and the ternary case share the same small maximum change difference $|y_i - x_i| \le 1$. Giving up this limitation allows for symbols to use a greater base. Pentary embedding, for instance, offers five options to change x_i (-2, -1, ± 0, $+1$, and $+2$). The *least significant pentary digit* of cover or stego values is determined using the function $\text{lspd}(\cdot)$:

$$\text{lspd}(x_i) \quad = \quad x_i \bmod 5 \qquad (2.9)$$
$$y_i \quad = \quad x_i + 2 - \text{lstd}(x_i + 2 - m_j) \qquad (2.10)$$

2.3 MINIMIZING EMBEDDING IMPACT—A SEPARATION PRINCIPLE

Most practical methods for multimedia steganography make efforts to reduce an embedding impact that more or less depicts the steganalytic detection abilities of its particular time. Beginning with fidelity aspects of the modified cover (LSB replacement, LSB matching) over the number of changes (matrix encoding [4]) and distinguished classes of altered positions in the cover (dry and wet, see Section 2.4.1), today the embedding impact is usually captured by a nonnegative additive distortion measure d. The embedding algorithm should find one of the stego data $\mathbf{y} \in Y_{\mathbf{m}}$ that communicates a given secret message $\mathbf{m}$ (2.11), while achieving the minimal value of d (2.12) [7]:

$$Y_{\mathbf{m}} \quad = \quad \{\mathbf{y} | \mathbf{m} = \text{ext}(\mathbf{y})\} \qquad (2.11)$$
$$\text{emb}(\mathbf{x}, \mathbf{m}) \quad = \quad \operatorname*{argmin}_{\mathbf{y} \in Y_{\mathbf{m}}} d(\mathbf{x}, \mathbf{y}) \qquad (2.12)$$

Distortion measures are subject to permanent revision and seem appropriate for a limited time, being a prominent research goal in information hiding. Hence it was a breakthrough when Fridrich and Filler introduced a way of separating an embedding method into the distortion measure (or cover model) and the actual coding part that is used in a practical implementation [8]. As a result of their work, steganographic algorithms can be improved by using better coding or by using a better cover model. With *syndrome trellis coding*, we have an embedding efficiency that is close to the theoretical bound even with nonuniform costs ρ_i (see Section 2.4). Detailed investigation and analysis of a cover model is possible without any coding by simulation. The coding is imitated by changing (i.e., applying the embedding operation, see Section 2.2) at each position with its corresponding probability p_i. With l being the length of the message **m** in bits, the probability p_i is given by:

$$p_i \;=\; \frac{1}{1 + e^{\lambda \rho_i}} \quad \text{where } \lambda \text{ is numerically obtained from} \qquad (2.13)$$

$$l \;=\; \sum_{i=1}^{n} \left(p_i \log_2 \frac{1}{p_i} + (1 - p_i) \log_2 \frac{1}{1 - p_i} \right) \qquad (2.14)$$

For a non-negative additive distortion measure d, the expected minimum distortion is given by

$$d_{\min}(\mathbf{x}, l) \;=\; \sum_{i=1}^{n} p_i \rho_i \;=\; \sum_{i=1}^{n} p_i d(\mathbf{x}, \mathbf{x}|_{y_i}) \qquad (2.15)$$

where $\mathbf{x}|_{y_i}$ is the cover **x** with its ith element steganographically altered to y_i. For nonadditive distortion functions d, we will run several "sweeps" of the Gibbs sampler [9] until the output, the change probability p_i for each pixel, becomes stable close to the stationary distribution. During a sweep, all cover elements are updated sequentially according to an appropriate visiting schedule. The Gibbs sampler allows for more general distortion measures to be used in practice, whereas the summands in (2.15) interact with each other. This method is borrowed from physics, where the Gibbs distribution is the one with the highest entropy for a given energy (λ corresponding to the temperature). Here, among all distributions of embedding changes, the Gibbs distribution offers the maximum message length.

The following sections present some prominent contemporary cost functions for different embedding domains, with and without side information.

2.3.1   Uniform Embedding

Uniform embedding [10] provides a cost function for JPEG images known as *uniform embedding distortion metric* (UED). The usual procedure of embedding follows a spread spectrum approach. The cover elements $x_{u,v}$ (DCT coefficients in JPEG images) are randomly chosen. However, DCT coefficients are Laplacian distributed (cf. the histogram in Figure 2.4(b)). Their frequency decreases with

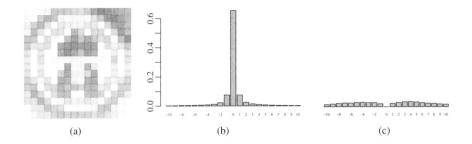

Figure 2.4 (a) Change probability of uniform embedding, approximated in spatial domain for 0.4 bits per nonzero AC coefficient (amounted absolute spatial contributions of DCT subbands that have been individually transformed back, darker means more probable), (b) histogram of quantized AC DCT coefficients, and (c) histogram of coefficients that have been changed by uniform embedding.

increasing absolute value. Hence, a random selection will concentrate most of the changes to small magnitudes in the histogram (first order statistics). In our example image, most of the non-zero AC coefficients (57%) have an absolute value of 1 or 2. Nevertheless, we have coefficients of 158 different magnitudes. For that same reason, random selection of coefficients will mainly affect a small region in the co-occurrence matrix (second order statistics) [11]. The cost function of uniform embedding strives to equalize the changes over the whole histogram, and, in the view of second order statistics, over the whole co-occurrence matrix uniformly. To equalize the choice between histogram bins, it inflicts higher costs on a smaller magnitude, roughly following the concept $1/|x_{u,v}|$. To achive uniform selection in the co-occurrence matrix, the neighborhood is included in the cost calculation:

$$\rho_{u,v}^{(UED)} = \sum_{(i,j) \in N_1} \frac{1}{|x_{u,v}| + |x_{i,j}| + \alpha_{\text{intra}}} + \sum_{(i,j) \in N_8} \frac{1}{|x_{u,v}| + |x_{i,j}| + \alpha_{\text{inter}}} \quad (2.16)$$

with $N_k = \{(u+k, v), (u-k, v), (u, v+k), (u, v-k)\}$, where N_1 is for the intra-block neighborhood (i.e., the coefficients of the neighboring DCT subbands of the same block) and N_8 for the inter-block neighborhood (i.e., the coefficients of same DCT subband of the neighboring blocks). $\alpha_{\text{intra}} = 1.3$ and $\alpha_{\text{inter}} = 1.0$ are adjusting parameters that have been determined experimentally. If a coefficient would be beyond the image boundary, it is excluded from the calculation in (2.16).

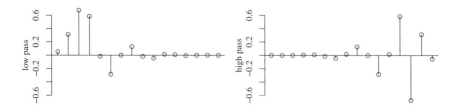

Figure 2.5   Filter coefficients for a Daubechies wavelet of class D16 **h** (left) and **g** (right).

2.3.2   Universal Wavelet Relative Distortion

The universal wavelet relative distortion function (UNIWARD [12]) is a generalization of wavelet-obtained weights (WOW [13]), which prevent embedding in
places where the content is predictable in at least one direction (e.g., clean edges).
It allows for embedding only if the content is unpredictable in every direction (e.g.,
textured areas). UNIWARD uses the same bank of filters (Daubechies wavelet,
Figure 2.5) to obtain directional residuals that are connected to the predictability
of a cover pixel. A distortion measure, which is determined from the pixel's local
neighborhood, introduces the necessary content adaptivity. While WOW provides
an effective prediction of embedding impact in the spatial domain, UNIWARD or-
ganizes the filters for measurement of distortion in an arbitrary domain and the use
with side-information. Consequently, there are several versions of UNIWARD:

- S-UNIWARD for embedding in the spatial domain;
- J-UNIWARD for embedding in JPEG images (DCT transform domain);
- SI-UNIWARD for embedding in JPEG images with side information.

All three variants of UNIWARD use a set of three linear shift-invariant 2D
directional filters, which are composed given the 1D filter coefficients (Figure 2.5)
as follows:

$$\mathbf{K}_{\mathrm{D16}}^{(1)} = \mathbf{hg}^{\mathrm{T}}, \quad \mathbf{K}_{\mathrm{D16}}^{(2)} = \mathbf{gh}^{\mathrm{T}}, \quad \text{and } \mathbf{K}_{\mathrm{D16}}^{(3)} = \mathbf{gg}^{\mathrm{T}} \qquad (2.17)$$

Note that the coefficients g_i are derived from h_i by $g_i = (-1)^i h_{17-i}$ with
$i \in \{1, \cdots, 16\}$. The filters in (2.17) perform the first-level undecimated wavelet
decomposition to the LH, HL, and HH subbands, respectively:

$$w^{(k)}(\mathbf{X}) = \mathbf{X} * \mathbf{K}_{\mathrm{D16}}^{(k)} \qquad (2.18)$$

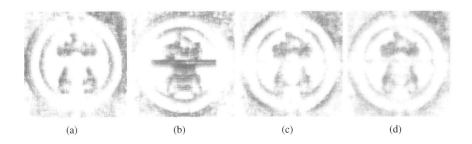

(a)   (b)   (c)   (d)

Figure 2.6   (a) Change probability with the partial cost function with the LH component only ($k = 1$ in (2.21)) for 0.4 bits per pixel, (b) with HL component only ($k = 2$), (c) with HH component only ($k = 3$), and (d) change probability with the complete UNIWARD cost function.

where "$*$" is a convolution that retains the size of the input matrix $\mathbf{X}$ by mirror-reflecting its elements across the matrix border (mirror padding).

The costs of altering with S-UNIWARD and J-UNIWARD are defined both using a spatial distortion function d_s:

$$\rho_{u,v}^{\text{(S-UNIWARD)}} = d_s(\mathbf{X}, \mathbf{X}|_{y_{u,v}}) \tag{2.19}$$

$$\rho_{u,v}^{\text{(J-UNIWARD)}} = d_s(j^{-1}(\mathbf{X}), j^{-1}(\mathbf{X}|_{y_{u,v}})) \tag{2.20}$$

where $\mathbf{X}|_{y_{u,v}}$ describes the cover in which one element $x_{u,v}$ has been replaced by its steganographic version $y_{u,v}$ at its particular position. The cover $\mathbf{X}$ contains pixels in the spatial case (2.19) and quantized DCT coefficients in the JPEG case (2.20). Before application of d_s, the cover elements are dequantized and transformed back to the spatial domain by the function j^{-1} (see Section 2.1.3) without rounding or limiting the resulting values.

UNIWARD's core distortion function d_s is the sum of (absolute) changes of all wavelet coefficients in proportion to their magnitude:

$$d_s(\mathbf{X}, \mathbf{Y}) = \sum_{k=1}^{3} \sum_{u=1}^{n_1} \sum_{v=1}^{n_2} \frac{|w^{(k)}(\mathbf{X})_{u,v} - w^{(k)}(\mathbf{Y})_{u,v}|}{\sigma + |w^{(k)}(\mathbf{X})_{u,v}|} \tag{2.21}$$

where σ is a stabilizing constant. It was determined experimentally $\sigma = 1$ for S-UNIWARD and $\sigma = 2^{-6}$ in the JPEG variants of UNIWARD [12]. The visualization of the change probabilities is shown in Figure 2.6.

The distortion function is nonadditive because the modification of one pixel will affect several wavelet coefficients (limited by the number of elements in the filter kernel). In addition, if one DCT coefficient is altered, up to 8×8 pixels will change. The filter kernels used here comprise 16×16 coefficients. Thus, the change of one DCT coefficient interacts with the wavelet coefficients for the pixels of this DCT block, the DCT blocks next to it, and even the DCT blocks after these.

As mentioned in Section 2.1.2, a lossy preprocessing function (e.g., JPEG compression) removes additional information (e.g., quantization error) that is part of the cover source $\mathbf{S}$. The sender can take this exclusive side information into account during embedding. It is not available to the recipient or any adversary, because it is not part of the stego data $\mathbf{Y}$. It is stripped off during the rounding step of the quantization $\dot{\mathbf{X}} \mapsto \mathbf{X}$, where $\dot{\mathbf{X}} = j(\mathbf{S})$ (see Section 2.1.3). The quantization error before and the total distortion after embedding will be denoted

$$
\begin{align}
e_{u,v} &= \dot{x}_{u,v} - x_{u,v} \tag{2.22} \\
e'_{u,v} &= \dot{x}_{u,v} - y_{u,v} \tag{2.23}
\end{align}
$$

respectively. SI-UNIWARD applies a technique known as *perturbed quantization* [5]. It either leaves the resulting quantized value unchanged or rounds it in the opposite direction with an extra distortion of $|e'_{u,v}| - |e_{u,v}| = 1 - 2|e_{u,v}|$. The cost function of SI-UNIWARD attempts to control the embedding by this extra distortion, which is modeled by the distortion function d_{si} involving side information:

$$
\begin{align}
\rho_{u,v}^{(\text{SI-UNIWARD})} &= d_{\mathrm{si}}(\dot{\mathbf{X}}|_{x_{u,v}}, \dot{\mathbf{X}}|_{y_{u,v}}) \tag{2.24} \\
d_{\mathrm{si}}(\mathbf{A}, \mathbf{B}) &= d_{\mathrm{s}}(\mathbf{S}, j^{-1}(\mathbf{B})) - d_{\mathrm{s}}(\mathbf{S}, j^{-1}(\mathbf{A})) \tag{2.25}
\end{align}
$$

2.3.3   HILL

The cost function of HILL [14] is realized using a high-pass filter followed by two low-pass filters, hence its name. Like WOW [13], the less predictable parts of a spatial image are identified by the high-pass filter. However, there are some pixels with high cost values in textured areas, which might be suitable for embedding changes. Hence, one low-pass filter connects textured, dense areas of low cost, while another, wider low-pass filter attenuates the low cost carefully across the borders to smooth regions. This spreading reduces the maximum change probability in conjunction with the probability of detection.

The Ker-Böhme predictor [15], which is often used in steganalysis, is adopted as the high-pass filter kernel $\mathbf{H}_{\mathrm{KB}}$ here (2.27). HILL's process of obtaining the cost

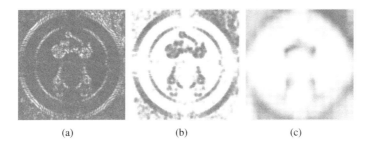

(a)   (b)   (c)

Figure 2.7 (a) HILL's cost function after application of the Ker-Böhme kernel $|\mathbf{X} * \mathbf{H}_{KB}|$, (b) change probability before application of $\mathbf{L}_2$, and (c) change probability with the complete HILL cost function for 0.4 bits per pixel.

values is given as:

$$\rho_{u,v}^{(\text{HILL})} = \left[\frac{1}{|\mathbf{X} * 4\mathbf{H}_{KB}| * \mathbf{L}_1} * \mathbf{L}_2 \right]_{u,v} \tag{2.26}$$

$$\mathbf{H}_{KB} = \frac{1}{4} \begin{bmatrix} -1 & 2 & -1 \\ 2 & -4 & 2 \\ -1 & 2 & -1 \end{bmatrix} \tag{2.27}$$

where $\mathbf{L}_1$ and $\mathbf{L}_2$ are both average filters. The best experimental results have been reached with filter sizes 3×3 and 15×15, respectively.

Figure 2.7(a) shows the predictability of the pixels measured by the Ker-Böhme kernel. The darker positions are predicted best, while the light positions are more suitable for steganography as they deviate from their prediction. The smaller low pass filter $\mathbf{L}_1$ (Figure 2.7(b)) ensures that all pixels within textural regions maintain relatively high change probability, while the wider $\mathbf{L}_2$ (Figure 2.7(c)) takes the mutual dependencies of neighboring pixels into account, which is spreading the low embedding costs appropriately.

2.3.4 Multivariate Generalized Gaussian Cover Model (MVGG)

This cover model [16] is an attempt to close the gap between the distortion function and the power of an optimal statistical detector, described in Section 3.1, (3.5). The performance of this detector is proportional to the Fisher information in the payload limit $\alpha \to 0$. It is assumed that the cover elements are independent realizations of quantized zero-mean generalized Gaussian random variables with a constant shape

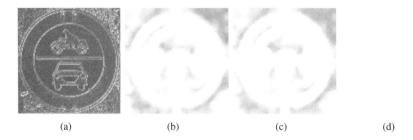

(a)   (b)   (c)   (d)

Figure 2.8 (a) MVGG's absolute noise residuals, (b) change probability for ternary embedding at 0.4 bits per pixel, (c) pentary embedding: probability for a change by ±1, and (d) same for a change by ±2.

parameter ν, distributed according to

$$f(x; b_n, \nu) \quad = \quad \frac{\nu}{2b_n \Gamma(1/\nu)} e^{-\left|\frac{x}{b_n}\right|^\nu} \tag{2.28}$$

where b_n is the width parameter linked to the variance $\sigma_n^2 = b_n^2 \Gamma(3/\nu)/\Gamma(1/\nu)$. However, since the variance of each pixel (the multivariate variance) is not known exactly, it will be estimated in two steps:

1. partly eliminate the image content using a denoising filter f, yielding $n_1 \times n_2$ noise residuals $\mathbf{R} = \mathbf{X} - f(\mathbf{X})$, and

2. approximate the variance for each pixel by the maximum likelihood estimation (MLE) from the pixel's neighborhood.

The filter f is implemented by a pixel-wise adaptive Wiener method based on statistics estimated from a 2×2 neighborhood of each pixel (Figure 2.8(a)). shows the absolute values of the resulting residuals $\mathbf{R}$. Since there is no center pixel in a 2×2 neighborhood, the statistic is south-east of the current location, half a diagonal pixel distance relocated. This results in a visible, unequal treatment of edges in main diagonal (NW to SE) and antidiagonal direction (NE to SW).

The second MLE step is matching the notation of the optimal detector. However, the local parametric model, which is implemented with two-dimensional discrete trigonometric polynomial functions, can be described with an $n_3 \times n_3$ DCT subband filter, which is more suitable for a comparison between the cost functions. The neighborhood $\mathbf{R}^{(u,v)}$ of each residual $r_{u,v}$ consists of $n_3 \times n_3$ residuals,

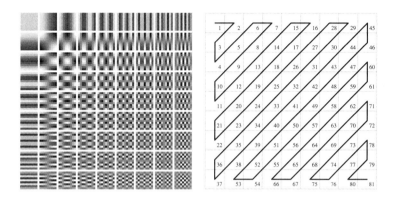

Figure 2.9 DCT basis images for block size 9×9 (left), "zigzag" order of DCT subbands (right).

including $r^{(u,v)}_{\lceil n_3/2 \rceil, \lceil n_3/2 \rceil} = r_{u,v}$ in the middle. It is transformed by the $n_3 \times n_3$ DCT. The best estimation was achieved for $n_3 = 9$; the corresponding basis images are depicted in Figure 2.9 (left). Following a zigzag path, the coefficients are ordered from DC and low frequencies to high frequencies (see Figure 2.9, right). The energy is compacted in the upper left coefficients: To further eliminate the image content, the first n_4 coefficients in zigzag order are deleted. The best choice among the experimental results was $n_4 = 45$. Let $\tilde{\mathbf{R}}^{(u,v)}$ be 9×9 residuals restored by inverse 9×9 DCT from the remaining $n_3^2 - n_4 = 36$ high frequency subbands (positions 46 to 81 in zigzag order). The variance $\sigma^2_{u,v}$ for $x_{u,v}$ and the steganographic Fisher information $\rho^{(\mathrm{MVGG})}_{u,v}$ is estimated by

$$\hat{\sigma}^2_{u,v} \;=\; \frac{1}{n_3^2 - n_4} \sum_{i=1}^{n_3} \sum_{j=1}^{n_3} \left(\tilde{r}^{(u,v)}_{i,j} \right)^2 \tag{2.29}$$

$$\rho^{(\mathrm{MVGG})}_{u,v} \;=\; \frac{1}{\hat{\sigma}^4_{u,v}} \tag{2.30}$$

With increasing change probability $p_{u,v}$, the relative entropy between cover $\mathbf{X}$ and stego data $\mathbf{Y}$ increases (see Section 2.5). The optimal change probabilities $p_{u,v}$ for ternary embedding are found by minimizing the relative entropy. We solve the root of its first derivative with respect to $p_{u,v}$ (2.31) numerically. The Lagrange multiplier λ is constrained by the message length l in bits (2.32, [17] for more detail):

$$0 = p_{u,v}\rho_{u,v}^{(MVGG)} - \frac{2}{\lambda}\log_2\left(\frac{1}{p_{u,v}} - 2\right) \tag{2.31}$$

$$l = \sum_{u=1}^{n_1}\sum_{v=1}^{n_2}\left(2p_{u,v}\log_2\frac{1}{p_{u,v}} + (1 - 2p_{u,v})\log_2\frac{1}{1 - 2p_{u,v}}\right) \tag{2.32}$$

Although the shape parameter ν has remarkable influence on the corresponding change probabilities, the experimental results showed similar empirical detectability. For $\nu = 2$, the change probabilities $p_{u,v}^{(k)}$ (of changing by $+k$ or $-k$; $k \in \{1,2\}$) for pentary embedding can be derived from the ternary Fisher information $\rho_{u,v}^{(MVGG)}$ (2.30) in the equation system ((2.33) and (2.34)), which is numerically solved using a parallelized Newton method. The Lagrange multiplier λ is determined numerically as well from the message length constraint (2.35):

$$0 = \rho_{u,v}^{(MVGG)}p_{u,v}^{(1)} + 4\rho_{u,v}^{(MVGG)}p_{u,v}^{(2)} - \frac{1}{\lambda}\log_2\frac{1 - 2p_{u,v}^{(1)} - 2p_{u,v}^{(2)}}{p_{u,v}^{(1)}} \tag{2.33}$$

$$0 = 4\rho_{u,v}^{(MVGG)}p_{u,v}^{(1)} + 16\rho_{u,v}^{(MVGG)}p_{u,v}^{(2)} - \frac{1}{\lambda}\log_2\frac{1 - 2p_{u,v}^{(1)} - 2p_{u,v}^{(2)}}{p_{u,v}^{(2)}} \tag{2.34}$$

$$l = \sum_{u=1}^{n_1}\sum_{v=1}^{n_2}\left(p_{u,v}^{(0)}\log_2\frac{1}{p_{u,v}^{(0)}} + 2\sum_{k=1}^{2}p_{u,v}^{(k)}\log_2\frac{1}{p_{u,v}^{(k)}}\right) \tag{2.35}$$

2.4 EMBEDDING BY SYNDROME TRELLIS CODING

The term "trellis" comes from the light lattice that is mounted at the walls of some houses to support vines or other climbing plants. It is used for the similar shape of a state diagram (see Figure 2.10), which is unrolled over the time axis. Repeated vertical bars support the branches (arcs forming a path) that grow from left to right between discrete levels (states). From time to time, the steganographic gardener comes and prunes back the branches according to the next bit to be embedded.

In our (binary) example, we select a parity check matrix

$$\mathbf{H} = \begin{pmatrix} 1 & 1 & 0 & 0 & 0 & 0 \\ 0 & 1 & 1 & 1 & 0 & 0 \\ 0 & 0 & 0 & 1 & 1 & 1 \end{pmatrix} \tag{2.36}$$

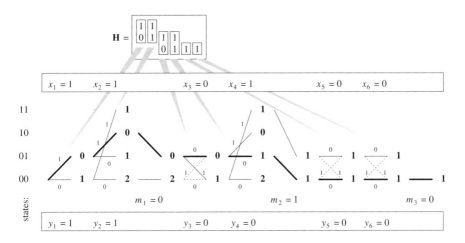

Figure 2.10 Trellis diagram.

such that each stego data **y** satisfying **m** = **Hy** corresponds to a path through the trellis. The optimal **y** closest to the cover data **x** is determined by the Viterbi algorithm. **H** is constructed by placing a 2×2 submatrix $\hat{\mathbf{H}}$ next to each other and shifted down by one row, which leads to a sparse banded parity check matrix. The height of $\hat{\mathbf{H}}$ is controlling the number of states in the trellis, which is typically in the range from 6 to 15, while its width $\lceil \alpha^{-1} \rceil$ is specified by the desired relative payload $\alpha = l/n$; in our example, $\alpha = 1/2$ specifies 2 as the width of $\hat{\mathbf{H}}$ [18].

In Figure 2.10, we want to embed the message **m** = $(0\ 1\ 0)^{\mathrm{T}}$ into the cover **x** = $(1\ 1\ 0\ 1\ 0\ 0)^{\mathrm{T}}$ with the least number of changes. The initial branch always springs up from the ground (state 00 in Figure 2.10) and grows to the right. For each column of $\hat{\mathbf{H}}$, the path grows one step to the right beforewe embed one message bit. This is repeated until the whole message is embedded. From the initial state 00, two states are reachable. For $y_1 = 1$ (i.e., when the first column of $\hat{\mathbf{H}}$ is added to the state (bitwise modulo 2, least significant bit at top of $\hat{\mathbf{H}}$)), we reach state 01. For $y_1 = 0$ (i.e., when the first column of $\hat{\mathbf{H}}$, is not added to the state), we reach state 00. Hence, we draw two edges labeled by the choice of y_1. (The appearance of the edges will be explained in a moment.) In the first case, where $x_1 = y_1 = 1$, we have no cost at all to reach state 01, whereas in the second case, to reach state 00, we have $x_1 \neq y_1 = 0$ (i. e., costs ofone change). The cumulated costs are denoted in the columns after each step by bold numbers.

In the second step, we can continue from two states (00 and 01) by either adding the right column of $\hat{\mathbf{H}}$ (reaching the states 11 or 10, respectively) or not. Since $x_2 = 1$, changing the state is again cheaper than staying in the same state. Now comes the decisive moment: we embed the first bit $m_1 = 0$, hence the states 01 and 11 can be discarded because their least significant bit does not match and will not change anymore. After embedding, we shift the state bits to the right (00 $\mapsto$ 00, 10 $\mapsto$ 01). At this point we have two options for embedding m_1: either at no costs or at the costs of two changes. However, because the total costs of embedding all message bits are to be minimized, we have to wait with the selection of the best path until the end.

After embedding $m_1 = 0$, we continue from the states 00 and 01 with the left column of $\hat{\mathbf{H}}$ again. From state 00, we reachstate 00 with $y_3 = 0$ at no additional costs (total costs 2), and state 01 at total costs 3. However, from state 01, we also reach state 00 by adding the left column at total costs 1, state 01 at total costs 0, which is cheaper. The branches from state 00 will not grow any further and dry out (hence the dotted lines). The continuation for y_4 contains no surprises. We embed $m_2 = 1$, keeping only the states 01 and 11 with the matching least significant bit, then shifting the state bits to the right (01 $\mapsto$ 00, 11 $\mapsto$ 01).

For the last two cover elements x_5 and x_6, the columns of $\hat{\mathbf{H}}$ are already clipped to their LSB. Hence, their processing is similar to x_3, yielding only two stages 00 and 01. Only state 00 is kept at the end because its LSB is matching $m_3 = 0$.

Now ,we follow from left to right the path through the trellis, marking its edges bold, because this is the path with the lowest cost. Finally, only y_4 will be changed from 1 to 0.

2.4.1 Wet Paper Channel

Writing on wet paper [19] is a communication channel for steganography that is similar to writing in memory with defective cells [20]. In this metaphor, the cover is a piece of paper that is sprinkled with raindrops. The sender restricts her writing to the dry spots. Writing on the wet spots will cause runny ink. On account of that, the warden would convict the sender of using steganography. During delivery, the paper dries. The recipient has no information about the dry spots. Thus, he cannot and does not need to take into account the side information that is available only at the sender side.

The cost of changing wet cover elements are set to ∞, preventing the embedding algorithm from modifying them. In our example, we will only mark the

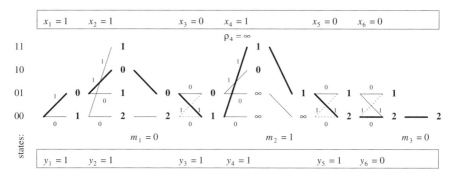

Figure 2.11   Trellis diagram for the same cover with one "wet" position.

changed position as wet by setting $\rho_4 = \infty$ (Figure 2.11). Consequently, all branches that need to set $y_4 = 0 \neq x_4$ result in total costs ∞, taking away their offsprings' livelihood. This increases the total cost of embedding to another possible path, changing both y_3 and y_5 from 0 to1, while keeping the wet position $y_4 = x_4 = 1$. There is a pathwith equal costs, changing y_6 instead of y_5, that could have been selected.

2.4.2   Perturbed Quantization

As already mentioned in Section 2.3.2, SI-UNIWARD uses perturbed quantization embedding with side information [5]. Table 2.1

gives an example of this technique.[1] Ten cover source elements s_i are quantized to the cover elements x_i, leaving the quantization errors $e_i = x_i - s_i$. If the LSB of a cover element has to be flipped, s_i is rounded in the opposite direction with an extra distortion (cost) of $\rho_i = 1 - 2|e_i|$. If s_i is exactly in the middle of two quantized values, flipping the LSB causes no embedding costs ($\rho_2 = 0$ in the upper section of the table). This is the only changed cover element in our example.

Zero embedding costs are mainly reproduced in four DCT subbands, which is easily checked in Eq. 2.1: For $u, v \in \{0, 4\}$, the cosines are either 1 or $\frac{1}{2}\sqrt{2}$, which give—multiplied with the weights w_k—a rational number. The coefficients in DCT subband $(0, 0)$ are always a multiple of $\frac{1}{4}$, in subband $(0, 4)$ or $(4, 0)$ a multiple of $\frac{1}{8}$, and in subband $(4, 4)$ a multiple of $\frac{1}{16}$. All other subbands produce irrational numbers. Embedding in coefficients with zero embedding costs will strongly prefer

---

1   Some details are omitted. A three bit message is embedded, the parity check matrix is constructed using a 4×3 submatrix $\hat{\mathbf{H}}$.

Table 2.1

Example of embedding using costs with side-information.

i	1	2	3	4	5	6	7	8	9	10
s_i	7.25	5.50	6.72	1.20	6.47	5.00	5.33	4.87	9.42	1.75
x_i	7	6	7	1	6	5	5	5	9	2
$|e_i|$	0.25	0.50	0.28	0.20	0.47	0.00	0.33	0.13	0.42	0.25
ρ_i	0.50	0.00	0.44	0.60	0.06	1.00	0.34	0.74	0.16	0.50
$\mathrm{lsb}(x_i)$	1	0	1	1	0	1	1	1	1	0
$\mathrm{lsb}(y_i)$	1	1	1	1	0	1	1	1	1	0
y_i	7	5	7	1	6	5	5	5	9	2
ρ_i'	0.50	∞	0.44	0.60	0.06	1.00	0.34	0.74	0.16	0.50
$\mathrm{lsb}(y_i)$	0	0	1	1	0	1	0	1	1	0
y_i	8	6	7	1	6	5	6	5	9	2

these four DCT modes. This artifact increases with higher quality of JPEG images (smaller quantizers in **Q**) and is escalated by fast integer implementations of DCT. A lower detectability is achieved by replacing zero costs in these DCT subbands by very large costs (marking them as wet: $\rho_2' = \infty$, cf. the lower section of the table). In our example, x_2 is left untouched now. Two changes are produced in y_1 and y_7 at total costs of $\rho_1' + \rho_7' = 0.84$.

2.5 SECURITY

Less distortion is believed to result in less detectable stego data, though this postulation is hard to prove in general, and pathologic counterexamples are easy to find [21]. For instance, the change of a single pixel might be discovered, if a spatial image has been derived from a JPEG image by decompression—because of broken "JPEG compatibility" [22]—, while several changes in other images might not.

Cachin proposed the relative entropy $D(P_c||P_s)$, between the probability distributions P_c of covers and P_s of stego data, to quantify the security of a steganographic system against passive attacks [23, 24]. This distance measure, which is also called Kullback-Leibler divergence, is connected to the detectability of steganographic changes. If $D(P_c||P_s) = 0$, the steganographic system is perfectly secure against all possible detectors. If $D(P_c||P_s) \leq \epsilon$, it is called ϵ-secure against passive adversaries. The probability of missed detection is $p_{MD} \geq 2^{-\epsilon}$ for a probability of false positives $p_{FP} = 0$.

2.5.1 Perfectly Secure Steganography

There are some examples of how Cachin's information-theoretic model fulfills the needs of real-world applications. Perfectly secure steganographic systems require a probabilistic model of covers. This is true for artificial covers. Imagine two scientists that exchange data of radioactive decay. The observations cannot be predicted, but their probabilities can be specified. Craver put forward the supraliminal channel [25], the art of smuggling ciphertext into pseudorandom data of applications. In particular, there are especially two very nice examples.

Apple's iChat instant messaging software, bundled with OS X version 10.5, allowed the user to apply special effects (camera distortion, various image filters) to a video chat session. Such computer-generated backdrops can be driven by pseudorandom number generators. Craver et al. implemented an option to replace the pseudo-random data with ciphertext to establish a supraliminal channel within the video chat application [26]. While the backdrop can be as simple as color-changing blocks, animated rain clouds have been among the user's favorites.

In another example, a walkie-talkie app for the iPhone optionally allows for encrypted messages in pseudorandom effects like the characteristic "chhht" appended to each radio message [27].

2.5.2 ϵ-Secure Steganography

In this chapter, we presented typical systems for multimedia steganography that either heuristically approximate the cover distributions or use probabilistic models. The distribution of empirical covers cannot be estimated from a finite set. Because of this incognizable nature, the information-theoretic bounds mentioned in Section 2.5 cannot be calculated in practice. Important for practical steganography is the empirical indistinguishability between (a finite set of) observed stego objects and an estimated (from finite observations) cover distribution [21].

The secure embedding rate is asymptotically vanishing [28] for $n \to \infty$: For a constant level of low detectability, the message length l should be proportional to $\sqrt{n}$, which is called the "square root law."

References

[1] Zöllner, J., et al., "An Information-Theoretic Model for Steganography," in *Information Hiding (2nd International Workshop)*, Vol. 1525 of *LNCS*, Berlin Heidelberg: Springer-Verlag, 1998, pp. 306–318.

[2] Ker, A. D., "A Fusion of Maximum Likelihood and Structural Steganalysis," in *Information Hiding (9th International Workshop)*, Vol. 4567 of *LNCS*, Berlin Heidelberg: Springer-Verlag, 2007, pp. 204–219.

[3] Sharp, T., "An Implementation of Key-Based Digital Signal Steganography," in *Information Hiding (4th International Workshop)*, Vol. 2137 of *LNCS*, Berlin Heidelberg: Springer-Verlag, 2001, pp. 13–26.

[4] Westfeld, A., "F5—A Steganographic Algorithm: High Capacity Despite Better Steganalysis," in *Information Hiding (4th International Workshop)*, Vol. 2137 of *LNCS*, Berlin Heidelberg: Springer-Verlag, 2001, pp. 289–302.

[5] Fridrich, J., M. Goljan, and D. Soukal, "Perturbed Quantization Steganography with Wet Paper Codes," in *Proc. of ACM Multimedia and Security Workshop*, Magdeburg, Germany, September, 20–21 2004, pp. 4–15.

[6] Fridrich, J., T. Pevný, and J. Kodovský, "Statistically Undetectable JPEG Steganography: Dead Ends, Challenges, and Opportunities," in *Proc. of ACM Multimedia and Security Workshop 2007, MM&Sec07, Dallas, Texas, USA*, New York: ACM Press, September, 20–21 2007, pp. 3–14.

[7] Pevný, T., T. Filler, and P. Bas, "Using High-Dimensional Image Models to Perform Highly Undetectable Steganography," in *Information Hiding (12th International Conference)*, Vol. 6387 of *LNCS*, Berlin Heidelberg, 2010, pp. 161–177.

[8] Fridrich, J., and T. Filler, "Practical Methods for Minimizing Embedding Impact in Steganography," in *Security, Steganography and Watermarking of Multimedia Contents IX (Proc. of SPIE)*, San Jose, CA, January 2007, pp. 650502-1–650502-15.

[9] Filler, T., and J. Fridrich, "Gibbs Construction in Steganography," *IEEE Trans. on Information Forensics and Security*, Vol. 5, December 2010, pp. 705–720.

[10] Guo, L., J. Ni, and Y. Q. Shi, "An efficient JPEG steganographic scheme using uniform embedding," in *IEEE International Workshop on Information Forensics and Security (WIFS)*, Tenerife, Spain, December 2012, pp. 169–174.

[11] Fridrich, J., "Feature-Based Steganalysis for JPEG Images and Its Implications for Future Design of Steganographic Schemes," in *Information Hiding (6th International Workshop)*, Vol. 3200 of *LNCS*, Berlin Heidelberg: Springer-Verlag, 2004, pp. 67–81.

[12] Holub, V., J. Fridrich, and T. Denemark, "Universal distortion function for steganography in an arbitrary domain," *EURASIP Journal on Information Security*, 2014.

[13] Holub, V., and J. Fridrich, "Designing steganographic distortion using directional filters," in *IEEE International Workshop on Information Forensics and Security (WIFS)*, Tenerife, Spain, December 2012, pp. 234–239.

[14] Li, B., et al., "A new cost function for spatial image steganography," in *IEEE International Conference on Image Processing ICIP 2014*, CNIT La Défense, Paris, France, October 2014, pp. 4206–4210.

[15] Ker, A. D., and R. Böhme, "Revisiting Weighted Stego-Image Steganalysis," in *Media Forensics and Security (Proc. of SPIE)*, San Jose, CA, January 2008, pp. 681905-1–681905-17.

[16] Sedighi, V., J. Fridrich, and R. Cogranne, "Content-Adaptive Pentary Steganography Using the Multivariate Generalized Gaussian Cover Model," in *Media Watermarking, Security, and Forensics (Proc. of SPIE)*, San Francisco, CA, January 2015, pp. 94090H-1–94090H-13.

[17] Fridrich, J., and J. Kodovský, "Multivariate Gaussian Model for Designing Additive Distortion for Steganography," in *IEEE International Conference on Acoustics, Speech, and Signal Processing (Proc. of ICASSP)*, Vancouver, British Columbia, Canada, May 2013, pp. 2949–2953.

[18] Filler, T., J. Judas, and J. Fridrich, "Minimizing Additive Distortion in Steganography Using Syndrome-Trellis Codes," *IEEE Trans. on Information Forensics and Security*, Vol. 6, September 2011, pp. 920–935.

[19] Fridrich, J., et al., "Writing on Wet Paper," in *Security, Steganography and Watermarking of Multimedia Contents VII (Proc. of SPIE)*, San Jose, CA, January, 16–20 2005, pp. 328–340.

[20] Kusnetsov, A. V., and B. S. Tsybakov, "Kodirowanie v Pamiati s Defektnymi Iacheikami (Coding in a Memory with Defective Cells)," *Problemy Peredachi Informatsii*, Vol. 10, 1974, pp. 132–138.

[21] Böhme, R., *Advanced Statistical Steganalysis*, Information Security and Cryptography, Berlin Heidelberg: Springer-Verlag, 2010.

[22] Fridrich, J., M. Goljan, and R. Du, "Steganalysis Based on JPEG Compatibility," in *Multimedia Systems and Applications IV (Proc. of SPIE)*, Vol. 4518, San Jose, CA, 2001, pp. 275–280.

[23] Cachin, C., "An Information-Theoretic Model for Steganography," in *Information Hiding (2nd International Workshop)*, Vol. 1525 of *LNCS*, Berlin Heidelberg: Springer-Verlag, 1998, pp. 306–318.

[24] Cachin, C., "An Information-Theoretic Model for Steganography," *Information and Computation*, Vol. 192, 2004, pp. 41–56.

[25] Craver, S., "On Public-Key Steganography in the Presence of an Active Warden," in *Information Hiding (2nd International Workshop)*, Vol. 1525 of *LNCS*, Berlin Heidelberg: Springer-Verlag, 1998, pp. 355–368.

[26] Craver, S., et al., "A Supraliminal Channel in a Videoconferencing Application," in *Information Hiding, 10th International Workshop, Proceedings*, Vol. 5284 of *LNCS*, Berlin Heidelberg: Springer-Verlag, 2008, pp. 283–293.

[27] Li, E., and S. Craver, "Supraliminal Channel in a Wireless Phone Application," in *Proc. of ACM Multimedia and Security Workshop 2009, MM&Sec09, Princeton, NJ*, New York: ACM Press, September, 7-8 2009, pp. 151–154.

[28] Filler, T., A. D. Ker, and J. Fridrich, "The Square Root Law of Steganographic Capacity for Markov Covers," in *Media Forensics and Security (Proc. of SPIE)*, San Jose, CA, January 2009, pp. 725408-1–725408-11.

Chapter 3

Steganalysis

Jessica Fridrich

Steganalysis is the art of discovering the presence of secret messages. In the narrow sense of this word, the objective is to identify whether a given object contains a secretly embedded message. Once the presence of the message can be established, the steganalyst's job has ended. This is how the word "steganalysis" is currently understood in the research literature. From the practical point of view, we may, however, be interested in additional information that goes beyond establishing the mere presence of the secret. For example, a forensic analyst may be interested in which steganographic tool was used to embed the secret, how long the message is, what the actual message is, and may possibly desire to recover the secret stego key. These tasks formally belong to the field of "forensic steganalysis," which encompasses steganalysis in the narrow sense. Finally, one may rightfully argue that current detection tools may not be good enough to reliably detect the presence of secrets in individual media objects, and what one should really strive for is to discover the users of steganography rather than individual stego-objects. This makes a lot of sense because, even when our detection tools are not very accurate, it should be possible to identify the steganographers with increasing degree of certainty given enough observed traffic. Indeed, since steganography is, by definition, a repetitive process, even weak evidence will accumulate over time.

The warden's ability to detect messages heavily depends on her knowledge of the entire steganographic channel, especially whether or not she knows the embedding method and how much she knows about the source of cover objects. It should be obvious that, unless the steganography is somehow fundamentally flawed, short messages should be more difficult to detect than longer messages. The statistical detectability of embedding is very strongly influenced by the embedding algorithm and its embedding operation. We will see that LSB replacement is in general much easier to detect than LSB matching. The source of cover objects also plays a very important role. For example, scans of photographs are rather noisy and mask the artifacts that are introduced during message embedding very well. On the other hand, pixels in a decompressed JPEG image or an image that has undergone a color interpolation without any additional processing exhibit quite strong relationships that may allow a steganalyst to reliably detect even a very short message.

In this chapter, we will work with digital images as typical examples of digital media objects with the caveat that many concepts, techniques, and algorithms can be adapted to other digital media objects, including video and audio. This constraint was consciously made because the vast majority of steganalysis attacks for digital media were designed for digital images.

In the next section, we formulate steganalysis as statistical signal detection and give a simple example of a state-of-the-art detector built as the likelihood ratio test. Steganalysis works with compact representations of images, which is the subject of Section 3.2, where we describe modern representations using rich models and general techniques for constructing powerful statistical descriptors of images in spatial and JPEG domains, including calibration, parity awareness, and JPEG-phase awareness. Section 3.3 deals with quantitative attacks that are capable of estimating the secret message length. In Section 3.3.1, we describe an example of structural steganalysis, including quantitative steganalyzers built as regressors in a selected feature space (Section 3.3.2). In Section 3.3.3, we explain the properties and distributions of the estimation error. Section 3.4 is devoted to selected special topics, such as the cover source mismatch, compatibility attacks (which can be quite powerful under special circumstances), multiclass steganalysis, batch steganography and pooled steganalysis, and techniques aimed at practical deployment of steganalysis in the real world. Finally, in Section 3.5, we delve into the topic of steganalysis in the wider sense (forensic steganalysis), as well as system attacks based on stego-software signatures.

3.1   STEGANALYSIS AS SIGNAL DETECTION

In this section, we formulate steganalysis as a signal detection problem and explain how the performance of detectors is evaluated in practice using ROC curves and some useful scalar quantities. We also give an example of a detector derived as a likelihood ratio using statistical hypothesis testing.

The first step in building a detector of steganography is to choose a representation of images. The detector can work directly with pixels, histograms of pixels or pixel pairs, or with some other quantities derived from them, such as sample joint statistics (co-occurrences) of noise residuals or transform coefficients. In the past, researchers have investigated a large number of possible representations and their suitability for detecting a particular form of embedding. Here, we will simply assume that the representation is chosen and that it is possible to estimate the statistical distribution of cover images p_c. This is, in fact, a quite strong assumption, which limits the representation one that can use in practice. The topic of choosing suitable statistical descriptors of images appears in the next section.

If the warden has no information about the stego-system, the steganalysis problem essentially becomes a composite test for whether the observed representation $\mathbf{X}$ is compatible with the distribution of covers:

$$H_0 : \quad \mathbf{X} \sim p_c \tag{3.1}$$

$$H_1 : \quad \mathbf{X} \nsim p_c \tag{3.2}$$

If the knowledge available to the warden allows her to estimate the distribution of stego-objects, p_s, then the detection problem leads to simple hypothesis testing

$$H_0 : \quad \mathbf{X} \sim p_c \tag{3.3}$$

$$H_1 : \quad \mathbf{X} \sim p_s \tag{3.4}$$

This presumes, of course, that the warden knows the embedding algorithm (or at least its inner working) and is able to work out the stego-distribution p_s. She also needs to know the payload size or its distribution. In this case, the optimal detector is the likelihood ratio (LRT) test

$$\text{Decide } H_1 \text{ when } L(\mathbf{X}) = \frac{p_s(\mathbf{X})}{p_c(\mathbf{X})} > \gamma \tag{3.5}$$

where γ is a threshold that controls the trade off between the false-alarm rate, P_{FA} (the probability that a cover image will be identified as stego), and the missed-detection rate, $P_{\mathrm{MD}} = 1 - P_{\mathrm{D}}$, which is the probability of erroneously marking a stego-image as cover. The threshold γ is determined from costs of errors and prior probabilities or by a bound on the false alarm within the Neyman–Pearson setting. Bayesian detectors are more problematic to use (in practice) because the prior probabilities of encountering a cover or stego-image can rarely be accurately estimated. The Neyman–Pearson framework is much more relevant, as it is important that any detector have a very small false alarm rate. This is because images detected as potentially containing secret messages will be likely subjected to further forensic analysis aimed at determining the steganographic software used to embed the message, the stego-key, and extracting the secret message. This may require brute-force dictionary attacks that can be quite expensive and time-consuming. Thus, it is more valuable to have a detector with a very low false-alarm rate, even though its probability of missed detection may be quite high (e.g., $P_{\mathrm{MD}} > 0.5$ or higher). Because steganographic communication is typically repetitive, even a detector with $P_{\mathrm{MD}} = 0.5$ will eventually amass enough evidence about the usage of steganography.

There exist many other possibilities that fall in between the two formulations above, depending on the information about the steganographic channel available to the warden. For example, she may know the embedding algorithm, but not the payload size. In this case, p_s will depend on the unknown relative message length R, and the warden will face a composite one-sided hypothesis testing problem

$$\mathrm{H}_0 : \quad R = 0 \tag{3.6}$$

$$\mathrm{H}_1 : \quad R > 0 \tag{3.7}$$

In practice, steganalysis detectors constructed as likelihood-ratio tests are a viable option only in rare cases, typically when the embedding algorithm uses LSB replacement (there is a fundamental reason for this, and it is explained in Section 3.1.1) or when the chosen image representation is low dimensional (see Section 3.3.1). For more complex (high-dimensional) image representations, it is impossible to estimate the cover distribution because the number of images required for an accurate estimation grows exponentially with the dimensionality of the representation. In this case, the problem of distribution estimation and detection using the LRT is typically reformulated as the much simpler problem of classification (pattern-recognition) and solved by training a classifier on a large database of cover and stego-images.

Regardless of the detector type, whether it is an LRT or a classifier, its performance is usually described using the function $P_{\mathrm{D}}(P_{\mathrm{FA}})$ called the Receiver Operating Characteristic (ROC) curve. A poor detector will have an ROC curve that is close to the diagonal line $P_{\mathrm{D}}(P_{\mathrm{FA}}) \approx P_{\mathrm{FA}}$ (the dashed line in Figure 3.1), while the ROC curve for very accurate detectors will come close to the point $(P_{\text{FA}}, P_{\text{MD}}) = (0, 1)$.

While some detectors can be unambiguously compared because their ROCs satisfy $P_{\text{D}}^{(1)}(P_{\text{FA}}) > P_{\text{D}}^{(2)}(P_{\text{FA}})$ for all $P_{\text{FA}} \in [0, 1]$, which means that Detector 1 is more accurate than Detector 2 for all false alarms, ROCs can intersect and then it may not be obvious which detector is better. To be able to unambiguously compare detectors, researchers have proposed several scalar measures of performance. The two most commonly used ones are:

- The minimal total average decision error under equal prior probabilities of cover and stego images

$$P_{\text{E}} = \min_{P_{\text{FA}} \in [0,1]} \frac{1}{2} \left(P_{\text{FA}} + P_{\text{MD}}(P_{\text{FA}}) \right) \tag{3.8}$$

The minimum is reached at a point where the tangent to the ROC curve has slope 1. In Figure 3.1, this point is marked with a circle.

- The false-alarm rate at probability of detection equal to $P_{\text{D}} = 1/2$, $P_{\text{D}}^{-1}(1/2)$. This point on the ROC curve is marked with a square in Figure 3.1.

The value $P_{\text{D}}^{-1}(1/2)$ is probably the most relevant for steganalysis because of the importance of the false-alarm rate for steganalysis. The P_{E} is very commonly used for benchmarking steganographic and steganalysis algorithms.

3.1.1 Weighted-Stego Image Detector

A good example of an excellent detector of LSB replacement constructed as the LRT is the weighted stego-image (WS) detector. Initially devised as a quantitative detector that outputs an estimate of the secret message in [1] , it was later improved in [2]. Finally, the detector was rederived as an LRT in [3], which we show in this section using simplified arguments.

Everywhere in this chapter, we will work with 8-bit grayscale cover and stego-images represented as $M \times N$ matrices $\mathbf{X}$ and $\mathbf{Y}$ with $n = MN$ pixels with values x_{ij}, $y_{ij} \in \{0, \ldots, 255\}$. By a common abuse of language, we will speak of pixel x_{ij} meaning the grayscale value x_{ij} of the i, jth pixel. The symbol $\beta \geq 0$ will denote the change rate defined as the relative number of modified pixels.

The key insight is to model noise residuals instead of the pixel values; those values depend heavily on content. A noise residual is computed for each pixel x_{ij} as the difference between the pixel value and its predicted value, which is obtained

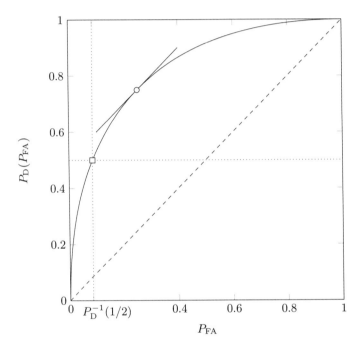

Figure 3.1 An example of an ROC curve with the square marking the point on the ROC curve corresponding to the criterion $P_D^{-1}(1/2)$, while the circle corresponds to the minimal total decision error P_E.

from neighboring pixels:

$$r_{ij} = x_{ij} - \text{Pred}(\mathcal{N}_{ij}), \tag{3.9}$$

where $\mathcal{N}_{ij}$ is a neighborhood of pixel x_{ij} that does not include x_{ij}. Virtually all steganalysis detectors, including classifiers, represent images using noise residuals rather than pixel values. Not only is the image content suppressed in the residual (which gives it a much narrower dynamic range and thus improves the stego-signal to noise ratio [1]) but, most importantly, residuals are much easier to model than pixel values. It is important not to involve the pixel itself in the prediction because we would be subtracting the stego-signal itself. In the most extreme case, the most accurate predictor of a pixel value is the value itself, which is obviously a completely useless prediction.

In practice, the operation in (3.9) is a high-pass filter. When implemented as a finite impulse response filter $\mathbf{K}$, the residual is obtained using convolution as

$$\mathbf{R}(\mathbf{X}) = \mathbf{X} - \text{Pred}(\mathbf{X}) = \mathbf{X} - \mathbf{K} \star \mathbf{X} \tag{3.10}$$

The convolution in (3.10) is evaluated so that it has the same dimensions as $\mathbf{X}$ by mirror-padding $\mathbf{X}$ at the image boundaries. A popular pixel predictor that can be shown optimal under the right assumptions (see Chapter 5 in [4]) uses the KB (Ker–Böhme) kernel:

$$\mathbf{K} = \frac{1}{4} \begin{pmatrix} -1 & 2 & -1 \\ 2 & 0 & 2 \\ -1 & 2 & -1 \end{pmatrix} \tag{3.11}$$

We furthermore introduce the concept of pixel parity defined as

$$\pi_{ij}(x_{ij}) = \bar{x}_{ij} - x_{ij} \in \{-1, 1\} \tag{3.12}$$

where the bar denotes the operation of LSB flipping (e.g., $\bar{5} = 4$, $\bar{8} = 9$, etc.).

For a cover image residual, we model r_{ij} as a sequence of independent realizations of zero-mean Gaussian random variables with variances σ_{ij}^2 discretized to $\mathcal{R} = \{k/4 \,|\, k \in \mathbb{Z}\}$. In particular, the probability mass function of pixel x_{ij} is

$$p_{ij}(k; \sigma_{ij}) = \frac{1}{Z} \exp\left(-\frac{(k/4)^2}{2\sigma_{ij}^2}\right), \quad Z = \sum_{k \in \mathbb{Z}} \exp\left(-\frac{(k/4)^2}{2\sigma_{ij}^2}\right) \tag{3.13}$$

---

1   Here, the noise is mainly the scene remainder in r_{ij}.

where k indexes all values in $\mathcal{R}$. Even though σ_{ij}^2 for the discrete Gaussian is not its variance, it can be shown by direct evaluation that, at least, in the range $\sigma_{ij}^2 \in [10^{-4}, 10^2]$, $Var[p_{ij}] \approx \sigma_{ij}^2$ within a few percent. We will estimate the variance from the 3×3 neighborhood as

$$\hat{\sigma}_{ij}^2 = \max\left(0, \frac{1}{|\mathcal{N}_{ij}|} \sum_{x'_{ij} \in \mathcal{N}_{ij} \cup \{x_{ij}\}} (x'_{ij} - \hat{\mu}_{ij})^2\right)$$

where $\hat{\mu}_{ij}$ is the sample mean of pixel values from $\mathcal{N}_{ij} \cup \{x_{ij}\}$.

A stego-image obtained by flipping LSBs of βn uniformly randomly selected pixels in **x** is

$$y_{ij} = x_{ij} + s_{ij}, \qquad (3.14)$$

where $s_{ij} \in \{0, \pi_{ij}\}$ are mutually independent realizations of random variables with $\Pr\{s_{ij} = 0\} = 1 - \beta$ and $\Pr\{s_{ij} = \pi_{ij}\} = \beta$, that are also independent of the cover.

Denoting a Gaussian random variable with zero mean and variance σ_{ij}^2 discretized to $\mathcal{R}$ as ξ_{ij}, our hypothesis test is

$$\mathrm{H}_0: \quad r_{ij} \sim \xi_{ij}, \quad \forall i, j \qquad (3.15)$$

$$\mathrm{H}_1: \quad r_{ij} \sim \pi_{ij} + \xi_{ij}, \; \forall i, j \qquad (3.16)$$

In other words, this test assumes that either we are looking at a cover image or an image whose *all* pixels have flipped LSBs. This is a simplifying step that allows us to avoid having to deal with a mixture for the alternative hypothesis and one which significantly simplifies the derivations.

Due to the independence of residuals (and the fact that $\pi_{ij}^2 = 1$), the log-LRT for our problem is

$$\sum_{i,j} \log \frac{A_{ij} \exp(-(r_{ij} - \pi_{ij})^2/(2\sigma_{ij}^2))}{A_{ij} \exp(-r_{ij}^2/(2\sigma_{ij}^2))} = \sum_{i,j} \frac{1}{2\sigma_{ij}^2} (2r_{ij}\pi_{ij} - 1) > \gamma \quad (3.17)$$

This means that an equivalent detection statistic is the generalized matched filter $\sum_{ij} r_{ij}\pi_{ij}/\sigma_{ij}^2$. Since, in practice, we will use variances estimated from the image, we need to stabilize the detector whenever the variance is too small, such as $\sum_{ij} r_{ij}\pi_{ij}/(1 + \sigma_{ij}^2)$.

It is rather interesting that this detection statistic normalized by the sum of the weights $\sum_{ij} w_{ij} = \sum_{ij} 1/(1 + \sigma_{ij}^2)$ is an estimate of the change rate. To see this, we split the summation over pixels that did not change and those that did change:

$$\sum_{i,j} w_{ij} r_{ij} \pi_{ij} = \left(\sum_{y_{ij}=x_{ij}} w_{ij} r_{ij} \pi_{ij} + \sum_{y_{ij}=\bar{x}_{ij}} w_{ij} r_{ij} \pi_{ij} \right)$$

The first sum is a linear combination of independent zero-mean random variables ξ_{ij}, which all have a zero mean, while the second sum is over $\approx n\beta$ pixels, for which $y_{ij} = \bar{x}_{ij}$ and thus $r_{ij} = \pi_{ij} + \xi_{ij}$:

$$\sum_{y_{ij}=\bar{x}_{ij}} w_{ij} r_{ij} \pi_{ij} = \sum_{y_{ij}=\bar{x}_{ij}} w_{ij} (\pi_{ij} + \xi_{ij}) \pi_{ij} \tag{3.18}$$

which is in expectation and after normalizing by $\sum_{i,j} w_{ij}$:

$$\frac{\sum_{y_{ij}=\bar{x}_{ij}} w_{ij} \pi_{ij}^2}{\sum_{i,j} w_{ij}} = \frac{\sum_{y_{ij}=\bar{x}_{ij}} w_{ij}}{\sum_{i,j} w_{ij}} \approx \beta \tag{3.19}$$

because the βn changed pixels were selected uniformly randomly.

A normalized version of this detector that is asymptotically universally most powerful was derived by Fillatre [5]. An LRT was also derived for JPEG-domain algorithms Jsteg [6] and OutGuess [7]. We note that the first detectors of LSB replacement built as LRTs using statistical hypothesis testing appeared in [8, 9]. In contrast to the WS detector, the models used in this prior art were adopted for the pixel values themselves, which are much more difficult to model than the noise residuals. The WS attack was also heuristically adapted to work for the detection of LSB replacement in JPEG images [10, 11] and for the detection of content-adaptive embedding that employs LSB replacement [12] (even though no such scheme is known to the author of this chapter) and for LSB replacement in color images [13].

We close this section with a rather important observation. Note that in (3.16) we are testing at each pixel whether the residual has a non-zero and known mean value. This is possible because of the character of the operation of LSB replacement. In contrast, for LSB matching, when the cover value is changed by 1 or -1 with the same probability, the expectation of the stego-pixel does not change, its variance only slightly increases. One can say that there is a fundamental difference between LSB replacement and matching when it comes to detection. The detection of the former is a test for a non-zero mean, while the latter is a test for increased variance. While many well-advanced techniques exist for estimating the pixel mean, the problem of estimating pixel variance at a specific pixel is much less developed, which makes detection of LSB matching much more challenging. Detectors of LSB matching based on statistical hypothesis testing are described in [14–16]. Another class of attacks on LSB matching based on the statistical impact of embedding on the pixel histogram uses the center of gravity of the histogram characteristic function [17–19].

3.2 IMAGE REPRESENTATIONS

Whether we build a detector as an LRT or a classifier using machine learning, it is always useful to represent images in some way other than large matrices of integers standing for the actual pixel values or the values of DCT coefficients (for JPEG images). This is because of the high dimensionality of the signal and a very low stego-signal-to-noise ratio. Steganalysts say that we represent images using features. In general, we desire a representation that is compact (for ease of building the detector), that reacts sensitively to steganographic embedding changes, and is insensitive to the image content. In the past, researchers have come up with a great variety of statistical descriptors for steganalysis. In this section, we introduce the most commonly used feature sets in the spatial and JPEG domain.

3.2.1 Spatial Domain

As already hinted in Section 3.1.1, it is natural to build image representations in the spatial domain from noise residuals such as (3.9). The noise residual has a much narrower dynamic range than pixels and the stego signal enjoys a larger SNR. Moreover, it is much easier to find a well-fitting model for noise residuals than for pixels.

The noise residual is, however, still a very high-dimensional signal of essentially the same dimensionality as the original image. Also, neighboring residual samples exhibit dependencies that are likely to be disturbed by embedding. Thus, it is not sufficient to form a first-order statistic (histogram) from the residual — one needs to capture the joint statistic of the residual samples. To this end, it has become customary to first quantize the residual to a small number of samples and then form the sample joint probability mass function (co-occurrence matrix). Since the number of bins in the co-occurrence increases exponentially with co-occurrence dimensionality and polynomially with regards to the number of quantizer centroids, one needs to be quite conservative with both parameters. Based on a large number of experiments on various image sources and with various steganographic schemes, re-searchers have converged to what is now called the Spatial Rich Model (SRM) [20] as a very strong statistical descriptor of images. It is formed by four-dimensional co-occurrence matrices of numerous quantized residuals. The multitude of residuals brings in diversity and the ability to detect embedding changes in diverse content. Below, we provide a brief description of the SRM, referring the reader to the original publication for more details [20].

The SRM contains two types of pixel predictors — linear and nonlinear ones. All linear predictors are realized as shift-invariant finite-impulse response linear filters captured by a kernel matrix, such as the KB kernel above or the 5×5 kernel

$$\mathbf{K}_5 = \frac{1}{12} \begin{pmatrix} -1 & 2 & -2 & 2 & -1 \\ 2 & -6 & 8 & -6 & 2 \\ -2 & 8 & 0 & 8 & -2 \\ 2 & -6 & 8 & -6 & 2 \\ -1 & 2 & -2 & 2 & -1 \end{pmatrix} \tag{3.20}$$

originally proposed in [21].

The SRM uses numerous other linear predictors. Most are derived by assuming that the image content locally follows a polynomial model. For example, the pixel predictors

$$\mathrm{Pred}(x_{ij}) = x_{i,j+1} \tag{3.21}$$
$$\mathrm{Pred}(x_{ij}) = (x_{i,j-1} + x_{i,j+1})/2 \tag{3.22}$$
$$\mathrm{Pred}(x_{ij}) = (x_{i,j-1} + 3x_{i,j+1} - x_{i,j+2})/3 \tag{3.23}$$

are based on the assumption that image content is locally constant, linear, and quadratic, respectively. Note that the residuals computed using these three predictors are all directional because they only utilize horizontally adjacent neighbors of x_{ij}. The vertical form of these residuals that uses only vertically adjacent pixels is obtained by simply swapping the subscripts in (3.21)–(3.23). In general, the kernel for the vertical predictor is a transpose of the one for the horizontal direction.

All nonlinear predictors in the SRM are obtained by taking the minimum (maximum) of the output of two or more residuals obtained using linear predictors. For example, given a horizontal residual $\mathbf{R}^{(h)} = (r_{ij}^{(h)})$ and a vertical residual $\mathbf{R}^{(v)} = (r_{ij}^{(v)})$, the non-linear residuals (residuals computed using a non-linear predictor) are computed as:

$$r_{ij}^{(\text{min})} = \min\{r_{ij}^{(\text{h})}, r_{ij}^{(\text{v})}\}, \ \forall i, j \tag{3.24}$$

$$r_{ij}^{(\text{max})} = \max\{r_{ij}^{(\text{h})}, r_{ij}^{(\text{v})}\}, \ \forall i, j \tag{3.25}$$

Before forming the final descriptors, the co-occurrence matrices, all residuals are quantized to a set of centroids $\mathcal{Q} = \{-Tq, (-T+1)q, \ldots, Tq\}$, where $T > 0$ is an integer truncation threshold and $q > 0$ is a quantization step:

$$z_{ij} \triangleq Q_{\mathcal{Q}}(r_{ij}), \ \forall i, j \tag{3.26}$$

It appears that the descriptors' ability to detect steganography is not very sensitive to the quantizer parameters T and q. There were some attempts to utilize non-uniform quantizers to improve the performance [22] and to make the features more compact [23]; however, these ideas did not lead to any significant improvement in detection accuracy.

The next step in forming the SRM feature vector involves computing a co-occurrence matrix of fourth order from four (horizontally and vertically) neighboring values of the quantized residual z_{ij} (3.26) from the entire image:

$$C_{d_0 d_1 d_2 d_3} = \sum_{i,j=1}^{M,N-3} [z_{i,j} = d_k, \forall k = 0, \ldots, 3] \tag{3.27}$$

Here, the square bracket is the so-called Iverson bracket meaning $[P] = 1$ when the statement P is true and zero otherwise. Note that, in general, a D-dimensional co-occurrence of residuals thresholded at T contains $(2T+1)^D$ bins. As argued in [20], diagonally neighboring values are not included in the SRM due to much weaker dependencies among residual samples along diagonal directions. To keep the co-occurrence bins well-populated and thus statistically significant, the co-occurrence dimensionality was kept at $D = 4$ and the truncation threshold $T = 2$. Five-dimensional co-occurrences do not necessarily bring better detection, as too many bins become underpopulated, while dimensions 3 or lower are not as powerful for steganalysis as the four-dimensional ones. While it is true that increasing the threshold T would further improve detection for one residual, it would also increase the feature dimensionality. For a fixed feature dimensionality, it is far better to increase the feature diversity by adding residuals from different predictors rather than to increase T for one residual.

Finally, symmetries of natural images are leveraged in order to further marginalize the co-occurrence matrix to decrease the feature dimension and better populate the SRM feature vector (see Section II.C of [20]).

With a single quantization step q, the dimensionality of SRM is $12,753$. When choosing $q = 1$, this representation is called SRMQ1. The abbreviation SRM is typically used for the bigger version of the features obtained by concatenating SRMQq with $q \in \{1, 1.5, 2\}$, which has the dimensionality of $34,671$.

Many extensions and modifications of the SRM were proposed in the literature. The Projection Spatial Rich Model (PSRM) uses the same set of residuals as the SRM, but represents them by using an alternative statistical descriptor. Instead of forming co-occurrences, the residuals are projected on random vectors and crudely quantized histograms are then taken as the features. When combined with the FLD ensemble classifier [24], the PSRM can achieve the same detection performance as the SRM with an order of magnitude fewer features or, with the same feature dimensionality, one can achieve a lower detection error. For a good performance, one needs to choose many random projections, which makes the PSRM feature vector quite expensive to compute (it requires computing tens of thousands of convolutions) and thus difficult to use in practice [25].

Another important modification of the SRM is its selection-channel aware version called the maxSRM for detection of content-adaptive steganography, which is a generalization of the descriptor originally proposed in [26]. If the warden can estimate the probabilities with which pixel x_{ij} was modified, $\hat{\beta}_{ij}$, then the maxSRM version of the SRM forms the co-occurrences by modifying (3.27) to

$$\tilde{C}_{d_0 d_1 d_2 d_3} = \sum_{i,j=1}^{M,N-3} \max_{k=0,\ldots,3} \hat{\beta}_{i,j+k} [z_{i,j} = d_k, \forall k = 0, \ldots, 3] \qquad (3.28)$$

The maxSRM is especially effective against highly content adaptive algorithms, such as WOW [27] and also against HILL [28].

For steganalysis of color images, the SRM has been modified to the so-called Color Rich Model (CRM) [29] by replacing the four-dimensional co-occurrences in the spatial domain with three-dimensional co-occurrences in the color domain. In other words, instead of forming co-occurrences from four spatially adjacent residuals, they are formed from the triplets $(z_{ij}^{(r)}, z_{ij}^{(g)}, z_{ij}^{(b)})$ of residuals computed in the red, green, and blue channels. The CRM can be added to the SRM evaluated for each color channel to improve steganalysis of color images. For images that exhibit traces of color interpolation, the dependencies among color channels are so much stronger than those in the spatial domain that the CRM alone has the majority of the detection power [29, 30].

The first feature set for steganalysis of images in the spatial domain involved image quality metrics and binary similarity measures [31, 32]. Feature-based steganalysis implemented with machine learning took off after the publication of the 72-dimensional feature vector computed from the prediction errors (essentially residuals) in the quadrature mirror decomposition of the image [33]. Co-occurrences were proposed for steganalysis for the first time in [34–36]. Statistical moments of wavelet coefficients were proposed in [37].

3.2.2 JPEG Domain

JPEG images are represented via coefficients of the Discrete Cosine Transform (DCT). As such, with the exception of the DC coefficient (which is the average intensity in a 8×8 pixel block), the remaining 63 AC coefficients are outputs of 63 high-pass filters. Thus, they can be considered as quantized "noise residuals" obtained using large-support kernels subsampled to the 8×8 grid. Therefore, it is no wonder that features proposed to represent JPEG images for steganalysis are typically formed by co-occurrences of DCT coefficients. There are, however, important differences between noise residuals and DCT coefficients.

First, because the coefficients are computed on disjoint pixel blocks, there are two types of dependencies among DCT coefficients: inter-block and intra-block. It is important to capture both for steganalysis. The dependencies are, however, much weaker than in the spatial domain because of the subsampling by 8. Because DCT kernels are orthogonal, the coefficients are largely decorrelated, too. Indeed, any dependencies among them would mean that the JPEG format could be further losslessly compressed. Second, due to the much weaker dependencies, it does not make sense to form co-occurrences of an order higher than two. Third, due to the different nature of each coefficient, a JPEG image is essentially formed by 64 channels of different statistical properties that are weakly dependent. This limits what a steganalyst can use for detection.

In the past, many different feature sets of various complexity were proposed. In this section, we briefly describe the JPEG Rich Model (JRM) and then review other statistical descriptors.

Because the JRM is quite complicated, we limit our description to a high-level exposition. The JRM is built as a collection of two-dimensional inter- and intra-block co-occurrences of absolute values of DCT coefficients and their differences by splitting them into DCT modes. Only the low and medium spatial frequencies are

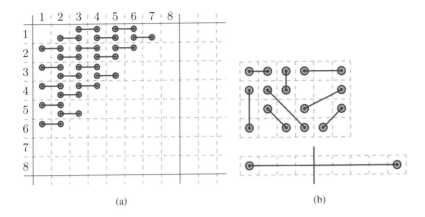

Figure 3.2 Pairs of DCT coefficients from which JRM co-occurrences are formed. The dots symbolically mark pairs of (intra or inter) neighboring coefficients or their differences.

used, as they typically hold the majority of non-zero DCT coefficients. Figure 3.2(a) shows the low and medium frequency coefficients that participate in computing a horizontal co-occurrence. Figure 3.2(b) shows all types of co-occurrences used in the JRM. The marked neighbors are used for both inter- and intra-block co-occurrences. All these co-occurrences are split into submodels based on the DCT mode (frequency). To keep the submodels well populated, the co-occurrences are symmetrized leveraging the natural symmetries of images and a small value of the truncation threshold T is used ($T = 3$ for co-occurrences of absolute values of coefficients and $T = 2$ for co-occurrences of differences of their absolute values). To allow the JRM to "see beyond small values of T," it contains co-occurrences computed from all DCT modes (the so-called integral components) with a larger value of $T = 5$. The final dimensionality of the JRM is 11,255, and, after adding reference features (see Cartesian calibration in Section 3.2.3), the final dimensionality of the JRM feature vector is doubled to $2 \times 11,255 = 22,510$.

Other popular feature representations of JPEG images include the 486-dimensional feature by Chen [38], which is an extension of the descriptor proposed by Shi et al. [35], formed by sample transition probability matrices (the so-called "Markov features") to capture both intra- and inter-block dependencies; the 216-dimensional feature proposed by Liu [39], which incorporated a more elaborate version of calibration and calibration by ratio; the 274-dimensional PF feature vector that originated from [34] and [35]; the Cross Domain Features (CDF) of dimensionality 1,234 (a merger of the Cartesian-calibrated PF feature vector and the 686-dimensional second-order SPAM feature [40]) [41]; and the CF* model (7,850) [24].

JRM is more effective against older steganography that introduces artifacts into the distribution of JPEG DCT coefficients. Modern embedding methods, such as J-UNIWARD [42] or UED [43], are less accurately detected in the DCT domain and are better detected using spatial-domain features, such as the SRM, the phase-aware PHARM features [44], and combinations of spatial and JPEG features [45].

3.2.3 Reference Representations

There exist general methods for "upgrading" steganalysis features that make them more sensitive to steganographic embedding changes and thus lead to more accurate detection. They are generally recognized as calibration or reference methods. The idea is to supply a reference feature vector to an existing feature vector with the hope that the machine learning will learn the relationship between both parts of the feature vector.

In JPEG domain, researchers introduced[2] an idea, schematically depicted in Figure 3.3, that allows one to approximately achieve such a feat. A stego JPEG image is first decompressed to the spatial domain, then cropped by 4 pixels on each side, and finally recompressed using the same quantization table. This image will be visually similar to the original cover (and stego) image but, because of the recompression on a shifted grid, the effects of embedding will be suppressed. A feature extracted from such an image will intuitively be a useful reference. This reference helps especially when the steganography violates first-order distribution of JPEG coefficients, such as OutGuess [47], Jsteg, or F5 [48]. In this case, the histogram of the reference image may in fact be closer to the histogram of the cover image than the histogram of the stego image.

In the original proposal in [46], the calibrated feature was computed as an L2 norm of the difference between the features computed from the stego image and the reference image. Later, it was discovered that it is more beneficial to skip the norm and use the difference between features directly for steganalysis [49]. In [41], the authors proposed to concatenate the original and reference features in what was termed "Cartesian calibration" as the best way to calibrate in the JPEG domain. The Cartesian calibration proved especially effective against YASS [50, 51], a steganographic algorithm originally designed to be (nearly) undetectable using features calibrated by difference. We note that Cartesian calibration has the effect

---

2   The concept of calibration was behind the first published attack on F5 [46].

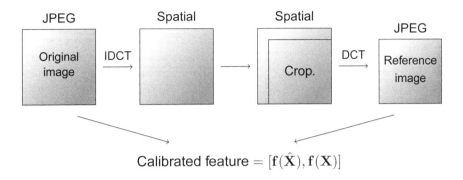

Calibrated feature $= [\mathbf{f}(\hat{\mathbf{X}}), \mathbf{f}(\mathbf{X})]$

Figure 3.3 Calibration in JPEG domain.

of doubling the feature dimensionality while calibration by difference preserves the feature dimension.

The beneficial effect of calibration strongly depends on the stego method, as well as on the feature vector being calibrated. The way calibration works (or does not work) is quite complex. The reader is referred to [41] for an in-depth study of calibration, its mechanism, and cases when it may actually hurt the detection.

There were also proposals to apply a similar concept in the spatial domain. In one such proposal, the embedding changes are partially suppressed by low-pass filtering the image (downsampling by a factor of 2) [18]. A different idea proposed by Ker [52] is to calibrate using images with overlapping or similar content.

Calibration was also proved to be extremely useful for feature-based detection of LSB replacement. The work of Fridrich et al. [53] described a general method for making any feature set "parity aware" in order to improve its ability to detect LSB replacement. Indeed, because most features in the spatial domain are formed from noise residuals, they are blind to the difference between LSB replacement and LSB matching. By supplying the feature vector with a feature extracted from the same image with zeroed out LSBs, one again provides a very useful reference. Parity-aware features with the ensemble classifier were shown to even outperform other targeted detectors of LSB replacement, such as the WS detector (Section 3.1.1) or structural detectors (Section 3.3.1). The obvious disadvantage of such detectors is common to all detectors built as classifiers — the necessity to train the detector —

which means that the steganalyst needs to have sufficiently many examples from the cover source.

The last idea recently proposed to improve steganalysis of JPEG images is the concept of "phase-awareness." Modern JPEG steganographic algorithms, such as J-UNIWARD [42] and UED [43] seem more detectable in the spatial domain rather than the JPEG domain. Based on the studies that appeared in [44, 54], what is essential for spatial-domain features to be effective against JPEG steganography is their awareness of the underlying 8×8 grid. The PHARM feature vector splits random projection of noise residuals based on their position with respect to the grid. This works because in a decompressed JPEG image, the pixels are not shift invariant and their statistical properties depend on their position or "phase" with respect to the compression grid.

3.3   QUANTITATIVE STEGANALYSIS

As introduced in Section 3.1, a steganalysis detector is a mapping that assigns a binary output (cover versus stego-image) to the inspected object by thresholding the value of the test statistic. We also learned that the test statistic of the WS detector is an estimate of the relative number of embedding changes, the change rate. In general, steganalysis designed to estimate the relative number of embedding changes, the change rate, is called "quantitative". Quantitative techniques can be important in forensic steganalysis because the estimated change rate can be related to the length of the embedded secret message if the details of the embedding algorithm are known (e.g., the codes used to embed the message). For instance, when the warden obtains estimates of payload size from multiple images that cluster around multiples of some typical cipher block lengths, she can deduce that the message is encrypted and even narrow down the possibilities for the encryption algorithm. In this section, we first describe one example of a quantitative attack on LSB replacement based on structural steganalysis, and then we will talk about the statistical properties of quantitative steganalyzers. We close the section with a general approach to quantitative steganalysis based on regression in feature spaces.

3.3.1   Structural Steganalysis of LSB Replacement

Structural detectors are all based on the observation that it is possible to divide pixels into two or more disjoint classes of groups of pixels whose cardinalities in the cover image are known in expectation, but start deviating from their nominal values when LSB replacement is applied. The first such method was the RS Analysis [55]. The simplest case of RS Analysis, Sample Pairs Analysis (SPA), was later rederived [56] in a way that enabled multiple extensions and improvements [57–65].

In this section, we briefly describe the structural steganalysis framework by Ker [60], and then discuss possible extensions while referring the reader to the literature.

Let P be the set of all horizontally or vertically adjacent pixels. We divide P into three types of the so-called trace sets C, E, and O, indexed by i, which is an integer measure of the difference between the two pixel values:

$$C_i = \{(r, s) \in P \mid \lfloor r/2 \rfloor - \lfloor s/2 \rfloor = i\} \tag{3.29}$$

$$E_i = \{(r, s) \in P \mid r - s = i, \ s \text{ is even}\} \tag{3.30}$$

$$O_i = \{(r, s) \in P \mid r - s = i, \ s \text{ is odd}\} \tag{3.31}$$

The set C_i contains all pairs whose values differ by i after performing a right bitshift of their binary representation or, equivalently, after dividing by 2 and rounding down. When both r and s are even or both are odd, then $r - s = 2i$. On the other hand, when r is even and s odd, $r - s = 2i - 1$, and $r - s = 2i + 1$ when r is odd and s even. Therefore, each C_i can be written as a disjoint union of four trace subsets

$$C_i = E_{2i} \cup O_{2i-1} \cup E_{2i+1} \cup O_{2i} \tag{3.32}$$

Now notice that C_i is invariant with respect to LSB embedding because the value of $\lfloor r/2 \rfloor$ does not depend on the LSB of r. The four trace subsets of C_i are, however, not invariant. Figure 3.4 shows the transition diagram between the four trace subsets, including the transition probabilities between them.

After changing a random portion of β of LSBs in the image, the expected values of the cardinalities of the trace sets can be derived from the transition diagram. They can be written in the following convenient matrix form ($a = \beta$, $b = 1 - \beta$):

$$\begin{pmatrix} E[|E'_{2i}|] \\ E[|O'_{2i-1}|] \\ E[|E'_{2i+1}|] \\ E[|O'_{2i}|] \end{pmatrix} = \begin{pmatrix} b^2 & ab & ab & a^2 \\ ab & b^2 & a^2 & ab \\ ab & a^2 & b^2 & ab \\ a^2 & ab & ab & b^2 \end{pmatrix} \begin{pmatrix} |E_{2i}| \\ |O_{2i-1}| \\ |E_{2i+1}| \\ |O_{2i}| \end{pmatrix} \tag{3.33}$$

The trace sets are built in such a way that, for a cover image, we should have for the cardinalities $|E_j| \approx |O_j|$. This is because the number of pixel pairs with

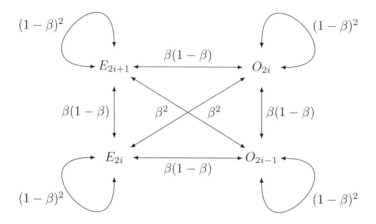

Figure 3.4 Transitions and their probabilities for the four trace sets forming C_i.

$r - s = j$ should not depend on whether s is even or odd. It can be easily verified that LSB replacement violates this condition only for odd values of $j = 2i + 1$. The condition $|E_{2i+1}| \approx |O_{2i+1}|$ can thus be used as a "zero-message hypothesis" or "cover hypothesis" that will constrain the unknown value of β. All one needs to do is to write the cardinalities of the trace sets in the cover image as functions of the corresponding cardinalities in the stego image by inverting (3.33). Executing the steps, one thus obtains the following quadratic equation for β for each $j = 2i + 1$:

$$
\begin{aligned}
\beta^2 \left(|C_i| - |C_{i+1}| \right) & \\
+ \beta \left(|E'_{2i+2}| + |O'_{2i+2}| - 2|E'_{2i+1}| + 2|O'_{2i+1}| - |E'_{2i}| - |O'_{2i}| \right) & \\
+ \left(|E'_{2i+1}| - |O'_{2i+1}| \right) = 0 &
\end{aligned}
\tag{3.34}
$$

When adding these equations over all indices i and solving the resulting single quadratic equation, one obtains a generalized version of SPA proposed by Dumitrescu [58]. Alternatively, one could solve (3.34) for some small values of $|i|$ (e.g., $|i| \leq 2$), obtaining individual estimates $\hat{\beta}_i$, and estimate the final change rate as $\hat{\beta} = \min_i \hat{\beta}_i$. This choice has been shown to provide more stable results compared with SPA [59]. Finally, (3.34) could be solved in the least-square sense [60, 65].

The approach described above can be extended to groups of more than two pixels. The triples analysis and quadruples analysis [60, 61] were reported to provide slightly more accurate change-rate estimates, especially for short messages. An alternative extension of SPA to groups of multiple pixels appeared in [57]. Structural steganalysis has also been extended to detection of embedding in two LSBs in [64, 66].

3.3.2 Quantitative Detectors as Regressors

Both the WS detector and the structural detector described in the previous section are hand-crafted, heavily utilizing the properties of LSB replacement. There is an alternative method to constructing quantitative detectors that is general and works for essentially any steganography. It is based on regression in the feature representation of images. Its disadvantage is that one needs sufficiently many examples from the cover source for training.

The basic idea is quite simple. As the embedded payload increases, the difference between the feature vectors of the cover and stego image also increases. Thus, instead of building a classifier that distinguishes cover and stego features, one could build a regressor that learns the relationship between the feature position and the embedded payload (change rate).

Let us assume that we have L stego images embedded with change rates β_i represented with d-dimensional feature vectors $\mathbf{f}^{(i)} = (f_1^{(i)}, \ldots, f_d^{(i)})$, $1 \leq i \leq L$. In the simplest possible formulation, the change rate will be linear in the features, $\hat{\beta}_i = \mathbf{f}^{(i)} \cdot \mathbf{p}, \forall i$, where $\mathbf{p} \in \mathbb{R}^d$ is a column vector of unknown parameters and "·" is the dot product. The unknown vector parameter $\mathbf{p}$ can be determined by minimizing the total square error $\sum_{i=1}^{L} (\mathbf{f}^{(i)} \cdot \mathbf{p} - \beta_i)^2$. This problem has a well-known solution

$$\mathbf{p} = (\mathbf{F}'\mathbf{F})^{-1}\mathbf{F}'\boldsymbol{\beta} \tag{3.35}$$

where $\mathbf{F}$ is a $L \times d$ matrix whose rows are the image features, $F_{ij} = f_j^{(i)}$, and $\boldsymbol{\beta} = (\beta_1, \ldots, \beta_L)$.

Change-rate estimators constructed in this fashion typically exhibit very good accuracy, which generally depends on how well the features react to embedding. Note that, in contrast to hand-crafted attacks, here the steganalyst does not need any information about the embedding algorithm; all that is needed is a set of cover and the corresponding stego images with known change rates. The reader is referred to [67] for more details about this approach to quantitative steganalysis. This reference also contains an alternative and little more accurate implementation using methods of support vector regression [68].

3.3.3   Statistical Properties of Quantitative Detectors

The output of a quantitative detector is a random variable and, as such, has some expectation and statistical spread. As shown in [69, 70], the error of quantitative steganalyzers has two components: the within-image error and the between-image error,

$$\hat{\beta} - \beta = W + B \qquad (3.36)$$

The within-image error, which we denote as W, is caused by random correlations between the image and the message, as well as the fact that the embedding visits a different part of the image each time we embed. Its behavior is well-modeled with a Gaussian distribution. To explain this error in more detail, imagine that the embedding modifies a pseudo-random fraction β of pixels in the cover image. The actual modifications will depend on the secret message itself and the embedding key. If this is repeated n times, the variations in the change-rate estimate are due to the within-image error. Its distribution depends on the image content (how homogeneous it is), as well as on the relative payload. When using an image with uniform content, such as a sky image, the variations due to the image content will be smaller than in an image with many different textures and objects. With larger change rate (payload size), the contribution of the image content to this type of error becomes smaller.

The distribution of the between-image error is connected to properties of natural images. It is essentially the estimator bias. Because the within-image error is Gaussian, one can isolate the between-image error by averaging all n estimates from the previous paragraph. The distribution of this error is obtained by sampling over many images. A good fit for the distribution of the between-image error is the Student's t-distribution, and this holds true for just about any quantitative detector ever described in the literature.

3.4   SPECIAL TOPICS

In this section, we list selected topics in steganalysis that received significant attention from researchers. The exposition is kept rather brief due to space constraints. The topics include the problem of the cover source mismatch, compatibility attacks, multiclass detectors, and batch steganography and pooled steganalysis.

3.4.1 Cover Source Mismatch

Currently, the most accurate detectors for modern steganographic schemes are constructed using machine learning as classifiers in a feature space. This is because modern steganography avoids introducing easily identifiable (and modelable) artifacts. The evidence for embedding becomes strong only when representing the digital media object with a rich representation (see Section 3.2). A big disadvantage of detectors constructed as classifiers is the need for the training phase, which means that the steganalyst has access to sufficiently many images from the cover source from which the steganographer is drawing the covers. This makes the detector "overspecialized" (not overtrained) to the chosen cover source. Even though the detector may be astonishingly accurate on the source on which it was trained, it may be disastrously inaccurate on images from a never-before-seen source. The situation when a steganalyzer is trained on one source of images and used to detect steganography in a different source of images usually results in a detection performance loss due to the so-called cover source mismatch (CSM).

The impact of CSM depends on (too) many factors, such as the source properties, which include the image resolution, format, processing, hardware and its settings, and environmental conditions. A very influential factor is the detector itself, its construction, and the chosen feature space. Last but not least, the impact of the CSM also depends on the steganographic algorithm.

The negative impact of the CSM has been known to the steganography community for a long time [37, 71–77]. It is not an exaggeration to state that the CSM is one of the main factors that is negatively affecting the successful deployment of steganalysis in the real world.

The problem of a mismatched detector in signal detection is rather old. Techniques, such as robust statistical hypothesis testing [78], were proposed to address this issue within statistical signal detection, and domain adaptation [79, 80] and domain generalization [81] in machine learning. The problem with applying the techniques developed in machine learning community is that they address only a "small" or "mild" mismatch, while in steganalysis the distribution mismatch is usually gross. This is because the variety of different processing that one can apply to images is simply too large. Images processed using a denoising filter will have extremely different statistical properties from those processed using sharpening, for example. A very useful insight was brought by the authors of [77], who realized that a large portion of the performance loss can be recovered by first applying some global transform, such as shift or scaling, to the features before analyzing them with a classifier. Other ideas proposed to mitigate the impact of the CSM include expanding the diversity of the training set and training a bank of classifiers for different sources and then selecting the one whose cover distribution is most compatible with the tested images [82, 83].

3.4.2 Compatibility Attacks

There exist cover sources in which steganography can be detected with an astonishingly small detection error, even for extremely small payloads. This is usually due to constraints that strongly limit the admissible values of pixels. The first such "compatibility" attack was described in [84]. It applies when the steganographer hides data by slightly changing the pixel values in a cover image that is a decompressed JPEG. The key observation enabling the compatibility attack is the fact that JPEG compression is a many-to-one mapping. Because of the rounding of DCT coefficients during JPEG compression, a large number of images will compress to the exact same JPEG image. This means that the pixels in a decompressed JPEG image are highly constrained. Changing even a single pixel (for example, by flipping its LSB), will produce an image about which one could, in principle, prove that it cannot be the result of decompressing any JPEG file while still bearing a strong artifact of the JPEG compression. Indeed, even though the information about the JPEG quantization table (and other parameters of JPEG compression, such as color downsampling or the type of implementation of the DCT) is lost by storing a decompressed JPEG in a raster format, one can estimate the entries in the quantization table by identifying the clusters of unquantized DCT coefficients surrounding integer multiples of quantization steps.

The JPEG compatibility attack relies on a procedural mistake of the steganographer: that she will embed her message in an image that was originally stored as a JPEG. However, this situation may not be as "niche" as it might appear at the first sight because the vast majority of users store their digital photographs in the JPEG format. However, the capacity of steganographic algorithms that hide data in DCT coefficients of JPEG images is generally much lower in comparison with spatial-domain steganographic techniques. Moreover, while basically all publicly available steganographic tools are capable of hiding messages in raster formats, not all allow for the hiding of messages in JPEGs. And none, as far as the author of this chapter is aware, take into account the compatibility issue.

Realizing the JPEG compatibility attack in practice is not, however, easy. This is because the actual values of the pixels may depend on the implementation of the inverse DCT and even on the computer platform. Also, it may not be easy or even possible to estimate the quantization steps of DCT coefficients of high frequencies simply because of lack of any non-zero DCT coefficients. Plus, the JPEG format allows for the subsampling of the chrominance channels, which, technically, should also be estimated. The final complication is that color images may have up to three quantization tables (one for luminance and two for the two chrominance channels) that need to be estimated in a compatibility attack. The final difficulty is that proving that a no JPEG image could decompress to an existing raster image may require a very expensive search.

Researchers thus developed variants of the compatibility attack that are not based on an incompatibility proof. As explained above, most of them start by estimating the parameters, c, of the JPEG compression, including the JPEG quality factor (the luminance quantization table), DCT (e.g., slow vs. fast), chrominance tables, and color subsampling. Then, using the estimated JPEG compression parameters, the raster image $\mathbf{Y}$ is recompressed to obtain $\hat{\mathbf{Y}} = \mathrm{JPEG}_{\mathbf{c}}^{-1}\left(\mathrm{JPEG}_{\mathbf{c}}(\mathbf{Y})\right)$. In [10], $\hat{\mathbf{Y}}$ was used as a pixel predictor in the WS detector implemented with uniform weights. This version of the compatibility attack is limited to detection of LSB replacement.

A different approach was proposed in [85], where the authors used $\hat{\mathbf{Y}}$ to directly estimate the change rate as a polynomial function of the relative number of differences between $\mathbf{Y}$ and $\hat{\mathbf{Y}}$: $1/n\left|\{(i,j)|y_{ij} \neq \hat{y}_{ij}\}\right|$. This attack can detect embedding operations other than LSB replacement, but is less robust to inaccurate estimates of c. Moreover, it does not distinguish between embedding changes and natural recompression artifacts. This problem was alleviated in [86] by using a more complex descriptor of the recompression artifacts in the form of a histogram of the number of mismatched pixels over all 8×8 blocks. Because recompression artifacts usually manifest as specific patterns rather than individual changed pixels, this attack can markedly improve the detection accuracy, especially for small payloads.

A different type of compatibility attack was recently discovered for color images that exhibit traces of color interpolation. Some color interpolation algorithms, such as AHD (adaptive homogeneity-directed) and PPG (patterned pixel grouping) available in ufraw version 0.18 with dcraw version 9.06, introduce rather strong artifacts that allow extremely accurate detection of even small change rates. This attack is not limited to LSB replacement. In [30], it was shown that the "minmax41c" submodel of the color rich model (Section 3.2.1) contains eight "violator bins" that are nearly empty in covers and get populated by embedding.

In general, compatibility attacks are always based on some singular property of the cover source. One could say that such cover sources (such as decompressed JPEGs and color images obtained using certain color interpolation algorithms) are simply unsuitable for steganography and should not be used for embedding. If the steganographer needs to use such images, the common advice is to subject them to additional processing, such as downsampling in order to suppress or eliminate the strong compatibility constraints. One, however, needs to be careful of what type of processing is used, as [53] showed that images processed using low-pass filtering and especially median filtering are susceptible to powerful attacks using low-dimensional features.

3.4.3   Multiclass Detectors

So far, the steganalysis problem has always been considered as a binary hypothesis test. One can, of course, consider more general cases when the steganalyst tests between several classes, such as the covers, and stego images embedded with several different embedding techniques. This is the problem of multiclass detection. Indeed, within the framework of feature-based classifiers, the position of the feature vector may be indicative of the stego technique used. This will be important to forensic investigators in their effort to identify the stego software and/or extract the secret message.

A binary classifier can be extended in order to classify classes into $k > 2$ by building $\binom{k}{2}$ binary classifiers distinguishing between every pair of classes and then fusing the results using a classical voting system. This method for multiclassification is known as the Max–Wins principle [87]. The topic of multiclass detection has been studied in [88–90].

3.4.4   Batch Steganography and Pooled Steganalysis

Looking at the secret communication from the point of view of long term use, one quickly discovers important "meta" issues. Knowing that the warden is closely inspecting all traffic between Alice and Bob (and many more innocent users), the steganographers face the problem of how to minimize the risk of being detected over an extended period of time when the warden can accumulate evidence about their use of steganography. In particular, how should Alice and Bob distribute their payload among the images they exchange? For sure, it would be an extremely bad idea to always embed the largest possible message into every image that they attach to their e-mails as the warden would quickly reach the point, where the secret communication would become virtually certain. The best strategy for the steganographers should depend on the warden's detector. For example, if the detector error has thick tails, it might be a good idea to keep sending cover images, and once in a while embed a large message into one image rather than spread the payload uniformly. Moreover, the steganographers should probably taper off their communication rate to zero over time, as a fixed rate would eventually become detectable due to the square root law of imperfect steganography [91–94]. This problem is recognized as batch steganography, and remains largely unsolved up to now.

The corresponding problem on the side of the warden is called "pooled steganalysis". It pertains to the problem of making decisions about the usage of steganography over time after analyzing the traffic. The first step towards a "pooled detector" was taken in [95], where the authors proposed a shift from identifying individual stego images to identifying stego users. They analyzed 800,000 JPEG images, all with quality factor 85 from 4,000 users of a social network. The steganographer was simulated to use F5 [48], no-shrinkage F5 (nsF5) [96], JP Hide and Seek, OutGuess [47], and Steghide [97], at 0–0.25 bpnzac (bits per non-zero AC DCT coefficient). Four embedding strategies for spreading payload among multiple covers (batch steganography) were studied. The warden performed pooled steganalysis under the assumption that most users were nonguilty. The images were represented using the 274-dimensional PF feature vector [49]. The idea was to let the nonguilty users help identify the steganographer as an outlier in the feature space. This was achieved by computing the local outlier factor (LOF) for each user. The steganographer was always ranked near the top on the list of the most suspicious users.

3.5 STEGANALYSIS IN THE WIDE SENSE

The goal of steganalysis is to detect the presence of a secret message in a given cover object. In practice, however, the warden will likely wish to know more. The warden may want to determine the steganographic algorithm and the stego key, and eventually extract the message. Such activities belong to forensic steganalysis or steganalysis in the wide sense, which can be loosely defined as a collection of tasks needed to identify individuals who are communicating in secrecy, the stegosystem they are using, its parameters (the stego key), and the message itself.

The success of this effort may be significantly increased by incorporating forensic evidence at the detector. For example, when a suspect's computer is seized, the stego tool may still reside on the computer, or its traces may be recoverable even after it has been uninstalled (e.g., using the utility called Gargoyle by Wetstone Tech). In this case, the warden may have more information, such as a pair of cover and stego images, which may greatly help her in recovering the stego key by searching and comparing the locations of embedding changes in the resulting stego image with those in the stego image under investigation.

A weak stego key space can compromise an otherwise hard-to-attack steganographic scheme. The stego key usually determines a pseudo-random path through the image where the message bits are embedded. It can also be used for encrypting the message itself. Depending on the size of the stego key space, the warden can go through all stego keys or use a dictionary attack. For each key tried, the warden extracts an alleged message. Once she obtains a legible message, she will know that Alice and Bob use steganography, and she will have the correct stego key, too.

This attack will not work if the message is encrypted prior to embedding because the warden cannot reliably distinguish between a random bit stream and an encrypted message. However, encrypting the message using a strong encryption scheme with a secure key still does not mean that the stego key does not have to be strong. This is because the warden can determine the stego key by other means than inspecting the message [98]. She can still run through all stego keys as above; however, this time she will be checking the statistical properties of the pixels along the pseudo-random path rather than the extracted message bits. The statistical properties of pixels along the true embedding path should be different than the statistical properties of a randomly chosen path, as long as the image is not fully embedded. [3]

A different variant of this attack was described in [99]. Assuming that a quantitative detector of steganography is available (a detector that estimates the message length), one could first estimate the message length (the number of embedding changes), and then attempt to read the embedded message length from the header and check for its consistency with the estimated message length. Since the error distribution of quantitative steganalyzers is known and can be estimated, one can quickly accumulate evidence for a specific stego key from multiple stego images embedded with the same key. The authors argue that it is rather hard to eliminate this type of attack unless the steganographers use strong stego keys and adopt a procedure for frequent key renewal.

When the steganographers reuse the stego-key and always embed in images of the same size, with enough stego-images, it may become possible to estimate the embedding path and identify which pixels carry the secret payload. This idea was proposed by Ker [100, 101] and then further analyzed by Quach (see [102] and the references therein).

Forensic analysts may also use system attacks in addition to the attacks described in previous sections. By system attacks, we understand a class of detectors

---

3   Fully embedded images can most likely be reliably detected using other methods.

that leverage some mistakes in how a specific steganographic algorithm is implemented or used in practice. Instead of identifying subtle statistical anomalies due to the embedding changes themselves, system attacks look for characteristic "fingerprints" of the embedding software and flaws in the implementation of the steganographic algorithm itself. One may also take advantage of reused stego keys and/or improperly chosen cover images, such as a publicly available image. Such attacks, when applicable, can be very powerful and much more accurate than statistical steganalysis of pixels or DCT coefficients.

The authors of [103–105] and [106] give examples of other unintentional fingerprints left in stego images by various stego products. Bell et al. [107] describe a general method for identifying signatures of steganographic software.

References

[1] Fridrich, J., and M. Goljan, "On Estimation of Secret Message Length in LSB Steganography in Spatial Domain," in *Proceedings SPIE, Electronic Imaging, Security, Steganography, and Watermarking of Multimedia Contents VI*, Vol. 5306, San Jose, CA, January 19–22, 2004, pp. 23–34.

[2] Ker, A. D., and R. Böhme, "Revisiting Weighted Stego-Image Steganalysis," in *Proceedings SPIE, Electronic Imaging, Security, Forensics, Steganography, and Watermarking of Multimedia Contents X*, Vol. 6819, San Jose, CA, January 27–31, 2008, pp. 5 1–17.

[3] Zitzmann, C., et al., "Statistical Decision Methods in Hidden Information Detection," in *Information Hiding, 13th International Conference*, Lecture Notes in Computer Science, Prague, Czech Republic, May 18–20, 2011, pp. 163–177.

[4] Böhme, R., *Advanced Statistical Steganalysis*, Berlin Heidelberg: Springer-Verlag, 2010.

[5] Fillatre, L., "Adaptive Steganalysis of Least Significant Bit Replacement in Grayscale Images," *IEEE Transactions on Signal Processing*, Vol. 60, No. 2, 2011, pp. 556–569.

[6] Thai, T., R. Cogranne, and F. Retraint, "Statistical Model of Quantized DCT Coefficients: Application in the Steganalysis of Jsteg Algorithm," *Image Processing, IEEE Transactions on*, Vol. 23, No. 5, May 2014, pp. 1–14.

[7] Thai, T., R. Cogranne, and F. Retraint, "Optimal Detection of OutGuess using an Accurate Model of DCT Coefficients," in *Sixth IEEE International Workshop on Information Forensics and Security*, Atlanta, GA, USA, December 3–5 2014.

[8] Chandramouli, R., and N. D. Memon, "A Distributed Detection Framework for Steganalysis," in *Proceedings of the 3rd ACM Multimedia & Security Workshop*, Los Angeles, CA, November 4, 2000, pp. 123–126.

[9] Dabeer, O., et al., "Detection of Hiding in the Least Significant Bit," *IEEE Transactions on Signal Processing*, Vol. 52, 2004, pp. 3046–3058.

[10] Böhme, R., "Weighted Stego-Image Steganalysis for JPEG Covers," in *Information Hiding, 10th International Workshop*, Vol. 5284 of Lecture Notes in Computer Science, Santa Barbara, CA: Springer-Verlag, New York, June 19–21, 2007, pp. 178–194.

[11] Westfeld, A., "Generic Adoption of Spatial Steganalysis to Transformed Domain," in *Information Hiding, 10th International Workshop*, Vol. 5284 of Lecture Notes in Computer Science, Santa Barbara, CA: Springer-Verlag, New York, June 19–21, 2007, pp. 161–177.

[12] Schöttle, P., S. Korff, and R. Böhme, "Weighted Stego-Image Steganalysis for Naive Content-Adaptive Embedding," in *Fourth IEEE International Workshop on Information Forensics and Security*, Tenerife, Spain, December 2–5, 2012.

[13] Kirchner, M., and R. Böhme, "Steganalysis in Technicolor: Boosting WS Detection of Stego Images from CFA-Interpolated Covers," in *Proc. IEEE ICASSP*, Florence, Italy, May 4–9, 2014.

[14] Cogranne, R., et al., "Statistical Detection of LSB Matching Using Hypothesis Testing Theory," in *Information Hiding, 14th International Conference*, Vol. 7692 of Lecture Notes in Computer Science, Berkeley, California, May 15–18, 2012, pp. 46–62.

[15] Cogranne, R., and F. Retraint, "Application of Hypothesis Testing Theory for Optimal Detection of LSB Matching Data Hiding," *Signal Processing*, Vol. 93, No. 7, July, 2013, pp. 1724–1737.

[16] Cogranne, R., and F. Retraint, "An Asymptotically Uniformly Most Powerful Test for LSB Matching Detection," *IEEE Transactions on Information Forensics and Security*, Vol. 8, No. 3, 2013, pp. 464–476.

[17] Harmsen, J. J., and W. A. Pearlman, "Steganalysis of Additive Noise Modelable Information Hiding," in *Proceedings SPIE, Electronic Imaging, Security and Watermarking of Multimedia Contents V*, Vol. 5020, Santa Clara, CA, January 21–24, 2003, pp. 131–142.

[18] Ker, A. D., "Resampling and the Detection of LSB Matching in Color Bitmaps," in *Proceedings SPIE, Electronic Imaging, Security, Steganography, and Watermarking of Multimedia Contents VII*, Vol. 5681, San Jose, CA, January 16–20, 2005, pp. 1–15.

[19] Ker, A. D., "Steganalysis of LSB Matching in Grayscale Images," *IEEE Signal Processing Letters*, Vol. 12, No. 6, June 2005, pp. 441–444.

[20] Fridrich, J., and J. Kodovský, "Rich Models for Steganalysis of Digital Images," *IEEE Transactions on Information Forensics and Security*, Vol. 7, No. 3, June 2011, pp. 868–882.

[21] Kodovský, J., J. Fridrich, and V. Holub, "On Dangers of Overtraining Steganography to Incomplete Cover Model," in *Proceedings of the 13th ACM Multimedia & Security Workshop*, Niagara Falls, NY, September 29–30, 2011, pp. 69–76.

[22] Pevný, T., "Co-occurrence steganalysis in high dimension," in *Proceedings SPIE, Electronic Imaging, Media Watermarking, Security, and Forensics 2012*, Vol. 8303, San Francisco, CA, January 23–26, 2012, pp. 0B 1–13.

[23] Chen, L., et al., "A Novel mapping Scheme for Steganalysis," in *Proc. 11th International Workshop on Digital-Forensics and Watermarking*, Vol. 7809 of Lecture Notes in Computer Science, Shanghai, China: Springer-Verlag, New York, October 31–November 3, 2012, pp. 19–33.

[24] Kodovský, J., J. Fridrich, and V. Holub, "Ensemble Classifiers for Steganalysis of Digital Media," *IEEE Transactions on Information Forensics and Security*, Vol. 7, No. 2, 2012, pp. 432–444.

[25] Ker, A. D., "Implementing the projected spatial rich features on a GPU," in *Proceedings SPIE, Electronic Imaging, Media Watermarking, Security, and Forensics 2014*, Vol. 9028, San Francisco, CA, February 3–5, 2014, pp. 1801–1810.

[26] Tang, W., et al., "Adaptive Steganalysis Against WOW Embedding Algorithm," in *2nd ACM IH&MMSec. Workshop*, Salzburg, Austria, June 11–13, 2014.

[27] Holub, V., and J. Fridrich, "Designing Steganographic Distortion Using Directional Filters," in *Fourth IEEE International Workshop on Information Forensics and Security*, Tenerife, Spain, December 2–5, 2012.

[28] Li, B., M. Wang, and J. Huang, "A new cost function for spatial image steganography," in *Proceedings IEEE, International Conference on Image Processing, ICIP*, Paris, France, October 27–30, 2014.

[29] Goljan, M., R. Cogranne, and J. Fridrich, "Rich Model for Steganalysis of Color Images," in *Sixth IEEE International Workshop on Information Forensics and Security*, Atlanta, GA, December 3–5, 2014.

[30] Fridrich, J., and M. Goljan, "CFA-aware Features for Steganalysis of Color Images," in *Proceedings SPIE, Electronic Imaging, Media Watermarking, Security, and Forensics 2015*, Vol. 9409, San Francisco, CA, February 8–12, 2015.

[31] Avcibas, I., N. D. Memon, and B. Sankur, "Steganalysis Using Image Quality Metrics," in *Proceedings SPIE, Electronic Imaging, Security and Watermarking of Multimedia Contents III*, Vol. 4314, San Jose, CA, January 22–25, 2001, pp. 523–531.

[32] Avcibas, I., et al., "Image Steganalysis with Binary Similarity Measures," *EURASIP Journal on Applied Signal Processing*, Vol. 17, 2005, pp. 2749–2757.

[33] Farid, H., and L. Siwei, "Detecting Hidden Messages Using Higher-Order Statistics and Support Vector Machines," in *Information Hiding, 5th International Workshop*, Vol. 2578 of Lecture Notes in Computer Science, Noordwijkerhout, The Netherlands: Springer-Verlag, New York, October 7–9, 2002, pp. 340–354.

[34] Fridrich, J., "Feature-Based Steganalysis for JPEG Images and its Implications for Future Design of Steganographic Schemes," in *Information Hiding, 6th International Workshop*, Vol. 3200 of Lecture Notes in Computer Science, Toronto, Canada: Springer-Verlag, New York, May 23–25, 2004, pp. 67–81.

[35] Shi, Y. Q., C. Chen, and W. Chen, "A Markov Process Based Approach to Effective Attacking JPEG Steganography," in *Information Hiding, 8th International Workshop*, Vol. 4437 of Lecture Notes in Computer Science, Alexandria, VA: Springer-Verlag, New York, July 10–12, 2006, pp. 249–264.

[36] Zou, D., et al., "Steganalysis based on Markov model of thresholded prediction-error image," in *Proceedings IEEE, International Conference on Multimedia and Expo*, Toronto, Canada, July 9–12, 2006, pp. 1365–1368.

[37] Goljan, M., J. Fridrich, and T. Holotyak, "New Blind Steganalysis and its Implications," in *Proceedings SPIE, Electronic Imaging, Security, Steganography, and Watermarking of Multimedia Contents VIII*, Vol. 6072, San Jose, CA, January 16–19, 2006, pp. 1–13.

[38] Chen, C., and Y. Q. Shi, "JPEG image steganalysis utilizing both intrablock and interblock correlations," in *Circuits and Systems, ISCAS 2008. IEEE International Symposium on*, Seattle, WA, May, 18–21, 2008, pp. 3029–3032.

[39] Liu, Q., "Steganalysis of DCT-embedding based adaptive steganography and YASS," in *Proceedings of the 13th ACM Multimedia & Security Workshop*, Niagara Falls, NY, September 29–30, 2011, pp. 77–86.

[40] Pevný, T., P. Bas, and J. Fridrich, "Steganalysis by Subtractive Pixel Adjacency Matrix," in *Proceedings of the 11th ACM Multimedia & Security Workshop*, Princeton, NJ, September 7–8, 2009, pp. 75–84.

[41] Kodovský, J., and J. Fridrich, "Calibration Revisited," in *Proceedings of the 11th ACM Multimedia & Security Workshop*, Princeton, NJ, September 7–8, 2009, pp. 63–74.

[42] Holub, V., and J. Fridrich, "Universal Distortion Design for Steganography in an Arbitrary Domain," *EURASIP Journal on Inf. Sec., Spec. Issue on Revised Selected Papers of 1st ACM IH&MMS Workshop*, Vol. 2014:1, 2014.

[43] Guo, L., J. Ni, and Y.-Q. Shi, "An Efficient JPEG Steganographic Scheme Using Uniform Embedding," in *Fourth IEEE International Workshop on Information Forensics and Security*, Tenerife, Spain, December 2–5, 2012.

[44] Fridrich, J., and M. Goljan, "Phase-Aware Projection Model for Steganalysis of JPEG Images," in *Proceedings SPIE, Electronic Imaging, Media Watermarking, Security, and Forensics 2015*, Vol. 9409, San Francisco, CA, February 8–12, 2015.

[45] Holub, V., and J. Fridrich, "Challenging the Doctrines of JPEG Steganography," in *Proceedings SPIE, Electronic Imaging, Media Watermarking, Security, and Forensics 2014*, Vol. 9028, San Francisco, CA, February 3–5, 2014, pp. 02 1–8.

[46] Fridrich, J., M. Goljan, and D. Hogea, "Steganalysis of JPEG Images: Breaking the F5 Algorithm," in *Information Hiding, 5th International Workshop*, Vol. 2578 of Lecture Notes in Computer Science, Noordwijkerhout, The Netherlands: Springer-Verlag, New York, October 7–9, 2002, pp. 310–323.

[47] Provos, N., "Defending Against Statistical Steganalysis," in *10th USENIX Security Symposium*, Washington, DC, August 13–17, 2001, pp. 323–335.

[48] Westfeld, A., "High Capacity Despite Better Steganalysis (F5 – A Steganographic Algorithm)," in *Information Hiding, 4th International Workshop*, Vol. 2137 of Lecture Notes in Computer Science, Pittsburgh, PA: Springer-Verlag, New York, April 25–27, 2001, pp. 289–302.

[49] Pevný, T., and J. Fridrich, "Merging Markov and DCT Features for Multi-Class JPEG Steganalysis," in *Proceedings SPIE, Electronic Imaging, Security, Steganography, and Watermarking of Multimedia Contents IX*, Vol. 6505, San Jose, CA, January 29–February 1, 2007, pp. 3 1–14.

[50] Solanki, K., A. Sarkar, and B. S. Manjunath, "YASS: Yet Another Steganographic Scheme that Resists Blind Steganalysis," in *Information Hiding, 9th International Workshop*, Vol. 4567 of Lecture Notes in Computer Science, Saint Malo, France: Springer-Verlag, New York, June 11–13, 2007, pp. 16–31.

[51] Sarkar, A., K. Solanki, and B. S. Manjunath, "Further Study on YASS: Steganography Based on Randomized Embedding to Resist Blind Steganalysis," in *Proceedings SPIE, Electronic Imaging, Security, Forensics, Steganography, and Watermarking of Multimedia Contents X*, Vol. 6819, San Jose, CA, January 27–31, 2008, pp. 16–31.

[52] Whitaker, J. M., and A. D. Ker, "Steganalysis of overlapping images," in *Proceedings SPIE, Electronic Imaging, Media Watermarking, Security, and Forensics 2015*, Vol. 9409, San Francisco, CA, February 8–12, 2015.

[53] Fridrich, J., and J. Kodovský, "Steganalysis of LSB Replacement Using Parity-Aware Features," in *Information Hiding, 14th International Conference*, Vol. 7692 of Lecture Notes in Computer Science, Berkeley, California, May 15–18, 2012, pp. 31–45.

[54] Holub, V., and J. Fridrich, "Low Complexity Features for JPEG Steganalysis Using Undecimated DCT," *IEEE Transactions on Information Forensics and Security*. Under review.

[55] Fridrich, J., M. Goljan, and R. Du, "Detecting LSB Steganography in Color and Gray-Scale Images," *IEEE Multimedia, Special Issue on Security*, Vol. 8, No. 4, October–December 2001, pp. 22–28.

[56] Dumitrescu, S., X. Wu, and N. D. Memon, "On Steganalysis of Random LSB Embedding in Continuous-Tone Images," in *Proceedings IEEE, International Conference on Image Processing, ICIP 2002*, Rochester, NY, September 22–25, 2002, pp. 324–339.

[57] Dumitrescu, S., and X. Wu, "LSB Steganalysis Based on Higher-Order Statistics," in *Proceedings of the 7th ACM Multimedia & Security Workshop*, New York, NY, August 1–2, 2005, pp. 25–32.

[58] Dumitrescu, S., X. Wu, and Z. Wang, "Detection of LSB Steganography via Sample Pairs Analysis," in *Information Hiding, 5th International Workshop*, Vol. 2578 of Lecture Notes in Computer Science, Noordwijkerhout, The Netherlands: Springer-Verlag, New York, October 7–9, 2002, pp. 355–372.

[59] Ker, A. D., "Improved Detection of LSB Steganography in Grayscale Images," in *Information Hiding, 6th International Workshop*, Vol. 3200 of Lecture Notes in Computer Science, Toronto, Canada: Springer-Verlag, Berlin, May 23–25, 2004, pp. 97–115.

[60] Ker, A. D., "A General Framework for Structural Analysis of LSB Replacement," in *Information Hiding, 7th International Workshop*, Vol. 3727 of Lecture Notes in Computer Science, Barcelona, Spain: Springer-Verlag, Berlin, June 6–8, 2005, pp. 296–311.

[61] Ker, A. D., "Fourth-order structural steganalysis and analysis of cover assumptions," in *Proceedings SPIE, Electronic Imaging, Security, Steganography, and Watermarking of Multimedia Contents VIII*, Vol. 6072, San Jose, CA, January 16–19, 2006, pp. 25–38.

[62] Ker, A. D., "A Fusion of Maximal Likelihood and Structural Steganalysis," in *Information Hiding, 9th International Workshop*, Vol. 4567 of Lecture Notes in Computer Science, Saint Malo, France: Springer-Verlag, Berlin, June 11–13, 2007, pp. 204–219.

[63] Ker, A. D., "Optimally Weighted Least-Squares Steganalysis," in *Proceedings SPIE, Electronic Imaging, Security, Steganography, and Watermarking of Multimedia Contents IX*, Vol. 6505, San Jose, CA, January 29–February 1, 2007, pp. 6 1–6 16.

[64] Ker, A. D., "Steganalysis of Embedding in Two Least Significant Bits," *IEEE Transactions on Information Forensics and Security*, Vol. 2, 2007, pp. 46–54.

[65] Lu, P., et al., "An Improved Sample Pairs Method for Detection of LSB Embedding," in *Information Hiding, 6th International Workshop*, Vol. 3200 of Lecture Notes in Computer Science, Toronto, Canada: Springer-Verlag, Berlin, May 23–25, 2004, pp. 116–127.

[66] Yang, C., et al., "Steganalysis Frameworks of Embedding in Multiple Least-Significant Bits," *IEEE Transactions on Information Forensics and Security*, Vol. 3, 2008, pp. 662–672.

[67] Pevný, T., J. Fridrich, and A. D. Ker, "From Blind to Quantitative Steganalysis," in *Proceedings SPIE, Electronic Imaging, Media Forensics and Security*, Vol. 7254, San Jose, CA, January 18–21, 2009, pp. 0C 1–0C 14.

[68] Smola, A. J., and B. Schölkopf, "A tutorial on support vector regression," NeuroCOLT2 Technical Report NC2-TR-1998-030, 1998.

[69] Böhme, R., *Improved Statistical Steganalysis Using Models of Heterogeneous Cover Signals*, Ph.D. thesis, Faculty of Computer Science, Technische Universität Dresden, Germany, 2008.

[70] Böhme, R., and A. D. Ker, "A Two-Factor Error Model for Quantitative Steganalysis," in *Proceedings SPIE, Electronic Imaging, Security, Steganography, and Watermarking of Multimedia Contents VIII*, Vol. 6072, San Jose, CA, January 16–19, 2006, pp. 59–74.

[71] Cancelli, G., et al., "A Comparative Study of ±1 Steganalyzers," in *Proceedings IEEE International Workshop on Multimedia Signal Processing*, Cairns, Australia, October 8–10, 2008, pp. 791–796.

[72] Fridrich, J., et al., "Steganalysis of Content-Adaptive Steganography in Spatial Domain," in *Information Hiding, 13th International Conference*, Lecture Notes in Computer Science, Prague, Czech Republic, May 18–20, 2011, pp. 102–117.

[73] Fridrich, J., et al., "Breaking HUGO – the process discovery," in *Information Hiding, 13th International Conference*, Lecture Notes in Computer Science, Prague, Czech Republic, May 18–20, 2011, pp. 85–101.

[74] Gül, G., and F. Kurugollu, "A New Methodology in Steganalysis : Breaking Highly Undetactable Steganograpy (HUGO)," in *Information Hiding, 13th International Conference*, Lecture Notes in Computer Science, Prague, Czech Republic, May 18–20, 2011, pp. 71–84.

[75] Ker, A. D., et al., "Moving Steganography and Steganalysis from the Laboratory into the Real World," in *1st ACM IH&MMSec. Workshop*, Montpellier, France, June 17–19, 2013.

[76] Lubenko, I., and A. D. Ker, "Steganalysis with mismatched covers: Do simple classifiers help," in *Proc. 13th ACM Workshop on Multimedia and Security*, Coventry, UK, September 6–7 2012, pp. 11–18.

[77] Ker, A. D., and T. Pevnýý, "A mishmash of methods for mitigating the model mismatch mess," in *Proceedings SPIE, Electronic Imaging, Media Watermarking, Security, and Forensics 2014*, Vol. 9028, San Francisco, CA, February 3–5, 2014, pp. 1601–1615.

[78] Wilcox, R. R., *Introduction to Robust Estimation and Hypothesis Testing, Third Edition (Statistical Modeling and Decision Science)*, Elsevier, 2012.

[79] Gong, B., K. Grauman, and F. Sha, "Connecting the Dots with Landmarks: Discriminatively Learning Domain-Invariant Features for Unsupervised Domain Adaptation," in *Proceedings of the 30th International Conference on Machine Learning*, Vol. 28, Atlanta, GA, June 16–21, 2013.

[80] Gong, B., et al., "Geodesic Flow Kernel for Unsupervised Domain Adaptation," in *Proceedings of the IEEE Conference on Computer Vision and Pattern Recognition (CVPR)*, Providence, RI, June 16–21, 2012.

[81] Muandet, K., D. Balduzzi, and B. Schölkopf, "Domain Generalization via Invariant Feature Representation," in *Proceeding of the 30th International Conference on Machine Learning (ICML 2013)*, Atlanta, GA, June 16–21 2013.

[82] Pevný, T., and J. Fridrich, "Detection of Double-Compression for Applications in Steganography," *IEEE Transactions on Information Forensics and Security*, Vol. 3, No. 2, 2008, pp. 247–258.

[83] Kodovský, J., V. Sedighi, and J. Fridrich, "Study of Cover Source Mismatch in Steganalysis and Ways to Mitigate its Impact," in *Proceedings SPIE, Electronic Imaging, Media Watermarking, Security, and Forensics 2014*, Vol. 9028, San Francisco, CA, February 3–5, 2014, pp. OJ 1–12.

[84] Fridrich, J., M. Goljan, and R. Du, "Steganalysis Based on JPEG Compatibility," in *Special Session on Theoretical and Practical Issues in Digital Watermarking and Data Hiding, SPIE Multimedia Systems and Applications IV*, Vol. 4518, Denver, CO, August 20–24, 2001, pp. 275–280.

[85] Luo, W., Y. Wang, and J. Huang, "Security Analysis on Spatial ±1 Steganography for JPEG Decompressed Images," *IEEE Signal Processing Letters*, Vol. 18, No. 1, 2011, pp. 39–42.

[86] Kodovský, J., and J. Fridrich, "JPEG-Compatibility Steganalysis Using Block-Histogram of Recompression Artifacts," in *Information Hiding, 14th International Conference*, Vol. 7692 of Lecture Notes in Computer Science, Berkeley, California, May 15–18, 2012, pp. 78–93.

[87] Hsu, C., and C. Lin, "A Comparison of Methods for Multi-Class Support Vector Machines," Technical report, Department of Computer Science and Information Engineering, National Taiwan University, Taipei, Taiwan, 2001.

[88] Pevný, T., and J. Fridrich, "Multiclass Blind Steganalysis for JPEG Images," in *Proceedings SPIE, Electronic Imaging, Security, Steganography, and Watermarking of Multimedia Contents VIII*, Vol. 6072, San Jose, CA, January 16–19, 2006, pp. O 1–O 13.

[89] Pevný, T., and J. Fridrich, "Towards Multi-Class Blind Steganalyzer for JPEG Images," in *International Workshop on Digital Watermarking*, Vol. 3710 of Lecture Notes in Computer Science, Siena, Italy: Springer-Verlag, Berlin, September 15–17, 2005.

[90] Pevný, T., and J. Fridrich, "Multiclass Blind Steganalysis for JPEG Images," in *Proceedings SPIE, Electronic Imaging, Security, Steganography, and Watermarking of Multimedia Contents VIII*, Vol. 6072, San Jose, CA, January 16–19, 2006, pp. 257–269.

[91] Ker, A. D., "A Capacity Result for Batch Steganography," *IEEE Signal Processing Letters*, Vol. 14, No. 8, 2007, pp. 525–528.

[92] Ker, A. D., et al., "The Square Root Law of Steganographic Capacity," in *Proceedings of the 10th ACM Multimedia & Security Workshop*, Oxford, UK, September 22–23, 2008, pp. 107–116.

[93] Filler, T., A. D. Ker, and J. Fridrich, "The Square Root Law of Steganographic Capacity for Markov Covers," in *Proceedings SPIE, Electronic Imaging, Media Forensics and Security*, Vol. 7254, San Jose, CA, January 18–21, 2009, pp. 08 1–11.

[94] Ker, A. D., "The Square Root Law in stegosystems with imperfect information," in *Information Hiding, 12th International Conference*, Vol. 6387 of Lecture Notes in Computer Science, Calgary, Canada: Springer-Verlag, New York, June 28–30, 2010, pp. 145–160.

[95] Ker, A. D., and T. Pevný, "Steganographer is the outlier," *IEEE Transactions on Information Forensics and Security*, Vol. 9, No. 9, July 2014, pp. 1424–1435.

[96] Fridrich, J., T. Pevný, and J. Kodovský, "Statistically Undetectable JPEG Steganography: Dead Ends, Challenges, and Opportunities," in *Proceedings of the 9th ACM Multimedia & Security Workshop*, Dallas, TX, September 20–21, 2007, pp. 3–14.

[97] Hetzl, S., and P. Mutzel, "A Graph-Theoretic Approach to Steganography," in *Communications and Multimedia Security, 9th IFIP TC-6 TC-11 International Conference, CMS 2005*, Vol. 3677 of Lecture Notes in Computer Science, Salzburg, Austria, September 19–21, 2005, pp. 119–128.

[98] Fridrich, J., et al., "Forensic Steganalysis: Determining the Stego Key in Spatial Domain Steganography," in *Proceedings SPIE, Electronic Imaging, Security, Steganography, and Watermarking of Multimedia Contents VII*, Vol. 5681, San Jose, CA, January 16–20, 2005, pp. 631–642.

[99] Ker, A. D., and T. Pevný, "Steganographic key leakage through payload metadata," in *2nd ACM IH&MMSec. Workshop*, Salzburg, Austria, June 11–13, 2014.

[100] Ker, A. D., "Locating Steganographic Payload via WS Residuals," in *Proceedings of the 10th ACM Multimedia & Security Workshop*, Oxford, UK, September 22–23, 2008, pp. 27–32.

[101] Ker, A. D., and I. Lubenko, "Feature Reduction and Payload Location with WAM Steganalysis," in *Proceedings SPIE, Electronic Imaging, Media Forensics and Security*, Vol. 7254, San Jose, CA, January 18–21, 2009, pp. 0A 1–0A 13.

[102] Quach, T.-T., "Cover estimation and payload location using Markov random fields," in *Proceedings SPIE, Electronic Imaging, Media Watermarking, Security, and Forensics 2014*, Vol. 9028, San Francisco, CA, February 3–5, 2014, pp. H1–9.

[103] Johnson, N. F., and S. Jajodia, "Exploring Steganography: Seeing the Unseen," *IEEE Computer*, Vol. 31, February 1998, pp. 26–34.

[104] Johnson, N. F., and S. Jajodia, "Steganalysis: The Investigation of Hidden Information," in *Proceedings IEEE, Information Technology Conference*, Syracuse, NY, September 1–3, 1998.

[105] Johnson, N. F., and P. Sallee, "Detection of hidden information, covert channels and information flows," in *Wiley Handbook of Science Technology for Homeland Security*, New York: Wiley & Sons, Inc, April 4, 2008.

[106] Kipper, G., *Investigator's Guide to Steganography*, Boca Raton, FL: CRC Press, 2004.

[107] Bell, G., and Y.-K. Lee, "A Method for Automatic Identification of Signatures of Steganography Software," *IEEE Transactions on Information Forensics and Security*, Vol. 5, No. 2, June 2010, pp. 354–358.

Chapter 4

Network Steganography

Wojciech Mazurczyk and Luca Caviglione

4.1 INTRODUCTION

The pervasive nature of modern networks makes communication protocols one of the most important scenarios where steganography can be applied. In fact, the Internet is characterized by two major properties that are mandatory for the successfulness of the information hiding process:

- *Availability of carriers*: nowadays, communication networks are used to transfer data, voice, and multimedia by means of a highly integrated framework. Also, end nodes range from standard desktops to a composite set of appliances, thus using a wide variety of protocols. Therefore, a modern networked environment offers many carriers to be exploited for steganography and data hiding purposes, possibly also in a combined manner.

- *High masking capacity*: network services are used daily by billions of people to communicate, establish or maintain social relationships, and for business/entertainment purposes. Besides, the advent of online social networks (OSNs) and the cloud paradigm lead to an intensified usage, because many operations and assets are no longer used in-house, but are remotely accessed [1]. As a consequence, the related volume of exchanged data offers an extreme masking capacity, since hidden communications can pass unnoticed when buried in the bulk of exchanged information.

However, relying on some form of information hiding is not a recent need. In fact, throughout the years, different protocols, architectures, and methodologies have been defined to make the Internet a secure worldwide service. For example, users must have a proper degree of privacy guaranteed when communicating, and sensitive services, such as those exchanging financial data, must be secured. Nevertheless, developing techniques to prevent censorships have been one of the most important topics in the research agenda in the last decade.

As a consequence, network engineers already had — at least partially — addressed the following problems affecting the Internet:

- *i*) obfuscation — to make the traffic ambiguous and difficult to understand,

- *ii*) anonymity — to make the sources of a conversation hard to recognize, and

- *iii*) stealthiness — to make the flow of data not visible from an observer.

For the case *i*) the *de-facto* standard paradigm involves *cryptography*, which does not cloak the existence of the communication, but makes it unreadable for any third part observer. It must be noted that information hiding mechanisms can be used jointly with cryptography in order to assure that the information would be unreadable if spotted. At the same time, a cryptographic flow can be used as a carrier that is exploitable to cloak secrets.

In a similar extent, to cope with the requirement of *ii*), many solutions to provide *anonymity* have been proposed. Examples include, ad-hoc protocols, complex overlay routing mechanisms, and proxying architectures. In some cases, cryptography can be also used to make the anonymization process more effective and secure. Information hiding can be also adopted to purse the anonymization of endpoints connected to a communication networks.

Finally, to assure *iii*) *communication hiding* methods are of primary importance, because they enable to hide the very existence of the information exchange process. This is where *network steganography* definitely plays the most relevant role. It can be defined as a group of techniques aiming to conceal information in communication networks by creating a covert channel for the purpose of hidden data exchange.

The major details and techniques concerning such process are the focus of this chapter; Section 4.2 introduces data hiding in networks with emphasis on the TCP/IP protocol architecture and IEEE standards, and Section 4.3 showcases the major applications of network steganography. Section 4.4 deeply discusses the most popular methods used to hide data within each layer of the protocol stack, and Section 4.5 outlines some techniques used to perform the detection of a hidden communication, as well as how to develop possible countermeasures. Lastly, Section 4.6 concludes the chapter by offering a summary of the presented network steganography methods.

4.2 UNDERSTANDING NETWORK STEGANOGRAPHY

In order to provide a general introduction, preliminary we present a similitude between network steganography and a real-world situation. Hence, let us consider a crowded airport, that can resemble a set of routers of a communication network. For some duties, it even behaves in a similar manner. In fact, instead of packets, an airport dispatches passengers to different destinations, usually targeting boarding gates. As required for the Internet, an airport must assure a proper degree of security. To this aim, passengers are inspected like datagrams; for example, to prevent boarding illegal objects, such as weapons or drugs. To assure a proper throughput and to increase comfort, people are seldom physically searched. On the contrary, scanners are used to inspect them under their clothes in a quick and respectful fashion. Unfortunately, despite technological advancements, someone is sometimes able to bring forbidden objects onboard. This is mainly achieved by deceiving a scanner, and by precisely knowing the security protocols deployed for airport security. This requires a thorough understanding of both technologies and practices used to detect illegal objects. In other words, one can hide a secret only by finding a precise behavior (or weakness) to exploit. For this example, knowing how a given scanner model works could lead to the engineering of an ad-hoc packaging to reflect the electromagnetic waves. In general, the same principle is at the basis of network steganography. In order to successfully transmit data in a covert manner, the sender must embed the secret somewhere within the network traffic. Obviously, so as not to reveal the transmission, modifications should not be visible by intermediate devices or end users.

In this perspective, we consider the term "network steganography" as a hyponym of grouping all techniques that conceal information in communication networks by creating a covert (steganographic) channel for the purpose of hidden data exchange. Such a covert message is inseparably bound to the data carrier. To be more precise, the network flow embedding the secret is a sequence of information sent from a given source(s) to a particular destination(s). Accordingly, it can be a single overt traffic flow exchanged between the covert sender and receiver or a multidimensional conversation. In this case, different subcarriers are concurrently used to increase the opportunity of injecting secrets, as well as to increase the performance of the overall cloaked communication process. This also implies that network steganography techniques serve as a way to create network covert (steganographic) channels for hidden communication. However, such covert channels cannot exist in communication networks without steganography.

4.2.1   Hiding Opportunities Within the Protocol Stack

According to the ISO/OSI model, each functional layer offers specific carriers where data can be hidden. For example, well-defined fields of the protocol data units (PDUs) produced by the transport layer can be judiciously altered as to store secrets. In a similar manner, the behavior of the medium access control (MAC) sublayer within the Data Link layer can be properly forced in order to transmit covert information over the physical medium. In any case, each functional layer offers advantages and disadvantages, which will be addressed in Section 4.4. Moreover, a technique specifically designed for working with a given protocol often will not be general enough to be reused in different portions of the OSI stack. This highlights one of the most important features of steganographic methods: they are profoundly coupled with the used carrier. This also implies that it is hard to develop detection techniques or countermeasures that are able to work on a wide spectrum of methods at once.

Even if the ISO/OSI model is exceptionally suitable for describing network architectures, the *de-facto* standard suite is the TCP/IP stack that is used in the Internet. Therefore, we only focus on its protocols and applications.

Compared with other steganography techniques (see Chapter 2), such as those using digital media, network steganography offers additional benefits. In fact, a network traffic flow does not have clear boundaries, thus leading to a carrier that is potentially without limits. Moreover, a network is supposed to be a "permanent" infrastructure, and it is not uncommon to have covert exchanges lasting for weeks or months. As a consequence, it is possible to leak information for long periods, or decide to "spread" a small amount of data to be exfiltrated over long timeframes. Therefore, network steganography is not trivial to detect. It also raises critical challenges in the field of the digital forensics, given that wide area networks are typically spread among different States having mixed legislations.

Figure 4.1 depicts a general view of the TCP/IP architecture and classical examples of features that can be exploited to perform network steganography. As shown, each layer offers different opportunities, that can be properly manipulated to embed data. To provide a general idea, the most classical usages are:

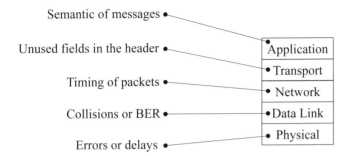

Figure 4.1 Paradigmatic examples of the utilization of the TCP/IP stack for network steganography.

- *The Physical Level* encodes information into medium-dependent signals. Then, secrets can be sent over the medium in forms of additional delays among symbols or ad-hoc bursts of errors conveying information.

- *The Data Link Layer* is mainly responsible for packing bits into frames and granting a collision-free transmission over multiple access channels. Therefore, data can be injected in the padding that is used to have well-sized frames, or by forcing collisions on the medium.

- *The Network Layer* enables one to address and route data over a best-effort network. Thus, a possible place to hide information is within the generation rate of packets (e.g., to have inter-packet times encoding information).

- *The Transport Layer* is responsible of maintaining the end-to-end semantic between the involved endpoints of a communication. Also, it performs flow control and error recovery. As a consequence, protocols like TCP have many fields in the header, that can be hijacked to carry secret data.

- *The Application Layer* embraces all the functionalities needed to exchange data through the network. As a consequence of a huge variety of protocols, many opportunities for embedding secrets rely within on this layer. A possible example exploits the case-insensitive nature of many protocol implementations (i.e., secrets can be retrieved from patterns like `<attribute>`, `<Attribute>` or `<attriBute>`).

Obviously, when developing network steganography methods, it is frequent to use several cloaking techniques, each one exploiting a different layer of the protocol stack. In this case, we refer to such methods as *cross-layer*.

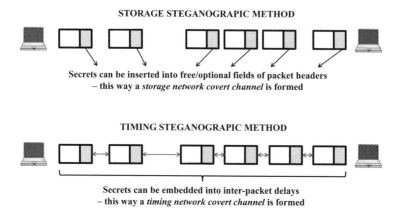

STORAGE STEGANOGRAPIC METHOD

Secrets can be inserted into free/optional fields of packet headers
– this way a *storage network covert channel* is formed

TIMING STEGANOGRAPIC METHOD

Secrets can be embedded into inter-packet delays
– this way a *timing network covert channel* is formed

Figure 4.2   Reference use-cases for storage and timing methods.

While the previous taxonomy is effective in order to locate the layer where the steganographic process takes place, it does not give enough information on *how* the network covert channel is built. In other words, it fails to reveal if the secret is exchanged through the network by means of an alteration of *places* (i.e., where the altered data is located) or *time* (i.e, how the alteration relates within the flow of events). For such reasons, we do introduce an additional step in order to better describe where the steganography techniques affect the creationof a network covert channel:

- If a technique affects the "location" of the hidden data carrier, then a *storage network covert channel* is created.

- If a technique affects a timing of "events" of the hidden data carrier, then a *timing network covert channel* is created.

Figure 4.2 depicts the reference use-cases for the aforementioned classes of network cover channels.

4.2.2   Reference Scenario for Network Steganography Information Exchange

As presented in Section 1.5.1, the stego-key can also be the knowledge on "how" the information hiding technique operates. Wendy, the warden, can try to reveal

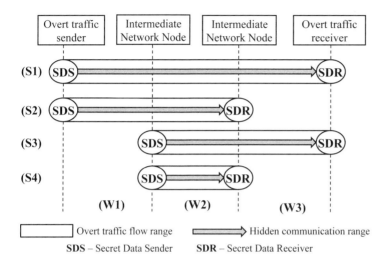

Figure 4.3 Possible communication scenarios for network steganography.

the secret by performing a particular type of inspection called *steganalysis*. In particular, Wendy:

- Is aware that Alice and Bob can utilize hidden communication to exchange data in a covert manner.

- Has a knowledge of all existing steganographic methods, but not of the one used by Alice and Bob (this, as mentioned earlier, is assumed to be their stego-key).

- Is able to try detecting and/or interrupting the hidden communication.

As illustrated in Figure 4.3, network steganography usually considers four hidden communication scenarios. Possible locations of the warden are denoted as W1 – W3. In more details a node acting as a warden performs steganalysis (see, Section 4.5 for detection methods), and it can be placed near the sender, or at some intermediate node in order to intercept the overt communication. Moreover, it can monitor the network traffic from a single point of collection (centralized approach or centralized warden) or in multiple places (distributed approach or distributed warden). In general, both the location and the number of wardens influence their effectiveness.

Regarding these scenarios, the first one (labeled as S1) is the most common: the overt sender and receiver perform plain transmission while simultaneously exchanging secret data. The conversation path is the same one of the hidden data exchange. For the three remaining scenarios (labeled as S2 – S4), only a part of the end-to-end flow transported by the network is used for the covert communication. As a consequence, both the overt sender and receiver are, in principle, unaware of the steganographic data exchange.

4.2.3   Fundamental Properties

As it happens for other applications of information hiding, all the methods used to perform network steganography are also characterized by the three fundamental properties as follows:

- *Steganographic bandwidth* (called, in digital media steganography, *capacity*): the volume of secret data that can be sent per time unit upon fixing the method.

- *Undetectability* (or *security*): the inability to detect the secret data within a certain carrier.

- *Robustness*: the number of alterations that the hidden message can withstand before being destroyed.

Ideally, the perfect method should be both robust and hard to detect, and should also offer the highest attainable bandwidth. Alas, it is impossible to maximize such properties simultaneously, as they are related according to the *magic triangle* relationship. In more detail, this relationship states that it is impossible to increase a performance index without lowering the remaining two [2]. Demonstrating in a closed form the magic triangle is still an open research problem, especially due to the tight relation between the properties and the used methods. Yet, an intuitive interpretation could be given with the following example, partially borrowed from [3]. Let us consider using some bits of an image as a method to embed secrets. Alterations result in noise, which must be kept under a given threshold in order to remain undetected. Yet, the more bits that are used for the secret (the bandwidth increases), the more the noise would increase, thus making the method more fragile (detectable).

Lastly, an additional metric, usually not explicitly considered by the magic triangle is the *steganographic cost*. It considers how applying network steganography affects the hidden data carrier. More specifically, it indicates the degradation or distortion caused by the application of a steganographic method to the specific carrier. For example, when hiding secret data in digital image, audio, or video, the parameters MSE (mean-square error) or PSNR (peak signal-to-noise ratio) are utilized for this purpose. However, they cannot be directly applied to dynamic, diverse carriers like transport layer connections. For the case of steganography applied to VoIP (voice over IP) conversations, this cost can be expressed via a measure of the degradation perceived in the quality of the conversation due to the hidden data embedding. Besides, in the case of using certain fields within the protocol header as hidden data carrier, the cost is expressed as a potential loss of protocol functionality.

4.3   MAJOR APPLICATIONS OF NETWORK STEGANOGRAPHY

In general, information hiding can be used both for legitimate and illegal purposes, and the main application of network steganography is to provide a channel for performing clandestine communication. Reasons could be mixed, ranging from legal to illicit activities. For instance, relying upon network steganography could lead to important benefits that guarantee the privacy of individuals, but, at the same time, also to empower threats aiming at people, enterprises, or financial institutions, as well as entire states. Therefore, when developing/deploying techniques involving information hiding, one might meticulously consider complex ethical, legal, and technological issues. Still, such a discussion is outside the scope of this chapter and interested readers should refer to Section 1.3.

4.3.1   Legitimate Purposes

A classical legitimate application of network steganography is when communicating parties believe that the detection of the existence of a secret message can be harmful. A typical scenario involves journalists and censors (usually acting within a dictatorship). In this case, creating a hidden channel would give protection without raising the attention due to visible and encrypted messages.

Another relevant field of application is the one aiming at enriching/improving a specific portion of an Internet service, or the functionalities of a network protocol. In this vein, network steganography has proven to be effective in order to mitigate the impact of packet losses in VoIP communications, to improve voice quality [4], [5], to increase the bandwidth for carrying the voice [6], and to enhance the security of cryptographic keys distribution procedures [7]. In a similar extent, [8] proposed to apply steganography within unused fields in the header of the real-time transport protocol (RTP). Also, authors developed a method using digital watermarking to embed additional information into the RTP traffic in order to provide authentication and content integrity features. To this aim, the needed information was embedded, besides RTP, also in unused fields of the IP, UDP as well as in the vocal stream generated by the codec. Moreover, the work also proposed to save the transmission bandwidth used by the VoIP conversation by implementing some basic functionalities of the RTCP (real-time transport control protocol) through covert channels.

4.3.2 Illegal Purposes

As said, network steganography can be also applied for malicious purposes (e.g., for criminal communication, confidential data exfiltration from secured or monitored systems, cyber weapon exchange and control, and industrial espionage). In this perspective, malware is definitely the archetypal example of tools used for illegal purposes. In fact, researchers are increasingly observing the adoption of network steganography methods used to improve their stealthiness [9], mainly to hide signaling flows exchanged with a remote command and control (C&C) facility (i.e., the entity gathering stolen information and sending commands to compromised hosts), or the leaking of sensitive data.

For the sake of brevity, in the following, we briefly report the most relevant malware using network steganography:

- Feederbot (discovered in 2011) communicates to its C&C by means of ad-hoc queries against a domain name system (DNS) servers. W.32.Morto exploits a similar techniques by high-jacking the TXT records of DNS.

- Linux.Fokirtor (discovered in 2013) injects data within the secure shell (SSH) traffic to leak information to its C&C infrastructure.

- Regin (discovered in 2014, but dated back *a posteriori* in 2008) is characterized by a high degree of sophistication and exploits four different channels to leak data or communicate with its C&C servers. Specifically:

  - it can embed information in lieu of legitimate ICMP/ping data;

  - it can inject a proprietary payload within an UDP datagram;

  - similar to the previous case, but using TCP;

  - it can encode secret data within cookies (e.g., by properly altering `WINKER`, `TIMESET` and `LASTVISIT`).

To summarize, relying on network steganography to improve the stealthiness of malicious software is a trend that will continue in the future [9], especially on portable devices, such as smartphones.

4.4 A REVIEW OF NETWORK STEGANOGRAPHY METHODS

In this section, we provide a compact review of the most popular or successful network steganography methods taken from the reference scientific literature.

4.4.1 Physical Layer Methods

When deployed in the physical layer, steganographic techniques can exploit material features of communication channels and/or imitate their imperfectness. We point out that the same also partially applies to the data link layer, see Section 4.4.2.

One of the most successful techniques relies upon the alteration of a physical behavior of fiber optics. Accordingly, this class of methods has been called *optical steganography*, and it is used to hide signals within existing public links in order to avoid any eavesdropping attempts from a third party attacker/observer. In general, the stealth channel is "buried" within the noise that already exists in the system, thus requiring one to adopt a stealth signal typically $10-20$ dB lower than the allotted one [10]. As an example of such an approach, [11] proposed to stretch short optical pulses in order to cause a chromatic dispersion phenomena, which can remain concealed within the system noise of the link.

Another approach exploits wireless channels, especially those using the IEEE 802.11 standard. This is the case of WiPad (wireless padding) [12], which hides information in the wireless link by inserting secrets in the padding field that is used to have trials of symbols generated by the modulator of well-defined sizes. Depending on the transmission data rate, the number of encoded bits per symbol ranges from 24 to 216. Experimental campaigns have been done on IEEE 802.11g links at 54 Mbit/s, and results indicate a steganographic bandwidth of 1.1 Mbit/s for secrets embedded in data frames, and 0.44 Mbit/s for those embedded in ACK frames. Hence, by combining the two network flows, it is possible to achieve a steganographic channel that is able to sustain rates up to 1.54 Mbit/s.

The presented methods require low-level modifications. Thus, such intrinsic complexity could limit their applicability on a wide range of devices or use-cases.

4.4.2   Data Link Layer Methods

One of the earliest (and popular) techniques has been introduced in [13] and exploited the carrier sense multiple access collision detection (CSMA/CD) mechanism used in Ethernet. In essence, colliding frames produce a jamming signal trig-
gering an exponential back-off procedure to randomly select waiting times, in order
to avoid two (or more) senders to synchronize. In this case, the covert station tries
to jam packets of another node and, if a collision happens, it uses back-off delays
that are equal to zero or the maximum value. Therefore, all the frames sent through
the link will either precede or lag the remaining traffic, essentially creating a one-
bit-per frame covert channel. The receiver can recover the information by counting
the number of collisions and analyzing the order of the frame.

In a similar way, the mechanism presented in [14] tries to hide data within
wireless LANs (WLANs) scenarios. The proposed approach has been called HIC-
CUPS (hidden communication system for corrupted networks) and exploits the
broadcast nature of wireless channels (i.e., all the terminals can "hear" data con-
tained in frames transmitted over the medium). The main idea is that frames with a
bad checksum are discarded, whereas terminals aware of the use of the steganographic method may preserve them in order to extract the secret data from the
payload. In this perspective, HICCUPS uses frames with intentionally corrupted
checksums in order to establish covert communication. Thus, when the receiver
gets a packet, it checks for errors by using the frame check sequence (FCS) and
then extracting the hidden data. The method can be potentially spotted because it
can lead to anomalous bursts of errors. HICCUPS can enable transmission in a
covert channel with a rate of 1.27 Mbit/s for an IEEE 802.11g 54 Mbit/s network
with 10 hosts.

We point out that — since such methods exploit a portion of the stack
acting on an hop-by-hop basis — they have a scope limited to the local network.
Besides, they are also difficult to implement because they often require relevant
customizations in the device drivers.

4.4.3   Network Layer Methods

Methods exploiting carriers available at the network layer are very popular, even
if highly overlapped in functionalities. In fact, many of them share the basic idea
of embedding data within unused fields of the header. Therefore, we only present
methods that have to be considered as an archetype of a more wider set.

The first one has been proposed in [15] and exploits the DF (don't fragment) flag of the IPv4 header. In order to properly work, the secret sender must generate PDUs with a size smaller than the MTU (maximum transfer unit) of a given path (i.e., it must avoid that intermediate routers will fragment the traffic). Another example (which is conceptually similar) uses IPv6 [16], where 22 potential information hiding methods were identified and rely on its various headers fields. Moreover, in [17], Servetto and Vetterli demonstrated a timing channel by intentionally introducing packet losses at the sender side. To detect losses, this technique exploits the packet sequence number (i.e., the Identification field within the IP header). Erasures within the produced flow are then realized at the sender side by artificially losing packets. The hidden communication is established as the covert sender encodes binary 1 in a lost packet and binary 0 in the contrary.

Nevertheless, secret data can be also encoded by varying packet rates, which is equivalent to modulating the packet timing (the interpacket gap) as proposed in many research papers, including [18]. To this aim, at fixed time intervals, the covert sender varies its rate of PDUs among well-defined quantities. Then, the receiver can decode the covert information by measuring the observed data rate. This approach allows one to create network covert channels with different steganographic bandwidths according to the used encoding scheme. For example, a binary channel can transmit one bit per time interval, whereas a multirate channel can transmit $\log_2 r$ bits per time interval, where r is the number of artificial rates utilized. For such techniques, it is important to note that both the sender and the receiver need a mechanism for the synchronization of the time intervals.

Methods of hiding data within the network layer provide end-to-end covert communication through the whole network. This could lead to difficulties in the implementation phase, because it requires a tight interaction with the underlying OS, as well the as proper tools to manipulate and inspect the traffic (e.g., to perform decoding). Note that such issues also apply to techniques exploiting the transport layer.

4.4.4 Transport Layer Methods

With regard to applying network steganography at the transport layer, in [19] Mazurczyk et al. developed a method called RSTEG (retransmission steganography), which uses specific behaviors of the TCP as a carrier. The main idea of RSTEG is to drop the acknowledgement of successfully received segments in order to intentionally cause retransmissions. As a result, such segments contain secret data hidden within the payload. As it happens for similar methods (e.g., those presented in Section 4.4.2) retransmission events that are too aggressive would lead to the revealing of the steganographic activity. Coherently, authors estimated that a fair amount of intentional retransmissions should be less than the 0.1%, hence leading to a rate of 200 segments/s and a resulting steganographic bandwidth of about 1.4 kbit/s.

The same approach can be applied also to the stream control transmission protocol (SCTP) [20], whose fields in the header can be vulnerable to the same information injecting approaches discussed for the network layer (see Section 4.4.3). As of today, SCTP is implemented (natively or as an add-on) for the most popular OSes and provides a reliable, in-sequence transport of messages with congestion control. However, its main advantages include capabilities of multi-streaming (i.e., the ability to use one or more streams to transfer data via unidirectional logical channels between SCTP endpoints) and multihoming (i.e., the ability of a host to have more than one IP address in order to increase the reliability of data transfer). A rigorous analysis revealed steganographic vulnerabilities in these features. In particular, 19 different storage and timing covert channels were identified.

Before discussing the most effective methodologies presented in [20], we do briefly introduce some technical details of the protocol. Specifically, each SCTP packet consists of a main header and one or more chunks. The latter can be of two types: data chunks containing user-generated information, and control chunks used to rule the data transfer. In both cases, each one consists of type-specific fields and parameters. In SCTP, the multistreaming (for ordered delivery) is implemented by utilizing two identifiers: the stream identifier (SI) to uniquely mark the stream, and the stream sequence number (SSN) to ensure the correct order of packets at the receiver. Despite these two identifiers, each chunk containing data also adopts a transmission sequence number (TSN), which is independently assigned. With such a preamble, we then introduce two of the most effective SCTP-based network steganography techniques:

Multistreaming-based method: it exploits a determined assignment of TSNs for every chunk distributed along different streams. SIs in subsequent DATA chunks will represent hidden data bits. During the initialization phase of the SCTP association, users negotiate the number of streams to be utilized. Hence, each stream is assigned a binary sequence and the order of the chunks is determined by the TSN number. At this point, the secret is encoded by selecting which stream will be used to effectively send the data. We underline that the actual time of the packet arrival is not essential to the correct reception of the secret message.

Multihoming based method: in this case, two users establish an SCTP association. According to the protocol specification, each association can be bound to one or more NICs (network interface cards). If at least two NICs are available, each one can be associated to a secret bit. Thus, by sending data from different NICs a secret message can be delivered from the hidden sender to its destination.

4.4.5 Application Layer Methods

With the advent of different proprietary/open services (such as those for audio/video communication, on-line gaming and cloud computing, and the diffusion of peer-to-peer architectures), the number of methods using the application layer has dramatically inflated. As an example of how such channels are intimately bound against the used application/protocol, we mention [21], where Zander et al. created a covert channel by using the popular Quake III Arena first-person shooter game. To this aim, an instrumented client manipulated some bits of the angles used to locate the orientation of a player within the game world. This method can achieve a steganographic bandwidth up to 18 bit/s. Higher values cannot be reached without adding too much noise from preventing players correctly moving around the map.

Another popular approach relies on the HTTP (hypertext transfer protocol) [22]. It offers many possibilities to perform steganography; specifically, some unused/not set fields in the header can be modified (as it happens for protocols utilized in network and transport layers) or reordered. Case-insensitive information can be manipulated in order to encode data (e.g., each permutation of `<meta>`, `<Meta>` or `<mEta>` represents a secret bit of information). The presence/absence of optional header fields, as well as its sequence can cloak information.

As a final example of a method exploiting a "closed" but very popular application, we briefly showcase SkyDe (Skype Hide) [23]. In essence, it hides data by substituting the silence of VoIP conversations with secrets. Even if encrypted, Skype traffic still reveals silence/talk periods, since they are highly correlated with the sizes of packets, as voice needs more data than silence. As a consequence, a third party can identify packets by simply inspecting the size of the PDUs composing the flow. In addition, Skype does not utilize any silence suppression algorithm, allowing the use of packets for steganographic purposes: this is how SkyDe operates. In more detail, PDUs carrying silence are identified and used to convey secret data (i.e., by replacing the silence with an arbitrary sequence of bits representing the encrypted covert message). As reported, this approach has a low impact on the perceived quality because it only affects voice samples in a very minimal manner. In order to deploy this method in real-world scenarios, a proper selection of how many packets will be hijacked by SkyDe is fundamental, and basically requires a trade-off among Skype call quality, desired steganographic bandwidth, and undetectability. Experimental results demonstrated that SkyDe offers a steganographic bandwidth of up to 1.8 kbit/s (for 30% utilization of packets with silence), while introducing almost no distortion to the Skype call. Moreover, authors have proven that under such circumstances, the method remains undetectable.

Application layer steganographic methods behave similarly to network and transport layer ones. However, their implementation is typically easier because it requires performing only changes in the application itself without the need of modifying functionalities within the lower layers.

4.4.6   Cross-Layer Methods

In this section, we complete our discussion on techniques used for network steganography by showcasing methods simultaneously utilizing features belonging to different layers of the protocol stack.

The first method is called PadSteg (padding steganography) [24], and it relies heavily upon the Etherleak vulnerability, which was first reported in 2003 [25]. Specifically, PadSteg utilizes Ethernet, the address resolution protocol (ARP) and protocols like TCP, UDP, or ICMP (or other network protocols that typically cause Ethernet frames to be padded) to conceal data. Regarding the Ethernet portion of the approach, it exploits ambiguities within the standardization that causes differences in implementation of the padding strategies of Ethernet frames. In fact, some systems have padding operations that are directly handled by the NIC (often defined as "auto padding"), others have them performed via software (e.g., by device drivers). Moreover, some drivers handle frame padding incorrectly and fail to fill it with zeros. Data inserted in padding by Etherleak is considered unlikely to contain any valuable information; therefore, it does not pose serious threats to network security. However, it creates a perfect candidate for carrying hidden data. Thus, PadSteg enables a hidden group to secretly communicate across a LAN. In this scenario, each host should be able to locate and identify other hidden hosts. In PadSteg, ARP protocol (together with improper Ethernet frame padding are) is used to provide localization and identification of the members of such a hidden group. To exchange steganograms, improper Ethernet padding is utilized in frames that use TCP, ARP or ICMP in upper layers. While the secret communication occurs, hidden nodes can switch between carrier/protocols in order to minimize the risk of disclosure. The experimental steganographic bandwidth was roughly estimated to be 32 bit/s.

Another example of a cross-layer steganographic method is iStegSiri [26]. We will discuss it in detail, because voice-assisted tools for smartphones are becoming widespread and popular. In order to embed secrets, it relies on modulating the audio used to impart commands to the iOS native service called Siri. As a result of such modulation, it is possible to control the characteristics of the produced network traffic. To better understand how it can be used as a tool for network steganography, we will briefly describe the Siri application. In essence, it allows one to interact with the device using voice to issue commands or to dictate text. To offload the hardware, the translation of voice inputs to text is performed remotely in a server farm. To this aim, the device samples the voice, sends it to the remote facility, and waits for a response containing the recognized text, a similarity score, and a time stamp. From the perspective of the produced traffic, this resembles a sort of one-way VoIP stream encrypted and encapsulated within HTTP [27].

Hence, the iSiriSteg functioning can be characterized by three different steps:

1. The secret message is converted into an audio sequence based on the proper alternation of voice and silence.

2. By using the internal microphone, the sound pattern is provided to Siri as the input. Consequently, the device will produce traffic towards the remote server to require the audio-to-text conversion.

3. The recipient of the secret communication passively inspects the conversation and — by observing a specific set of features — applies a decoding scheme to extract the secret information.

Steps 1) and 2) require a proper matching between the offered audio and the produced throughput. To this extent, authors have discovered that the overall traffic must be split into different components by using a set of ranges for the protocol data units (PDUs) produced by Siri. Specifically, PDUs in the range of $800 - 900$ bytes were effective in representing talk periods, while PDUs in the range of $100 - 700$ bytes silence periods. With such a partition, the method can be used to arbitrarily encode 1 and 0 within the traffic (i.e., by alternating talk/silence periods in order to increase/decrease the number of PDUs belonging to each defined range). Nevertheless, some form of voice activity detection (VAD) impedes high symbol rates (i.e., the speed at which voice and silence alternates). To complete Step 3), the covert listener must capture the traffic and decode the secret. The former can be achieved in several ways (e.g., via transparent proxies, or by using probes dumping traffic for off-line processing). Authors achieved a steganographic bandwidth of about 0.5 b/s. We underline that this method is general enough to be used with other vocal assistants (e.g., Google Voice or Cortana) deployed in many modern smartphones and tablets.

As a remark, cross-layer steganographic methods require the modification of multiple parts of the stack, thus their implementation is more complex than single-layer counterparts. Obviously, the needed effort varies according to the involved protocols, since, as said, acting on lower layers is more complex than the case of higher ones.

4.5   DETECTION AND COUNTERMEASURES

According to the required degree of security, being able to interfere/affect/prevent network steganography could be a core requirement. Unfortunately, such a process is greatly influenced by the network topology, the underlying technology, and the effective availability of countermeasures. In this section, we introduce some general steps to building a strategy for counteract network steganographic communications. Yet, we underline that *there are no universal mechanisms*, because, as showcased in Section 4.4, each specific method is tightly coupled within the used carrier.

In general, taming network steganography requires the following steps [28]:

Identification: requires one to gain awareness of the existence of a hidden communication process within the observed/managed network. Without such knowledge, even a naive steganographic method will remain covert. Still, without a proper identification approach, network covert channels may be spotted by means of general-purpose anomaly detection methods, even if we are not aware of products effectively addressing such an issue (at the time of this writing). On the contrary, several formal methods were developed to reveal the presence of covert channels acting within operating systems (both for desktop and mobile versions) or in third-party applications. Following the same approach, existing works also offer some algorithms to recognize whether information hiding is ongoing within some network protocols.

From the authors' best knowledge, the prime way to identify the presence of (possible) network channels is to assess them during the design phase of a protocol or an Internet service. Specifically, designers should eliminate semantic ambiguities, unnecessary redundancies, and unclear specifications. Alas, this is not an easy task; rather, it is error-prone, hence requiring some type of automated formal identification procedures. Existing techniques can be grouped into the following categories: information flow analysis and noninterference analysis [29], shared resource matrix (SRM) [30] and covert flow tree (CFT) [31] methods. As of today, they have been seldom applied to network protocols, thus their effectiveness when used in production quality environments is still unclear. Consequently, the best option to identify a network of covert channels is still relying on ad-hoc mechanisms.

Documentation: makes everyone aware of the existence of the specific threat. We underline that precisely documenting a channel is an effective deterrent, since many techniques are based on the "security by obscurity" paradigm.

Auditing (Monitoring): aims at observing network traffic to compare its behavior against a dataset that is considered representative of a normal (clean) scenario. To this aim, a common approach takes advantage of some form of machine learning (ML) technique in order to extract a reduced set of features of interest. However, many of the algorithms made available in the reference literature are still tailored towards specific covert channels (i.e., they only work for a given steganographic technique used with a certain type of covert traffic). Often, they also require training examples for normal traffic and covert channels acquired in a controlled environment, which could be a very complex task, especially for large-scale networks. Luckily, recent advancements of the research community allow for the development of more generic detection approaches. When auditing a network channel in an automatic manner, the main issue is how to decide whether the observed traffic is legitimate. In this vein, when using ML or other statistical approaches, the decision boundary usually must be determined manually (by a human) during the training, and for some approaches proposed in the literature, it is unclear as to how to effectively accomplish such task. In contrast, ML methods determine the decision threshold automatically during the training phase, yet it can be very hard to interpret.

Nevertheless, for all detection methods, it is important to avoid engineering a detector that performs very well for the training data, but does not perform well for the actual observed traffic. Additionally, a number of detection techniques are based on statistical approaches using a variety of mechanisms, such as regularity metric, the Kolmogorov-Smirnov test, entropy, entropy rate, Welch's t-test, autocorrelation, and modified chi-square tests (see, e.g., [3] and references therein).

Elimination or Limitation: accounts for the effective removal of the channel. If not possible, some techniques aim to aggressively limit the steganographic bandwidth, making the cover communication difficult or disadvantageous. To this aim, the most effective approach is to rely on a tool performing normalization of the network traffic. For instance, it can be used to alter certain timing statistics of the PDUs, or to overwrite unused fields in headers in order to destroy the steganographic information. Alas, using traffic normalizers may result in side effects because the normalization of protocol headers often includes setting some fields to default values, which makes the latter unusable even for legitimate purposes [32].

Regarding network entities where normalization can happen, it can be performed by end hosts or by network devices, such as firewalls or proxies. The literature divides normalizers into stateless and stateful ones. Stateless normalizers focus on one packet at a time and do not take the "past history" into account. Instead, stateful normalizers keep information of previously received packets to evaluate traffic based on current and historical information, and can detect more covert channels.

Another important characteristic of normalizers concerns the transparency of the overall process. For instance, a "blind" normalization (i.e., applied to the whole traffic without a specific knowledge of the hidden channel to be defeated), can be used if it does not significantly affect the characteristics of the flow. Consequently, this approach can only eliminate a small group of network steganography threats. Yet, if accurate detection methods exist, known covert channels can be eliminated or limited using targeted normalization or even disruptive measures (e.g., the overt traffic could simply be blocked).

A relevant portion of normalization methods proposed in the related literature performs normalization on the network and transport protocol level [32], [16] (i.e., they act over certain header fields of IP, UDP, and TCP.) Moreover, the same concept can be used for eliminating covert channels in application protocols. For example, [33] proposed to eradicate HTTP covert channels by enforcing protocol-compliant behaviors, such as imposing the usage of response headers from a fixed set. Also, they propose to verify response header fields against the corresponding object meta-data and the client's request.

For what concerns the limitation of network convert channels, this is often a difficult process because it could require one to slow down an entire portion of a network, influence the behavior of an intermediate node (e.g., a router), or massively affect the performance of an entire computing system. Notwithstanding, some limitation techniques have proven to be very effective, especially for timing steganographic methods. Wei-Ming [34] introduced a fuzzy-time mechanism to make all clocks in a system noisy, while Wang et al. [35] proposed to eliminate inter-packet timing channels by deploying a stateful traffic controller that randomized inter-packet times on a per-flow basis. Channels using storage methods can be impeded or limited by using similar techniques. Also in this case, side effects can impair the performance or prevent a specific service from working properly.

Finally, the aforementioned actions can be performed independently or mixed according to the dangerousness of the threat and constraints imposed by the underlying network infrastructure. Moreover, we underline that each task could utilize active techniques (allowing one to actively manipulate the network traffic), passive techniques (providing only observation capabilities of the network traffic), or a combination of the two.

4.6 SUMMARY

In this chapter, we discussed network steganography and showcased how the proposed methods can be used both for legal or fraudulent purposes. In the latter case, we discussed how malware is the most rapidly growing hazard affecting network steganography.

As presented, several features of each layer of the protocol architecture can be exploited to act as a carrier for hiding data. Consequently, the majority of steganographic techniques are tightly coupled with the specific carrier, thus making the development of "general" countermeasures very difficult. In fact, network steganography can be prevented by deploying ad-hoc mechanisms according to the channel needing to be eradicated.

References

[1] Caviglione, L., "Can satellites face trends? The case of web 2.0," in *Satellite and Space Communications, 2009. IWSSC 2009. International Workshop on*, IEEE, 2009, pp. 446–450.

[2] Fridrich, J., T. Pevný, and J. Kodovský, "Statistically undetectable jpeg steganography: dead ends challenges, and opportunities," in *Proceedings of the 9th workshop on Multimedia & Security*, ACM, 2007, pp. 3–14.

[3] Mazurczyk, W., and L. Caviglione, "Steganography in Modern Smartphones and Mitigation Techniques," *Communications Surveys Tutorials, IEEE*, 2014.

[4] Komaki, N., and T. Yamamoto, "A packet loss concealment technique for VoIP using steganography," *IEICE TRANSACTIONS on Fundamentals of Electronics, Communications and Computer Sciences*, The Institute of Electronics, Information and Communication Engineers, Vol. 86, No. 8, 2003, pp. 2069–2072.

[5] Aoki, N., "VoIP packet loss concealment based on two-side pitch waveform replication technique using steganography," in *TENCON 2004. 2004 IEEE Region 10 Conference*, Vol. 100, IEEE, 2004, pp. 52–55.

[6] Aoki, N., "Potential of value-added speech communications by using steganography," in *Proceedings of the Third International Conference on International Information Hiding and Multimedia Signal Processing (IIH-MSP 2007)-Volume 02*, IEEE Computer Society, 2007, pp. 251–254.

[7] Huang, Y., et al., "Key distribution over the covert communication based on VoIP," *Chinese Journal of Electronics*, Vol. 20, No. 2, 2011, pp. 357–360.

[8] Mazurczyk, W., and Z. Kotulski, "New VoIP traffic security scheme with digital watermarking," in *Computer Safety, Reliability, and Security*, Springer, pp. 170–181, 2006.

[9] Mazurczyk, W., and L. Caviglione, "Information Hiding as a Challenge for Malware Detection," *IEEE Security and Privacy Magazine*, 2015.

[10] Wu, B., et al., "Optical steganography based on amplified spontaneous emission noise," *Optics Express*, Vol. 21, No. 2, 2013, pp. 2065–2071.

[11] Wu, B. B., and E. E. Narimanov, "A method for secure communications over a public fiber-optical network," *Optics Express*, Vol. 14, No. 9, 2006, pp. 3738–3751.

[12] Szczypiorski, K., and W. Mazurczyk, "Hiding data in ofdm symbols of IEEE 802.11 networks," in *Multimedia Information Networking and Security (MINES), 2010 International Conference on*, 2010, pp. 835–840.

[13] Handel, T. G., and M. T. Sandford II, "Hiding data in the OSI network model," in *Information Hiding*, Springer, 1996, pp. 23–38.

[14] Szczypiorski, K., "HICCUPS: Hidden communication system for corrupted networks," in *International Multi-Conference on Advanced Computer Systems*, 2003, pp. 31–40.

[15] Kundur, D., and K. Ahsan, "Practical Internet steganography: data hiding in IP," in *Proceedings of the Texas Workshop on Security of Information Systems*, Vol. 2, 2003.

[16] Lucena, N. B., G. Lewandowski, and S. J. Chapin, "Covert channels in IPv6," in *Privacy Enhancing Technologies*, Springer, 2006, pp. 147–166.

[17] Servetto, S. D., and M. Vetterli, "Communication using phantoms: covert channels in the Internet," in *Information Theory, 2001. Proceedings. 2001 IEEE International Symposium on*, IEEE, 2001, p. 229.

[18] Wolf, M., "Covert channels in LAN protocols," in *Local Area Network Security*, Springer, pp. 89–101, 1989.

[19] Mazurczyk, W., M. Smolarczyk, and K. Szczypiorski, "Retransmission steganography and its detection," *Soft Computing*, Springer, Vol. 15, No. 3, 2011, pp. 505–515.

[20] Fraczek, W., W. Mazurczyk, and K. Szczypiorski, "Hiding information in a stream control transmission protocol," *Computer Communications*, Elsevier, Vol. 35, No. 2, 2012, pp. 159–169.

[21] Zander, S., G. Armitage, and P. Branch, "Covert channels in multiplayer first person shooter online games," in *Local Computer Networks, 2008. LCN 2008. 33rd IEEE Conference on*, IEEE, 2008, pp. 215–222.

[22] Van Horenbeeck, M., "Deception on the network: thinking differently about covert channels," in *Information Warfare and Security Conference*, 2006, p. 174.

[23] Mazurczyk, W., M. Karaś, and K. Szczypiorski, "SkyDe: a Skype-based Steganographic Method," *International Journal of Computers Communications & Control*, Vol. 8, No. 3, 2013, pp. 432–443.

[24] Jankowski, B., W. Mazurczyk, and K. Szczypiorski, "PadSteg: Introducing inter-protocol steganography," *Telecommunication Systems*, Springer, Vol. 52, No. 2, 2013, pp. 1101–1111.

[25] Arkin, O., and J. Anderson, "EtherLeak: Ethernet frame padding information leakage," *Online: http://www. rootsecure. net/content/downloads/pdf/atstake etherleak report. pdf*, 2003.

[26] Caviglione, L., and W. Mazurczyk, "Understanding information hiding in iOS," *Computer*, IEEE, Vol. 48, No. 1, 2015, pp. 62–65.

[27] Caviglione, L., "A first look at traffic patterns of Siri," *Transactions on Emerging Telecommunications Technologies*, Wiley Online Library, 2013.

[28] Zander, S., G. Armitage, and P. Branch, "A survey of covert channels and countermeasures in computer network protocols," *Communications Surveys & Tutorials, IEEE*, IEEE, Vol. 9, No. 3, 2007, pp. 44–57.

[29] Gligor, V. D., *A guide to understanding covert channel analysis of trusted systems*, The Center, 1994.

[30] Kemmerer, R. A., "A practical approach to identifying storage and timing channels: Twenty years later," in *Computer Security Applications Conference, 2002. Proceedings. 18th Annual*, IEEE, 2002, pp. 109–118.

[31] Kemmerer, R. A., and P. A. Porras, "Covert flow trees: A visual approach to analyzing covert storage channels," *Software Engineering, IEEE Transactions on*, IEEE, Vol. 17, No. 11, 1991, pp. 1166–1185.

[32] Handley, M., V. Paxson, and C. Kreibich, "Network Intrusion Detection: Evasion, Traffic Normalization, and End-to-End Protocol Semantics." in *USENIX Security Symposium*, 2001, pp. 115–131.

[33] Schear, N., et al., "Glavlit: Preventing exfiltration at wire speed," *IRVINE IS BURNING*, Citeseer, 2006, pp. 133.

[34] Hu, W.-M., "Reducing timing channels with fuzzy time," *Journal of computer security*, IOS Press, Vol. 1, No. 3, 1992, pp. 233–254.

[35] Wang, Y., et al., "Traffic controller: A practical approach to block network covert timing channel," in *Availability, Reliability and Security, 2009. ARES'09. International Conference on*, IEEE, 2009, pp. 349–354.

Chapter 5

Robust Watermarking

Gwenaël Doërr

5.1 INTRODUCTION

The steganographic methods presented in Chapters 2 and 4 focus on the statistical undetectability of the hidden information by an automated inspection process. Moreover, they usually assume that the stego content is left untouched when it is delivered to the recipient (passive warden scenario). In contrast, *robust watermarking* [1] refers to another category of information hiding techniques characterized by the fact that:

- the alterations made to the cover signal shall be imperceptible by the senses of a human being,

- and it should be possible to recover the hidden information even if the watermarked cover has been subsequently altered.

Fundamentally, it corresponds to a different compromise for the fidelity vs. robustness vs. embedding rate trade-off that underpins all information hiding techniques.

Although early traces of robust watermarking were found as early as 1954 [2], the interest for this technology was revived in the 1990s, when the entertainment industry was facing increased piracy. The music industry had to cope with MP3 versions of their songs exchanged on peer-to-peer file sharing platforms [3], whereas the film industry had just seen the protection for digital versatile disks (DVD) being broken [4]. In this context, robust watermarking has been considered as a candidate

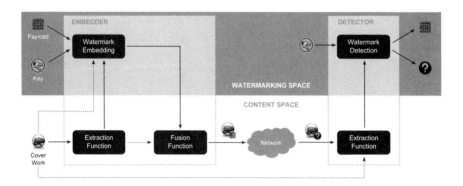

Figure 5.1   Generic watermarking architecture separated in two layers. A content adaptation layer is in charge of processing the input content to map it to the content space to the watermarking space, where the communications layer is in charge of modifying the content to introduce/detect the watermark.

technology to complement conventional cryptography-based content protection. A common shortcoming of content protection systems is indeed that multimedia content has to be eventually decrypted in order to be presented to the consumers. At that point, the content is available in the clear and is vulnerable to piracy (e.g., simply by placing a camcorder in front of the screen displaying copyrighted content). Incorporating digital watermarks would then provide a means to bind copyright information within the essence of the content itself that would be detectable by authorized devices in charge of enforcing usage rules set by content owners. As such, a key requirement of robust watermarking is historically to withstand the so-called *analog hole* (i.e., digital–analog–digital conversion, such as print-and-scan for printed material, acoustic path transmission for audio content, and camcorder recapture for video).

   After two decades of research, digital watermarking is now mature and well understood. Ignoring fine-grained details for the sake of simplicity, watermarking systems can usually be summarized using the layered architecture depicted in Figure 5.1. To begin with, an extraction function modifies the representation of the original content (also referred to as the *cover*) to map it from the content space to the watermarking space. In general, it amounts to applying some transform to the cover and selecting a number of transform coefficients. These coefficients are then modified using some watermarking routine, that may be constrained by some perceptual characteristics of the original cover. These modifications are in charge of encoding the desired watermark information (also referred to as the *payload*) and are controlled by a secret key in order to prevent adversaries from getting access to the watermark. The modified transform coefficients are then mapped back to the content space to form the watermarked content, possibly incorporating portions of the signal that were left untouched. When a copy appears on unauthorized distribution platforms, it is mapped to the watermarking space using the same extraction function as the one used on the embedder side, and the resulting transform coefficients are then fed to the watermark engine to check for the presence of a watermark and extract it. Ideally, the detector is expected to operate in a *blind* manner (i.e., without access to the original content). Watermarking systems that require the original content for detection are referred to as *non blind*.

The content-dependent components of a watermarking system form the content adaptation layer. Typical examples detailed in Section 5.2 are the transforms used to map between the content and the watermarking spaces, and the perceptual models which limit the modifications that can be made to the content. Abstracting this content adaptation layer, digital watermarking can then be assimilated to a communications channel in charge of transmitting the watermark payload from an emitter to a receiver. In particular, watermarking is characterized by specific communications models detailed in Sections 5.3 and 5.4, and dedicated resynchronization strategies described in Section 5.5. The remainder of this chapter then discusses relevant aspects of watermarking beyond the core technology design. Section 5.6 recalls good practices for benchmarking the different building blocks of a watermarking system, and Section 5.7 surveys application use cases where watermarking has been considered. A research outlook is given in Section 5.8 to provide interested readers with avenues for potential investigations.

5.2 THE CONTENT ADAPTATION LAYER

The content adaptation layer encompasses all the components of a watermarking system that need to be adapted depending on the type of content to be watermarked. In other words, it refers to the building blocks that will be different in a watermarking system, depending on if it is intended to watermark still images, moving pictures, audio tracks, 3D meshes, or anything else. In practice, two technology bricks incarnate this content dependency:

1. the transform applied to the input content to map it from the content space to the watermarking space,

2. and the perceptual model that will provide constraints for the modifications applied to the cover content.

5.2.1   Mapping to the Watermarking Space

The *raw* representation of multimedia content refers to how the content is digitally
described prior to any processing (e.g., immediately after capture). For instance, a
still image is routinely represented as an array of pixels (i.e., integer values encoded
using eight bits to cover values in $\{0, \ldots, 255\}$ that indicate how much light
should be emitted to render each pixel). Similarly, digital audio is represented by
a temporal sequence of integer values that relate to the sound pressure sampled by
a microphone at different instants in time. Watermarking systems directly altering
such raw representation are said to operate in the *spatial domain* or in the *temporal
domain*, depending on the type of content. This strategy essentially amounts to
modifying the natural representation of the signal. For still images, it is somehow
equivalent to placing a few brush strokes directly on the canvas of a painting. This
closeness to the content explains why this approach received a lot of attention in the
early ages of watermarking.

However, nowadays, it is common practice to apply some kind of transform to
obtain an alternate representation of the content. The objective of such a transform
is to abstract relevant properties of the raw signal in order to map the content
to a space where it will be more convenient and effective to apply watermark
embedding techniques. To be readily usable, the transform needs to satisfy several
requirements.

5.2.1.1   Energy Compaction

One limitation of the raw representation is that all samples are equally important.
As a result, it is not straightforward to prioritize the placement of the watermark
signal. To alleviate this issue, one objective of the mapping function is therefore
to concentrate the energy of the content onto a few transform coefficients. In other
words, the cover signal is reduced to a few *perceptually significant* components, and
their alteration would strongly impair the content. Intuitively, such coefficients are
the worst possible choice to host the watermark. Because of the fidelity constraint, it
is tempting to embed the watermark in perceptually insignificant components of the
cover content (e.g., introducing the watermark in the blue channel of an image since
the human eye is less sensitive to such changes [5]). However, the gain in fidelity
is counter-balanced by the fact that the adversary also has much more freedom to
devise attacks without compromising the perceived quality of the content. This is
the reason why perceptually significant transform coefficients are routinely selected
to host the watermark signal in practice. In this case, altering the watermark would

require modifying perceptually significant components of the cover content and would thus yield unacceptable distortion.

5.2.1.2 Independence

Another shortcoming of the raw signal is that it generally features a high level of redundancy. A possible strategy is then to make the watermark coherent with the host content to mimic its self-similarities [6, 7]. However, it may be cumbersome to achieve in practice, and an alternate strategy is therefore to rely on a mapping function that abstracts the redundancy of the content to yield independent transform coefficients. It is then possible to alter individual coefficients without caring for interdependencies during the watermark embedding process. Sometimes, though, transforms generate correlated coefficients by design (e.g., the popular short time Fourier transform (STFT) in audio processing). In such cases, if the watermarking system does not account for this dependency, the round trip between the watermarking and content spaces that naturally occurs prior to detection is likely to damage the embedded watermark, possibly impairing detection performances [8].

5.2.1.3 Invertible

The mapping function to the watermarking space is only a means to derive an interim representation of the content, that is easier to manipulate. Once the transform coefficients have been altered to encode the desired watermark payload, the content actually needs to be mapped back to the content space for storage or transmission. It is therefore helpful if the transform is invertible to facilitate such inverse mapping. The virtue of this property is particularly vibrant for 3D meshes where mapping functions are routinely content-dependent (e.g., the manifold harmonics [9] or the distribution of radial distances [10]). As a result, alterations to the content in the watermarking space may impair the definition of the transform itself, thereby causing instability. It is then necessary to introduce some iterative embedding procedure, whose convergence may not be guaranteed in practice.

In this context, most conventional transforms used in signal processing have been considered for watermarking (e.g., the discrete cosine transform (DCT), the discrete Fourier transform (DFT), the discrete wavelet transform (DWT), the discrete contourlet transform, the discrete ridgelet transform, etc.). Reusing such well-established transforms is motivated by the fact that they are routinely used in signal processing primitives involved in the watermarking pipeline. For instance, they can be used to define perceptual models or employed in lossy compression

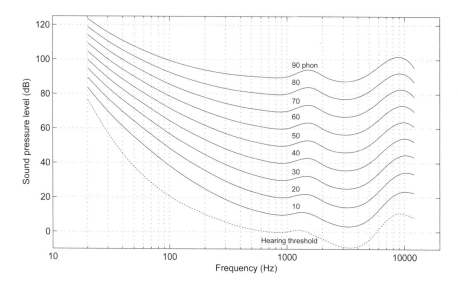

Figure 5.2 Sensitivity of the human ear as given by the equal loudness contour curve of ISO 226:2003 [11]. The curves show the sound pressure level required at different frequencies to perceive a given level of loudness, given in phon. The curve at the bottom indicates the hearing threshold.

algorithms. In the latter case, the coding engine usually relies on an alternate representation instead of the raw signal, and it is therefore desirable to embed the watermark directly in this space to avoid unnecessary mappings between content representation spaces. These transforms typically represent signals as a collection of frequency components, and watermarking systems that rely on them are thus said to operate in the *frequency domain*.

5.2.2 Perceptual Modeling

The second content-dependent building block in a watermarking system is the perceptual model, that is used to constrain the embedding changes introduced in the watermarking space. Keeping in mind that the watermark is expected to be imperceptible, it is important to understand the human sensory system in order to predict what will be the perceived impact of the modifications made to the content and thus guide the watermark placement throughout the content. In practice, the objective is to obtain for each individual transform coefficient a *perceptual slack* that indicates how much the coefficient can be modified. The computation of these slacks rely on perceptual models that attempt to account for various properties of the human sensory system [1], such as:

- frequency sensitivity,

- intensity sensitivity,

- and masking.

The human ear and the human eye do not respond equally to direct stimuli signals, depending on their frequency. Figure 5.2 illustrates the sensitivity of the ear as a function of the frequency. The graph clearly indicates a sweet spot around 3 kHz where the ear is most sensitive, whereas sensitivity declines rapidly at very low (20 Hz) and very high (20 kHz) frequencies. For visual content, the situation is more complex because the frequency sensitivity can be decomposed as a combination of spatial frequency response, spectral sensitivity response (color), and temporal frequency response (motion/flicker). Similarly to audio, the contrast sensitivity function (CSF [12]) indicates that the human eye is most sensitive to luminance changes at mid-range frequency, around 6 cycles per degree in the field of vision, and that human sensitivity decreases at lower/higher frequencies. Moreover, it is well established that human vision is much more reactive to edges having a horizontal or vertical orientation in an image than to lines in the oblique direction [13, 14]. Finally, with respect to colors, the human eye is less sensitive to variations in the blue channel than in the red or green ones.

Additionally, several physiology studies revealed that frequency sensitivity is usually dependent on the intensity of the stimulus. For instance, human hearing has been found to be able to discern smaller changes when the average intensity of the audio stimulus is louder compared to quieter signals. This phenomenon is revealed in Figure 5.2 by the equal loudness contour curves getting closer to one another when the loudness increases, especially around 100 Hz. In the Watson model for visual content [15], luminance adaptation (also referred to as *contrast masking*) is based on a power version of Weber-Fechner's law. This law essentially states that, if the luminance of a test stimulus is just noticeable from the surrounding luminance, then the ratio of the luminance difference to the surrounding luminance is approximately constant. In other words, changes in bright areas are less noticeable than in dark areas.

The last major component of any perceptual model relates to masking. It accounts for the fact that the perception of a given stimulus may be affected by the presence of another interfering stimulus. For example, a person talking in a bathroom may be heard from a nearby room, but will be inaudible as soon as water is running in the bathtub. This masking mechanism of nearby tones is one of the baseline tricks exploited in MP3 compression, where non audible components of the signal are simply not encoded [16]. Additionally, the perception of a sound may be masked by another sound that occurred in the past or that will occur in the future! A similar principle holds for visual content. It is well-established that high-frequency noise is more visible in uniform regions than in textured areas of an image. This property motivates an empirical watermarking paradigm that consists of amplifying the watermark in textured regions of an image [17].

The objective of a perceptual metric is then to aggregate the influence of all these perceptual mechanisms in order to derive a perceptibility threshold for each transform coefficient (also known as the *perceptual slack*). In other words, it shall indicate what is the largest change that can be applied to a coefficient before getting a just noticeable difference (JND).

Many perceptual models have been proposed and reused in watermarking. Among them, Watson's model – routinely used in image/video compression – relies on an abacus that specifies the frequency sensitivity for each mode of the 8×8 block DCT and then incorporates luminance and contrast masking using a couple of equations to obtain the perceptual slacks [15]. In MPEG-1 Layer model for audio, the perceptual slacks for individual STFT coefficients are obtained by comparing an absolute threshold of hearing in a noiseless environment and a masking threshold derived from a spectral analysis of the signal per frequency bands called *critical bands* [18]. The masking thresholds are adjusted according to the noise-like or tone-like nature of the audio frame.

5.3 SPREAD-SPECTRUM COMMUNICATIONS

From a pure communication perspective, the best transmission performances of the watermark would be achieved by sending only the watermark signal. However, in real life, the whole challenge is to send the watermark together with some cover content, which is often copyrighted and/or valuable material, and whose quality therefore needs to be preserved. As a result, the content hosting the watermark signal can be seen as a source of large power noise that interferes with watermarking communications. In military communications, signal jamming refers to the deliberate effort by an adversary to impair communications on the battlefield. To cope with this threat, *spread spectrum communications* rely on a key-seeded modulation that spreads the signal across a larger bandwidth than required [19]. By assimilating the cover content to a jammer in watermarking communications, this paradigm led to a first generation of watermarking systems[1].

5.3.1 Baseline Spread Spectrum Watermarking System

Typically, the coefficients selected to host the watermark offer a good fidelity vs. robustness trade-off according to some perceptual model. For example, it is common practice to watermark the middle-low frequency band of an image. Additionally, the order of these coefficients can be shuffled according to a secret key in an effort to make the watermarking channel inaccessible to non authorized parties. After these channel selection and channel obfuscation steps, the cover content is typically represented by a vector $\mathbf{c}_o$, referred to as the original cover content, which contains an ordered sequence of transform coefficients.

The spread spectrum watermark embedding operation can then be expressed as an additive or multiplicative process, depending on the properties of the watermarking space [20]:

$$\mathbf{c}_w = \mathbf{c}_o + \alpha \mathbf{w}_K \tag{5.1}$$
$$\mathbf{c}_w = \mathbf{c}_o(1 + \alpha \mathbf{w}_K) \tag{5.2}$$

where $\alpha > 0$ is a scalar embedding strength, $\mathbf{w}_K$ is the watermark signal, and $\mathbf{c}_w$ is the resulting watermarked content. The watermark $\mathbf{w}_K$, also referred to as the *carrier signal*, is generated pseudo-randomly using a secret key K according to some probability law. For example, the samples of the watermark are normally distributed with zero mean and unit variance.

On the receiver side, the detector receives a version $\mathbf{c}_n$ of the content that may or may not be watermarked, and that may be corrupted by noise (i.e., $\mathbf{c}_n = \mathbf{c}_o + \epsilon \alpha \mathbf{w}_K + \mathbf{n}$ where $\epsilon \in \{0, 1\}$ indicates if the content is watermarked and $\mathbf{n}$ is a noise vector). Using the same secret key K as the embedder, the detector then generates the watermark pattern $\mathbf{w}_K$ and computes a correlation score with $\mathbf{c}_n$, for example:

$$\rho_{lc}(\mathbf{c}_n, \mathbf{w}_K) = \frac{\mathbf{c}_n^T \mathbf{w}_K}{N} = \frac{1}{N} \sum_{i=1}^{N} \mathbf{c}_n[i].\mathbf{w}_K[i] \tag{5.3}$$

---

1   Spread spectrum communications come in different flavors: direct-sequence spread spectrum (DSSS), frequency-hopping spread spectrum (FHSS), time-hopping spread spectrum (THSS), chirp spread spectrum (CSS), and their combinations. They all have to rely on pseudo-random generators to determine and control how the signal is spread across the allocated bandwidth. They offer resistance to various types of jamming. Watermarking usually relies on DSSS.

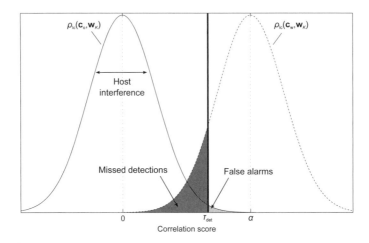

Figure 5.3 Illustration of the typical distribution of spread spectrum watermark detection scores for original and watermarked content (wihout any subsequent attack). In general, they cannot be perfectly separated with a threshold τ_{det} because of the host interference. As a result, the detection process yields false alarms and missed detections.

where $\rho_{\text{lc}}(.,.)$ is the linear correlation function, ^{T} is the transpose operator, and N is the number of components in the vectors. Exploiting the linearity of the detection process, the correlation score can thus be decomposed in three terms:

$$\rho_{\text{lc}}(\mathbf{c}_{\text{n}}, \mathbf{w}_K) = \underbrace{\rho_{\text{lc}}(\mathbf{c}_{\text{o}}, \mathbf{w}_K)}_{\text{host interference}} + \epsilon \underbrace{\alpha \rho_{\text{lc}}(\mathbf{w}_K, \mathbf{w}_K)}_{\text{watermark power}} + \underbrace{\rho_{\text{lc}}(\mathbf{n}, \mathbf{w}_K)}_{\text{noise interference}} \approx \epsilon \alpha \qquad (5.4)$$

The pseudo-random watermark pattern $\mathbf{w}_K$ is expected to be statistically independent with the cover content $\mathbf{c}_{\text{o}}$ and the noise signal $\mathbf{n}$. The first and third terms in (5.4) are thus drawn from two Gaussian distributions having zero mean and standard deviation $\sigma_{\mathbf{c}_{\text{o}}}/\sqrt{N}$ and $\sigma_{\mathbf{n}}/\sqrt{N}$, respectively, where $\sigma_{\mathbf{c}_{\text{o}}}$ and $\sigma_{\mathbf{n}}$ are the standard deviations of the cover content $\mathbf{c}_{\text{o}}$ and the attack noise $\mathbf{n}$. The correlation score $\rho_{\text{lc}}(\mathbf{c}_{\text{n}}, \mathbf{w}_K)$ statistically reduces to zero or α, depending on whether or not the content is watermarked. In practice, however, such perfect detection statistics are impaired by two interfering terms, one originating from the cover content and the other from the alterations made to the content after watermarking, whose influences are inversely proportional to the square root of the spreading length N. The more the watermark $\mathbf{w}_K$ is spread on a large number of samples, the less watermarking communications are affected by host and noise interference.

In any case, detecting the presence of the watermark pattern $\mathbf{w}_K$ can be achieved by comparing the detection score $\rho_{\mathrm{lc}}(\mathbf{c}_\mathrm{n}, \mathbf{w}_K)$ to a threshold $\tau_{\det}$. Figure 5.3 illustrates this detection procedure using mock distributions for the watermark detection scores $\rho_{\mathrm{lc}}(.,.)$. In line with (5.4), the distribution of detection scores for original content is centered on zero, whereas the one for watermarked content is centered on α. As mentioned earlier, the host interference term is not exactly equal to zero and creates a dispersion of the detection scores around these average values. As a result, the threshold-based decision engine can make errors: original content can be mistaken for watermarked content (*false alarms*) and, conversely, watermarked content can be mistaken for original content (*missed detections*). The compromise between these two types of errors is usually captured by a receiver operating characteristic (ROC) curve that depicts the different operating points of the system for different thresholds $\tau_{\det}$ [21]. Interestingly, Figure 5.3 also exemplifies the watermarking fidelity vs. robustness trade-off. To decrease detection errors (i.e., to increase robustness), the two distributions should be as separated as possible, which can be achieved by raising the embedding strength α. However, the flip side of the coin is that fidelity is then degraded. Another strategy would be to somehow cancel host interference in order to reduce the dispersion of the watermark detection scores.

This baseline spread spectrum watermarking strategy is present in most commercially-deployed systems today. Looking back into the mirror, it can even be found in early ad-hoc watermarking designs. For example, the Patchwork algorithm and its follow-up differential energy incarnations essentially amount to pseudo-randomly separating the coefficients of the cover signal $\mathbf{c}_\mathrm{o}$ in two equal sets and enforcing some difference between the average values of those two sets [22, 23]. In essence, it is equivalent to spread spectrum watermarking using a binary antipodal watermark pattern $\mathbf{w}_K$ (i.e., $\mathbf{w}_K[i] \in \{-1, 1\}$).

5.3.2 Add-Ons for Improved Fidelity and Robustness

A natural enhancement of this system is to incorporate perceptual considerations during the embedding procedure. Assuming that a perceptual model provides perceptual slacks $\{\mathbf{s}[i]\}_{1 \leq i \leq N}$ for the different coefficients of the cover content $\mathbf{c}_\mathrm{o}$, the embedding process can be revised to modulate the embedding strength α according to the sensitivity of individual transform coefficients $\mathbf{c}_\mathrm{o}[i]$:

$$\mathbf{c}_\mathrm{w}[i] = \mathbf{c}_\mathrm{o}[i] + \alpha(\mathbf{s}[i])\mathbf{w}_K[i] \tag{5.5}$$

A straightforward strategy consists of amplifying the watermark for less sensitive coefficients and attenuating it otherwise [17]. Another approach is to bridle the embedder so that the amplitude of the embedding changes never exceeds the perceptual constraints [24], for example:

$$\mathbf{c}_w[i] = \mathbf{c}_o[i] + \text{sign}(\mathbf{w}_K[i]) \min(\alpha|\mathbf{w}_K[i]|, \mathbf{s}[i]) \qquad (5.6)$$

where $\text{sign}(x) = x/|x|$ is the sign operator. In some specific cases, it is possible to *perceptually shape* the watermark pattern $\mathbf{w}_K$ in a way that optimizes the fidelity vs. robustness trade-off. For example, assuming that detection relies on linear correlation and that fidelity is evaluated using some weighted L_p norm, it can be shown that the optimal embedding equation is given by (cf. E_PERC_OPT in [1]):

$$\mathbf{c}_w[i] = \mathbf{c}_o[i] + \alpha \left(\mathbf{w}_K[i]\mathbf{s}[i]^p\right)^{\frac{1}{p-1}} \qquad (5.7)$$

From a geometrical perspective, the underlying rationale is that it is advantageous to slightly adjust the watermark pattern in a direction that yields less perceptual distortion in order to get a higher correlation score $\rho_{lc}(\mathbf{c}_w, \mathbf{w}_K)$.

By design, spread spectrum watermarking systems have a limitation due to the fact that the original cover content $\mathbf{c}_o$ is considered to be interfering noise. It translates in a host interfering term that impairs the detection statistics as illustrated in (5.4) and Figure 5.3. Nevertheless, the original content is not a random source of noise. As a matter of fact, it is available at embedding and it is actually possible to compute the host interference $\rho_{lc}(\mathbf{c}_o, \mathbf{w}_K)$ beforehand. Canceling this component is then simply a matter of revising the baseline embedding process as follows:

$$\mathbf{c}_w = \mathbf{c}_o + \left(\alpha - \lambda\rho_{lc}(\mathbf{c}_o, \mathbf{w}_K)\right)\mathbf{w}_K \qquad (5.8)$$

where $\lambda \in [0, 1]$ is a parameter used to control how much of the host interference is canceled [25]. For example, with $\lambda = 1$, the host interference is fully canceled and the distribution of detection scores for watermarked content reduces to a Dirac impulse at α. This being said, in practice, it is recommended to relax this control parameter in order to optimize the fidelity vs. robustness trade-off. On the receiver side, it is also common practice to apply a *whitening filter* to the content prior to computing the watermark detection score [26]. This operation has the virtue of reducing host interference, especially when the watermark is not placed in the highest frequencies, but rather in the lower-mid-frequency band (e.g., for improved robustness). In such cases, cross-talk between the watermark and the cover is much more likely and this prefiltering operation somehow helps compensate for it.

For the sake of simplicity, the detection procedure for spread spectrum watermarking has been described using linear correlation. This detection metric is, however, naturally flawed against valuemetric scaling. If all the coefficients of the cover content $\mathbf{c}_\mathrm{o}$ are scaled down by a value $\beta < 1$, the detection score is also scaled accordingly, and may fall below the detection threshold τ_det. Such valuemetric scaling occurs on a regular basis in everyday life (e.g., when lowering the brightness of visual content or turning down the volume of an audio track). This is the reason why alternate metrics, such as the normalized correlation or the correlation coefficient, that provides natural immunity against scaling, are used in practice. In general, this change also requires modifying the embedding procedure, although the baseline principles remain the same.

5.3.3 Transmitting Watermark Information

Strictly speaking, the watermarking system described so far does not transmit information. It simply assesses whether a specific watermark pattern $\mathbf{w}_K$ is present in a tested cover $\mathbf{c}_\mathrm{n}$ and is routinely referred to as *zero-bit watermarking* [27]. However, most application use cases actually require to send a multibit watermark payload $\mathbf{p}$, which is the output of formating a binary message $\mathbf{m}$. The formating process may include encryption for confidentiality, appending an authentication code for integrity, and/or channel coding to cope with transmission errors [28, 29]. Transmitting a single bit of information can be achieved by updating the baseline embedding procedure as follows:

$$\mathbf{c}_\mathrm{w} = \mathbf{c}_\mathrm{o} + \alpha b \mathbf{w}_K \qquad (5.9)$$

where $b \in \{-1, 1\}$ is the antipodal mapping of the bit to embed. On the receiver side, the detection procedure is then performed in two steps:

$$|\rho_\mathrm{lc}(\mathbf{c}_\mathrm{n}, \mathbf{w}_K)| \lessgtr \tau_\mathrm{det} \quad \text{and} \quad \hat{b} = \mathrm{sign}(\rho_\mathrm{lc}(\mathbf{c}_\mathrm{n}, \mathbf{w}_K)) \qquad (5.10)$$

where $\hat{b}$ is the extracted payload bit. In other words, the detector first compares the amplitude of the watermark detection score to assess whether or not the watermark pattern $\mathbf{w}_K$ is present, and then looks at the sign of the score to recover the payload bit.

To transmit multiple bits, a strategy referred to as *time/space-division multiplexing* consists of dividing the cover content $\mathbf{c}_\mathrm{o}$ into disjoint segments and embedding one payload bit per segment using (5.9). In contrast, *code-division multiplexing* can be seen as repeatedly embedding full coverage watermarks, each watermark pattern $\mathbf{w}_{K_p}$ being associated with one bit of the payload $\mathbf{p}$ and generated using a different key K_p:

$$\mathbf{c}_\mathrm{w} = \mathbf{c}_\mathrm{o} + \frac{\alpha}{\sqrt{P}} \sum_{p=1}^{P} \mathbf{p}[p]\mathbf{w}_{K_p} \qquad (5.11)$$

where P is the number of payload bits. The normalization of the embedding strength by $1/\sqrt{P}$ guarantees that the watermark distortion is calibrated to α.

Both approaches have pros and cons. With time/space-division multiplexing, if one segment of the cover is lost during transmission, the corresponding payload bit cannot be recovered. Moreover, keeping in mind that the host interference term in (5.4) scales inversely to the square root of the spreading length N, it is possible to appreciate the trade-off between the embedding rate and robustness. For a fixed number of samples, more payload bits could be embedded by reducing the watermark spreading length, but this also incurs larger host interference from the cover content. On the other hand, with code-division multiplexing, there could be cross-talk between the watermark patterns $\{\mathbf{w}_{K_p}\}_{1 \leq p \leq P}$, and it is therefore recommended to apply some orthogonalization procedure during the generation process in order to avoid interferences. Another shortcoming originates from the embedding strength calibration, which essentially brings the distributions of the watermark detection scores for original and watermarked content in Figure 5.3 closer, and thereby increases the likelihood of detection errors.

5.4 COMMUNICATIONS WITH SIDE INFORMATION

In spread-spectrum watermarking, the communications model does not account for the fact that one of the sources of noise, namely the cover signal, is actually known by the embedder. In 1983, Costa [30] studied a communications channel that consisted of two additive white Gaussian noise sources. The first one was perfectly known by the transmitter, whereas the receiver had no knowledge about it. In this seminal paper, information transmission over this channel is compared to "writing on dirty paper." Imagine a sheet of paper covered with a normally-distributed pattern of dirt. This dirt is the first noise source, which the transmitter can examine. The transmitter writes a message on this paper and sends it to a receiver. Along the way, the paper may acquire a second layer of dirt, corresponding to the second noise source. The receiver cannot distinguish between dirt and the ink used to write the message. Surprisingly, the first noise source (i.e., the *dirty paper*) has no effect on channel capacity [30, 31]. In the context of watermarking, it suggests that the host

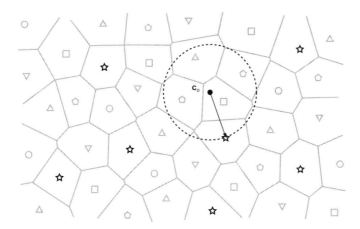

Figure 5.4 Dirty paper watermarking. The watermarking space is partitioned in cells, and any content falling in a cell is considered to be carrying the message associated with the corresponding codeword. Here, the original content c_o is considered to be conveying the message `square`. To embed the message `star`, the watermarking process (i) isolates all cells encoding the desired message, (ii) identifies the cell that is the closest to c_o, and (iii) moves the content within this cell.

content does not have to interfere with the watermark signal. This paradigm change triggered the creation of a second generation of watermarking systems.

5.4.1 Dirty Paper Watermarking

The magic behind dirty paper watermarking comes from the use of so-called *dirty paper codes*. In contrast with conventional codes, dirty paper codes offer a one-to-many mapping between messages and codewords. In other words, the codebook contains several alternate codewords for each message, and the encoder therefore has the flexibility to select one or the other depending on available side-information, namely the original cover content c_o in the context of watermarking. For example, the watermarking module may select the codeword that introduces the least distortion in an attempt to preserve fidelity. This mechanism is illustrated in Figure 5.4 for reference purposes.

In more detail, the embedder and the detector agree on a codebook $\mathcal{C}$ which is the union of several sets $\mathcal{C}_p$ of codewords encoding the same payload p. To embed a watermark, the embedder now has the choice between codewords that encode the desired payload, and it can exploit available side-information (e.g., derived from the cover content) to select which one of them to use. In practice, the embedder first prunes the codebook to keep only one subset $\mathcal{C}_\mathbf{p}$ that contains all codewords encoding the desired payload, and then identifies the codeword $\mathbf{q}^*$ that is the closest to the original cover content $\mathbf{c}_\mathrm{o}$:

$$\mathbf{q}^* = \arg\min_{\mathbf{q}\in\mathcal{C}_\mathbf{p}} \mathrm{D}_\mathrm{enc}(\mathbf{c}_\mathrm{o}, \mathbf{q}) \tag{5.12}$$

where $\mathrm{D}_\mathrm{enc}(.,.)$ is a distance used at the encoding stage that potentially accounts for perceptual properties. This selected codeword is associated with a detection cell, defined as the portion of the watermarking space where any content is considered to be encoding the codeword $\mathbf{q}^*$ by the watermark detector. The actual watermark embedding procedure then consists of moving the cover content inside this detection cell. One strategy would be to apply pure quantization (i.e., $\mathbf{c}_\mathrm{w} = \mathbf{q}^*$). However, to achieve capacity, communications theory instructs one to relax this embedding rule:

$$\mathbf{c}_\mathrm{w} = \alpha\mathbf{q}^* + (1-\alpha)\mathbf{c}_\mathrm{o} = \mathbf{q}^* + (1-\alpha) \underbrace{(\mathbf{c}_\mathrm{o} - \mathbf{q}^*)}_{\text{quantization error}} \tag{5.13}$$

where $\alpha \in [0,1]$ is the so-called *distortion compensation* parameter that restores a portion $(1-\alpha)$ of the quantization error. In other words, the embedding process now moves the content towards the selected codeword according to a parameter α. For $\alpha = 1$, it reduces to simple quantization. Due to this connection with quantization, such watermarking systems are routinely referred to as *binning schemes*. It should be noted that, according to this description, the embedding process is completely deterministic and an adversary has direct access to the watermarking channel. To avoid attacks, it is therefore common practice to *dither* the codebook to obfuscate the watermarking channel. For instance, the codewords can all be offset by a pseudo-randomly generated dither vector $\boldsymbol{\delta}_K$: $\mathbf{q} \leftarrow \mathbf{q} + \boldsymbol{\delta}_K$.

On the receiver side, the watermark detector does not have access to any side-information and therefore has to consider the whole codebook $\mathcal{C}$. As a result, the detector first identifies the codeword $\hat{\mathbf{q}}$ which is the closest to the tested content $\mathbf{c}_\mathrm{n}$:

$$\hat{\mathbf{q}} = \arg\min_{\mathbf{q}\in\mathcal{C}} \mathrm{D}_\mathrm{dec}(\mathbf{c}_\mathrm{n}, \mathbf{q}) \tag{5.14}$$

where $\mathrm{D}_\mathrm{dec}(.,.)$ is a distance that may be different from the one used during embedding, typically the Euclidean distance. To recover the embedded payload $\hat{\mathbf{p}}$, the watermark detector then simply needs to look up at the index of the codebook subset $\mathcal{C}_\mathbf{p}$ to which the codeword $\hat{\mathbf{q}}$ belongs:

$$\hat{\mathbf{q}} \in \mathcal{C}_\mathbf{p} \implies \hat{\mathbf{p}} = \mathbf{p} \tag{5.15}$$

5.4.2 Structured Codes for Binning Watermarking Schemes

Binning watermarking schemes involve two nearest neighbor searches: one at embedding given by (5.12) and another one at detection given by (5.14). In case of a random code, this would require an exhaustive search over all codewords, which would be too computationally prohibitive to be used in practice. This is the reason why binning schemes routinely rely on structured codes. It is then possible to leverage on the structure of the codebook to perform the nearest neighbor search on the embedder side efficiently.

The most simple example is *dither modulation* (DM), also referred to as *scalar Costa scheme* (SCS) [32]. In its simplest incarnation, dither modulation operates on scalar values and embed one bit of payload per cover coefficient $\mathbf{c}_o[i]$. The codebook subsets $\mathcal{C}_0$ and $\mathcal{C}_1$ associated to the different payload bit values are composed of codewords placed on a scalar quantization grid with step size Δ, and are offset with respect to each other by $\frac{\Delta}{2}$. Thanks to this structure, the nearest neighbor search reduces to a single quantization operation:

$$
\begin{aligned}
\mathbf{q}^*[i] &= \Delta . \left\lfloor \frac{\mathbf{c}_o[i] - \boldsymbol{\delta}_K[i] - b\frac{\Delta}{2}}{\Delta} \right\rceil + \boldsymbol{\delta}_K[i] + b\frac{\Delta}{2} \\
&= Q_\Delta\big(\mathbf{c}_o[i], b, \boldsymbol{\delta}_K[i]\big), \quad 1 \le i \le N
\end{aligned}
\tag{5.16}
$$

where $b \in \{0,1\}$ is a payload bit, $\boldsymbol{\delta}_K[i] \in [-\frac{\Delta}{2}, \frac{\Delta}{2}]$ is a pseudo-randomly selected dithering offset, and $\lfloor . \rceil$ denotes the nearest integer rounding operator. The quantization step size Δ has a direct impact on the watermarking fidelity vs. robustness trade-off. While larger step size values grant improved robustness, they also translate into reduced fidelity, even if this side-effect can be somehow mitigated by relying on distortion compensation. Ignoring the dithering and distortion compensation and assuming that $\Delta = 2$, the watermarking process then reduces to making the cover content coefficients $\mathbf{c}_w[i]$ odd or even depending on the payload bit b to embed. In other words, it amounts to least significant bit (LSB) watermarking, one of the baseline steganographic technique described in Chapter 2.

On the receiver side, the embedded payload bit can also be recovered with a few quantization operations:

$$
\begin{aligned}
\hat{b} &= \arg \min_{b \in \{0,1\}} \big\| \mathbf{c}_n[i] - Q_\Delta\big(\mathbf{c}_o[i], b, \boldsymbol{\delta}_K[i]\big) \big\|_2 \\
&= \left\lfloor \frac{\mathbf{c}_n[i] - \boldsymbol{\delta}_K[i]}{\frac{\Delta}{2}} \right\rceil \mod 2
\end{aligned}
\tag{5.17}
$$

where $\|.\|_2$ denotes the Euclidean norm. The last equation clearly indicates that the payload information is entirely conveyed by the quantization index, which explains why binning watermarking schemes are sometimes referred to as *quantization index modulation* (QIM). Depending on the watermarking space, it may be useful to introduce a mechanism called *spread transform* to gain robustness [32]. The baseline idea is to project the cover coefficients $\mathbf{c_o}$ onto a random direction $\mathbf{w}_K$ in a manner similar to spread-spectrum watermarking prior to applying dither modulation watermark embedding in order to attenuate the impact of interfering noise. For a single bit, it amounts to changing the embedding and detection equations as follows:

$$\mathbf{c_w} = \mathbf{c_o} + \alpha \left(Q_\Delta \left(\mathbf{c_o^T w}_K, b, \delta_K \right) - \mathbf{c_o^T w}_K \right) \mathbf{w}_K \qquad (5.18)$$

$$\hat{b} = \arg \min_{b \in \{0,1\}} \left| \mathbf{c_n^T w}_K - Q_\Delta \left(\mathbf{c_n^T w}_K, b, \delta_K \right) \right| \qquad (5.19)$$

where α is the distortion compensation parameter and δ_K is a scalar dithering value.

To embed several bits, one could simply apply dither modulation independently to each coefficient of the cover content $\mathbf{c_o}$. However, from a multidimensional perspective, this strategy yields codes that are suboptimal in terms of sphere packing [33]. State-of-the-art watermarking systems therefore rely on multidimensional structured codes, such as lattice codes [34] or trellis codes [35].

5.4.3   Add-Ons for Improved Fidelity and Robustness

A major limitation of binning schemes is their natural weakness against valuemetric scaling. This distortion makes the communication convention between the watermark embedder and the detector – namely the codebook $\mathcal{C}$ – obsolete. This is somewhat similar to the desynchronization problem that will be discussed in Section 5.5. If the scaling factor used by the adversary is known, the detector can then extract the embedded payload either by inverting the scaling operation or by using an appropriately scaled codebook. Such side-information about the piracy parameters is usually not available to the detector and therefore needs to be estimated [36, 37]. The counterpart of this strategy is that the robustness of the system is now dependent of two components – the watermark modulation mechanism and the scaling estimation technique – which may result in increased instability overall. Another countermeasure against scaling consists of applying dither modulation to a ratio of cover content coefficients [38]. Such a ratio is indeed left unaffected by valuemetric scaling and the watermarking system is therefore oblivious to the distortion. Alternately, the binning scheme can be modified to use dirty paper spherical codes [35, 39]. In this case, the watermark information is encoded by the direction of the content $c_w/\|c_w\|_2$ and the system is immune to scaling by construction.

Another shortcoming of dither modulation is its lack of perceptual adaptation. In its crudest version, all cover content coefficients $c_o[i]$ are equally subject to embedding changes without any regard for any perceptual model that may indicate that some coefficient should be less modified than others. In dirty paper watermarking, perceptual considerations could be possibly incorporated at two different stages:

1. During the coding step, the codeword q^* that is (perceptually) the closest to the original cover content c_o is identified.

2. During the embedding step, the cover content is moved (along a perceptually tuned direction) inside the detection cell of the selected codeword q^*.

In general, the first item is difficult to tackle and only workarounds have been proposed so far (e.g., by using codebooks $\mathcal{C}$ that are adapted to human perception). For example, nonuniform quantization could be used to have a quantization error that scales with the amplitude of the cover content coefficient in order to be in line with human vision, which is less sensitive to changes in bright regions when compared to darker ones [40]. Alternately, the uniform quantization step size Δ of each coefficient could be modulated according to its corresponding perceptual slack, thereby allowing more quantization error for less perceptible coefficients [41]. In this latter case, though, it should be noted that the definition of the quantizers is now content-dependent. This may cause instability on the detector side; the perceptual slacks have to be recomputed for decoding, and they are likely to differ from the ones used on the embedder side. To some extent, incorporating perceptual considerations during the embedding step is better understood today, especially if the system incorporates some spread-spectrum-like component. In this case, well-established solutions can be reused to perceptually shape the direction of modification (e.g., using (5.7)) [35, 41].

5.5 WATERMARK SYNCHRONIZATION MECHANISMS

Both watermark modulation mechanisms presented in Sections 5.3 and 5.4 are highly sensitive to desynchronization. In spread spectrum watermarking, if the watermark pattern w_K is not aligned with the watermark present in the cover c_w, the correlation score computed by the detector (such as the one given by (5.3)) is likely to be below the detection threshold τ_{det}, thereby resulting in a missed detection. In binning schemes, using a mismatching dither δ_K at detection results in incorrect payload bits extraction. Such desynchronization naturally occurs when manipulating content (e.g., scaling or rotating an image, increasing/decreasing the playback speed of an audio track, changing the aspect ratio of a video, etc.). However, these routine operations disrupt the underlying watermark communications convention and the detector no longer sees the watermark although it is still present.

As a result, there is a key component in any watermarking system that is in charge of maintaining this synchronization. A challenging aspect is that desynchronization attacks in the content space usually translate in hard-to-predict alterations in the watermarking space, and off-the-shelf solutions from other research communities cannot be readily reused. The next sections detail the main synchronization mechanisms that are routinely used for watermarking systems. While the main idea of these techniques can be applied to any type of media content, individual implementations need to incorporate some content-specific adjustments to account for the nature of the cover content.

5.5.1 Exhaustive Search

The most straightforward strategy to tackle desynchronization is exhaustive search. In some application use cases, it is possible to specify the type of distortion to which the watermark should be immune. For example, the objective could be to detect the watermark conveyed by the audio track played back by the loudspeakers of a TV set after a microphone capture on a mobile devices [24]. In such a scenario, the watermark detection may be affected by the Doppler effect due to the movement of the user. However, the amplitude of the distortion is limited by the regular walking speed of a consumer in a living room. If the desynchronization distortion can be modeled with a set of parameters θ, the exhaustive search then amounts to launching the detection procedure after compensating for the distortion, with parameters in an admissible set $\mathcal{T}$. If the watermark is detected for one of these tests, the content is considered to be carrying a watermark.

A major drawback of this strategy is its computational complexity due to the large number of calls to the watermark detector. This complexity is inherently tied to the bounds of the search window, which relates to the intended robustness of the watermarking system, as well as the resolution at which the search window is scanned. This, in turn, relates to the natural robustness of the watermark to the distortion of interest. This search space can be somewhat reduced by incorporating regularization constraints (e.g., to account for the fact that distortions in spatially connected regions of an image are not completely unrelated [42, 43]). Another important issue with exhaustive search relates to the probability of false alarms, which may be raised to unacceptable levels due to the multiple calls to the detector [44]. These two aspects impose severe restrictions on the size of the search space, in particular if watermark detection is expected to run in real-time. This is why efficient uses of exhaustive search are usually the ones that can reduce to small searches.

5.5.2 Invariance to Desynchronization

Instead of struggling a posteriori to recover synchronization that may have been lost along the processing pipeline, it could be advantageous to design components of the watermarking system in such a way that they are immune to desynchronization attacks. For example, the watermarking space could be defined so that the transform coefficients are left unaltered by desynchronization operations in the content space. With still images, this can be achieved by ignoring all geometrical information when representing the content. Considering that an image reduces to a bag of independent values with no relation between them, it can then be represented by its histogram of pixel values. This compact representation is oblivious to geometrical transformations such as rotation, scale, and translation (RST), and can thus serve as a powerful medium for watermarking [45]. In a similar way, one could modulate the frame average luminance along the time axis to watermark a video and thus be robust against perspective transforms introduced by handheld cameras [46]. Another well-known example of invariant watermarking space is the Fourier-Mellin transform, which leverages on the properties of the Fourier transform and log-polar mapping to construct an image representation invariant to RST. A watermarking system can then rely on the full Fourier-Mellin transform to build an invariant watermark [47], or only use a portion of it to make RST attacks reduce to shifts that can be tackled with exhaustive search while alleviating some of the shortcomings of the full transform [48].

Another way of achieving invariance to desynchronization is commonly referred to as *implicit resynchronization* and relies on features naturally present in the cover content to guide the resynchronization process. For example, for a still image, it is possible to define geometric moments as follows:

$$m_{p,q} = \sum_{x,y} x^p y^q \mathbf{i}[x, y] \tag{5.20}$$

where (p, q) are the moment order and (x, y) are the pixel coordinates in the image **i**. These image geometric moments are robust quantities against rotation and scaling attacks as long as the amount of cropping remains reasonable. As a result, they can be used as reference indicators to define a canonical geometric coordinate system that is intrinsic to the cover content and is robust against desynchronization attacks. The watermark can then be embedded and read in this specific referential [49]. While this approach performs relatively well against global desynchronization attacks, it is not really appropriate to deal with space- or time-varying attacks, such as the random bending attack, Stirmark, that emulates the print-and-scan process for still images for example [50]. This limitation has motivated the design of resynchronization mechanisms that consider local features instead. Salient points in an audio track can serve as anchors for the watermark signal and thereby provide robustness to time delay [51]. Feature points in an image can also be used to guide the watermarking process. They can, for example, be exploited to define a partition over the image, wherein each element of the partition will host a portion of the watermark [52, 53].

5.5.3   Resynchronization Template

A drawback of implicit resynchronization is that it inherently relies on some features which are naturally present in the cover content. As a result, the resynchronization capabilities can be content-dependent which, in turn, may yield undesired instability in practice. To alleviate this shortcoming, another synchronization strategy is to rely on synthetic features introduced at the embedding stage. In other words, the final watermark signal is now composed of two elements: (i) a *pilot watermark* for synchronization purposes and (ii) a *payload watermark* to convey information.

A popular approach for still images is to repeatedly embed a small watermark pattern in the image [54, 55]. In the magnitude of the Fourier transform, such repetitive embedding translates into a constellation of peaks that would not be observed in natural images. Figure 5.5 illustrates this mechanism when the peaks are aligned onto a rectangular grid[2]. Thanks to the properties of the Fourier transform, RST attacks applied to the image induce an RST transformation to the constellation of peaks. In other words, recovering these peaks in an attacked image provides a powerful tell-tale indicator to reverse-engineer the parameters of the RST attack applied to the image (e.g., by realigning the detected constellation of peaks onto the reference resynchronization template). The flip side of the coin is that these peaks

---

2   As a somewhat relevant side note, the image used in this illustration is derived from a photograph of a Swedish woman named Lena Sjööblom, which appeared in the November 1972 issue of *Playboy Magazine*. The so-called *Lena image* was later digitized at the University of Southern California as one of many possible images for use by the research community. Such unauthorized used of copyrighted material triggered some tension with Playboy Enterprises, which eventually decided to overlook the large use of this particular centerfold for research purposes.

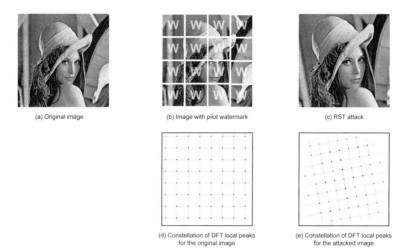

(a) Original image

(b) Image with pilot watermark

(c) RST attack

(d) Constellation of DFT local peaks
for the original image

(e) Constellation of DFT local peaks
for the attacked image

Figure 5.5 Resynchronization relying on a pilot watermark. Repetitive embedding of the same watermark pattern $\mathbf{w}_K$ creates a constellation of local peaks in the frequency domain, which can be used as a reference template to infer the parameters of the RST attack applied to the watermark prior to detection.

are accessible in plain sight and an adversary can simply remove them to disrupt the resynchronization mechanism and thereby impair watermark communications [56].

To avoid this pitfall, one could simply finely interleave the pilot watermark with the payload watermark, and then rely on an exhaustive search of the pilot watermark to obtain realignment parameters to extract the payload watermark [42, 43]. Interestingly, the false alarm bias of an exhaustive search is no longer an issue. If the search for the pilot watermark yields a false alarm, the detection procedure of the payload watermark will indeed remain unsuccessful, and the content will be considered as not watermarked. Moreover, recent advances in template matching enables coping with nonrigid geometric transforms, such as Stirmark. Still, template-based watermarking usually implies embedding the same pilot watermark in different cover content several times, and thus opens the door to watermark estimation remodulation attacks, such as the one discussed in Chapter 6.

5.5.4 Synchronization with Forensic Metadata

The last strategy to recover lost synchronization is to rely on side-information about the original content (i.e., non blind detection). This strategy should be avoided when possible because it drastically narrows the usability of the watermarking system. Requiring access to content-dependent metadata at detection does indeed preclude most watermarking applications that usually rely on standalone live detectors. The only notable exception is forensic watermarking, whose objective is to identify a posteriori the party who has leaked a copy of a content. However, even in this case, it is desirable to not require access to the actual original content. Watermark detection is indeed likely to be operated by a third party in practice, and providing access to the original would simply create another potential source of piracy for copyright holders. This situation has therefore motivated the creation of *semi blind* resynchronization mechanisms that only require access to a digest of the original content, such as content fingerprints which are routinely used for content identification and indexing. For example, the time index of video key frames could serve as reliable anchors to guide a coarse temporal realignment process [57, 58]. It is even possible to achieve fine-grained realignment by incorporating contextual constraints and to add spatial realignment by considering the feature points of the key frames [59]. The key challenge is then to minimize the amount of forensic metadata required at detection while preserving resynchronization accuracy.

5.6 BENCHMARKING WATERMARKING SYSTEMS

Similar to other information hiding techniques, robust watermarking involves a trade-off between various performance indicators, namely (i) the data embedding rate, (ii) the fidelity of the watermark embedding process, and (iii) the robustness of the embedded watermark. As a matter of fact, security aspects that will be discussed at length in Chapter 6 make the situation even more complex. As a result, it is quite challenging to provide a fair comparison between different watermarking systems. Setting aside the embedding rate that is easier to control, the next sections detail good practices on how to benchmark the imperceptibility and robustness of embedded watermarks.

5.6.1 Fidelity Assessment

One of the characterizing features of watermarking is that alterations made to the content should remain imperceptible to human beings. Due to our imperfect understanding of human perception, such perceptual fidelity is actually quite difficult to evaluate in real life. In practice, calibrating the embedding distortion is usually a three-stage process. To begin with, the watermark embedding distortion is evaluated using objective quality metrics. For example, although the mean squared error and the (weighted) peak signal-to-noise ratio are known to correlate poorly with human vision, they are still routinely used to adjust the amount of watermark energy inserted in still images to obtain a specified distortion. While more advanced metrics do exist, they may be ill-fitted to assess watermark distortion because they have usually been designed for coding applications [60]. Even if these metrics are imperfect, some of them are good enough to calibrate distortion based on large-scale automated experimentation.

Once the watermark fidelity has been calibrated using objective quality metrics, it is then necessary to validate these particular settings using subjective quality evaluation tests. These tests involve presenting original and/or watermarked content to human users to evaluate whether the embedded watermark is perceptible or not, and how annoying the distortion is. Various subjective evaluation protocols have been proposed in the literature [61]. For instance, in the ABX test for audio, the user is first presented with the original content (A) and the watermarked content (B), in any order. Next, the user is presented with either the original or the watermarked content (X=A or B) and asked to label this last content as either A or B. By repeating this test several times, it is possible to determine if users perceive any distortion by looking if there is any consistent bias in their answers. Subjective evaluation is tedious and time-consuming to conduct, but is usually a prerequisite prior to commercial deployment. Moreover, it offers potential to optimize the local embedding strength of the watermark with respect to the perception threshold [62].

In some cases (e.g., for premium content), such subjective evaluation is complemented by an inspection from individuals with extremely acute vision or hearing, the so-called *golden eyes* and *golden ears*, that may have the final go or no-go business decision. These people can pick up very small distortions that most users would overlook. Copyright owners sometimes rely on them before adopting a watermark technology in order to make sure that it will not impair the artistic value of their work. These evaluations are highly subjective and may feel somehow irrational (e.g., it is not unheard of that a golden ear preferred a stronger watermark because "the perceived noise is better aligned with the signature *sound* of the studio"). Still, these individuals are very well respected in the entertainment industry and a watermarking technology may struggle if it does not meet their fidelity criteria.

Table 5.1

Performance Indicators for Various Components of a Watermarking System.

System component	Performance indicator
Watermarking space	Instability of transform coefficients
Watermarking communications	Correlation score / detection score
	Bit error rate
	Message error rate
Watermark resynchronization	Accuracy compared to the ground truth

5.6.2 Robustness Evaluation

Once the fidelity of a watermarking system has been calibrated to yield the desired level of distortion, the next step is to evaluate the ability of the embedded watermark to survive subsequent signal processing. Since such subsequent operations are prone to degrading detection performances, they are routinely referred to as *attacks* and are classified into two categories:

1. Synchronous attacks that affect the value of the transform coefficients conveying the watermark (e.g., filtering, noise addition, valuemetric scaling, lossy compression, etc.).

2. Asynchronous attacks that affect the location of the transform coefficients and may disrupt the watermark synchronization (e.g., RST attacks, temporal/spatial jitter, perspective transform, tempo, time stretching, etc.).

Benchmarking a watermarking system then consists of applying attacks to a large number of watermarked contents and recording some detection performance indicator. It is then possible to look at the mean/median performance to infer the nominal regime of the system, to measure the dispersion of the scores to assess the performance stability for different contents, and to isolate outliers showcasing particularly poor robustness to understand the limitations of the system (and possibly fix them). Moreover, for a given attack, it is important to investigate more than a single attacking strength. Indeed, a key objective of robustness benchmarks is to identify the critical value for the attacking strength at which watermark detection performances collapse (i.e., the tipping point where the system derails).

Robustness evaluation is highly computationally intensive and several benchmarking tools have been developed: Stirmark [63], Certimark [64], Checkmark [65], Optimark [66], and WET [67]. Unfortunately, these tools only partially address the needs of watermark designers. They consider watermarking systems as black boxes and benchmark them as a whole, whereas it may be desirable in practice to evaluate each component separately and to tune each one of them accordingly. Table 5.1 lists a number of performance indicators relevant for the main components of a watermarking system. To assess the suitability of a particular transform for watermarking, it makes sense to evaluate how much attacks impact the value of transform coefficients. At the communications layer, transmission performances are assessed by the detection scores obtained after watermark demodulation, by the raw bit error rate obtained after simple decoding of the detection scores, and by the message error rate recorded after error correction. When desynchronization attacks are simulated, the performances of the synchronization module are evaluated by measuring how much the estimated resynchronization parameters deviate from the actual ground truth. Such compartmentalized benchmarking provides greater insight with respect to the pros and cons of each component and highlights the weakest points in the design that need to be fixed.

While the ability to survive the analog hole is one of the selling arguments of robust watermarking, robustness against D/A-A/D conversion is still hardly evaluated nowadays because it involves tedious experimental campaigns and cumbersome logistics. To alleviate this problem, there have been some efforts to model the analog hole for different types of content. The print-and-scan process for still images content introduces a combination of a global geometric transform, local shearing, and random jitter due to the imperfections of the devices [50]. Acoustic transmission of audio files will be affected by the impulse response of the room as well as ambient noise [68]. Placing a camcorder in front of an LCD screen rendering a video clip introduces global geometric and photometric transform, but also a spatio-temporal flicker originating from the interplay between the backlight of the screen and the rolling shutter of camcorder [69]. Thanks to passive forensic techniques such as the ones described in Chapter 9, it is possible to estimate the parameters of the D/A-A/D piracy path in a particular setting and then to build a simulator to reproduce its effects. It can then be incorporated with an automated benchmark to approximate the robustness against this attack.

5.7 APPLICATIONS

In essence, digital watermarking can be seen as a means to irremediably attach relevant information to multimedia content. Compared to transmitting information in some metadata header of a file format that can be lost, a robust watermark travels along the cover content regardless of any subsequent processing. In the mid

90s, digital watermarking received a lot of attention in the context of applications relating to copyright protection. This new technology was indeed perceived as a promising mechanism to combat piracy. This being said, over the last few years, robust watermarking has received renewed interest in slightly different application use cases, namely to enrich content. In this context, the watermark is no longer perceived as an annoying feature inserted by copyright holders, but rather becomes an asset valued by the consumers that provides added value.

5.7.1   Copyright Protection

As mentioned in the introduction of this chapter, the interest for watermarking was initially triggered by increasing MP3 song piracy and by the release of the DeCSS hack to circumvent DVD protection. In this context, the entertainment industry has considered watermarking as a candidate technology to provide playback and copy control functionalities. The underlying rationale was to "keep honest people honest." The strategy was thus to embark watermark readers in consumer electronics devices that would not authorize playback of pirated content or recording of protected content [70]. In other words, the watermark was intended to *prevent* the creation of pirate copies as well as their consumption to force consumers to duplicate their equipment if they wanted to consume both authorized and unauthorized content. Several standardization organizations tested such solutions, most notably the Copy Protection Technical Working Group for DVD [71] and the Secure Digital Music Initiative [72]. Unfortunately, these standardization efforts have been unsuccessful for a variety of reasons: lack of robustness [73], competing interests between various industry stakeholders, and public backlash against content protection technologies. Regardless of the overall context, from a technical perspective, releasing watermark detectors to the public provides adversaries with an oracle that could be used to remove the embedded watermark [74, 75]. That being said, this threat can be somehow mitigated in practice and, for instance, Verance's Cinavia audio watermark is present on some Blu-ray disks today to provide control capabilities [76].

Television broadcast raises unique challenges relating to copyright: advertisers want to verify that the ads that they have paid for are actually aired, content owners want to know when their property is broadcast to collect royalties accordingly, and advertisers want to know accurate measurements of the audience to be charged accordingly by the TV channels. Several technical solutions exist to provide these services, and digital watermarking is one of them. For example, to monitor broadcast content, one simply needs to encode a unique content identifier with a watermark. As a result, whenever this content will be aired, the monitoring station listening to the broadcast will detect the watermark and report about it together with the date and time of diffusion [77]. Such monitoring services are widely deployed nowadays; for example, using Civolution's Teletrax watermarking technology [78]. Similarly, reliable audience measurement can be achieved by slightly modifying the broadcast workflow so that each channel inserts a watermark encoding the unique channel identifier as well as some timing information in any content before diffusion. By placing watermark readers in the homes of the panelists, it is possible to infer which channels they are looking at simply by collecting the detected watermarks. Such watermark-based audience measurement systems have been deployed by major market analysis agencies over the world [79].

Another watermarking application to combat piracy is traitor tracing. The baseline idea is to serialize cover contents with a unique identifier to serve various end users with individual copies. If a copy surfaces on an unauthorized distribution platform, content owners can locate the origin of the leak and take appropriate remedial actions [80]. In contrast with the playback/record control use case, the embedded watermark does not prevent piracy actions from the consumers. They can virtually manipulate the content in any way they want, but are warned that they could be caught if they distribute illegal copies. This *deterrence mechanism* is widely deployed in the movie industry (e.g., to distribute pre-release screeners to journalists, actors, directors, voting members of the Oscar academy). Movies projected in cinemas are also forensically watermarked to encourage theater owners to enforce a "no camcorder" policy [81]. In the near future, content distributed to consumers is also likely to contain forensic watermarks since MovieLabs, representing major motion picture studios, recently released a specification that mandates the use of watermarking for the next generation of video formats [82]. An important requirement of such tracing systems is that the tracing algorithm should never frame innocent users. This may require relying on *anti collusion codes* that will be fully detailed in Chapter 7.

5.7.2 Content Enrichment

Robust watermarks for copyright protection are a typical example of adversarial signal processing. The information conveyed by the watermarks may be undesired by some stakeholders in the ecosystem, and therefore there is motivation for an adversary to remove such watermarks (e.g., to restore some playback capabilities or to evade the accusation procedure of some traitor tracing process). However, from a down-to-earth perspective, digital watermarking is simply an auxiliary communications channel embedded within multimedia content, and it could be

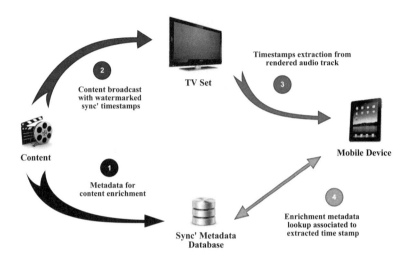

Figure 5.6 Synchronization watermarks for second screen applications. Prior to diffusion, the content provider feeds a database with relevant information to display or actions to perform at specified time stamps. The content is subsequently broadcast together with the time stamps specified by the content owner using an audio watermarking technique. Any companion device can then retrieve the time stamps using its built-in microphone to listen to the audio track. To display the content associated with the current time stamp, the device simply needs to query the metadata database.

used to convey any kind of information. For example, watermarks could be use to enhance costly-to-upgrade legacy system. Along this line, Eurocontrol considered using watermarks to digitally transmit the aircraft call-sign along with the pilot voice messages and thereby avoid time-consuming reidentification requests in air traffic control [83].

Another strategy is to insert watermarks to enrich multimedia content and thus provide added value to the consumers. This paradigm flourished around 2010, when tablets became popular and content owners and broadcasters were looking for technical means to display relevant content on such companion devices when consumers are watching movies and TV shows on television. To do so, they were looking for a technology that would enable them to synchronize the devices. Among other technologies, robust watermarking appeared as a quick-to-deploy backward-compatible solution that could be used while waiting for dedicated transport protocols [24]. Figure 5.6 depicts the typical workflow for watermark-enabled companion screen synchronization. In essence, the content owner inserts some watermarks encoding a unique identifier at specific time stamps in the program where he wants to display additional content (e.g., behind-the-scene bonus material, advertisement, trivia, etc.). When the second screen hears or sees the watermark, it is able to fetch the information to display based on the detected watermark.

This enrichment paradigm has even been extended to physical goods. For example, Digimarc developed a watermarking technology that is widely deployed for printed visual content. Their Discover application for mobile phones allows users to take snapshots of magazines to be interactively redirected to relevant content online. At some point, they even considered watermarking to provide some level of interactivity for toys [84]. Later, the same idea was extended to audio by Philips [85]. More recently, Digimarc introduced a watermarking system for retail packaging to complement legacy bar codes and showcased drastic improvement with respect to the checkout time, thereby creating potential for cost savings [86]. These examples illustrate the increasing maturity of watermarking, which is slowly becoming yet another baseline tool in the default signal processing toolbox. In the future, for an increasing number of multimedia systems, watermarking will simply be a utility that provides a convenient functionality and will no longer be the capstone of the system. A good example is Dialogic's VideoVision quality monitoring system: watermarking is a mere detail of the full system and only provides synchronization capabilities [87].

5.8   RESEARCH OUTLOOK

This chapter is intended to provide a high-level overview on digital watermarking to students, researchers, and practitioners who want to learn about this technology. For conciseness and pedagogy, some parts have been somewhat over-simplified and do not necessarily represent the latest results of the state-of-the-art. Interested readers who would like to further learn about watermarking are therefore encouraged to read the seminal research papers listed in the references and even to read more in-depth manuals [1].

Although robust watermarking is now a mature technology, there are still a number of enduring challenges that need to be addressed. Several lines of research are indicated below for students and researchers who would be interested to work in this area.[3]

---

3   Outliving the future when laying down a research agenda rarely occurs. Hopefully, some of the suggested research lines in this section will still be relevant in the next few years. The reader should be forgiving and remember that this chapter was finalized in summer 2015.

- *Watermarking correlated samples.* In many cases, it is not possible to completely remove the redundancy of the cover content, and there is therefore some remaining correlation between the transform coefficients that are watermarked. Efficient watermarking methods that account for such correlation still need to be invented.

- *Perceptual accommodation.* Overall, there is limited research effort to evaluate the perceptual impact of watermarking, although it has been clearly established that watermarking distortion differs from compression distortion. There are new types of content appearing on the market (e.g., stereo video content, light-field imaging, high-dynamic range, ultra wide gamut, high order ambisonic, etc.). Understanding how to perceptually accommodate the specificities of these content will be necessary in watermarking.

- *Multidimensional watermark modulation.* State-of-the-art watermarking systems essentially map the input content to a 1D representation (i.e., a sequence of transform coefficients) prior to embedding the watermark. In the best case scenario, the resynchronization module may account for the multidimensional nature of the content. Watermark designs that would deviate from this generic blueprint may provide new functionalities and may be more appropriate for manifold representations of content (e.g., 3D meshes).

- *Theory vs. practice.* Several theoretical results clearly indicate that dirty-paper watermarking is expected to outperform spread-spectrum watermarking. Nevertheless, most commercially deployed systems still rely on spread spectrum. Empirical practice indeed suggests that there is a gap between theory and practice. Further research is needed to figure out whether and how this discrepancy can be fixed.

- *Coping with nonglobal attacks.* State-of-the-art watermarking techniques are able to cope with global attacks (e.g., gamma correction, perspective geometry, etc.). However, detection performances may be adversely affected by locally varying distortions, such as local luminance alterations due to camcord recapture flicker or irregular temporal resampling due to screencasting. There is therefore a need for new mechanisms to cope with such alterations.

- *Piracy path modeling.* A large majority of research contributions in watermarking limit benchmarking to conventional attacks (e.g., noise addition, filtering, lossy compression, and RST attack) that are hardly in line with the different workflows set in place by the pirates. For example, camcorder recapture can be crudely modeled as the combination of a global geometric transform, temporal resampling, noise addition, and loss compression. However, it does not account for spatio-temporal luminance flicker, temporal shaking for handheld cameras, or nonglobal luminance changes due to parasite lighting. Tackling such realistic distortions is instrumental to improve the robustness of watermarking systems in real life.

- *Complexity and integration effort.* An aspect that is regularly overlooked by the academic research community is the computational complexity and the memory footprint of their proposals. You can have the best watermarking system, but if it is too computationally intensive and is not able to meet real-time/live requirements, it will not be considered. If it requires one to change the whole workflow of the client, it will not be deployed. The challenge is then to achieve the best fidelity/robustness trade-off under constrained resources.

References

[1] Cox, I. J., et al., *Digital Watermarking and Steganography*, Morgan Kaufmann, 2nd ed., 2007.

[2] Hembrooke, E. F., "Identification of Sounds and Like Signals," US Patent US3004104 A, 1961.

[3] Lam, C. K. M., and B. C. Y. Tan, "The Internet is Changing the Music Industry," *Communications of the ACM*, Vol. 44, No. 8, August 2001, pp. 62–68.

[4] Patrizio, A., "Why the DVD Hack Was a Cinch," *Wired*, November 1999.

[5] Kutter, M., F. Jordan, and F. Bossen, "Digital Watermarking of Color Images using Amplitude Modulation," *Journal of Electronic Imaging*, Vol. 7, No. 2, April 1998, pp. 326–332.

[6] Doërr, G., J.-L. Dugelay, and D. Kirovski, "On the Need for Signal-Coherent Watermarks," *IEEE Transactions on Multimedia*, Vol. 8, No. 5, October 2006, pp. 896–904.

[7] Koz, A., C. Cigla, and A. A. Alatan, "Watermarking of Free-view Video," *IEEE Transactions on Image Processing*, Vol. 19, No. 7, July 2010, pp. 1785–1797.

[8] Chen, X.-M., et al., "Efficient Coherent Phase Quantization for Audio Watermarking," in *Proceedings of the IEEE International Conference on Acoustics, Speech and Signal Processing*, May 2011, pp. 1844–1847.

[9] Liu, Y., B. Prabhakaran, and X. Guo, "A Robust Spectral Approach for Blind Watermarking of Manifold Surfaces," in *Proceedings of the ACM Workshop on Multimedia and Security*, September 2008, pp. 43–52.

[10] Rolland-Nevière, X., G. Doërr, and P. Alliez, "Triangle Surface Mesh Watermarking based on a Constrained Optimization Framework," *IEEE Transactions on Information Forensics and Security*, Vol. 9, No. 9, September 2014, pp. 1491–1501.

[11] TC 43 Acoustics, "Acoustics – Normal Equal-Loudness-Level Contours," Technical Report 226:2003, ISO, 2003.

[12] Mannos, J. L., and D. J. Sakrison, "The Effects of a Visual Fidelity Criterion on the Encoding of Images," *IEEE Transactions on Information Theory*, Vol. IT-20, No. 4, July 1974, pp. 525–536.

[13] Taylor, M. M., "Visual Discrimination and Orientation," *Journal of the Optical Society of America*, Vol. 53, No. 6, June 1963, pp. 763–765.

[14] Campbell, F. W., and J. J. Kulikowski, "Orientational Selectivity of the Human Visual System," *The Journal of Physiology*, Vol. 187, No. 2, November 1966, pp. 437–445.

[15] Watson, A. B., "DCT Quantization Matrices Visually Optimized for Individual Images," in *Human Vision, Visual Processing, and Digital Display IV*, Vol. 1913 of *Proceedings of SPIE*, January 1993, pp. 202–216.

[16] Musmann, H. G., "Genesis of the MP3 Audio Coding Standard," *IEEE Transactions on Consumer Electronics*, Vol. 52, No. 3, August 2006, pp. 1043–1049.

[17] Voloshynovskiy, S., et al., "A Stochastic Approach to Content Adaptive Digital Image Watermarking," in *International Workshop on Information Hiding*, Vol. 1768 of *Lecture Notes in Computer Science*, September 1999, pp. 211–236.

[18] JTC1/SC29/WG11, "Information Technology – Coding of Moving Pictures and Associated Audio for Digital Storage Media at up to About 1,5 Mbit/s – Part 3: Audio," Technical Report 11172-3, ISO/IEC, 1993.

[19] Pickholtz, R. L., D. L. Schilling, and L. B. Milstein, "Theory of Spread-Spectrum Communication – A Tutorial," *IEEE Transactions on Communications*, Vol. 30, No. 5, May 1982, pp. 855–884.

[20] Cox, I. J., et al., "Secure Spread Spectrum Watermarking for Multimedia Content," *IEEE Transactions on Image Processing*, Vol. 6, No. 12, December 1997, pp. 1673–1687.

[21] Fawcett, T., "ROC Graphs: Notes and Practical Considerations for Data Mining Researchers," Technical Report HPL-2003-4, HP Laboratories, January 2003.

[22] Bender, W., et al., "Techniques for Data Hiding," *IBM Systems Journal*, Vol. 35, No. 3&4, 1996, pp. 313–336.

[23] Langelaar, G. C., and R. L. Lagendijk, "Optimal Differential Energy Watermarking of DCT Encoded Images and Video," *IEEE Transactions on Image Processing*, Vol. 10, No. 1, January 2001, pp. 148–158.

[24] Arnold, M., et al., "A Phase-Based Audio Watermarking System Robust to Acoustic Path Propagation," *IEEE Transactions on Information Forensics and Security*, Vol. 9, No. 3, March 2014, pp. 411–425.

[25] Malvar, H. S., and D. A. F. Florêncio, "Improved Spread Spectrum: A New Modulation Technique for Robust Watermarking," *IEEE Transactions on Signal Processing*, Vol. 51, No. 4, April 2003, pp. 898–905.

[26] Depovere, G., T. Kalker, and J.-P. Linnartz, "Improved Watermark Detection Reliability using Filtering Before Correlation," in *Proceedings of the IEEE International Conference on Image Processing*, Vol. I, October 1998, pp. 430–434.

[27] Furon, T., "A Constructive and Unifying Framework for Zero-Bit Watermarking," *IEEE Transactions on Information Forensics and Security*, Vol. 2, No. 2, June 2007, pp. 149–163.

[28] Menezes, A. J., P. C. van Oorschot, and S. A. Vanstone, *Handbook of applied Cryptography*, CRC Press, 1996.

[29] Moon, T. K., *Error Correction Coding: Mathematical Methods and Algorithms*, Wiley, 2005.

[30] Costa, M. H. M., "Writing on Dirty Paper," *IEEE Transactions on Information Theory*, Vol. 29, No. 3, May 1983, pp. 439–441.

[31] Gelfand, S. I., and M. S. Pinsker, "Coding for Channel with Random Parameters," *Problems of Control and Information Theory*, Vol. 9, No. 1, 1980, pp. 19–31.

[32] Chen, B., and G. W. Wornell, "Quantization Index Modulation: A Class of Provably Good Methods for Digital Watermarking and Information Embedding," *IEEE Transactions on Information Theory*, Vol. 47, No. 4, May 2001, pp. 1423–1443.

[33] Conway, J., and N. J. A. Sloane, *Sphere Packings, Lattices and Groups*, Springer, 1998.

[34] Moulin, P., and R. Koetter, "Data-Hiding Codes," *Proceedings of the IEEE*, Vol. 93, No. 12, December 2005, pp. 2083–2126.

[35] Miller, M. L., G. J. Doërr, and I. J. Cox, "Applying Informed Coding and Embedding to Design a Robust High-capacity Watermark," *IEEE Transactions on Image Processing*, Vol. 13, No. 6, June 2004, pp. 762–807.

[36] Lee, K., et al., "EM Estimation of Scale Factor for Quantization-based Audio Watermarking," in *Proceedings of the International Workshop on Digital Watermarking*, Vol. 2939 of *Lecture Notes in Computer Science*, October 2003, pp. 316–327.

[37] Shterev, I. D., and R. L. Lagendijk, "Amplitude Scale Estimation for Quantization-Based Watermarking," *IEEE Transactions on Signal Processing*, Vol. 54, No. 11, November 2006, pp. 4146–4155.

[38] Pérez-González, F., et al., "Rational Dither Modulation: A High-Rate Data-Hiding Method Invariant to Gain Attacks," *IEEE Transactions on Signal Processing*, Vol. 53, No. 10, October 2005, pp. 3960–3975.

[39] Ourique, F., et al., "Angle QIM: A Novel Watermark Embedding Scheme Robust Against Amplitude Scaling Distortions," in *Proceedings of the IEEE International Conference on Acoustics, Speech, and Signal Processing*, Vol. II, March 2005, pp. 797–800.

[40] Oostveen, J., T. Kalker, and M. Staring, "Adaptive Quantization Watermarking," in *Security, Steganography, and Watermarking of Multimedia Contents VI*, Vol. 5306 of *Proceedings of SPIE*, January 2004, pp. 296–303.

[41] Li, Q., and I. J. Cox, "Using Perceptual Models to Improve Fidelity and Provide Resistance to Valuemetric Scaling for Quantization Index Modulation Watermarking," *IEEE Transactions on Information Forensics and Security*, Vol. 2, No. 2, June 2007, pp. 127–139.

[42] Caldelli, R., et al., "Coping with Local Geometric Attacks by Means of Optic-flow-based Resynchronization for Robust Watermarking," in *Security, Steganography, and Watermarking of Multimedia Contents VII*, Vol. 5681 of *Proceedings of SPIE*, January 2005, pp. 164–174.

[43] Dugelay, J.-L., et al., "Still Image Watermarking Robust to Local Geometric Distortions," *IEEE Transactions on Image Processing*, Vol. 15, No. 9, September 2006, pp. 2831–2842.

[44] Lichtenauer, J. F., et al., "Exhaustive Geometrical Search and the False Positive Watermark Detection Probability," in *Security and Watermarking of Multimedia Contents V*, Vol. 5020 of *Proceedings of SPIE*, January 2003, pp. 203–214.

[45] Coltuc, D., and P. Bolon, "Robust Watermarking by Histogram Specification," in *Proceedings of the IEEE International Conference on Image Processing*, Vol. 2, October 1999, pp. 236–239.

[46] Haitsma, J., and T. Kalker, "A Watermarking Scheme for Digital Cinema," in *Proceedings of the IEEE International Conference on Image Processing*, Vol. 2, October 2001, pp. 487–489.

[47] Ó Ruanaidh, J. J. K., and T. Pun, "Rotation, Scale, and Translation Invariant Digital Image Watermarking," *Signal Processing*, Vol. 66, No. 3, May 1998, pp. 303–317.

[48] Lin, C.-Y., et al., "Rotation, Scale, and Translation Resilient Watermarking for Images," *IEEE Transactions on Image Processing*, Vol. 10, No. 5, May 2001, pp. 767–782.

[49] Alghoniemy, M., and A. H. Tewfik, "Geometric Distortion Correction Through Image Normalization," in *Proceedings of the IEEE International Conference on Multimedia and Expo*, Vol. 3, August 2000, pp. 1291–1294.

[50] Petitcolas, F. A. P., R. J. Anderson, and M. G. Kuhn, "Attacks on Copyright Marking Systems," in *Proceedings of the International Workshop on Information Hiding*, Vol. 1525 of *Lecture Notes in Computer Science*, April 1998, pp. 218–238.

[51] Wu, C.-P., P.-C. Su, and C.-C. J. Kuo, "Robust and Efficient Digital Audio Watermarking using Audio Content Analysis," in *Security and Watermarking of Multimedia Content II*, Vol. 3971 of *Proceedings of SPIE*, January 2000, pp. 382–392.

[52] Dittmann, J., T. Fiebig, and R. Steinmetz, "New Approach for Transformation-invariant Image and Video Watermarking in the Spatial Domain: Self-Spanning Patterns (SSP)," in *Security and Watermarking of Multimedia Contents II*, Vol. 3971 of *Proceedings of SPIE*, January 2000, pp. 176–185.

[53] Bas, P., J.-M. Chassery, and B. Macq, "Geometrically Invariant Watermarking using Feature Points," *IEEE Transactions on Image Processing*, Vol. 11, No. 9, September 2002, pp. 320–323.

[54] Rhoads, G. B., "Steganography Methods Employing Embedded Calibration Data," US Patent US5636292 A, 1995.

[55] Kutter, M., "Watermarking Resistance to Translation, Rotation, and Scaling," in *Multimedia Systems and Applications*, Vol. 3528 of *Proceedings of SPIE*, January 1999, pp. 423–431.

[56] Herrigel, A., S. V. Voloshynovskiy, and Y. B. Rytsar, "Watermark Template Attack," in *Security and Watermarking of Multimedia Contents III*, Vol. 4314 of *Proceedings of SPIE*, January 2001, pp. 394–405.

[57] Delannay, D., C. de Roover, and B. Macq, "Temporal Alignment of Video Sequences for Watermarking Systems," in *Security and Watermarking of Multimedia Contents V*, Vol. 5020 of *Proceedings of SPIE*, January 2003, pp. 481–492.

[58] Harmanci, O., M. Kucukgoz, and M. K. Mihcak, "Temporal Synchronization of Watermarked Video Using Image Hashing," in *Security, Steganography, and Watermarking of Multimedia Contents VII*, Vol. 5681 of *Proceedings of SPIE*, January 2005, pp. 370–380.

[59] Baudry, S., B. Chupeau, and F. Lefèbvre, "A Framework for Video Forensics Based on Local and Temporal Fingerprints," in *Proceedings of the IEEE International Conference on Image Processing*, November 2009, pp. 2889–2892.

[60] Pankajakshan, V., and F. Autrusseau, "A Multi-purpose Objective Quality Metric for Image Watermarking," in *Proceedings of the IEEE International Conference on Image Processing*, September 2010, pp. 2589–2592.

[61] Le Callet, P., F. Autrusseau, and P. Campisi, "Visibility Control and Quality Assessment of Watermarking and Data Hiding Algorithms," in *Multimedia Forensics and Security*, IGI Global, IX, pp. 163–192, July 2008.

[62] Autrusseau, F., S. David, and V. Pankajakshan, "A Subjective Study of Visibility Thresholds for Wavelet Domain Watermarking," in *Proceedings of the IEEE International Conference on Image Processing*, September 2010, pp. 201–204.

[63] Petitcolas, F. A. P., "Watermarking Schemes Evaluation," *IEEE Signal Processing Magazine*, Vol. 17, No. 5, September 2000, pp. 58–64.

[64] Vorbruggen, J. C., and F. Cayre, "Certimark Benchmark: Architecture and Future Perspectives," in *Proceedings of the IEEE International Conference on Multimedia and Expo*, Vol. 2, August 2002, pp. 485–488.

[65] Pereira, S., et al., "Second Generation Benchmarking and Application Oriented Evaluation," in *Proceedings of the Information Hiding Workshop*, Vol. 2137 of *Lecture Notes in Computer Science*, April 2001, pp. 340–353.

[66] Solachidis, V., et al., "A Benchmarking Protocol for Watermarking Methods," in *Proceedings of the IEEE International Conference on Image Processing*, Vol. 3, October 2001, pp. 1023–1026.

[67] Guitart, O., H. C. Kim, and E. J. Delp, III, "Watermark Evaluation Testbed," *Journal of Electronic Imaging*, Vol. 15, No. 4, December 2006, pp. 041106–1–13.

[68] Arnold, M., et al., "Simulating Large-scale Acoustic Path Benchmarking," in *Media Watermarking, Security, and Forensics XIV*, Vol. 8303 of *Proceedings of SPIE*, January 2012, pp. 83030T–1–12.

[69] Baudry, S., et al., "Modeling the Flicker Effect in Camcorded Videos to Improve Watermark Robustness," in *Proceedings of the IEEE Workshop on Information Forensics and Security*, December 2014, pp. 42–47.

[70] Bloom, J. A., et al., "Copy Protection for DVD," *Proceedings of the IEEE*, Vol. 87, No. 7, July 1999, pp. 1267–1276.

[71] Bell, A. E., "The Dynamic Digital Disk," *IEEE Spectrum*, Vol. 36, No. 10, October 1999, pp. 28–35.

[72] Secure Digital Music Initiative, "SDMI Portable Device Specification – Part 1," 1999.

[73] Craver, S. A., et al., "Reading Between the Lines: Lessons from the SDMI Challenge," in *Proceedings of the Conference on USENIX Security Symposium*, Vol. 10, August 2001, pp. 1–12.

[74] Kalker, T., J.-P. Linnartz, and M. van Dijk, "Watermark Estimation Through Detector Analysis," in *Proceedings of the IEEE International Conference on Image Processing*, Vol. 1, October 1998, pp. 425–429.

[75] Comesaña, P., L. Perez-Freire, and F. Pérez-González, "Blind Newton Sensitivity Attack," *IEE Proceedings on Information Security*, Vol. 153, No. 3, September 2006, pp. 115–125.

[76] Verance, "Cinavia Technology," http://www.cinavia.com, 2010.

[77] Depovere, G., et al., "The VIVA Project: Digital Watermarking for Broadcast Monitoring," in *Proceedings of the IEEE International Conference on Image Processing*, Vol. 2, October 1999, pp. 202–205.

[78] Civolution, "Teletrax – Television Monitoring," http://www.civolution.com/solution/digital-watermarking-fingerprinting-for-television-monitoring/ 2014.

[79] Médiamétrie, "Watermarking Technology," http://www.mediametrie.com/innovation/pages/watermarking-technology.php?p=7,112,78&page=81, 2009.

[80] Furon, T., and G. Doërr, "Tracing Pirated Content on the Internet: Unwinding Ariadne's Thread," *Security & Privacy*, Vol. 8, No. 5, September/October 2010, pp. 69–71.

[81] Digital Cinema Initiatives, LLC, *Digital Cinema System Specification*, 1st ed., March 2008.

[82] Motion Picture Laboratories, Inc., "MovieLabs Specification for Enhanced Content Protection," 2013.

[83] Hering, H., M. Hagmüller, and G. Kubin, "Safety and Security Increase for Air Traffic Management Through Unnoticeable Watermark Aircraft Identification Tag Transmitted with the VHF Voice Communication," in *Proceedings of the Digital Avionics Systems Conference*, Vol. 1, October 2003, pp. 4.E.2–1–10.

[84] Sharma, R. K., and S. Decker, "Practical Challenges for Digital Watermarking Applications," in *Proceedings of the IEEE Workshop on Multimedia Signal Processing*, October 2001, pp. 237–242.

[85] Lemma, A., et al., "Watermarking for Content Aware Intelligent Toys," in *Proceedings of the IEEE International Conference on Consumer Electronics*, January 2008, pp. 1–2.

[86] Rodriguez, T., D. Haaga, and S. Calhoon, "Automation and Workflow Considerations for Embedding Digimarc Barcodes at Scale," in *Media Watermarking, Security, and Forensics 2015*, Vol. 9409 of *Proceedings of SPIE*, February 2015, pp. 940905–1–13.

[87] Dialogic, "Measuring and Tracking Perceptual Video Quality," White Paper, 2012.

Chapter 6

Watermarking Security

Teddy Furon

This chapter deals with applications where watermarking is a security primitive included in a larger system protecting the value of multimedia content. In this context, there might exist dishonest users, in the sequel so-called attackers, willing to read/overwrite hidden messages or simply to remove the watermark signal.

The goal of this section is to play the role of the attacker. We analyze means to deduce information about the watermarking technique that will later ease the forgery of attacked copies. This chapter first proposes a topology of the threats in Section 6.1, introducing three different concepts: robustness, worst-case attacks, and security. Chapter 5 has already discussed watermark robustness. We focus on worst-case attacks in Section 6.2, on the way to measure watermarking security in Section 6.3, and on the classical tools to break a watermarking scheme in Section 6.4. This tour of watermarking security concludes by a summary of what we know and still do not know about it (Section 6.5) and a review of oracle attacks (Section 6.6). Last, Section 6.7 deals with protocol attacks, a notion which underlines the illusion of security that a watermarking primitive might bring when not properly used in some applications.

6.1 INTRODUCTION

Chapter 5 already mentioned the term "attacks." This introduction defines a topology to clearly underpin how different the "attacks" of this chapter are. This topology has three classes: robustness attacks, worst-case attacks, and security attacks. They range from the case where the attacker knows nothing about the watermarking technique (robustness) to the case where the attacker is willing to disclose all its internals and especially its secret key (security).

6.1.1 Robustness

The previous chapter calls an attack any process modifying multimedia content which may decrease the performance of the watermark detection or decoding. This acts as the communication channel that the watermark signal goes through. Many such processes are expected in the lifetime of multimedia content. They are routinely used during editing or rendering without the intention to hurt the watermark. They are not designed for watermarking removal but for source compression, denoising, filtering, etc. These attacks are *blind* in the sense that one uses them not having the slightest idea about what watermarking is. Section 5.6.2 classified them into synchronous (or valuemetric) attacks that change the value of the samples and the asynchronous (or geometric) attacks. The localization of the watermark signal in the spatial/time and/or frequency domain has moved so that the decoder will not look for it at the right place.

State-of-the-art watermarking techniques are very robust against synchronous or asynchronous attacks; being robust to a combination of both is more challenging. In details, watermarking modifies the samples in the embedding domain as follows:

$$\mathbf{c}_\mathrm{w} = \mathbf{c}_\mathrm{o} + \mathbf{w}(\mathbf{c}_\mathrm{o}, \mathbf{s}, \mathbf{m}, K) \tag{6.1}$$

where $\mathbf{c}_\mathrm{o} = (\mathbf{c}_\mathrm{o}[1], \ldots, \mathbf{c}_\mathrm{o}[N])$ and $\mathbf{c}_\mathrm{w} = (\mathbf{c}_\mathrm{w}[1], \ldots, \mathbf{c}_\mathrm{w}[N])$ are the host and watermarked samples, respectively, extracted from the original and the watermarked pieces of content. Function $\mathbf{w}(\cdot)$ is the embedding scheme that creates the watermark signal from the host $\mathbf{c}_\mathrm{o}$, the perceptual masking slack $\mathbf{s}$, the message to be hidden $\mathbf{m}$, and the secret key K. The embedding distortion is denoted D_e. A synchronous attack produces some noise in the embedding domain:

$$\mathbf{c}_\mathrm{z} = \mathbf{c}_\mathrm{w} + \mathbf{n} \tag{6.2}$$

We can quantify its impact by measuring how the performance P of the watermarking scheme decreases as the amount of distortion D_a between the watermarked and the attacked contents increases.

- P is often measured in practice by the bit error rate (BER) or the message error rate (MER) in watermark decoding, or the probability of a miss P_miss in watermark detection. In theoretical papers, it is expressed in terms of mutual information or capacity for watermark decoding or Kullback-Leibler or Bhattacharyya distances for watermarking detection.

- D_a is often the mean square error (MSE) between watermarked and attacked (or watermarked and original) contents, be it translated into PSNR in still image watermarking, or SNR in audio watermarking, or the expectation of the Euclidean distance in theoretical papers.

As is often the case, the attack is parametrized by a setup θ_a, giving birth to the operating curve $(P(\theta_a), D_a(\theta_a))$. For example, as the quality factor θ_a of a JPEG compression goes down, the distortion $D_a(\theta_a)$ between the compressed and the watermarked image gets bigger, while the performance $P(\theta_a)$ of the watermarking decoder or detector smoothly decreases.

6.1.2 Worst-Case Attacks

The concept of worst case attacks is summarized into one question: for a given attack distortion D_a, which process minimizes the watermarking performance P?

This concept is of utmost importance, as it yields a fair benchmark. Imagine that watermarking technique A is more robust to JPEG compression than technique B, but the latter is more robust to JPEG2000. Which technique is more robust? Not considering a particular attack, but on the contrary, focusing on the one that hurts most, reveals the intrinsic robustness of a particular watermarking scheme. Techniques A and B do not have the same worst-case attack, but their ultimate robustness allows to predict how they will resist against an *informed* attacker. This last word is the keystone of the concept. The nature of the worst-case attack mostly depends on the information available to the attacker.

The worst-case attack should be defined as the most damaging attack at a given distortion budget and for a given level of knowledge on the watermarking technique.

The literature always looks for the worst-case attack, assuming that the attacker knows the embedding domain and the watermarking scheme. In other words, he has access to the samples that carry the watermarking signal (6.1). Then, the attacker looks for the noise signal $\mathbf{n}$ to be added (6.2) to degrade, at most, the system performance. It is therefore tweaked for a particular watermarking embedding $\mathbf{w}(\cdot)$. Yet, the attacker does not know secret key K and cannot set $\mathbf{n} = -\mathbf{w}(\mathbf{c}_o, \mathbf{s}, \mathbf{m}, K)$. Signal $\mathbf{n}$ is thus a random noise that produces a given performance P for an expected attack distortion D_a. The goal is to find the distribution of random noise that maximizes the loss of performance at a given distortion budget.

Examples of worst-case attacks against two well known watermarking schemes (spread spectrum and quantization index modulation) are detailed in Section 6.2.

6.1.3   Security Attacks

6.1.3.1   Differences Between Robustness and Security

The concept of watermarking security has slowly emerged because it was often misunderstood as a synonym of robustness; this is because both terms deal with attacks. The intention of removing the watermark or the malice of the attacker are not sufficient enough to make a clear cut between the two concepts.

During security attacks, the attacker proceeds in two steps: he first observes some protected contents in order to disclose some information about the watermarking technique and its secret key. He then forges attacked contents thanks to a worst-case attack based on this new knowledge.

Security becomes a concern when the attacker observes many pieces of content watermarked with the same technique and the same secret key.

6.1.3.2   An Analysis Based on Attacker's Knowledge

Following Kerckhoffs' principle [1], an expert in charge of measuring the security level of a technique starts with the assumption that the attacker knows everything except the secret key. It means that the attacker knows how to extract the feature vectors carrying the watermark signal of (6.1). The only thing the attacker knows about the secret key is its sample set (the set of possible key values). We must clarify what the secret is. Almost all techniques create some key-variables (such as the secret direction for spread spectrum, or the dither for quantization index modulation) from a pseudo-random generator seeded with a secret binary word called the "seed." This is a very simple way to restitute these key-variables whenever needed at the embedding and the decoding sides. It is these key-variables which allow anyone to read, write, and erase watermarks. The seed is only an auxiliary variable. The ultimate secret to be disclosed is thus these key-variables.

The first issue of the security assessment is to state whether or not the attacker can disclose some information about this secret key when observing protected contents. This is called "information leakage". The consequence is that the attacker can improve his knowledge about the secret key. At the beginning, he only knows its sample domain. While carrying on observing protected contents, he can theoretically reduce this set (i.e., refine his estimation of the secret key). The second issue is the speed of this accumulation of knowledge as a function of the number of observations.

This theoretical security assessment results in the number of protected contents that the attacker needs to observe for disclosing the secret key up to a given accuracy. This theoretical study is very hard to conclude, and usually the watermarking scheme and the statistics of the host are simplified to the maximum. Another drawback is that this theoretical study may not give any clue about practical algorithms that take real protected contents as input and outputs the estimated secret key.

For this reason, a third issue is to build such an estimator. On the same over-simplified setup, the estimator performance is lower than foreseen because the theory gives a lower bound of its estimation accuracy. This proves the existence of one estimator doing the job within a limited complexity.

6.1.3.3 Classes of Security Attacks

In order to generalize security assessment to many applications, academics have listed typical scenarios of attacks. These categories are based on the type of observations to which the attacker has access in order to refine his knowledge about the secret key. Here is a nonexhaustive list:

- *Watermarked Only Attack:* the observations are pieces of content watermarked with the same technique and secret key. In most security oriented applications this attack is a threat.

- *Known Original Attack:* the observations are pairs of original host and its watermarked version. For example, a movie trailer might not be watermarked, while a copy taken from a blue-ray may be watermarked.

- *Known Message Attack:* the observations are pairs of watermarked pieces of content and their hidden messages. For example, if the embedded message is the copy "status" of a movie, it is obviously known.

- *Chosen Original Attack:* the observations are pairs of watermarked and original contents chosen by the attacker. This happens when the attacker has access to a watermark embedder as a sealed black box.

- *Multiple Watermarked Attack:* the observations are multiple watermarked versions with different messages of some original contents.

- *Chosen Watermarked Attack:* this is another name for the oracle attack (see Section 6.6).

Not all classes listed above have been analyzed; only a few have been studied (watermarked only attack, known message attack, known original attack) for some watermarking schemes (spread spectrum and quantization index modulation). Section 6.3 presents the three main approaches that have been proposed to measure the theoretical level of security of a watermarking scheme. Section 6.4 lists the main algorithms used to estimate secret keys in practice.

6.1.3.4   The Remaining Uncertainties

An information leakage about the secret key does not mean that the attacker will eventually disclose the secret key. For a multibit watermarking scheme, the watermarked only attack and the known original attack usually estimate the secret up to some uncertainties. In spread spectrum or quantization index modulation, for example, this allows the attacker to read the hidden symbols up to a permutation over their alphabet. In other words, this uncertainty prevents the attacker from embedding and decoding hidden messages. Yet, he can notice when two pieces of content are watermarked with different messages, he can flip some bits (not knowing which of them), and most importantly he can erase the watermark signal without introducing too much distortion.

Cayre and Bas [2] have built categories of watermarking schemes based on their remaining uncertainties under a watermarked only attack. They have also designed two variants of spread spectrum (called natural and circular watermarking) offering much more remaining uncertainties than the original scheme. Therefore, they can be considered more secure [3].

6.2   EXAMPLES OF WORST-CASE ATTACKS

This section details worst-case attacks against the two most well-known watermarking schemes: spread spectrum (see Section 5.3) and quantization index modulation (see Section 5.4.2).

6.2.1   Spread Spectrum

References about worst-case attacks against spread spectrum watermarking include the works of Le Guelvouit and Pateux [4], Su and Eggers [5], and Moulin et al. [6, 7]. Their analyses are similar, but with different flavors, because they assume different host distributions (white or correlated), performance metric P (BER or capacity), and attack distortion metric D_a (MSE or weighted MSE). They typically use the Lagrange multiplier method to minimize P at a given D_a, which ends up with a worst-case attack being a mixture of three strategies as detailed below.

Example: Spread spectrum with Gaussian host samples [4].
Suppose the following model: Host samples are statistically independent and Gaussian distributed with their own variance: $c_o[j] \sim \mathcal{N}(0, \sigma[j]^2)$. The embedding is as follows

$$c_w[j] = c_o[j] + \frac{s[j]}{\sqrt{N}} \sum_{i=1}^{P} b_i w_i[j] \qquad (6.3)$$

with $b_i \in \{-1, 1\}$ the antipodal modulation of the ith bit to be embedded, $\{w_1, \ldots, w_P\}$ the orthonormal secret carriers modulating one bit each (i.e., $w_k^\top w_\ell = \delta_{\{k=\ell\}}$), and $s[j] \geq 0$ a perceptual shaping weight. Then the worst-case attack can be written as $c_z[j] = \gamma[j] c_w[j] + n[j]$, with $\gamma[j] \geq 0$ a scaling factor and $n[j] \sim \mathcal{N}(0, \rho[j]^2)$. This creates the attack distortion

$$D_a = \mathbb{E}(\|c_z - c_o\|^2) = \sum_{j=1}^{N} \sigma[j]^2 (1 - \gamma[j])^2 + P\gamma[j]^2 s[j]^2 + \rho[j]^2 \qquad (6.4)$$

The optimal expression of the parameters $(\gamma[j], \rho[j]^2)$ can be derived from three strategies:

- *Erasure:* If the jth sample carries a lot of watermark power compared to the power of the host signal, canceling this coefficient lowers the watermark to noise power ratio while creating a small distortion: $(\gamma[j], \rho[j]^2) = (0, 0)$.

- *Wiener filtering:* If the jth sample carries a small watermark power compared to the power of the host signal, estimating the host sample by a Wiener filtering lowers the distortion while not modifying the watermark to noise power ratio: $(\gamma[j], \rho[j]^2) = (\gamma_W[j], 0)$ with

$$\gamma_W[j] = \frac{\sigma[j]^2}{\sigma[j]^2 + Ps[j]^2} \qquad (6.5)$$

- *SAWGN (Scale and Add White Gaussian Noise):* In between these two previous cases, the optimal $(\gamma[j], \rho[j]^2)$ are

$$\gamma^\star[j] = \frac{\lambda\sigma[j]^2 - \mathbf{s}[j]}{\lambda\mathbf{s}[j]^2}, \quad \rho^\star[j]^2 = \gamma^\star[j]\left(\gamma_W[j] - \gamma^\star[j]\right)\left(\sigma[j]^2 + P\mathbf{s}[j]^2\right)$$
(6.6)

where λ is a Lagrange multiplier.

The attacker plays the following game: he starts setting λ to a very small value, such that $\gamma^\star[j] < 0$ for $\forall j, 1 \le j \le N$. This means that all coefficients should be erased, producing a maximum of total distortion. Then, by slowly increasing λ, it is possible to apply the SAWGN strategy to the indices where both $\gamma^\star[j]$ and $\rho^\star[j]^2$ have positive values, reducing the total distortion $D_a(\lambda)$. By increasing λ again, some indices will see $\rho^\star[j]^2 < 0$ but $\gamma^\star[j] > 0$, so that the best strategy becomes the Wiener filtering. The attacker will stop when $D_a(\lambda)$ is lower or equal to its distortion budget. In the end, depending on this budget and the model's parameters $\{\sigma[j]^2, \mathbf{s}[j]\}$, the worst case attack is a mix of three strategies: erasure, Wiener filtering, and SAWGN.

6.2.2   Quantization Index Modulation (QIM)

A nonexhaustive list of papers on the worst-case attack against QIM with cubic lattices, such as DC-DM (distortion-compensation dither modulation) or scalar Costa scheme (see Section 5.4.2), is [8–10], and against QIM with arbitrary good lattices [11].

Example: Binary QIM with scalar quantizer and the "3 delta attacks" [8]. The embedding of bit 0 (resp. 1) uses the codebook $\mathcal{C}_0 = \mathbb{Z}\Delta + \delta_K$ (resp. $\mathcal{C}_1 = \mathbb{Z}\Delta + \Delta/2 + \delta_K$), where δ_K is the secret dither. The distortion compensation is α (see (5.13)) and to gain some robustness we assume $1/2 \le \alpha \le 1$. The decoding uses the union of codebook $\mathcal{C}_0 \cup \mathcal{C}_1$. A decoding error happens if $|\mathbf{c}_z[j] - Q_b(\mathbf{c}_z[j])| > \Delta/4$ when bit b is embedded in the jth host sample.

   If the attacker knows (Δ, α) but not the secret dither δ_K, the worst-case attack restricted on the addition of noise $\mathbf{c}_z[j] = \mathbf{c}_w[j] + \mathbf{n}[j]$ consists in drawing independent and identically distributed noise samples according to the probability mass function:

$$\mathbb{P}(\mathbf{n}[j] = -T) = \mathbb{P}(\mathbf{n}[j] = T) = A, \quad \mathbb{P}(\mathbf{n}[j] = 0) = 1 - 2A \qquad (6.7)$$

The expected attack distortion per sample is $d_a = D_a/N = 2AT^2$. For a given d_a, the parameters maximizing the BER are

$$T^\star = \begin{cases} \Delta\left(\alpha - \frac{1}{2}\right) & \text{if } \frac{1}{2} \le \alpha \le \frac{5}{6} \\ \frac{\Delta}{2}\left(\frac{3}{2} - \alpha\right) & \text{if } \frac{5}{6} \le \alpha \le 1 \end{cases} \quad \text{and } A^\star = \frac{d_a}{2T^{\star 2}} \tag{6.8}$$

producing the maximum BER:

$$\text{BER} = \begin{cases} \min\left(\frac{d_a}{\Delta^2} \frac{1}{2(1-\alpha)\left(\alpha - \frac{1}{2}\right)}, 1\right) & \text{if } \frac{1}{2} \le \alpha \le \frac{5}{6} \\ \min\left(\frac{d_a}{\Delta^2} \frac{4}{\left(\frac{3}{2} - \alpha\right)^2}, 1\right) & \text{if } \frac{5}{6} \le \alpha \le 1 \end{cases} \tag{6.9}$$

The worst-case attack depends on the embedding scheme and its parameters denoted by θ_e. In the previous example, the optimal noise distribution depends on $\theta_e = (\Delta, \alpha)$. Under an attack of parameter θ_a, the performance is given by $P(\theta_e, \theta_a)$. Therefore, a natural question arises: what is the best embedding setup θ_e in the sense that its lowers the impact of the induced worst-case attack? This defines a game between the watermark designer and the attacker where these actors have distortion budgets D_e and D_a, respectively:

$$\max_{\theta_e : D_e(\theta_e) \le D_e} \min_{\theta_a : D_a(\theta_a) \le D_a} P(\theta_e, \theta_a) \tag{6.10}$$

The answer for spread spectrum for colored host samples results in the rule of thumb called "power spectrum condition": the power spectrum of the watermark signal should be proportional to the power spectrum of the host [5]. Indeed, the situation is much more involved and cannot be detailed here. The following citations are the most detailed articles on this topic, assuming different host distributions and metrics for performance and distortion [4–7].

Example: Binary QIM with scalar quantizer and the "3 delta attacks" [8]. Instead of fixing (Δ, α), as in the previous example, we suppose that the watermark fulfills a constraint on the expected embedding distortion per sample: $d_e = \alpha^2 \Delta^2 / 12$. Then the optimal embedding parameters are

$$\alpha^\star = \frac{2}{3} \quad \text{and} \quad \Delta^\star = \sqrt{27 * d_e} \tag{6.11}$$

yielding a maxmin BER of $\min(d_a/3d_e, 1)$. In other words, the "3 delta attack" kills the watermark channel (i.e., BER $= 0.5$) with an attack distortion only $3/2$ times bigger than the embedding distortion.

6.3   HOW TO MEASURE WATERMARKING SECURITY

This section details three different ways to measure the security levels of a water-marking scheme. In this context, security attacks define more the way the attacker steals knowledge about the secret key rather than the exploitation of this stolen knowledge to decode, embed, modify or remove watermarks without authorization.

6.3.1   Fisher Information

This approach considers the secret key as fixed and the observations $o^{N_o} = \{o_1, \ldots, o_{N_o}\}$ as random variables whose distribution is denoted by $f(o; K)$. This makes sense under the watermark only attack; for example, not knowing the host content, the watermarked content appears to be a random variable. The embedding transforms the distribution of the host into the distribution of the watermarked content, which depends on the secret key. The goal of the attacker is to estimate this parameter of the distribution. Hidden messages and perceptual masks might be modeled as nuisance parameters.

The attacker cannot estimate the secret key if the problem is not identifiable: Suppose that $\forall (K', K) \in \mathcal{K}_0 \times \mathcal{K}_0$, $f(o; K') = f(o; K)$. Just by analyzing the observations, the attacker may disclose the set of keys $\mathcal{K}_0$, but this does not grant him the power to uniquely identify which key is the true secret key K inside this subset.

Suppose now that the estimation problem is identifiable. The works [12, 13] use the Cramer-Rao bound to measure watermarking security. Any unbiased estimator $\hat{K}$ of the secret key computed from a sample of N_o independent observations has a covariance matrix (reflecting the estimation noise) $\mathbf{R}_{\hat{K}} \geq N_o^{-1} M_{FI}(K)^{-1}$, in the sense of nonnegative definiteness of the difference matrix. $M_{FI}(K)$ is the Fisher Information Matrix defined as

$$M_{FI}(K) = \mathbb{E}[\psi(K)\psi(K)^{\perp}], \quad \text{with } \psi(K) = \nabla_K f(o; K) \tag{6.12}$$

The mean square error $\mathbb{E}[\|\hat{K} - K\|^2]$ equals the trace of $\mathbf{R}_{\hat{K}}$, its lower bound decreases to zero as N_o^{-1} with a proportional constant $Tr\left(M_{FI}(K)^{-1}\right)$. This last constant is proposed as a measurement of watermarking security in [12]. The more information about the secret key that leaks from the observations, the lower the security level. The main critics are the following:

- Vector $\psi(K)$ has an expression if distribution $f(o; K)$ is derivable with respect to K. This is not possible when K is a discrete variable.

- This measurement of watermarking security fails to capture the impact of remaining uncertainties. Indeed, they often turn the Fisher Information Matrix noninvertible.

6.3.2 Equivocation

A second attempt to define security in watermarking has been a translation of the seminal work proposed by Shannon [14] for cryptography during the 40s to the world of watermarking. The analogy is the following: like a crypto-system producing cipher texts that are functions of the clear texts and the secret key, a watermarking embedder produces watermarked contents from messages to be hidden, original contents, and the secret key.

The attacker knows nothing about the secret key K except its sample domain $\mathcal{K}$ and the way it has been generated, which amounts to its distribution p_K (a probability mass function if K is discrete, or a probability density function if it is continuous). This motivates the assumption that the secret key is a random variable K for the attacker. The entropy of this variable measures the amount of the attacker's uncertainty[1]: $H(K) = -\sum_{\mathcal{K}} p_K(k) \log p_K(k)$, expressed in bits if the logarithm is to the base of 2.

Depending on the class of the attack (see Section 6.1.3.3), the attacker has N_o observations of a given nature, denoted as $o^{N_o} = \{o_1, \ldots, o_{N_o}\}$. This transforms the a priori distribution $p_K(k)$ into a posteriori distribution $p_K(k|o^{N_o})$. The equivocation, $H(K|O^{N_o}) = \mathbb{E}_{O^{N_o}}[H(K|o^{N_o})]$ measures the amount of the remaining uncertainty from the attacker point of view. We are interested in how it decreases with the number of observations and we define $h(N_o) = H(K|O^{N_o})$ for $N_o \geq 1$, and $h(0) = H(K)$.

6.3.2.1 Discrete Random Variable

The secret key is a discrete random variable. Then, equivocation $h(N_o)$ is a nonnegative and nonincreasing function. It converges to a minimum value h_∞ as $N_o \to \infty$. If this minimum is $h_\infty = 0$, it means that by carrying on observing data, the attacker will gather enough information to uniquely determine the secret key K. If not, the attacker will reduce the key space $\mathcal{K}$ to a subset of size at least 2^{h_∞} (when the equivocation is expressed in bits). If the equivocation is a constant function (i.e.,

---

1   The expression $\sum_{\mathcal{X}} g(x)$ means $\sum_{x \in \mathcal{X}} g(x)$ if X is a discrete variable ($\mathcal{X}$ is finite or countable) and $\int_{\mathcal{X}} g(x) \partial x$ if X is continuous.

$h(N_o) = H(K))$, it proves that observations bring no information about the secret key. The watermarking scheme is then perfectly secure.

Example: Substitution scheme with binary data [12].
Vector $\mathbf{c}_o$ is a binary word of length N. The secret key is a P-uple containing distinct indices in $\{1, \cdots, N\}$: $K = (k[1], \cdots, k[P])$. The embedding substitutes some bits in the host cover, whose indices are given by the secret key, by message bits:

$$\mathbf{c}_w[k[i]] = b[i] \quad \forall 1 \leq i \leq P, \text{ otherwise } \mathbf{c}_w[j] = \mathbf{c}_o[j] \tag{6.13}$$

We denote by $\mathbf{c}_w^{(K)}$ the restriction of $\mathbf{c}_w$ over the set of indices given by K s.t. we can rewrite the embedding as $\mathbf{c}_w^{(K)} = \mathbf{b}$. Let us compute $H(K)$ first. The secret key, as a discrete random variable, is uniformly distributed. There are $|\mathcal{K}| = N!/(N-P)!$ possible values. Therefore, $p_K(k) = |\mathcal{K}|^{-1}$, and

$$H(K) = \sum_{k \in \mathcal{K}} -p_K(k) \log p_K(k) = \log |\mathcal{K}| \tag{6.14}$$

Watermarked Only Attack. The observations denoted by o^{N_o} are N_o random watermarked content. The message to be hidden $\mathbf{b}$ is uniformly distributed with probability $1/2^P$. We have:

$$p(\mathbf{c}_w|K) = \sum_{\mathbf{b}} p(\mathbf{c}_w|\mathbf{b}, K) p(\mathbf{b}|K) = \sum_{\mathbf{b}} p(\mathbf{c}_w|\mathbf{b}, K) p(\mathbf{b}) \tag{6.15}$$

$$= \sum_{\mathbf{b}} \frac{\delta_{[\mathbf{c}_w^{(K)} = \mathbf{b}]}}{2^{(N-P)}} \frac{1}{2^P} = \frac{1}{2^N} \tag{6.16}$$

and also

$$p(\mathbf{c}_w) = \sum_{K} p(\mathbf{c}_w|K) p_K(K) = \frac{1}{2^N} \sum_{K} p_K(k) = \frac{1}{2^N}. \tag{6.17}$$

Therefore, by Bayes rule, $p_K(k|\mathbf{c}_w) = p_K(k)$, which implies that $I(K; o^{N_o}) = 0$ and $h(N_o) = H(K)$ for all $N_o > 0$. This shows that no information about the secret key leaks from watermarked contents.

Known Original Attack. The situation is less secure as $h(N_o)$ decreases and converges to $\log_2(P!)$ (see [12]). This amounts for the remaining uncertainty: the attacker eventually discloses the indices of K, but not their ordering. He cannot read or write messages, yet, he can observe whether two contents share the same hidden message, or he can modify the hidden message (not knowing what he is writing).

Known Message Attack. The situation is even less secure as $h(N_o)$ decreases and converges to zero asymptotically (see [12]). Within $N_o \approx \log_2(PN)$ observations he has theoretically enough information for uniquely identifying the secret key.

6.3.2.2 Continuous Random Variable

The interpretation of the equivocation is less straightforward in this case. Equivocation $h(N_o)$ is a nonincreasing function, but it can be negative. Pérez-Freire and Pérez-González [15] give a complete analysis under this framework for spread spectrum like schemes with and without side informed embedding, whereas Pérez-Freire et al. [16, 17] cover quantization index modulation.

Example: Additive spread spectrum without side information [15].
The embedding is described in (6.3), where $P = 1$. The secret K generates a secret carrier $\mathbf{w}$ modeled as a white Gaussian vector of variance $\sigma_w^2 = 1/N$. The host cover follows the same distribution with variance σ_o^2, while the perceptual shaping weight is assumed to be constant: $\mathbf{s}[j] = s$. Observing independent samples $\{\mathbf{c}_{\mathbf{w}_i}, b_i\}_{i=1}^{N_o}$, the best estimator is:

$$\hat{\mathbf{w}} = \frac{\sigma_w^2}{\sigma_o^2 + N_o \sigma_w^2} \sum_{i=1}^{N_o} b_i \mathbf{c}_{\mathbf{w}_i} \tag{6.18}$$

in the sense that $\hat{\mathbf{w}}$ follows the same distribution as $\mathbf{w}$. This produces the following equivocation:

$$h(N_o) = \frac{N}{2} \log \left(2\pi e \frac{\sigma_w^2 \sigma_o^2}{\sigma_o^2 + N_o \sigma_w^2} \right) \tag{6.19}$$

A interesting interpretation of the equivocation for continuous secret signal makes the connection with estimation theory [15]. Denote by σ_e^2 the variance per dimension of the attacker's estimation of the secret. The equivocation gives a lower bounds of this variance:

$$\sigma_e^2 \geq \frac{1}{2\pi e} \exp \left(\frac{2}{N} h(N_o) \right) \tag{6.20}$$

By using (6.19) and for large N_o, we find back the Cramer-Rao bound mentioned in Section 6.3.1 for additive spread spectrum. This lower bound holds whatever the estimator used by the attacker. However, due to the remaining uncertainties (especially under WOA), the accuracy of the estimator can be much bigger.

6.3.3   Effective Key Length

Watermarking and cryptography are two security primitives. It is not surprising that the previous security analysis framework is deeply inspired by the similar work Shannon did in cryptanalysis. However, there is a big difference.

The notion of *estimated secret key* does not make sense in cryptography. The attacker must find the unique key that decodes cipher texts. It is an "all or nothing" game. In watermarking, one might be able to read, write, or erase watermarks with an estimated key, which is not exactly the secret key. Of course, the more accurate the estimation, the more reliable the access to the watermarking channel.

Example: Spread spectrum scheme with binary watermark signal [18].
Suppose that the secret direction $\mathbf{w}$ is a vector of N components taking ± 1 values. In other words, $\mathcal{K} = \{-1, +1\}^N$. There are $|\mathcal{K}| = 2^N$ possible secret directions. Finding this secret key over of such a large set has a complexity equaling N in logarithmic scale. Suppose now that an attack is successful, provided that the attacker finds a key close to the secret direction; their correlation with the true secret direction equals ρN, with $-1 \leq \rho \leq 1$. This means that the estimated and secret keys agree on $N_+ = N(1 + \rho)/2$ components. There are indeed $\binom{N}{N_+}$ keys in $\mathcal{K}$ meeting this constraint. Finding one of these in $\mathcal{K}$ has a logarithmic complexity $\approx N(1 - h_2((1 + \rho)/2))$ in logarithmic scale (asymptotically as $N \to \infty$, thanks to the Stirling formula), where $h_2(p)$ is the entropy in bits of a random Bernoulli binary random variable X s.t. $\mathbb{P}(X = 1) = p$. If $\rho = 0.4$, the logarithmic complexity is $0.12N$ bits, which is a much smaller security level than N bits.

The framework presented in Section 6.3.2 assumes that the aim of the attacker is to disclose the key used at the embedding side thanks to the observations. Yet, the last section shows a pitfall in this approach: the decoding key can be different from the embedding key. How accurate should the estimated key be to successfully hack the watermarking scheme? This section details a new framework that was proposed recently. It aims to jointly consider the estimation of the secret key with its use in a worst case attack.

First, it starts by defining what a successful attack is. For example, the attacker is willing to decode hidden messages with a given probability of success

$1 - \eta$. Second, it turns this requirement into a set of keys, called the "equivalent keys" which achieve this goal. This set depends on the true secret key K and the requirement η, and is denoted $\mathcal{K}_{eq}(K, \eta)$. A successful attack is equivalent to the disclosure of one of these equivalent keys.

We now give the attacker a random sample of N_o observations, from which he derives an estimation $\hat{K}$ of the secret key. This is a random variable because the sample is random. We now compute the probability that this estimation is one of the equivalent keys: $\mathbb{P}(\hat{K} \in \mathcal{K}_{eq}(K, \eta))$. The *effective key length* measured in bits is defined by:

$$L \triangleq -\log_2 \mathbb{P}(\hat{K} \in \mathcal{K}_{eq}(K, \eta)) \tag{6.21}$$

This quantity measures '*the inability by an unauthorized users to have access to the raw watermarking channel,*' which is the way Kalker defined watermarking security in [19]. This also strengthens the analogy with cryptography: $1/2^L$ is the probability that a key randomly picked by a brute force attack is indeed the unique secret key, when keys are sequences of L bits.

Example: Decoding of spread spectrum with binary watermark signal.
We consider the same setup as in the previous example. We assume that the host samples are i.i.d. as $\mathcal{N}(0, \sigma^2)$ and the embedding of one bit is done as follows: $\mathbf{c}_w = \mathbf{c}_o + \frac{s}{\sqrt{N}} b\mathbf{w}$. The bit error rate for the legitimate decoder, which uses the secret direction $\mathbf{w}$, is given by:

$$\mathrm{BER}_D = \Phi\left(-\frac{s}{\sigma}\right) \tag{6.22}$$

Suppose that the attacker is now willing to decode the hidden bit using an estimated key $\mathbf{w}' \in \mathcal{K}$ s.t. $\mathbf{w}^\top \mathbf{w}' = N\rho$. This leads to the following $\mathrm{BER}_A = \Phi(-\rho \frac{s}{\sigma})$. The attack is deemed successful if $\mathrm{BER}_A \leq \eta$, which implies that $\mathbf{w}'$ is an equivalent key if $\rho \geq \rho_{\min} = \Phi^{-1}(\eta)/\Phi^{-1}(\mathrm{BER}_D)$. Contrary to the previous example, an equivalent key has a normalized correlation that is greater than or equal to a lower bound $\rho_{\min}$. If the attacker is randomly sampling $\mathcal{K}$, the probability of picking an equivalent key is the probability that a random variable distributed as a Binomial distribution $\mathcal{B}(N, 1/2)$ is bigger than $N(1 + \rho_{\min})/2$, which is approximately, for large N, $\approx \Phi(-\rho_{\min}\sqrt{N})$. This gives an effective key length in the order of

$$L \approx \frac{\rho_{\min}^2}{2\log(2)} N \tag{6.23}$$

As a consequence, for $\mathrm{BER}_D = 10^{-3}$ and $\eta = 10^{-1}$, we have $\rho_{\min} \approx 0.4$, so that $L \approx 0.115 * N$ bits. Again, we find back that the security level is proportional to N but with a small proportional constant.

Example: Detection of spread spectrum with binary watermark signal.
We consider the same setup as in the previous example but under a detection framework. The embedding is simply: $\mathbf{c_w} = \mathbf{c_o} + s_e \mathbf{w} \sqrt{N}$. At the detection side, the threshold τ is set to meet a requirement on the probability of false alarm: $\tau = \sqrt{N}/\sigma \Phi^{-1}(1 - P_{\mathrm{fa}})$. This fixes the probability of a miss detection: $P_{\mathrm{miss}} = \Phi(\Phi^{-1}(1 - P_{\mathrm{fa}}) - s_e/\sqrt{N}\sigma)$.

The goal of the attacker is to remove the watermark signal: $\mathbf{c_z} = \mathbf{c_w} - s_a \mathbf{w'}/\sqrt{N}$, with an attack distortion which is ν times more than the embedding distortion (i.e., $s_a = \sqrt{\nu}s_e$) and a probability of success of at least $1 - \eta$. This gives a constraint on the equivalent key: its normalized correlation with the true secret key $\mathbf{w}$ must be s.t.

$$\rho \geq \rho_{\min} = \frac{s_e}{s_a} \cdot \frac{\Phi^{-1}(1 - \eta) - \Phi^{-1}(P_{\mathrm{miss}})}{\Phi^{-1}(1 - P_{\mathrm{fa}}) - \Phi^{-1}(P_{\mathrm{miss}})} \qquad (6.24)$$

Consequently, for $P_{\mathrm{fa}} = 10^{-6}$, $P_{\mathrm{miss}} = 10^{-1}$, $\eta = 10^{-1}$ and $\nu = 2$, using approximation (6.23), we have $L \approx 0.06 * N$.

Both examples above assume a basic and simple model, especially because the attacker picks an estimated key in $\mathcal{K}$, whereas the general framework grants him N_o observations to increase the probability of picking an equivalent key. The analysis is then more cumbersome. We refer the reader to the following papers dealing with spread spectrum like schemes [20, 21] or QIM schemes [22].

To conclude this section, Fisher information, equivocation, and effective key length are not the only ways to gauge watermarking security. The other approaches, like [23], have been somehow less investigated.

6.4 ALGORITHMS AND TOOLS

The previous section surveyed approaches for quantifying watermarking security. For simple models, theoretical developments give close form expressions or bounds of the above-mentioned quantities. This section briefly reviews signal processing or machine learning tools that have been used to disclose the secret key in practice.

6.4.1 Spread Spectrum Like Schemes

The main principle of spread spectrum is to focus the watermark power in a subspace of small dimension, spanned by the secret carriers. The attacker leverages this principle by identifying the subspace of higher energy thanks to a principal component analysis (PCA) [24] or an independent component analysis (ICA) [12]. This works well when the watermark signal is independent from the host, but also against side informed embedding to some extend [25].

This kind of scheme usually produces watermarked signals deeply located inside decoding regions. Therefore, these signals are all concentrated along several directions of the space. The attacker leverages this pitfall by using clustering algorithms like k-means [25–27]. This idea has been pushed further with a total variational approach, minimizing a cost function modeling this concentration phenomenon by a conjugate gradient distance in the case of the ISS watermarking scheme [15].

6.4.2 Quantization Index Modulation

QIM schemes are also attacked with the principle that watermarked signals are packed around lattice codewords. Thanks to the periodicity of the lattice codewords, a lattice modulo operation folds the space such that the secret dither lies in a finite region around each watermarked signal (under the KMA or CMA scenarios). Set membership algorithms can then compute an approximate intersection of these feasible regions, which shrinks around the secret dither as the attacker analyzes more observations [16]. The attack is more involved under the watermarked-only attack (WOA) scenario [17].

6.5 WHAT WE KNOW SO FAR ABOUT WATERMARKING SECURITY

The following sections sum up the results known so far.

6.5.1 Differences Between WOA and KMA

The WOA is more difficult because the attacker has access to less data. WOA has two limitations:

- The estimation of the secret is harder. However, the difference when compared to KMA (known message attack) vanishes as the hidden message length is small.

- There are remaining uncertainties under WOA. Even after disclosing all parts of the secret, the attacker can't read or write a message because he does not know which part of the secret is coding which bit. He can, however, see if two hidden messages are the same; he can flip a bit (whose position in the hidden message is unknown) or remove the watermark signal.

6.5.2   Trade-Off Between Robustness and Security

Usually, for a given embedding scheme, there is a trade-off between robustness and security. There are some exceptions: under some specific setups, improved sprectrum spectrum (ISS) and correlation aware spread spectrum (CASS [28]) may witness a decrease of the security level as well as a decrease in robustness when fine-tuning their parameters for a given embedding distortion; see [15] or [20].

This comment holds for a given watermarking scheme. Yet, as far as we know, there is no theoretical analysis of a would-be optimum trade-off between security and robustness.

6.5.3   Orders of Magnitude

For spread spectrum like watermarking, the attacker needs some hundreds of watermarked contents when $N \approx 100$, and some thousands of them when $N \approx 100,000$ (for a given embedding distortion budget), to disclose the secret directions when a dozens of bits are hidden.

For quantization index modulation schemes, the security level may vary a lot; it can be very high if robustness is not an issue, but very low as soon as a good robustness is achieved. In this latter case, the security level is much lower than spread spectrum techniques, and ≈ 10 observations might be enough to disclose the secret dither.

These orders of magnitude are provided under the assumption that the attacker has access to the cover samples carrying the watermark signal.

6.6   ORACLE ATTACKS

In an oracle attack, the attacker has an unlimited access to a watermark detector or decoder enclosed in a sealed black box. The attacker has one of the three following goals:

1. To remove the watermark of a protected content.

2. To hide a message or to overwrite the message already hidden in a content.

3. To disclose a part of the secret key.

The first two goals are conceptually identical as soon as we imagine the set of all possible contents. This huge ensemble can be partitionned into regions of contents producing the same decoding / detection output. The attacker has a content not belonging to the desired decoding region. The aim is to shift it into another region. This is the region of unwatermarked content in goal (1), or the region of content hiding the desired message in goal (2). The attacker would like to find the closest content on the other side of the frontier enclosing the targeted region. We called this attack a *closest point attack* and it belongs to the category of worst-case attack of Section 6.1.2.

The third goal is totally different. We assume that any protected content is watermarked with the same secret key K. This secret parameter is also embedded in the sealed black box. The attacker feeds the decoder with contents and saves their outputs. These observations, pairs of content / output, may leak information about K [29]. We call this process the *chosen watermarked attack*, which pertains to the category of security attacks of Section 6.1.3.

6.6.1 Sensitivity Attack

Although chasing different goals, closest point attacks and chosen watermarked attacks resort to the same core process: the sensitivity attack, whose roots date back to [30]. The attacker "works" with extracted features whose space $\mathcal{F}$ is of dimension n_f, in the sense that he is able to modify a content such that its extracted features equal a given target. These features may not be the same as the ones used by the embedder for carrying the watermark signal in (6.1).

A naive oracle attack submits content whose feature vector $\mathbf{f}$ samples the feature space $\mathcal{F}$. This can be done by probing over a regular grid. The attacker creates a map of $\mathcal{F}$ with white points when the decision of the decoder is the desired one and black points otherwise. Having disclosed this map, he knows how to get outside the black region in order to reach the white region with the shortest path (i.e., with the minimum distortion). If the grid has a step Δ and $\overline{F}$ denotes the typical amplitude of features, then there are $(\overline{F}/\Delta)^{n_f}$ points to be tested. This is exponential with the number of features, and it does not lead to a tractable oracle attack in practice. The detector output discloses, on average, very little information. During the naive oracle attack, the attacker would see some long series of constant outputs. The useful information is indeed located when sampling near the frontier where the detector outputs change. Disclosing regions or their frontiers are equivalent problems. This is the goal of the sensitivity attack.

The first step in this attack is to find a point on the frontier. This is called a "sensitive content" because a small perturbation flips the detection output with a good probability. To find a sensitive vector, the attacker needs two pieces of content whose feature vectors f_1 and f_2 are not located in the same region. For goal (1), the attacker strongly distorts a protected content until it is deemed "nonwatermarked." For goal (2), he needs at least one piece of content watermarked with the desired hidden message. In the feature space $\mathcal{F}$, the line going from f_1 to f_2 intersects the frontier. A dichotomy line search repeatedly submits to the sealed black box content whose extracted feature is along this line, and according to the output, it will iterate and converge to the sensitive content.

Once a sensitive vector is found, the second step adds a small random perturbation to its features and submits the modified vector to the detector. By repeating this process, the attacker is then able to have a local approximation of the frontier in $\mathcal{F}$, only valid in the neighborhood of the sensitive point. This approximation is up to the first order: the frontier is approximated by a tangent hyperplane. Denote by $F_{\mathcal{F}}(.)$ the function describing the decoding region as $\{f \in \mathcal{F} | F_{\mathcal{F}}(f) > 0\}$. The normal vector of the hyperplane is the gradient of this function. This requires $O(n_f)$ iterations. Up to the second order, the attacker approximates the frontier by a quadric surface defined by the gradient and the Hessian of $F_{\mathcal{F}}(.)$. This requires $O(n_f^2)$ iterations.

6.6.2 Closest Point Attack

A first use of the sensitivity attack is the closest point attack (CPA): f_1 is the feature vector of the content to be hacked, f_2 is lying on the targeted region, but this content is too perceptually different. The sensitive content between f_1 and f_2 has a better quality. Once the frontier is locally estimated, the attacker knows in which direction he should push the extracted vector in order to get closer to f_1 while staying close to the frontier. From this new point f_3, the attacker again finds a sensitive vector, which should be nearer, and approximates again the frontier. This process is iterated until the improvement in quality of the sensitive content is no longer meaningful. Figure 6.1 shows the first iterations of the CPA in $n_f = 2$ dimensions.

This CPA is called BNSA (Blind Newton Sensitivity Attack) by its inventors [31, 32]. Its main advantage is that no assumption at all is needed with respect to the shape of the decoding region. Experimental simulations show that the algorithm quickly converges with the gradient option; around $M = 10$ iterations are needed.

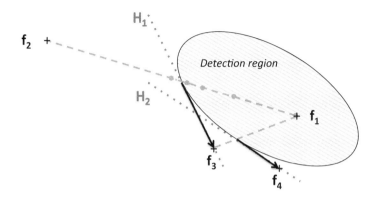

Figure 6.1 The closest point attack with $n_f = 2$. Tangent planes are sketched with dotted lines. The arrow shows the direction of the next move in order to get closer to $\mathbf{f}_1$.

This makes the Hessian estimation not worth it at all. The final sensitive content is of very good quality, although some differences exist depending on the watermarking scheme. Some techniques are more robust than others against the BNSA, in the sense that the final attacked content is more degraded. The researchers suspect that some watermarking schemes have bigger detection areas (for a given probability of false alarm) or more efficient embedders so that the watermarked feature vector $\mathbf{f}_1$ is more deeply located inside of the detection area. Another explanation is that the BNSA converges to the global minimum distortion if the decoding region is convex, and to a local minimizer otherwise.

The number of detector trials is $O(Mn_f)$ because, at each iteration, the sensitivity attack estimates the tangent hyperplane. Note that this estimation step can be done in parallel if the attacker has several decoders in hand. This attack works in theory, even if $\mathcal{F}$ is not the embedding domain. Yet, when performed on the spatial domain of real images, it needs millions of detection trials. The attacker should work with features of low dimension. Knowing that the watermarking technique does not modify some high frequencies' coefficients, for instance, is a crucial piece of information to make the attack work in practice. When not knowing the exact features used by the watermarking scheme, the attacker can play with his own features. If he gathers more features than needed, his attack lasts longer, but features carrying no watermark signal will almost not be distorted by the attack. If he works with too few features, the watermark signal will not be completely erased, and the quality of the final content is poorer.

This is the reason why Earl [33] introduced a notion of perceptual importance of the feature. The attacker performs his attack only with the most perceptually important features that are supposed to carry the biggest part of the watermark energy. This helps strike a better trade-off between the quality of the attacked content and the complexity of the attack. When tested on real images, this CPA needs some thousands of trials. Moreover, Earl proposed a method where the attacker does not have to wait for $O(n_f)$ detection trials (i.e., the end of a sensitivity attack estimating the tangent hyperplane) to submit an intermediate attacked content. However, this CPA cannot be run in parallel with several decoders.

An important feature of the CPA is that the quality of the attacked content keeps improving as the number of detection trials increases, but with an uneven speed. The quality improvement is huge for the first iterations, but then it stalls so that it requires a huge amount of trials to forge a copy with pristine quality.

We remind the reader that the goal of this attack is to remove (or modify) the watermark of a particular piece of content. The attack starts from scratch if another piece of watermarked content is to be attacked.

6.6.3 Chosen Watermarked Attack

The chosen watermarked attack (CWA) is in essence very different from the CPA, as it discloses the secret key, hence it is run only once. Moreover, this security attack needs knowledge of the algorithm, especially the embedding domain and the nature of the decoding regions (quadrants, cones, quadrics...). Formally, suppose that a content belongs to the decoding region if $F(\mathbf{c}, K) > \tau$. The attacker knows the generic function $F(.,.)$, but not the secret key K. With a sensitivity attack, he approximates the frontier around the sensitive vector $\mathbf{c}_\mathrm{s}$ with a tangent plane whose normal direction is the gradient of the function:

$$\mathbf{n}_{\mathbf{c}_\mathrm{s}} = \nabla_{\mathbf{c}_\mathrm{s}} F(\mathbf{c}_\mathrm{s}, k) \qquad (6.25)$$

This equation is vectorial, hence, it indeed gathers N scalar equations, and all variables are known except for the secret key. If the secret key is a vector of same length, then the attacker has theoretically enough information to disclose the secret key provided this equation has a unique solution. For instance, for the spread spectrum scheme, $F(\mathbf{c}, k) = \mathbf{c}^\top \mathbf{w}$, where $\mathbf{w}$ is the secret direction (or carrier). It immediately follows that $\mathbf{n}_{\mathbf{c}_\mathrm{s}} = \mathbf{w}$. Estimating the hyperplane gives the normal direction $\mathbf{n}_{\mathbf{c}_\mathrm{s}}$, which, in turn, reveals the secret parameter of the scheme. If the

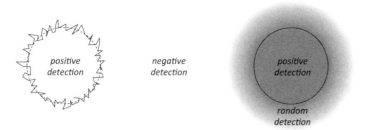

Figure 6.2 Left: The frontier of the detection region has been "fractalized." Right: The detection output is random when content is located in between positive and negative detection regions.

secret key is a $N \times N$ matrix (for instance, JANIS order 2 [34]), the attacker needs N sensitivity attacks yielding each N independent equations, for a total of $O(N^2)$ detector trials.

The CWA has only been studied with zero-bit watermarking schemes. Extension to multibit technique should be straightforward. The seminal paper is due to Kalker, Linnartz and van Dijk [35]. A more elaborated study is [36].

6.6.4 Countermeasures

The countermeasures proposed so far mainly focus on the core process of the oracle attacks: the sensitivity attack.

A first idea is to slow down the watermark detection. For example, Blu-ray disc players wait for 20 minutes before shutting down the playback of a copy deemed as pirated due to the presence of a watermark. It lets malicious users enjoy 20 minutes of content, but on the other hand, an oracle attack becomes impractical.

A second idea is to randomize the detection output in order to spoil the estimation of the tangent hyper-plane. Its success is mitigated; the sensitivity attack still works, but it needs more detection trials. Geometrically, a gray area is inserted along the frontier as sketched in Figure 6.2. In this gray area, the detection output is random: the detector flips a coin to take a decision. However, the frontier of the detection region does not change. The attacker needs to know on which side of the frontier a feature c_s lies. Hence, this feature vector is tested a few times to disclose whether the output is deterministic (always positive in detection region), or random (in the gray area). The number of detection trials is multiplied by a small constant, and it is still linear in N [37].

A third idea is to render the frontier more chaotic or less soft, so that the tangent plane is greatly changing or not even mathematically defined in the neighborhood of the sensitive content, see Figure 6.2. However, the decoding region cannot be fully chaotic because we need to accurately estimate the probability of a false alarm. Therefore, some researchers propose to start with a well-studied shape (i.e., quadrant or cone) whose impact on the probability of false alarm is well-understood, and to locally "fractalize" its frontier [38]. This counter-measure works poorly, as everything is a matter of scale. If the frontier looks chaotic when observed in great detail, it is still a soft surface when zooming out. The sensitivity attack still works, but with a bigger step (sensitive vectors are more distorted). The accuracy of the estimation of the tangent plane decreases, but not drastically.

The same idea can prevent a CPA, not on the estimation of the tangent plane, but on its convergence. If the decoding region is not convex, it converges to a local minimum that may not be the closest point. In its original design, the technique *broken arrow* uses some traps to stop oracle attacks [39]. Yet, it is not clear whether this design was proven useful during the BOWS2 competition [40]. However, this more complex decoding region raises the issue of the probability of a false alarm. Other researchers have reported a loss of robustness [41].

6.6.5   Some Comments on the Oracle Attack

The oracle attacks (CPA and CWA) are working in practice; they have been successful during both editions of the BOWS contest [40, 42]. However, it is a difficult attack in a practical setup. In a copy protection application, the watermark detector is inside a compliant device, like a DVD player. Therefore, in order to make a trial, the attacker has to create content, burn it on a blank disk, insert the disc in the device, and wait for the detection output. This certainly takes too long. The real issue is whether or not the attacker will be able to circumvent these constraints in order to speed up the oracle.

The most efficient countermeasures play with the practical setup. For example, most papers have implicitly considered that the detector is memoryless. A smart detector with some memory could refuse to give a decision when noticing that an oracle attack is going on [43].

6.7   PROTOCOL ATTACKS

This chapter has mostly assumed that the goal of the attacker is to remove a watermark. Disclosing the secret key also enables the attacker to decode hidden messages and to embed or modify hidden messages, such that an authorized decoder can retrieve them.

There are some other flaws, so-called *protocol attacks*, often stemming from misuses of watermarking technology. There is no general framework encompassing all protocol attacks. We present some of them through three case studies.

Example: The watermark copy attack.

This is the most well-known protocol attack [44]. It simply assumes a very robust watermarking scheme with no side informed embedding (e.g., additive spread spectrum). The watermark signal depends on the original cover only through the perceptual slack. A denoising algorithm is able to strip out a part of watermarking energy from the watermarked content. This part is not enough to remove the presence of the watermark thanks to the high robustness of the technique. Yet, this is not the goal of the attacker. The difference between the watermarked content and its denoised version is a rough estimation of the watermark signal. Inserting it into another content may result in a new watermarked content due to the high robustness of the technique. In other words, the attacker succeeds in copying and pasting the watermark.

Example: Proof of owernship.

Suppose a person claims ownership of the image $\mathbf{i}$ by exhibiting a watermark detector $d(\cdot, \cdot)$, a secret key K, and a threshold τ such that $d(\mathbf{i}, K) > \tau$. In other words, this image triggers the detection of a watermark.

First, we could be convinced that this proves this person has watermarked that image some time ago. It does not imply that this person is the true author or a legitimate copyright holder of this work. Anybody can watermark images with their own technique and secret key.

Second, we must be careful about the threshold τ. It is easy to first compute the score $d(\mathbf{i}, K)$ and then to pick a smaller threshold τ. We must verify the soundness of the value of τ by deriving the probability of false positive: $P_{\text{fa}} = \mathbb{P}(d(\mathbf{i}_o, K) > \tau)$, where $\mathbf{i}_o$ is an unwatermarked image. This probability should be small, but, for the sake of robustness, it cannot be zero. Usually, τ is set such that P_{fa} is in the order of 10^{-6}.

This means that, for a fixed K, over $\lceil 1/P_{\text{fa}} \rceil$ random images, one expects one false positive detection, and this person can claim ownership of that particular image. However, it is unlikely that this random image has some value. On the other hand, it also means that, for a fixed image $\mathbf{i}$, by testing N_K secret keys, the probability of finding at least one key producing a positive detection is $1 - (1 -$

$P_{\text{fa}})^{N_K} \approx P_{\text{fa}}N_K$. One sees that if N_K is in the order of $1/P_{\text{fa}}$, this person likely finds at least one secret key that triggers the detection.

This shows that the watermark detection brings a proof of low value in this context. To strengthen this proof, this person should show that the secret key was randomly drawn before the watermarking, independent of the image to be watermarked. For example, this key is also used to embed watermark in other photos which are known to be his previous works of the artist. As far as copyright protection is concerned, from a legal point of view, an author should belong to a society of authors where he registers his works. The deposit of the secret key to this society is a commitment that will bring trust in the watermark detection later on.

Example: Copy protection.
This example is about the playback of pirated content by the first version of some Blu-ray disc players. The detection of a watermarking in the audio streams of a nonciphered movie warns the Blu-ray player that the movie is pirated (camcorded in a theater, for example). The watermark detection only runs on audio streams encoded with the standard audio format. The format is labelled in the header of the audio stream. By just modifying this label, pirates succeed bypassing the watermark detector. The pirates then ask the player to output the audio stream to an external renderer, such as a PC, which decodes the audio stream without taking care of the corrupted format label in the header. This protocol attack benefits from an implementation flaw which has nothing to do with robustness, worst-case attack, or watermarking security.

6.8   CONCLUSION

Worst-case attacks, security attacks, and oracle attacks are three different concepts that are now well-understood in the watermarking community. However, research articles proposing new watermarking schemes almost never encompass their analysis. This restricts their use to applications where security is not a requirement.

Most robust watermarking schemes have a weak security level. Designing schemes where security is the top requirement is still in its infancy [3]. The research community is still missing the theoretical optimum trade-off between robustness and security.

References

[1] Kerckhoffs, A., "La cryptographie militaire," *Journal des Sciences Militaires*, Vol. 9, janvier 1883, pp. 5–38.

[2] Cayre, F., and P. Bas, "Kerckhoffs-based embedding security classes for WOA data-hiding," *IEEE Transactions on Information Forensics and Security*, Institute of Electrical and Electronics Engineers (IEEE), Vol. 3, No. 1, Mar. 2008, pp. 1–15.

[3] Mathon, B., et al., "Comparison of secure spread-spectrum modulations applied to still image watermarking," *Annales des Télécommunications*, Springer Verlag (Germany), Vol. 64, No. 11-12, Oct. 2009, pp. 801–813.

[4] Pateux, S., and G. Le Guelvouit, "Practical watermarking scheme based on wide spread spectrum and game theory," *Signal Processing: Image Communication*, Vol. 18, April 2003, pp. 283–296.

[5] Su, J., J. Eggers, and B. Girod, "Analysis of digital watermarks subjected to optimum linear filtering and additive noise," *Signal processing*, Elsevier, Vol. 81, 2001, pp. 1141–1175.

[6] Moulin, P., and A. Ivanovic, "The zero-rate spread-spectrum watermarking game," *Signal Processing, IEEE Transactions on*, Vol. 51, No. 4, Apr 2003, pp. 1098–1117.

[7] Moulin, P., and J. O'Sullivan, "Information-theoretic analysis of information hiding," *Information Theory, IEEE Transactions on*, Vol. 49, No. 3, Mar 2003, pp. 563–593.

[8] Vila-Forcén, J., et al., "Worst case additive attack against quantization-based data-hiding methods," in *Security, Steganography, and Watermarking of Multimedia Contents VII*, Vol. 5681 of *Proceedings of SPIE-IS&T Electronic Imaging*, SPIE, San Jose, CA, USA, 2005, pp. 136–146.

[9] Pérez-González, F., "The Importance of Aliasing in Structured Quantization Index Modulation Data Hiding," in *Digital Watermarking*, Vol. 2939 of *Lecture Notes in Computer Science*, Springer Berlin Heidelberg, pp. 1–17, 2004.

[10] Tzschoppe, R., et al., "Additive non-Gaussian noise attacks on the scalar Costa scheme (SCS)," in *Security, Steganography, and Watermarking of Multimedia Contents VII*, Vol. 5681 of *Proceedings of SPIE-IS&T Electronic Imaging*, SPIE, 2005, pp. 114–123.

[11] Moulin, P., and A. Goteti, "Block QIM watermarking games," *Information Forensics and Security, IEEE Transactions on*, Vol. 1, No. 3, Sept 2006, pp. 293–310.

[12] Furon, T., F. Cayre, and C. Fontaine, "Watermarking security: theory and practice," *Signal Processing, IEEE Transactions on*, Institute of Electrical and Electronics Engineers (IEEE), Vol. 53, No. 10, 2005, pp. 3976–3987.

[13] Zhang, D., J. Ni, and D.-J. Lee, "Security Analysis for Spread-Spectrum Watermarking Incorporating Statistics of Natural Images," in *Advances in Visual Computing*, Vol. 5359 of *Lecture Notes in Computer Science*, Springer Berlin Heidelberg, pp. 400–409, 2008.

[14] Shannon, C., "Communication theory of secrecy systems," *Bell System Technical Journal*, Vol. 28, October 1949, pp. 656–715.

[15] Pérez-Freire, L., and F. Pérez-González, "Spread-Spectrum Watermarking Security," *Information Forensics and Security, IEEE Transactions on*, Vol. 4, No. 1, March 2009, pp. 2–24.

[16] Pérez-Freire, L., et al., "Security of lattice-based data hiding against the Known Message Attack," *Information Forensics and Security, IEEE Transactions on*, Vol. 1, No. 4, December 2006, pp. 421–439.

[17] Pérez-Freire, L., and F. Pérez-González, "Security of Lattice-Based Data Hiding Against the Watermarked-Only Attack," *Information Forensics and Security, IEEE Transactions on*, Vol. 3, No. 4, Dec 2008, pp. 593–610.

[18] Cox, I., G. Doërr, and T. Furon, "Watermarking is not cryptography," in *Proceedings of the International Workshop on Digital Watermarking*, Vol. 4283 of *Lecture Notes in Computer Science*, Jeju Island, Korea, 2006, pp. 1–15.

[19] Kalker, T., "Considerations on watermarking security," in *Proceedings of the Fourth Workshop on Multimedia Signal Processing (MMSP)*, IEEE, Cannes, France, October 2001, pp. 201–206.

[20] Bas, P., and T. Furon, "A New Measure of Watermarking Security: The Effective Key Length," *Information Forensics and Security, IEEE Transactions on*, Institute of Electrical and Electronics Engineers (IEEE), Vol. 8, No. 8, Jul. 2013, pp. 1306 – 1317.

[21] Bas, P., and T. Furon, "Key length Estimation of zero-bit watermarking schemes," in *EUSIPCO - 20th European Signal Processing Conference*, Romania, Aug. 2012, pp. 1693–1697.

[22] Furon, T., and P. Bas, "A New Measure of Watermarking Security Applied on DC-DM QIM," in *IH - Information Hiding*, Berkeley, United States, May 2012, pp. 207–223.

[23] Katzenbeisser, S., "Computational security models for digital watermarks," in *Workshop on Image Analysis for Multimedia Interactive Services (WIAMIS)*, Montreux, Switzerland, April 2005, pp. 1261–1282.

[24] Doërr, G., and J. Dugelay, "Security pitfalls of frame-by-frame approaches to video watermarking," *Signal Processing, IEEE Transactions on*, Vol. 52, No. 10, Oct 2004, pp. 2955–2964.

[25] Bas, P., and A. Westfeld, "Two Key Estimation Techniques for the Broken-Arrows Watermarking Scheme," in *ACM Multimedia and Security Workshop 2009*, Princeton, NJ, United States, 2009, pp. 1–8.

[26] Bas, P., and G. Doërr, "Practical Security Analysis of Dirty Paper Trellis Watermarking," in *Information Hiding*, Vol. 4567 of *Lecture Notes in Computer Science*, Springer, June 2007, pp. 174–188.

[27] Bas, P., and G. Doërr, "Evaluation of an Optimal Watermark Tampering Attack Against Dirty Paper Trellis Schemes," in *ACM Multimedia and Security Workshop 2008*, United Kingdom, 2008, pp. 227–232.

[28] Valizadeh, A., and J. Wang, "Correlation-and-Bit-Aware Spread Spectrum Embedding for Data Hiding," *Information Forensics and Security, IEEE Transactions on*, Vol. 6, No. 2, June 2011, pp. 267–282.

[29] Linnartz, J.-P., and M. van Dijk, "Analysis of the Sensitivity Attack against Electronic Watermarks in Images," in *Information Hiding*, Vol. 1525 of *Lecture Notes in Computer Science*, Springer Berlin Heidelberg, pp. 258–272, 1998.

[30] Cox, I. J., and J.-P. Linnartz, "Public watermarks and resistance to tampering," in *Proceedings of the International Conference on Image Processing, ICIP'97*, Vol. 3, Oct 1997, pp. 3–6.

[31] Comesaña, P., L. Pérez-Freire, and F. Pérez-González, "Blind Newton Sensitivity Attack," *IEE Proc. on Information Security*, Vol. 153, No. 3, 2006, pp. 115–125.

[32] Comesaña, P., *Side-informed data hiding: robustness and security analysis*, Ph.D. thesis, Universidade de Vigo, 2006.

[33] Earl, J., "Tangential sensitivity analysis of watermarks using prior information," in *Security, steganography and watermarking of multimedia contents IX*, Vol. 6505 of *Proceedings of SPIE-IS&T Electronic Imaging*, 2007.

[34] Furon, T., G. Silvestre, and N. Hurley, "JANIS: Just Another N-order side-Informed Scheme," in *Proceedings of the International Conference on Image Processing, ICIP'02*, Vol. 2, Rochester, NY, USA, September 2002, pp. 153–156.

[35] Kalker, T., J.-P. Linnartz, and M. van Dijk, "Watermark estimation through detector analysis," in *Proceedings of the International Conference on Image Processing, ICIP'98*, Vol. 1, Oct 1998, pp. 425–429.

[36] El Choubassi, M., and P. Moulin, "Noniterative Algorithms for Sensitivity Analysis Attacks," *Information Forensics and Security, IEEE Transactions on*, Vol. 2, No. 2, June 2007, pp. 113–126.

[37] El Choubassi, M., and P. Moulin, "On Reliability and Security of Randomized Detectors Against Sensitivity Analysis Attacks," *Information Forensics and Security, IEEE Transactions on*, Vol. 4, No. 3, Sept 2009, pp. 273–283.

[38] Mansour, M., and A. Tewfik, "Secure detection of public watermarks with fractal decision boundaries," in *Signal Processing Conference, 2002 11th European*, Sept 2002, pp. 1–4.

[39] Furon, T., and P. Bas, "Broken Arrows," *EURASIP Journal on Information Security*, Hindawi, Vol. 2008, Oct. 2008, pp. ID 597040.

[40] Westfeld, A., "Fast Determination of Sensitivity in the Presence of Countermeasures in BOWS-2," in *Information Hiding*, Vol. 5806 of *Lecture Notes in Computer Science*, Springer Berlin Heidelberg, pp. 89–101, 2009.

[41] Choubassi, M. E., and P. Moulin, "On the fundamental tradeoff between watermark detection performance and robustness against sensitivity analysis attacks," in *Security, steganography, and watermarking of multimedia content VIII*, Vol. 6072 of *Proceedings of SPIE-IS&T Electronic Imaging*, SPIE, San Jose, CA, USA, 2006, p. 1I.

[42] Comesaña, P., and F. Pérez-González, "Breaking the BOWS Watermarking System: Key Guessing and Sensitivity Attacks," *EURASIP Journal on Information Security*, Vol. 2007, No. 2, February 2007. Article ID 25308.

[43] Barni, M., et al., "Are you threatening me? Towards smart detectors in watermarking," in *Proc. of SPIE Media Watermarking, Security, and Forensics*, San Francisco, CA, USA, Feb. 2014.

[44] Kutter, M., S. Voloshynovskiy, and A. Herrigel, "Watermark copy attack," in *Proc. SPIE Security and Watermarking of Multimedia Contents II*, Vol. 3971, 2000, pp. 371–380.

Chapter 7

Fingerprinting

Boris Škorić

When multiple malicious users join forces, it becomes possible to launch attacks on watermarks that are much more powerful than those described in Chapter 6. A group of attackers is referred to as a coalition or *colluders*, and their attack is called a *collusion attack*. The availability of multiple, differently watermarked copies of the same content allows the colluders to detect positions where their versions differ; this reveals a lot of information about the embedded watermarks that would not be available to a single attacker. The defence is to embed watermarking symbols according to a collusion-resistant code, also known as a *fingerprinting code*. Such a code can be seen as an error-correcting code, but in this case, it is for malicious noise instead of random noise.

In this chapter, we first present attack models. Then we discuss the history and state-of-the-art of fingerprinting codes, with a focus on the simplest attack model and the use of information-theoretic techniques from coding theory.

7.1 COLLUSION ATTACKS ON WATERMARKS

7.1.1 Joining Forces

In the case of a collusion attack, tracing the origin of unauthorized copies is much more difficult than in the case of a single attacker. The art of *collusion-resistant fingerprinting*, also known as *traitor tracing*, is to organize the watermarks in such

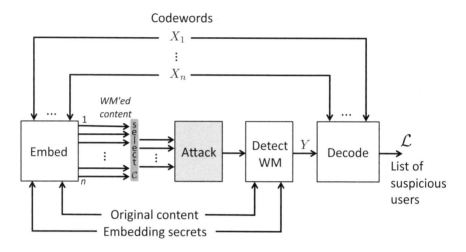

Figure 7.1 Information flow in a collusion attack and tracing.

a way that some degree of tracing is still possible even after the colluders have successfully attacked the locations where they detected differences.

We adopt the usual approach where (audio/video) content is modeled as a sequence of discrete *positions* into which watermark *symbols* can be embedded. As discussed in Chapter 5, the concept of a position is rather abstract. A position could be a set of locations in the content, spread out in time, or it could be a Fourier or wavelet component. Likewise, the concept of a symbol has no meaning other than being a label for the different marks. For simplicity, the number of different marks is assumed to be the same in each position. In this abstract description, the problem of collusion-resistant fingerprinting becomes a coding problem: how does one design a fingerprinting code that will resist coalitions up to a certain size.

Figure 7.1 shows the information flow in this setting. The content contains ℓ positions, into each of which a symbol from the finite alphabet $\mathcal{X}$ can be embedded. We write $q = |\mathcal{X}|$ for the size of the alphabet. There are n users. The coalition is a subset $\mathcal{C} \subset [n]$ of size $|\mathcal{C}| = c$. We refer to the party that tries to identify the colluders as the *tracer*. The tracer creates codewords $X_1, \ldots, X_n \in \mathcal{X}^\ell$. The watermarked content for user j is created by embedding X_j into the original content, using secret information, the "embedding secrets." Each user receives a uniquely watermarked copy of the content. The colluders combine their copies and create the "attacked content." The attack strategy is not known to the tracer.

The tracer uses a watermark detector to see which symbols are present in all the positions. This results in a sequence $Y \in \mathcal{Y}^\ell$, where the space $\mathcal{Y}$ is not necessarily equal to the alphabet $\mathcal{X}$. For example, erasures could occur, or multiple symbols may be detected in one position. An erasure is denoted as a special symbol ϵ. The sequence Y is called the attacked watermark. The detector is a *nonblind* detector (Section 5.1): it has access to the unwatermarked content. Finally, the tracer runs a *decoder* algorithm that looks at Y and all the user codewords to decide who should be included in a list $\mathcal{L} \subset [n]$ of suspicious users.

The term "decoder" reflects the similarities between traitor tracing and channel coding. The user identity is the message to be sent; the expansion into a watermark sequence together with the embedding encodes the message for transport; the collusion attack is a malicious form of noise, often called the *collusion channel*; and the decoder tries to reconstruct the message. Decoders can be grouped into two categories. *Simple decoders*, the most basic kind, assign a score to each user individually. *Joint decoders* are additionally allowed to investigate sets of users instead of individual users. Obviously, joint decoders can achieve better performance than simple decoders. However, performance comes at a cost. The run time of a simple decoder is linear in n, whereas checking all user tuples is polynomial in n.

It is possible that the colluders have no detailed knowledge of the embedding, detection, and decoding algorithm if the tracer succeeds in keeping such details hidden. Hence, Kerckhoffs's principle does not necessarily apply here.

7.1.2 Attacker Capabilities

The capabilities of the attackers depend on their processing power, as well as the tracer's choice of embedding and detection algorithms (and the coalition's knowledge about these algorithms). Various attacker models have been proposed. A very useful concept is the *detectable position*: this is defined as a position $i \in [\ell]$ where the colluders did not all receive the same watermark symbol. In an *undetectable position*, all colluders received the same symbol. In 1998, Boneh and Shaw [1] introduced the marking assumption (MA): in an undetectable position, the colluders can output only the symbol they have seen, and not (for example) an erasure or some other symbol. While in many situations the MA does not strictly hold, it is never far away from the truth. There are various models that furthermore specify what attacks are allowed in the *detectable* positions.

- The *General Digit Model* (GDM) allows the colluders to create any symbol in $\mathcal{X}$, or an erasure.

- The *Arbitrary Digit Model* (ADM) allows any symbol in $\mathcal{X}$.

- The *Unreadable Digit Model* (UDM) allows the symbols observed by the coalition, plus erasure.

- The *Restricted Digit Model* (RDM) allows only the observed symbols.

In the binary alphabet case, these four models are equivalent. For $q = 2$, an erasure informs the tracer that the colluders have received *both* symbols; hence, it is better for them to produce a single symbol than an erasure.

It is generally agreed that the GDM and ADM are not realistic for $q \geq 3$. In most watermarking systems, it is impossible to derive unobserved symbols from the observed ones. The combined digit model (CDM) [2, 3] is an extended attacker model that allows departure from the MA and comprises the UDM and RDM as special limiting cases. The data flow of the CDM in a single content position is illustrated in Figure 7.2. The colluders receive a subset of all symbols, $\Omega \subseteq \mathcal{X}$. Based on the symbols they received (and how many of each) they output attacked content created from a subset $\Psi \subseteq \Omega$ ($\Psi \neq \emptyset$) of the versions available to them (e.g., by averaging). Additionally, they insert noise. The CDM takes into account that the colluders do not know the consequences of their actions. (They do not know the embedding secrets and the unwatermarked content. Furthermore, the embedding and detection algorithm may not be entirely known to them.) The tracer's detector observes the presence of a *set* of symbols, $Y \subseteq \mathcal{X}$, with independent probabilities per symbol specified by $q + 1$ model parameters $r, t_1, \ldots, t_q \in [0, 1]$. The CDM has $\mathcal{Y} = 2^{\mathcal{X}}$, where the empty set corresponds to erasure. A symbol in Ψ gets detected with probability $t_{|\Psi|}$ (and erased with probability $1 - t_{|\Psi|}$), which reflects the noise strength and the effect of mixing $|\Psi|$ versions. Typically, $t_{|\Psi|}$ decreases with increasing $|\Psi|$. Due to the noise, a symbol not in Ψ has a small probability r of being detected.

The RDM is obtained from the CDM by setting $r = 0, t_1 = \cdots = t_q = 1$. The full visibility of every symbol in Ψ forces the colluders to set $|\Psi| = 1$, which then yields $\mathcal{Y} = \mathcal{X}$. The UDM is obtained by setting $r = 0, t_1 = 1, t_2 = \cdots = t_q = 0$.

The CDM is a very general and realistic model, but it is hard to analyze. It can be simplified by assuming that the colluders know enough about the tracer's detection procedure to avoid $|Y \cap \Psi| \geq 2$ events, which are very disadvantageous for them. In the *simplified CDM* (SCDM) the Ψ disappears, and the output space is $\mathcal{Y} = \mathcal{X} \cup \{\epsilon\}$. There is an $|\Omega|$-dependent probability $u_{|\Omega|}$ that the colluders are able to create an erasure. For each symbol in $\mathcal{X} \setminus \Omega$ independently there is a probability r that the they are able to output it.[1]

---

1   In a variant called the mixed digit model (MDM) [4], not only the erasure probability but also the
     probability of creating unseen symbols depends on $|\Omega|$.

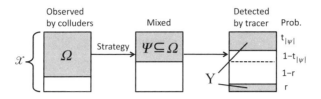

Figure 7.2   The combined digit model.

Whether the (S)CDM is closer to the RDM or to the UDM depends on the model parameters. Even the SCDM is hard to analyze. For $q \geq 3$ most work has concentrated on simpler models. The RDM is usually favored over the UDM. In the case of spread-spectrum sequences with a distortion constraint, possession of two symbols does not guarantee the ability to affect an erasure. Furthermore, in *dynamic* settings (such as unauthorized real-time redistribution of broadcasts), the colluders may not have time for extensive signal processing.

7.1.3   Attack Parametrization

The collusion attack may be nondeterministic. Hence, the most general description of the attack is a huge set of parameters

$$\Theta_{\psi|x_{\mathcal{C}}} \stackrel{\text{def}}{=} \Pr[\Psi = \psi | X_{\mathcal{C}} = x_{\mathcal{C}}] \tag{7.1}$$

that represent conditional probabilities. Here, $x_{\mathcal{C}} = (x_j)_{j \in \mathcal{C}}$ stands for the part of the code matrix x observed by the colluders. For an observation $x_{\mathcal{C}}$, the strategy parameter $\Theta_{\psi|x_{\mathcal{C}}}$ specifies the probability that the colluders output the sequence $\psi \in (2^{\mathcal{X}})^\ell$. In order to reduce the number of parameters, three simplifying assumptions are often introduced:

1. *Symbol symmetry.* The symbols in the alphabet $\mathcal{X}$ have no meaning other than as a label. As a consequence, the colluder strategy can be assumed to be invariant under permutation of the alphabet.

2. *Colluder symmetry.* The strategy is invariant under permutation of the colluders. The colluders equally share the risk. This assumption is motivated by the fact that breaking colluder symmetry will make it easier for the tracer to find at least one colluder.

3. *Position symmetry.* The same strategy is applied in each position $i \in [\ell]$, and it does not depend on any x_{jk} values with $k \neq i$. This assumption is motivated by the fact that, asymptotically, the optimal attack has position symmetry [5].

We define symbol tally vectors for the coalition as follows:

$$\mathbf{m}_i = (m_{i\alpha})_{\alpha \in \mathcal{X}}, \qquad m_{i\alpha} \overset{\text{def}}{=} |\{j \in \mathcal{C} : x_{ji} = \alpha\}| \qquad (7.2)$$

We denote the 1-norm of a vector as $|\cdot|$. It holds that $|\mathbf{m}_i| = c$. We define $\mathcal{M}_{qc} = \{\mathbf{m} \in \mathbb{N}^q : |\mathbf{m}| = c\}$.

When assumptions 2 and 3 hold, the strategy can be parametrized by a set of probabilities that depend only on the "local" tallies: in position i, the probability of outputting ψ_i is a function of only $\mathbf{m}_i$. Thus, a much smaller set of parameters $(\theta_{\psi|\mathbf{m}})_{\psi \in 2^{\mathcal{X}}, \mathbf{m} \in \mathcal{M}_{qc}}$ suffices to describe the collusion strategy,

$$\Theta_{\psi|x_{\mathcal{C}}} = \prod_{i=1}^{\ell} \theta_{\psi_i|\mathbf{m}_i} \qquad (7.3)$$

The $\theta_{\psi|\mathbf{m}}$ is the probability in an individual position that the colluders output ψ, given that they have observed tally $\mathbf{m}$; this parameter does not depend on the position. In the case of the SCDM, UDM, and RDM, the parametrization reduces to a set $(\theta_{y|\mathbf{m}})_{y \in \mathcal{Y}, \mathbf{m} \in \mathcal{M}_{qc}}$.

Furthermore, if assumption 1 holds as well, it is possible to further simplify the attack description because only the tally *values* matter, not to which symbol they belong [6]. In the RDM, this allows for a compact parametrization $(\Gamma_{b,s})_{b \in [c], s \in \mathcal{P}_{q-1}^{c-b}}$, where $\mathcal{P}_{q-1}^{c-b}$ stands for the partitions of the integer $c - b$ into at most $q - 1$ parts,

$$\Gamma_{b,s} \overset{\text{def}}{=} \theta_{y|\mathbf{m}} \quad \text{with } b = m_y \text{ and } \mathbf{s} = \text{Sort}(m_\alpha)_{\alpha \in \mathcal{X} \setminus \{y\}} \qquad (7.4)$$

The Γ_{bs} denotes the probability that the colluders output a symbol with tally b, given that the tally of all the other symbols is $\mathbf{s}$. Because of the MA, it holds that $\Gamma_{c0} = 1$.

An *eligible channel* is an attack parametrization allowed by the attack model under consideration. Table 7.1.3 shows the eligible channel for the most popular models.

We mention a number of often-considered attack strategies. In *minority voting*, the colluders choose the symbol with the lowest nonzero tally. In *majority voting*, they pick the symbol with the highest tally. In an *interleaving* attack, they

Table 7.1

Overview of Collusion Attack Models, Including Parameters and Constraints.

Model	Parameters	Constraints on the strategy
CDM	$\theta_{\psi\|\mathbf{m}}, r, t_1, \ldots, t_q$ $\psi \in 2^{\mathcal{X}} \setminus \emptyset$	$\sum_{\psi} \theta_{\psi\|\mathbf{m}} = 1$ If $\psi \setminus \Omega(\mathbf{m}) \neq \emptyset$ then $\theta_{\psi\|\mathbf{m}} = 0$
SCDM	$\theta_{y\|\mathbf{m}}, r, u_1, \ldots, u_q$ $y \in \mathcal{X} \cup \{\epsilon\}$	$\sum_{y} \theta_{y\|\mathbf{m}} = 1$ If $m_y = 0$ then $\theta_{y\|\mathbf{m}} \leq r$ $\theta_{\epsilon\|\mathbf{m}} \leq u_{\|\Omega(\mathbf{m})\|}$
MDM	$\theta_{y\|\mathbf{m}}, r_1, \ldots, r_{q-1},$ $u_1, \ldots, u_q$ $y \in \mathcal{X} \cup \{\epsilon\}$	$\sum_{y} \theta_{y\|\mathbf{m}} = 1$ $\sum_{y \in \mathcal{X} \setminus \Omega(\mathbf{m})} \theta_{y\|\mathbf{m}} \leq r_{\|\Omega(\mathbf{m})\|}$ $\theta_{\epsilon\|\mathbf{m}} \leq u_{\|\Omega(\mathbf{m})\|}$
UDM	$\theta_{y\|\mathbf{m}}$ $y \in \mathcal{X} \cup \{\epsilon\}$	$\sum_{y} \theta_{y\|\mathbf{m}} = 1$ If $m_y = 0$ then $\theta_{y\|\mathbf{m}} = 0$ If $\|\Omega(\mathbf{m})\| = 1$ then $\theta_{\epsilon\|\mathbf{m}} = 0$
RDM	$\theta_{y\|\mathbf{m}}$ $y \in \mathcal{X}$	$\sum_{y} \theta_{y\|\mathbf{m}} = 1$ If $m_y = 0$ then $\theta_{y\|\mathbf{m}} = 0$
RDM	$\Gamma_{b,\mathbf{s}}$ $b \in [c], \mathbf{s} \in \mathcal{P}^{c-b}_{q-1}$	$\sum_{y \in \Omega(\mathbf{m})} \Gamma_{m_y, (m_\alpha)_{\alpha \in \Omega(\mathbf{m}) \setminus \{y\}}} = 1$ $\mathbf{m} \in \mathcal{P}^c_q$

output the symbol of a randomly chosen colluder. This attack has $\theta_{y\|\mathbf{m}} = m_y/c$, and $\Gamma_{b,\mathbf{s}} = b/c$ independent of $\mathbf{s}$. In the *random symbol* attack, they output one of the observed symbols at random, not taking into account how many colluders receive each symbol; each symbol in Ω has probability $1/|\Omega|$ of being chosen.

7.2 TRAITOR TRACING CODES

7.2.1 Objectives and Error Types

The tracer's aim is usually one of the following: *catch-all*, where he wants to identify the whole coalition, or *catch-one*, where he wants to find at least one colluder. Catch-all is difficult to achieve if some of the colluders take very little risk. For equal-risk attack strategies, the difference between the two scenarios is minor. One defines two types of error: *false positive* (FP), meaning that the list $\mathcal{L}$ contains innocent users, and *false negative* (FN), meaning that $\mathcal{L}$ contains none of the colluders. The corresponding probabilities are

$$P_{\text{FP}} \overset{\text{def}}{=} \Pr[\mathcal{L} \setminus \mathcal{C} \neq \emptyset] \qquad P_{\text{FN}} \overset{\text{def}}{=} \Pr[\mathcal{L} \cap \mathcal{C} = \emptyset] \qquad (7.5)$$

For proof-technical reasons, another quantity is often used, the one-person FP probability. It is defined as the probability that a fixed innocent user ends up in $\mathcal{L}$,

$$P_{\mathrm{FP1}} \stackrel{\mathrm{def}}{=} \Pr[j \in \mathcal{L} \mid j \in [n] \setminus \mathcal{C}] \qquad (7.6)$$

Under the usual circumstances ($n \gg c$, $P_{\mathrm{FP}} \ll 1$), it holds that $P_{\mathrm{FP}} \approx (n-c)P_{\mathrm{FP1}}$.

The tracer's objective is to achieve low error probabilities in the face of a collusion attack with up to c_0 attackers, where c_0 is a design parameter. This has to be achieved with a code that is as short as possible. In the context of audio-video watermarking, the FP probability has to be very low (e.g., 10^{-6}) otherwise accused users can reasonably claim that they were framed or accused by accident. The FN is far less critical, since even a low probability of getting caught has a strong deterring effect. A scheme with $P_{\mathrm{FN}} \approx 0.5$ can be acceptable in practice.

Furthermore, a very desirable property is *no-framing*. A code is said to have the no-framing property if the FP probability does not depend on the actual coalition size. When c exceeds the design parameter c_0, the P_{FP} still stays low, while the P_{FN} increases. As a result, the list $\mathcal{L}$ is empty, which is an acceptable outcome.

7.2.2   A Very Short History of Collusion-Resistant Codes

The literature on collusion resistance goes back at least as far as the 1980s [7]. On the one hand, there is the effort to produce ever shorter codes. On the other hand, ever tighter bounds were proven on the minimum code length required to resist a collusion attack. We mention a few highlights without doing full justice to all these efforts.

In 1998, Hollmann et al. [8] developed identifiable parent property codes against coalitions of size $c_0 = 2$. In the same year, Boneh and Shaw [1] introduced a binary code formed by concatenating a deterministic outer code and a probabilistic inner code with sufficient code length $\ell = \mathcal{O}(c_0^4 \ln \frac{n}{P_{\mathrm{FP}}} \ln \frac{1}{P_{\mathrm{FP}}})$. They also proved a lower bound $\ell = \Omega(c_0 \ln \frac{1}{c_0 P_{\mathrm{FP}}})$. In the context of spread-spectrum watermarking, Kilian et al. [9] found a lower bound $\Omega(c_0^2 \ln n)$.

In 2001, Staddon et al. [10] presented a code of length $\ell = c_0^2 \log_q n$; however, the alphabet size had to be $q \geq \ell - 1$, which is not practical for audio/video watermarking. Peikert et al. [11] tightened the lower bound to $\Omega(c_0^2 \ln \frac{1}{c_0 P_{\mathrm{FP}}})$ for alphabet size independent of c_0.

In 2003, Gabor Tardos achieved a famous breakthrough [12, 13]. He proved a lower bound $\Omega(c_0^2 \ln \frac{1}{P_{\mathrm{FP1}}})$, and at the same time, introduced a binary construction achieving that bound. The code is built using two probabilistic steps and has length

$\ell = 100c_0^2 \lceil \ln \frac{1}{P_{\text{FP1}}} \rceil$. Apart from having asymptotically[2] optimal length, Tardos's code has other desirable properties: it is *no-framing* and new users can be added at any time. These results have had such an impact that one often speaks of a "pre-Tardos" and a "post-Tardos" era. In the post-Tardos era, work has concentrated on improving the code construction [14–16] and the decoder [17–21] in order to reduce the constant '100', as well as on analysis [22–27] and various generalizations [2, 3, 28–30]. The binary construction, which originally discarded positions with colluder output $y = 0$, has been made symmetric in the alphabet symbols and generalized to nonbinary alphabets [29].

The follow-up work has resulted in a whole class of codes which are often referred to as *Tardos codes* or *bias-based fingerprinting codes*. The most important recent advances are the information-theoretic analysis of the collusion channel, the use of hypothesis testing techniques, and the development of practical joint decoders. These topics are covered in Sections 7.3–7.5.

7.2.3 The q-ary Tardos Code

We briefly summarize the symmetrized version of Tardos's scheme and its generalization to nonbinary alphabets [29]. Tardos introduced the idea of *bias-based* code generation, which is entirely probabilistic and consists of two steps. First, for each position $i \in [\ell]$, independently, a bias vector $\mathbf{p}_i = (p_{i\alpha})_{\alpha \in \mathcal{X}}$ is randomly drawn from a probability density f, with $p_{i\alpha} \geq \tau$ and $|\mathbf{p}_i| \overset{\text{def}}{=} \sum_\alpha p_{i\alpha} = 1$. The $\tau \geq 0$ is a parameter called the cutoff; for $q = 2$ a nonzero cutoff is necessary for avoiding the occasional occurrence of extremely high innocent user scores. Tardos set it to $\tau = 1/(300c_0)$. In later works it was finetuned to $\tau \propto c_0^{-4/3}$ [25, 31].

The distribution f is a symmetric Dirichlet distribution with concentration parameter $\kappa > 0$,

$$f(\mathbf{p}) = N_{q\kappa\tau}^{-1} \prod_{\alpha \in \mathcal{X}} p_\alpha^{-1+\kappa} \tag{7.7}$$

Here $N_{q\kappa\tau}$ is a normalization constant. In the binary case one sets $\kappa = 1/2$, $\mathcal{X} = \{0, 1\}$, and f is given by the *arcsine distribution* $f(p_1) = p_1^{-\frac{1}{2}}(1 - p_1)^{-\frac{1}{2}}/(\pi - 4\arcsin\sqrt{\tau})$. For $\tau = 0$ the normalization constant is simply a Beta function, $N_{q\kappa 0} = [\Gamma(\kappa)]^q/\Gamma(q\kappa)$.

---

2 The term 'asymptotic' refers to the limit $c_0 \to \infty$.

In the second step of the code matrix generation, symbols are randomly generated column-wise according to the categorical distribution $\mathbf{p}_i$,

$$\Pr[X_{ji} = \alpha] = p_{i\alpha} \tag{7.8}$$

That is, for each user $j \in [n]$, independently, a symbol is drawn in position i by rolling a q-sided die that has bias $\mathbf{p}_i$. The overall distribution of the symbols X_{ji} is known as the multivariate Pólya distribution.

A simple decoder is specified for the case $\mathcal{Y} = \mathcal{X}$. For each position i, user j incurs a score $s_{ji} = g(x_{ji}, y_i, \mathbf{p}_i)$, and an overall score is computed for him by simply adding these together, $s_j = \sum_i s_{ji}$. A user j ends up in the list $\mathcal{L}$ if $s_j > Z$, where Z is a carefully chosen threshold. The *score function* g is given by[3]

$$g(x, y, \mathbf{p}) = (\frac{\delta_{xy}}{p_y} - 1)\sqrt{\frac{p_y}{1 - p_y}} \tag{7.9}$$

If $x = y$, the function is positive and grows when the probability of the event $x = y$ decreases. Likewise, if $x \neq y$, then the score is negative and becomes more negative the more unlikely the event $x \neq y$ is.

The score function (7.9), combined with the independence of the code matrix columns and (for given $\mathbf{p}_i$) the symbols within each column, makes the scheme very easy to analyze. For a given $\mathbf{p}$ and y, the expected score of an innocent user is zero, $p_y g(y, y, \mathbf{p}) + (1 - p_y)g(x \neq y, y, \mathbf{p}) = 0$. Furthermore, the variance is unity, $p_y g^2(y, y, \mathbf{p}) + (1 - p_y)g^2(x \neq y, y, \mathbf{p}) = 1$. Hence, the sum $s_j = \sum_i s_{ji}$ for an innocent user can be seen as a zero-mean, unit-variance random walk with statistics that depend very weakly on the coalition strategy. The threshold Z can be set in such a way that the P_{FP} is acceptable; even if $c \gg c_0$, the colluders have almost no influence on the false positive rate. Thus it is easily established that the Tardos scheme has the no-framing property.

The average single-position score of the whole coalition ("μ") is positive and depends on the collusion strategy. After ℓ steps of the random walk, a colluder's expected score is $\ell\mu/c$, while the innocent users' scores follow a distribution with zero mean and variance $\sqrt{\ell}$. Asymptotically, this distribution tends to be Gaussian. If ℓ is large enough, the colluders' scores (linear in ℓ) can be reliably distinguished from those of the innocents ($\propto \sqrt{\ell}$). Elementary analysis of Gaussian tails shows how the threshold Z and code length ℓ have to be set asymptotically as a function of c_0 and the desired error rate. Let β be a strategy-independent

---

3   The δ_{xy} stands for the Kronecker delta: 1 if $x = y$ and 0 otherwise.

lower bound on μ. Then a sufficient parameter setting is $\ell = (2/\beta^2)c_0^2 \ln(1/P_{\mathrm{FP1}})$, $Z = (2/\beta)c_0 \ln(1/P_{\mathrm{FP1}})$. For $q \geq 3$, the bound β is a complicated function of κ. In the binary case (with $\kappa = \frac{1}{2}$), however, it holds asymptotically that $\mu = 2/\pi$ independent of the strategy, yielding sufficient code length $\ell = \frac{\pi^2}{2}c_0^2 \ln(1/P_{\mathrm{FP1}})$.

Though the number $\frac{\pi^2}{2}$ is a lot smaller than the original constant '100' used by Tardos, the above scheme does not achieve capacity (see Section 7.3). It was found [16] for $q = 2$ that an improvement is obtained by taking a c_0-dependent discrete bias distribution instead of the continuous distribution (7.7). For $q \geq 3$, a scheme was found [32] that makes μ independent of the strategy. However, despite the simplification, the performance is much worse. It has turned out [33] that a rescaled version of the score function (7.9), namely $\delta_{xy}/p_y - 1$, does achieve asymptotic capacity. See Section 7.4 for a further discussion of decoders.

The nonasymptotic performance of the Tardos scheme is difficult to analyze. Provable upper bounds on the error rates are far from tight. The most accurate method to determine error rates, apart from simulations, is the convolution and series expansion technique [6, 34, 35], a seminumerical approach that makes use of the convolution-multiplication property of sums of independent variables.

7.3 INFORMATION-THEORETIC APPROACH

7.3.1 Fingerprinting Rate and Capacity

In analogy with channel coding, it is possible to define a *fingerprinting rate* and *fingerprinting capacity* for the collusion channel (Figure 7.1). The "message" to be sent is the identity of the colluders (i.e., the set $\mathcal{C} \subset [n]$). The entropy of this message, counted in q-ary symbols, is $\log_q \binom{n}{c}$. The number of symbols sent into the collusion channel is $c\ell$, namely the codewords given to the colluders. The fingerprinting rate R can be defined as the ratio of these two quantities,

$$R = \frac{\log_q \binom{n}{c}}{\ell c} \tag{7.10}$$

This rate represents the fraction of the sent symbols that actually carries useful information. For $n \gg c$, (7.10) gives $R \approx \ell^{-1} \log_q n$, which corresponds to the usual definition of code rate. The rate can be used as a fair metric for comparing codes that have different q.

In the theory of channel coding, Shannon's theorem [36] gives an upper bound on the achievable error probability P_{err} for the limit $\ell \to \infty$ at constant code rate:

$P_{\text{err}} \leq q^{-\ell(C-R)}$. Here, C is the *capacity* of the channel. As long as $R < C$, the error probability can be made arbitrarily small by increasing ℓ. From Shannon's theorem and the definition of R, it follows that the sufficient code length for resisting c_0 attackers at a certain error probability is given by

$$\ell_{\text{suff}}(q, c_0, P_{\text{FP}}) = \frac{\log_q \frac{n}{P_{\text{FP}}}}{C(q, c_0)} \tag{7.11}$$

in the limit $n \to \infty$. Here, the P_{FP} appears instead of P_{err} because, typically, a miscommunication of the "message" $\mathcal{C}$ causes accusation of innocents.

7.3.2 Mutual Information Maxmin Game

Next, we discuss how the fingerprinting capacity is determined. In the theory of ordinary channel coding, the achievable code rate is upper bounded by the mutual information between the input and the output of the noisy channel, given a known codebook. In our case, we have the code matrix $X \in \mathcal{X}^{n \times \ell}$ playing the role of the codebook, the collusion strategy θ that operates on X_C (the part of X received by the colluders) in the role of the channel, and the collusion output $Y \in \mathcal{Y}^\ell$. In analogy with channel coding, the quantity that upper-bounds the achievable fingerprinting rate is then $\frac{1}{\ell c} I(Y; X_C | X)$. The mutual information[4] $I(Y; X_C | X) = I(Y; \mathcal{C} | X) = I(XY; \mathcal{C})$ captures the "quality" of the code, as well as the strength of the collusion attack; it represents the amount of information about $\mathcal{C}$ that the tracer can get from his evidence X, Y. The factor ℓc is the same as in (7.10).

We write $I(Y; X_C | X) = H(Y | X) - H(Y | X_C)$. As n goes to infinity, $H(Y | X)$ tends[5] to $H(Y | \bar{\mathbf{P}})$, where $\bar{\mathbf{P}} \overset{\text{def}}{=} (\mathbf{P}_i)_{i \in [\ell]}$. Furthermore, as ℓ goes to infinity, there is perfect position symmetry in the realization of $\bar{\mathbf{P}}$ and X, from which it follows that the collusion strategy can be assumed to be position-symmetric. This makes X, Y, and $\bar{\mathbf{P}}$ split up into independent position components,

$$\frac{I(Y; X_C | X)}{\ell c} \to \frac{H(Y_i | \mathbf{P}_i) - H(Y_i | X_{Ci})}{c} \tag{7.12}$$

---

4   For the definition of Shannon entropy and mutual information see works on information theory, such as [37].

5   This can be seen as follows. We write $H(\bar{\mathbf{P}}XY) = H(\bar{\mathbf{P}}) + H(X | \bar{\mathbf{P}}) + H(Y | X)$. Here we have used that $H(Y | X\bar{\mathbf{P}}) = H(Y | X)$. We can also write $H(\bar{\mathbf{P}}XY)$ as $H(\bar{\mathbf{P}}) + H(Y | \bar{\mathbf{P}}) + H(X | \bar{\mathbf{P}}Y)$. Equating the two expressions for $H(\bar{\mathbf{P}}XY)$ gives $H(Y | \bar{\mathbf{P}}) - H(Y | X) = H(X | \bar{\mathbf{P}}) - H(X | \bar{\mathbf{P}}Y)$. With constant c and increasing n, the difference in the right-hand side tends to zero because Y is related to an ever smaller fraction of X. Hence $H(Y | \bar{\mathbf{P}}) - H(Y | X)$ tends to zero.

If we also assume colluder symmetry, then the dependence of Y_i on X_{Ci} is only through the tally vector $\mathbf{M}_i$, resulting in

$$\frac{I(Y; X_C|X)}{\ell c} \rightarrow \frac{H(Y_i|\mathbf{P}_i) - H(Y_i|\mathbf{M}_i)}{c} = \frac{I(Y_i; \mathbf{M}_i|\mathbf{P}_i)}{c} \qquad (7.13)$$

The fingerprinting capacity is precisely the maximum achievable value of expression (7.13) [5]. However, in contrast to ordinary noisy channels, the collusion channel is adversarial, and hence a worst-case scenario must be assumed. On one side, the tracer chooses the bias distibution f without knowing the attack θ. On the other side, the colluders know f and choose θ accordingly. This results in a maxmin game,

$$C(q, c) = \max_{f} \min_{\theta} \frac{1}{c} I(Y_i; \mathbf{M}_i|\mathbf{P}_i) \qquad (7.14)$$

Equation (7.14) holds for any of the attack models discussed in Section 7.1.2.

7.3.3 Saddlepoint Solutions

Next, we discuss solutions of the maxmin game (7.14). The expression $I(Y_i; \mathbf{M}_i|\mathbf{P}_i)$ is linear in f and convex in θ. By the minimax theorem [38], the game then allows a saddlepoint solution (f^{SP}, θ^{SP}). If the tracer uses a distribution f that is different from f^{SP}, then the colluders can choose an attack $\theta \neq \theta^{SP}$ that lowers the mutual information below the capacity. Similarly, if the tracer uses f^{SP} and the colluders apply an attack that is different from θ^{SP}, then the mutual information is higher than the capacity.

Numerical solutions are available in the literature, such as for the marking assumption with $q = 2$ and c up to 37 [39]. Figure 7.3 shows fingerprinting rates as a function of c. Figure 7.4 shows f^{SP} in cumulative distribution form, compared to the Dirichlet distribution (7.7). Figure 7.5 shows the attack θ^{SP} in the saddlepoint, compared to the Interleaving attack. The numerics suggest that, for growing coalition size, f^{SP} gets closer to the Dirichlet distribution, while θ^{SP} gets closer to Interleaving. This does not come as a surprise. In the limit $c \to \infty$, the expression $I(Y_i; \mathbf{M}_i|\mathbf{P}_i)$ becomes tractable, and an analytic solution can be obtained under certain regularity assumptions.[6] In the case of the RDM the result is[7] [14, 39, 42]

---

6   It is assumed that $\exists (g_y)_{y \in \mathcal{Y}} : \theta^{SP}_{y|\mathbf{m}} = g_y(\frac{\mathbf{m}}{c}) + o(\frac{1}{c})$ where the g_y are twice differentiable functions.

7   The binary capacity $(c^2 2 \ln 2)^{-1}$ was already conjectured in [40]. The conjecture was proven in [17, 41].

$$C_{\text{asymp}}^{\text{RDM}}(q,c) = \frac{1}{c^2} \cdot \frac{q-1}{2\ln q} + \mathcal{O}(c^{-5/2}) \tag{7.15}$$

$$f^{\text{SP,RDM}}(\mathbf{p}) \to \frac{\Gamma(q/2)}{\pi^{q/2}} \prod_{\alpha \in \mathcal{X}} p_\alpha^{-1/2} \quad ; \quad \theta_{y|\mathbf{m}}^{\text{SP,RDM}} \to \frac{m_y}{c} \quad \text{for } c \to \infty \tag{7.16}$$

For $q = 2$ the result is valid under the MA in general. Equations (7.11), (7.15) give the sufficient code length

$$\ell_{\text{suff}}^{\text{RDM}}(q, c_0 \to \infty, P_{\text{FP}}) = \frac{2}{q-1} c_0^2 \ln \frac{n}{P_{\text{FP}}} \tag{7.17}$$

Several points about the RDM results are interesting to note:

- The asymptotically optimal bias distribution is precisely of the form (7.7) with $\kappa = \frac{1}{2}$. In statistics, this distribution is known as the *Jeffreys prior*, asymptotically the *least informative* distribution for someone who tries to estimate the bias $\mathbf{p}_i$ from observing $X_{\mathcal{C}i}$. This makes intuitive sense: if the colluders could accurately estimate $\mathbf{p}_i$, then they would know how many users must typically have each symbol $\alpha \in \mathcal{X}$, and they would know the score values for each symbol. This would allow them to minimize their own collective score compared to that of the innocent users. It has been shown [43, 44] that the fingerprinting rate decreases exponentially in c if the colluders know $\mathbf{p}_i$.

  In Figure 7.4, we see that the number of discrete $\mathbf{p}$-values increases irregularly with increasing c. Asymptotically, the discrete distribution approaches a continuum distribution.

- Asymptotically, the optimal attack strategy gets ever nearer to Interleaving (Figure 7.5). This too makes intuitive sense: Interleaving is the strategy that makes the colluders statistically look like innocent users as closely as possible, given their knowledge $\mathbf{m}$; it makes sure that the colluder symbol y is Bernoulli-distributed with bias $\mathbf{m}/c$, which is an estimator for $\mathbf{p}$ that is asymptotically unbiased and has minimum asymptotic variance [39].

- Figure 7.3 shows that, with increasing c, the capacity gets closer to the asymptotic formula $1/(c^2 \cdot 2\ln 2)$.

- Figure 7.3 also shows that the two limiting procedures (i) compute the saddle-point and then take $c \to \infty$ and (ii) take the asymptotic θ^{SP} =interleaving, find

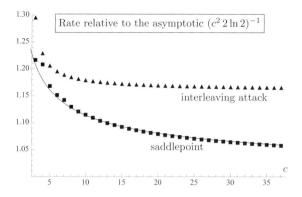

Figure 7.3 Binary fingerprinting rates as a function of c, normalized with respect to the asymptotic expression $1/(c^2 \cdot 2 \ln 2)$. The squares correspond to the saddlepoint solutions of the maxmin game (7.14) under the marking assumption. The line joining the squares is a curve-fit, $1 + 0.36/\sqrt{c}$. The triangles represent the highest achievable rate when the colluders use the interleaving strategy. Data from Figure 2a in [39].

the best f against interleaving, and then take $c \to \infty$, are not the same. In the latter case, there always exists a special f of the form $\frac{1}{2}\delta(p_1 - \frac{\alpha}{c}) + \frac{1}{2}\delta(p_1 - 1 + \frac{\alpha}{c})$, for some constant α, which achieves a rate that lies a constant fraction ≈ 1.16 above the asymptotic capacity formula.

- The rate of the Tardos scheme is significantly lower[8] than the capacity. Given that the Tardos scheme uses the right f, this means that its decoder is suboptimal.

- The capacity is an increasing function of q. Hence q-ary codes will, if implementation constraints allow it, perform better than binary codes.

In the UDM there is no gain in going to nonbinary alphabets, because erasures carry less information at large q. The maxmin game has also been studied for the CDM [45] and the SCDM/MDM [4]. The capacity gradually decreases from C^{RDM} when the non-MA attack strength parameters are increased. The f^{SP} is still the Dirichlet distribution, but the optimal attack departs from Interleaving [4].

8 For $q = 2$, this is obvious from the code length constant $\frac{\pi^2}{2}$ versus 2 (i.e., a factor ≈ 2.47). For $q \geq 3$, it takes more work to determine the asymptotic rate [31].

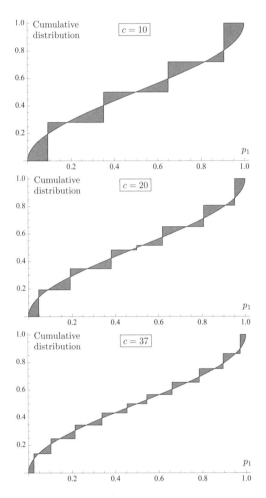

Figure 7.4 Convergence of the (discrete) binary $f^{\mathrm{SP}}(\mathbf{p})$ to the Dirichlet distribution. The cumulative distribution function (cdf) for the component p_1 is plotted as a function of p_1. The shaded area is the difference between the actual cdf at finite c and the cdf of the binary Dirichlet distribution, $\frac{2}{\pi}\arcsin\sqrt{p_1}$. Data from Figure 3a in [39].

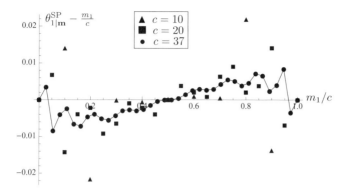

Figure 7.5 Attack parameters θ at finite-c saddlepoint solutions under the marking assumption, for $q = 2$ and various coalition sizes. On the vertical axis the difference is shown with respect to the interleaving attack. Data from Figure 4a in [39].

7.4 UNIVERSAL DECODERS

7.4.1 Neyman-Pearson Score

The saddlepoint solution tells the tracer which bias distribution f to use, but not how to build a decoder. An obvious approach to construct a decoder is to make use of the Neyman-Pearson lemma [46], a well-known result in statistics; if one has a body of evidence E and one must choose between two hypotheses H_0 and H_1, then the most powerful test is to look at the Neyman-Pearson score $\frac{\Pr[H_0|E]}{\Pr[H_1|E]}$. If the score lies above a certain threshold, choose H_0, otherwise choose H_1. Here "most powerful" means having the lowest possible false negative probability at the given false positive probability, as well as the other way round. In a simple decoder, the hypothesis we want to test is whether or not a user $j \in [n]$ is part of the collusion. The available evidence consists of $\bar{\mathbf{p}}$, x and y. The corresponding Neyman-Pearson score is

$$\frac{\Pr[j \in \mathcal{C}|\bar{\mathbf{p}}xy]}{\Pr[j \notin \mathcal{C}|\bar{\mathbf{p}}xy]} \tag{7.18}$$

If we assume colluder symmetry and position symmetry, then after some manipulations (7.18) can be rewritten as[9]

$$\frac{c}{n-c} \cdot \frac{\mathbb{E}_{\bar{\mathbf{m}}|x, j \in \mathcal{C}} \prod_i P_{y_i|\mathbf{m}_i}}{\mathbb{E}_{\bar{\mathbf{m}}|x, j \notin \mathcal{C}} \prod_i P_{y_i|\mathbf{m}_i}} \tag{7.19}$$

The notation $P_{y_i|\mathbf{m}_i}$ stands for $\sum_{\psi_i} \Pr[Y_i = y_i | \Psi_i = \psi_i] \theta_{\psi_i|\mathbf{m}_i}$ in the case of the CDM, and for $\theta_{y_i|\mathbf{m}_i}$ in all the other attack models. The expectations $\mathbb{E}_{\bar{\mathbf{m}}|x}$ in (7.19) involve a summation over all possible candidate coalitions, where each candidate is equally likely because of the tracer's lack of a priori information about the colluders. Such a summation has approximately $\binom{n}{c}$ terms and it is therefore completely impractical to compute the score in practice.

7.4.2   Keeping the Symbol Tallies as Evidence

The practicality of the Neyman-Pearson score changes completely if we "forget" most of the evidence in x and use evidence $\bar{\mathbf{p}}, x_j, y$ instead of $\bar{\mathbf{p}}, x, y$. Then the expectations in (7.19) are of the form $\mathbb{E}_{\bar{\mathbf{m}}|\bar{\mathbf{p}}}$, which nicely factors into $\prod_i \mathbb{E}_{\mathbf{m}_i|\mathbf{p}_i}$ without the need to sum over coalitions. The $\mathbf{m}_i|\mathbf{p}_i$ is multinomial-distributed and allows for relatively easy computations.

Here, we will consider a somewhat less drastic amnesia. We remember x_j and the tallies $\bar{\mathbf{t}} = (\mathbf{t}_i)_{i=1}^{\ell}$, where we write $\mathbf{t}_i = (t_{i\alpha})_{\alpha \in \mathcal{X}}$ with $t_{i\alpha} \stackrel{\text{def}}{=} |\{j \in [n] : x_{ji} = \alpha\}|$. In otrher words, $t_{i\alpha}$ counts how many users (innocent as well as colluders) received symbol α in position i. Now the expectations $\mathbb{E}_{\bar{\mathbf{m}}|x}$ in (7.19) turn to $\mathbb{E}_{\bar{\mathbf{m}}|\bar{\mathbf{t}}}$, which factors into $\prod_i \mathbb{E}_{\mathbf{m}_i|\mathbf{t}_i}$, and again the summation over candidate coalitions has disappeared. The distribution of $\mathbf{m}_i$ given $\mathbf{t}_i$ is a multivariate hypergeometric distribution. The probabilities are given by $\Pr[\mathbf{m}|\mathbf{t}] = \binom{n}{c}^{-1} \prod_{\alpha \in \mathcal{X}} \binom{t_\alpha}{m_\alpha}$. Properly taking care of the conditions $j \in \mathcal{C}$ (numerator) and $j \notin \mathcal{C}$ (denominator) in (7.19) yields [21] the following score[10] [11]

---

9   Notice that $\bar{\mathbf{p}}$ has disappeared from (7.19); this happens because $\bar{\mathbf{m}}$ follows directly from x.

10   Taking any monotonous function of a Neyman-Pearson score preserves the ROC curve (i.e., the balance of FP versus FN error probability in the hypothesis test). Here we have applied a linear function and a logarithm.

11   In the case where $\bar{\mathbf{p}}$ is taken as evidence, we get $\mathbf{t}_i \to n\mathbf{p}_i$ and $\mathbf{t}_i - \mathbf{m}_i \to (n-c)\mathbf{p}_i$, yielding a score of the form [18, 20, 33]

$$\sum_i w(x_{ji}, y_i, \mathbf{p}_i) \text{ with } w(x, y, \mathbf{p}) = \ln \frac{\mathbb{E}_{\mathbf{m}|\mathbf{p}}[m_x P_{y|\mathbf{m}}]}{cp_x \mathbb{E}_{\mathbf{m}|\mathbf{p}}[P_{y|\mathbf{m}}]} = \ln(1 + \frac{1}{c} \frac{\partial \ln P_{y|\mathbf{p}}}{\partial p_x}).$$

$$\sum_{i=1}^{\ell} \ln \frac{\mathbb{E}_{\mathbf{m}_i|\mathbf{t}_i} P_{y_i|\mathbf{m}_i} m_{ix_{ji}}}{\mathbb{E}_{\mathbf{m}_i|\mathbf{t}_i} P_{y_i|\mathbf{m}_i} (t_{ix_{ji}} - m_{ix_{ji}})} \tag{7.20}$$

7.4.3 Substituting the Interleaving Attack

The expression (7.20) has a serious drawback: it depends on the colluder strategy θ, which is not known to the tracer. Now a result [47] from the theory of compound discrete memoryless channels comes to the rescue: it suffices to build a decoder against the saddlepoint value θ^{SP}. This results in a *universal* decoder that achieves the saddlepoint rate and has reasonable performance against attacks $\theta \neq \theta^{SP}$. In Section 7.3.3, we saw that the RDM saddlepoint solution is complicated, but with θ^{SP} lying very close to Interleaving. Hence, substituting $\theta =$ Interleaving in (7.20) yields a near-optimal decoder for the RDM, which gets closer to optimal with increasing c_0. The resulting score system is as follows [21]. For each user, the score is computed as a sum, $u_j = \frac{1}{\ell} \sum_{i=1}^{\ell} u_{ji}$, with

$$u_{ji} = r(x_{ji}, y_i, \mathbf{t}_i) \quad ; \quad r(x, y, \mathbf{t}) = \delta_{xy} \ln(1 + \frac{1}{c_0 - 1} \cdot \frac{n-1}{t_y - 1}) \tag{7.21}$$

Unlike earlier individual-user score functions proposed in the literature, the decoder has the interesting property that user j's score depends on the tallies $\mathbf{t}_i$, which are influenced by the symbols of *all* users.

There is another interesting property. If in any position i only a single user j received symbol y_i, it follows that $t_{iy_i} = 1$ and hence $u_j = \infty$, meaning that user j can be accused with certainty.

For $n \to \infty$, the t_y tends to its expected value np_y and the function r reduces to $\delta_{xy} \ln(1 + \frac{1}{c_0-1} \cdot \frac{1}{p_y})$, a q-ary generalization of the Laarhoven score [20]. For $c_0 \to \infty$, this further reduces (up to an unimportant linear transformation) to the score of Oosterwijk et al. [33], $h(x, y, \mathbf{p}) = \delta_{xy}/p_y - 1$. The score h has been shown to achieve asymptotic capacity and to give rise to an f vs. θ maxmin game of the asymptotic rate, which has a saddlepoint exactly at the same place as the mutual information maxmin game of Section 7.3.3, namely Jeffreys prior vs. Interleaving.

7.4.4 Setting the Threshold

In contrast to the score function g as specified in (7.9), with its simple random walk, the score r yields complicated statistics for innocent users. The average and variance of the innocent user score depends on the collusion strategy. Consequently, the accusation criteria has to be more involved than simply setting a strategy-independent threshold.

A straightforward solution is to look at the histogram of scores of the *whole* population $[n]$ and to interpret it as the distribution belonging to the *innocent* population. (This is accurate as long as $n \gg c$ and the empirical scores considered are not the $\mathcal{O}(c)$ highest ones.) Optionally, the tracer may also generate a large set of new codewords, which are never distributed to anyone, for the purpose of determining the statistics of the (y-dependent) innocent user scores [48]. After this phase, the tracer sets an accusation threshold, such as by assuming a Gaussian distribution[12] or by more advanced statistical techniques.

There is another aspect that makes the decoding more complicated: the score function (7.21) contains the design parameter c_0, while the actual coalition size c is unknown. One way to deal with this is to start at $c_0 = 2$ and keep increasing c_0 while $\mathcal{L} = \emptyset$, of course making sure that c_0 is compatible with ℓ.

7.4.5   No-Framing

It is important to determine if the scheme with the discrete f^{SP} for finite c_0 combined with the universal score function (7.21) has the no-framing property. There is no formal proof of no-framing, but several arguments indicate that framing is practically impossible.

- For $c \ll n$, the attack has no discernible effect on the score histogram of the whole user base. While it is possible for a coalition of size $c > c_0$ to dilute its collective score and stay undetected, the attack cannot cause errors in the tracer's estimate of the innocent users' distribution. If the technique with the additional innocent codewords is used, then even for $c = \mathcal{O}(n)$ the colluders cannot influence the tracer's estimate.

- No matter how large c is, the bias-based construction of the code matrix makes sure that the colluders do not know the actual symbols received by the innocent users.

---

12 In contrast to the single-position innocent user score s_{ji}, which has a power-law probability tail, the distribution of u_{ji} has an exponential tail that falls off as $\exp(-\frac{5}{2}u)$ or faster [21]. Due to the central limit theorem, the distribution of the summed score $\sum_i u_{ji}$ is very close to Gaussian.

7.5 JOINT DECODERS

For $c_0 < \infty$, it is generally not possible for a simple decoder to achieve capacity [5]. The gap between the capacity and the achievable rate of the (universal) simple decoder must be bridged by using a *joint decoder*. Designing a joint decoder is far from trivial. Unlike the case of binary questions such as "is this user a colluder or not?" (for which the optimal Neyman-Pearson hypothesis test is available), no optimal test is known for more complicated problems where one has to choose from more than two hypotheses.

Although capacity-achieving joint decoders *have* been devised [5, 17], they need to test all candidate coalitions of size c_0, which takes $\mathcal{O}(n^{c_0})$ time. The best *practical* joint decoder to date was developed by Meerwald and Furon [19, 48]. In the catch-all scenario, this decoder works as follows: A list $\mathcal{L}$ is kept that is updated every time a new colluder is identified. The decoder looks at t-tuplets of increasing size t, starting at $t = 1$ (i.e., a simple decoder). Whenever $\mathcal{L}$ is updated, the empirical y and $\bar{p}$ together with $\mathcal{L}$ are used to infer which attack $\hat{\theta}$ by c_0 colluders is most likely to have happened. Whenever t or $\mathcal{L}$ changes, the score function is updated to a Neyman-Pearson score based on $\hat{\theta}$, which tests the hypothesis "are all user in this t-tuplet colluders," conditioned on the fact that the users in $\mathcal{L}$ are known to be colluders. A threshold is determined for the updated score function. If there are tuplets whose score exceeds the threshold, then from this tuplet, the user with the highest simple-decoder score is added to $\mathcal{L}$. If no tuplet exceeds the threshold, then t is increased. With every update of t the set of users is pruned to size $n(t)$, such that $\binom{n(t)}{t}$ is roughly constant. The pruning is done by eliminating users who have low scores.

The joint decoder of Meerwald and Furon catches significantly more colluders than simple decoders.

7.6 OUTLOOK / FURTHER READING

In a chapter like this, it is impossible to do full justice to all the work that has been done on fingerprinting. We did not discuss alternative models for the collusion channel [49]; or special constructions that exist for $c_0 = 2$ [17, 50] and $c_0 = 3$ [15]; or the body of simulation data that has been compiled over the years for all the invented schemes; or the various proof techniques for bounding the FP and FN error probabilities [31, 51]; or the different ways to set (tuple) scores for joint decoders [52]. There are whole fields of study that we did not mention, such as dynamic (also called sequential) traitor tracing [30, 53–55], in which both tracer and attacker are able to adapt their actions in response to events in previous positions; combining Tardos codes with buyer-seller watermarking schemes ("asymmetric fingerprinting") [28, 56–58], where the seller does not have full knowledge of the embedded watermark so that he is not able to frame innocent buyers; fingerprinting using error-correcting codes [59, 60]; the connection between traitor tracing and (medical) group testing [20, 21, 61, 62]; the connection between traitor tracing and differential privacy [63, 64].

Sections 7.3 through 7.5 may give the impression that fingerprinting is "solved" in the sense that—with the identification of the f vs. θ saddlepoints and the introduction of universal score functions—everything has been optimized to its theoretically achievable maximum. Though progress has been great, and the theoretically achievable bounds have been mostly charted, there are still some blank spots and loose ends.

The finite-c saddlepoint has not yet been studied for $q \geq 3$, and for $q = 2$, the results are only numerical. Furthermore, the maxmin game that has been studied pertains to the quantity $I(Y_i; \mathbf{M}_i|\mathbf{P}_i)$, while at finite n the mutual information $I(Y_i; \mathbf{M}_i|X_{-i})$ is the quantity of interest.

On the decoder side, various improvements are possible. To get an efficient procedure for setting thresholds, it is necessary to have a good theoretical understanding of the probability distribution of the scores; the tail of the innocent-user distribution is of special interest, because it determines the FP rate. The distribution of the universal scores has not been fully explored yet. Techniques like the CSE method [26] could be of help. Another research topic is to design (q-ary) practical decoders that come even closer to capacity.

ACKNOWLEDGMENTS

The author thanks Pierre Moulin and Yen-Wei Huang for providing the data for Figures 7.3, 7.4 and 7.5.

References

[1] Boneh, D., and J. Shaw, "Collusion-secure fingerprinting for digital data," *IEEE Transactions on Information Theory*, Vol. 44, No. 5, 1998, pp. 1897–1905.

[2] Škorić, B., et al., "Tardos fingerprinting codes in the Combined Digit Model," *IEEE Transactions on Information Forensics and Security*, Vol. 6, No. 3, 2011, pp. 906–919.

[3] Xie, F., T. Furon, and C. Fontaine, "On-off keying modulation and Tardos fingerprinting," in *Proc. 10th Workshop on Multimedia & Security (MM&Sec)*, ACM, 2008, pp. 101–106.

[4] Huang, Y.-W., and P. Moulin, "On the fingerprinting capacity games for arbitrary alphabets and their asymptotics," *IEEE Transactions on Information Forensics and Security*, Vol. 9, No. 9, 2014, pp. 1477–1499.

[5] Moulin, P., "Universal Fingerprinting: Capacity and Random-Coding Exponents," 2011. `http://arxiv.org/abs/0801.3837`.

[6] Simone, A., and B. Škorić, "Accusation probabilities in Tardos codes: beyond the Gaussian approximation," *Designs, Codes and Cryptography*, Vol. 63, No. 3, 2012, pp. 379–412.

[7] Blakley, G., C. Meadows, and G. Purdy, "Fingerprinting Long Forgiving Messages," in *Advances in Cryptology, CRYPTO '85*, Vol. 218 of *Lecture Notes in Computer Science*, Springer, 1985, pp. 180–189.

[8] Hollmann, H., et al., "On codes with the identifiable parent property," *Journal of Combinatorial Theory*, Vol. 82, 1998, pp. 472–479.

[9] Kilian, J., et al., "Resistance of Digital Watermarks to Collusive Attacks," in *IEEE International Symposium on Information Theory (ISIT)*, 1998, p. 271.

[10] Staddon, J., D. Stinson, and R. Wei, "Combinatorial properties of frameproof and traceability codes," *IEEE Transactions on Information Theory*, Vol. 47, No. 3, 2001, pp. 1042–1049.

[11] Peikert, C., A. Shelat, and A. Smith, "Lower bounds for collusion-secure fingerprinting," in *Proceedings of the 14th Annual ACM-SIAM Symposium on Discrete Algorithms (SODA)*, 2003, pp. 472–478.

[12] Tardos, G., "Optimal Probabilistic Fingerprint Codes," in *ACM Symposium on Theory of Computing (STOC)*, 2003, pp. 116–125.

[13] Tardos, G., "Optimal probabilistic fingerprint codes," *Journal of the ACM*, Vol. 55, No. 2, 2008, pp. 10:1–10:24.

[14] Huang, Y.-W., and P. Moulin, "Capacity-achieving fingerprint decoding," in *IEEE Workshop on Information Forensics and Security*, 2009, pp. 51–55.

[15] Nuida, K., "Short Collusion-Secure Fingerprint Codes against Three Pirates," in *Information Hiding*, Vol. 6387 of *Lecture Notes in Computer Science*, Springer, 2010, pp. 86–102.

[16] Nuida, K., et al., "An improvement of discrete Tardos fingerprinting codes," *Des. Codes Cryptography*, Vol. 52, No. 3, 2009, pp. 339–362.

[17] Amiri, E., and G. Tardos, "High rate fingerprinting codes and the fingerprinting capacity," in *ACM-SIAM Symposium on Discrete Algorithms (SODA)*, 2009, pp. 336–345.

[18] Charpentier, A., et al., "Expectation maximization decoding of Tardos probabilistic fingerprinting code," in *Media Forensics and Security*, Vol. 7254 of *SPIE Proceedings*, 2009, p. 72540.

[19] Meerwald, P., and T. Furon, "Towards joint Tardos decoding: the 'Don Quixote' algorithm," in *Information Hiding conference*, Vol. 6958 of *Lecture Notes in Computer Science*, 2011, pp. 28–42.

[20] Laarhoven, T., "Capacities and capacity-achieving decoders for various fingerprinting games," in *ACM Information Hiding and Multimedia Security Workshop (IH&MMSec)*, 2014, pp. 123–134.

[21] Škorić, B., "Tally-based simple decoders for traitor tracing and group testing," *IEEE Transactions on Information Forensics and Security*, Vol. 10, No. 6, 2015, pp. 1221–1233.

[22] Blayer, O., and T. Tassa, "Improved versions of Tardos' fingerprinting scheme," *Designs, Codes and Cryptography*, Vol. 48, No. 1, 2008, pp. 79–103.

[23] Furon, T., A. Guyader, and F. Cérou, "On the Design and Optimization of Tardos Probabilistic Fingerprinting Codes," in *Information Hiding*, Vol. 5284 of *Lecture Notes in Computer Science*, Springer, 2008, pp. 341–356.

[24] Furon, T., et al., "Estimating the minimal length of Tardos code," in *Information Hiding*, Vol. 5806 of *Lecture Notes in Computer Science*, 2009, pp. 176–190.

[25] Laarhoven, T., and B. de Weger, "Optimal symmetric Tardos traitor tracing schemes," *Des. Codes Cryptography*, Vol. 71, No. 1, 2014, pp. 83–103.

[26] Simone, A., *Error probabilities in Tardos codes*, Ph.D. thesis, Eindhoven University of Technology, June 2014.

[27] Škorić, B., et al., "Tardos fingerprinting is better than we thought," *IEEE Transactions on Information Theory*, Vol. 54, No. 8, 2008, pp. 3663–3676.

[28] Charpentier, A., et al., "An asymmetric fingerprinting scheme based on Tardos codes," in *Information Hiding*, Vol. 6958 of *Lecture Notes in Computer Science*, Springer, 2011, pp. 43–58.

[29] Škorić, B., S. Katzenbeisser, and M. Celik, "Symmetric Tardos fingerprinting codes for arbitrary alphabet sizes," *Designs, Codes and Cryptography*, Vol. 46, No. 2, 2008, pp. 137–166.

[30] Laarhoven, T., et al., "Dynamic Tardos traitor tracing schemes," *IEEE Transactions on Information Theory*, Vol. 59, No. 7, 2013, pp. 4230–4242.

[31] Škorić, B., and J.-J. Oosterwijk, "Binary and q-ary Tardos codes, revisited," *Designs, Codes, and Cryptography*, Vol. 74, No. 1, 2015, pp. 75–111.

[32] Škorić, B., J.-J. Oosterwijk, and J. Doumen, "The holey grail: A special score function for non-binary traitor tracing," in *Workshop on Information Forensics and Security (WIFS)*, IEEE, 2013, pp. 180–185.

[33] Oosterwijk, J.-J., B. Škorić, and J. Doumen, "Optimal suspicion functions for Tardos traitor tracing schemes," in *ACM Workshop on Information Hiding and Multimedia Security*, 2013, pp. 19–28.

[34] Simone, A., and B. Škorić, "False Positive probabilities in q-ary Tardos codes: comparison of attacks," *Designs, Codes and Cryptography*, Vol. 75, No. 3, Feb 2015, pp. 519–542.

[35] Simone, A., and B. Škorić, "False Negative probabilities in Tardos codes," *Designs, Codes, and Cryptography*, Vol. 74, No. 1, 2015, pp. 159–182.

[36] Shannon, C., "A mathematical theory of communication," *Bell Sys. Tech. Journal*, Vol. 27, 1948, pp. 379–423,623–656.

[37] Cover, T., and J. Thomas, *Elements of information theory, 2nd edition*, Wiley, 2006.

[38] Sion, M., "On general minimax theorems," *Pacific Journal of Mathematics*, Vol. 8, No. 1, 1958, pp. 171–176.

[39] Huang, Y.-W., and P. Moulin, "On the Saddle-Point Solution and the Large-Coalition Asymptotics of Fingerprinting Games," *IEEE Transactions on Information Forensics and Security*, Vol. 7, No. 1, 2012, pp. 160–175.

[40] Huang, Y.-W., and P. Moulin, "Saddle-point Solution of the Fingerprinting Capacity Game Under the Marking Assumption," in *IEEE International Symposium on Information Theory (ISIT)*, 2009, pp. 2256–2260.

[41] Huang, Y.-W., and P. Moulin, "Maximin Optimality of the Arcsine Fingerprinting Distribution and the Interleaving Attack for Large Coalitions," in *IEEE Workshop on Information Forensics and Security (WIFS)*, 2010, pp. 1–6.

[42] Boesten, D., and B. Škorić, "Asymptotic fingerprinting capacity for non-binary alphabets," in *Information Hiding*, Vol. 6958 of *Lecture Notes in Computer Science*, Springer, 2011, pp. 1–13.

[43] Somekh-Baruch, A., and N. Merhav, "Achievable error exponents for the private fingerprinting game," *IEEE Transactions on Information Theory*, Vol. 53, No. 5, 2007, pp. 1827–1838.

[44] Furon, T., and L. Pérez-Freire, "Worst case attacks against binary probabilistic traitor tracing codes," in *IEEE Workshop on Information Forensics and Security (WIFS)*, 2009, pp. 46–50.

[45] Boesten, D., and B. Škorić, "Asymptotic fingerprinting capacity in the Combined Digit Model," in *Information Hiding*, Vol. 7692 of *Lecture Notes in Computer Science*, Springer, 2012, pp. 255–268.

[46] Neyman, J., and E. Pearson, "On the Problem of the Most Efficient Tests of Statistical Hypotheses," *Philosophical Transactions of the Royal Society A: Mathematical, Physical and Engineering Sciences*, Vol. 231, 1933, pp. 694–706.

[47] Abbe, E., and L. Zheng, "Linear universal decoding for compound channels," *IEEE Transactions on Information Theory*, Vol. 56, No. 12, 2010, pp. 5999–6013.

[48] Meerwald, P., and T. Furon, "Towards practical joint decoding of binary Tardos fingerprinting codes," *IEEE Transactions on Information Forensics and Security*, Vol. 7, No. 4, 2012, pp. 1168–1180.

[49] Kuribayashi, M., "A new soft decision tracing algorithm for binary fingerprinting codes," in *Advances in Information and Computer Security - 6th International Workshop, IWSEC*, Vol. 7038 of *Lecture Notes in Computer Science*, Springer, 2011, pp. 1–15.

[50] Anthapadmanabhan, N., A. Barg, and I. Dumer, "On the fingerprinting capacity under the marking assumption," *IEEE Transactions on Information Theory*, Vol. 54, No. 6, 2008, pp. 2678–2689.

[51] Furon, T., and M. Desoubeaux, "Tardos codes for real," in *IEEE Workshop on Information Forensics and Security (WIFS)*, 2014, pp. 24–29.

[52] Oosterwijk, J., J. Doumen, and T. Laarhoven, "Tuple decoders for traitor tracing schemes," in *Media Watermarking, Security and Forensics*, Vol. 9028 of *Proc. of SPIE*, 2014, p. 90280C.

[53] Fiat, A., and T. Tassa, "Dynamic Traitor Tracing," *J. Cryptology*, Vol. 14, No. 3, 2001, pp. 211–223.

[54] Berkman, O., M. Parnas, and J. Sgall, "Efficient dynamic traitor tracing," in *Symposium on Discrete Algorithms*, ACM/SIAM, 2000, pp. 586–595.

[55] Laarhoven, T., J. Oosterwijk, and J. Doumen, "Dynamic traitor tracing for arbitrary alphabets: Divide and conquer," in *IEEE Workshop on Information Forensics and Security (WIFS)*, 2012, pp. 240–245.

[56] Pfitzmann, B., and M. Schunter, "Asymmetric fingerprinting," in *Advances in Cryptology, EURO-CRYPT '96*, Vol. 1070 of *Lecture Notes in Computer Science*, 1996, pp. 84–95.

[57] Pfitzmann, B., and M. Waidner, "Asymmetric Fingerprinting for Larger Collusions," in *ACM Conference on Computer and Communications Security*, 1997, pp. 151–160.

[58] Bianchi, T., and A. Piva, "TTP-Free asymmetric fingerprinting based on client side embedding," *IEEE Transactions on Information Forensics and Security*, Vol. 9, No. 10, 2014, pp. 1557–1568.

[59] Fernandez, M., and M. Soriano, "Identification of traitors in algebraic-geometric traceability codes," *IEEE Transactions on Signal Processing*, Vol. 52, No. 10, 2004, pp. 3073–3077.

[60] Tomàs-Buliart, J., et al., "Use of turbo codes with low-rate convolutional constituent codes in fingerprinting scenarios," in *IEEE Workshop on Information Forensics and Security (WIFS)*, 2011, pp. 1–6.

[61] Meerwald, P., and T. Furon, "Group testing meets traitor tracing," in *International Conference on Acoustics, Speech, and Signal Processing (ICASSP)*, IEEE, 2011, pp. 4204–4207.

[62] Laarhoven, T., "Efficient probabilistic group testing based on traitor tracing," in *Allerton Conference on Communication, Control, and Computing*, IEEE, 2013, pp. 1458–1465.

[63] Bun, M., J. Ullman, and S. Vadhan, "Fingerprinting codes and the price of approximate differential privacy," in *Symposium on Theory of Computing (STOC)*, ACM, 2014, pp. 1–10.

[64] Steinke, T., and J. Ullman, "Interactive fingerprinting codes and the hardness of preventing false discovery," 2015. http://arxiv.org/abs/1410.1228.

Chapter 8

Fragile and Authentication Watermarks

Martin Steinebach, Huajian Liu

The goal of data authentication is to verify the integrity of the multimedia content. To achieve this, one could use a cryptographic signature. However, media data is often subject to manipulations not changing its content but its binary representation. These manipulations will render the content unauthentic. In contrast to cryptographic solutions, we aim at authentication methods that are robust against content-preserving operations on the media.

Lossy compression algorithms, filter operations, and format changes are common examples for content-preserving operations. Nevertheless, authentication solutions should uncover content-changing manipulations, such as the removal of a relevant object or the insertion of an object from another work.

An important problem here is deciding if a change is content-preserving or content-changing. To detect the changes and to decide if a change of content has occurred, we can use features describing the content of the media. In image or video data, the position of edges—as well as color or lightness histograms—are examples of common features. Typical audio features are spectral distribution or loudness. There is no absolute borderline between content-preserving modifications and content-changing manipulations. Whether a manipulation belongs to one group depends on the application and the related requirements. For example, lossy compression surely is acceptable for a photo posted to a social network, but will be unacceptable for a medical picture.

In general, four concepts are known for data authentication. Figure 8.1 shows a simplified overview of these concepts. They differ with respect of complexity, as well as the nature of changes to the cover they can detect:

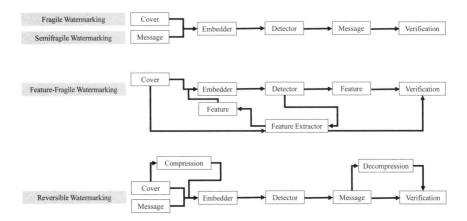

Figure 8.1   Typical concepts of the different authentication watermarking approaches.

- *Fragile Watermarking:* A watermark is embedded into the cover signal, which is not robust against manipulations and will therefore be destroyed when this occurs. Detecting the watermark verifies the integrity of the cover.

- *Reversible Watermarks:* This is a special kind of the fragile watermark. If the authenticity of the data can be verified, then the embedded watermark can be retrieved, inverted, and the original document can be reproduced.

- *Semifragile Watermarking:* Similar to fragile watermarking, the watermark is embedded and retrieved as a proof of integrity. The watermark is desired to be robust against allowed manipulations (e.g., lossy compression). Even if these manipulations occur, the watermark is still detectable.

- *Feature-Fragile Watermarking:* Here a robust watermark is used to embed a description of the covers content. This description is fragile against content-changing manipulations. A proof of integrity is achieved by comparing the embedded feature information with the cover actual features.

Fragile and invertible watermarking are almost as sensitive to changes of the cover as cryptographic hash functions. Semi- and feature-fragile watermarking are usually significantly more resistant against cover manipulations.

There is also a fifth concept mentioned in the literature: zero watermarking for authentication [1]. As this approach is more similar to robust hash extraction than to watermark embedding, we do not consider it in this chapter.

The organization of this chapter is as follows: first, we discuss common challenges for watermarking-based authentication with a focus on the different types of manipulation. Then, we provide a general overview of the concepts utilized here. Afterwards, we introduce the different approaches listed above and give examples of algorithms existing in literature. Finally, we briefly address (possible) applications of watermarking-based authentication.

8.1   COMMON CHALLENGES

The goal of authentication watermarking is to verify the integrity of a multimedia content while withstanding content-preserving cover changes. Furthermore, some schemes also allow one to estimate the impact of a change or localize cover modifications. One mutual challenge for authentication watermarking, therefore, is to distinguish between changes of the cover without a significant impact on its semantics and object changes executed for modifying perceived content. A visual example for these concepts is given in Figure 8.2, illustrating the difference between object removal and JPEG compression. In the following sections, we therefore discuss these two types of changes. It needs to be noted that not all authentication watermarks are robust against cover changes and fragile against object changes. It is rather a simplified ideal that helps to stress the challenges authentication watermarking often faces: to distinguish between content-preserving and content-changing operations. It is also worth mentioning that certain manifestations of both cover and object changes can be seen as part of the opposite set of operations; individual color correction of an object may not lead to a change of the perceived content, while very strong compression will remove much of the meaning of a cover.

8.1.1   Cover Changes

Lossy compression is the most common example of an operation that modifies the whole cover. Today it is applied to all media types. Most images (JPEG), videos (MPEG2, mp4), and audio (mp3, AAC) are all distributed in a format which reduces the required file size by dropping information of small relevance for human perception.

From the perspective of an authentication system, this can be seen as a continuous distortion of the signal. Often, the distortion is of similar strength for the whole signal or cover, but some formats allow a variable amount of compression controlled by human perception models. The usage of a lossy compression format

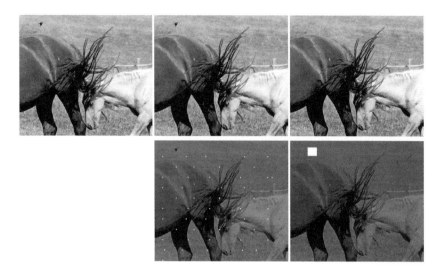

Figure 8.2   Example of cover and object changes. Top row, left to right: Original cover, JPEG converted cover, bird removed on the upper left. Bottom row: Ideal delta to be reported by authentication watermarking detector. JPEG causes small changes over the whole cover, object removal one strong change at the position of the removed bird.

is the main reason why cryptographic hash methods cannot be used for robust identification of digital media data: the presence of small changes over the whole file after re-compression disables the recognition even of small parts of the media.

There are many other operations that are of similar nature, but may have a different impact on the cover. For images, rotation, scaling, and global color corrections are typical examples. For audio, limited pitch shifting and time stretching, normalization, or equalization are common. All these operations potentially influence pixels or samples all over the cover. Therefore, they require resampling, which is further discussed by Popescu et al. in [2]. In most watermarking applications, they are typical challenges for robustness. In authentication watermarking, they also require the decision about the influence of the operation on the content. As stated above, they usually can be seen as content-preserving.

8.1.2   Object Changes

In contrast to cover changes, object changes focus on one limited area or section of the cover. The removal or replacement of objects is the usual goal of these operations. Well-known examples are the removal of persons from group photos, but also the pasting of fake UFOs on landscape photographies falls under this category. In audio, the removal of short segments of sound (e.g., a single word), is a common example. But also local pitch shifting and filtering for a single syllable can be content-changing; for example, the spoken word 'woman' can be changed to sound like 'women' by modifying the 'o' to an 'e'.

While object modifications cause strong changes in one limited area, the rest of the cover is theoretically unaffected. In practice, such a manipulation often requires decompression of the cover into a raw format and lossy compression as discussed above after the changes have been made. This can be challenging for localizing the actual area of the change, as lossy compression can have a masking effect. This stresses the need to distinguish between both types; an ideal authentication watermark would be able to identify the object change and would not be distracted by the cover change. Figure 8.2 illustrates the concept: a JPEG compression as an example of a cover change only creates a noise-like pattern over the whole cover at the watermark detector, while object removal (a bird, in this case) leads to a concentrated area that is easily identified. At least any information in this area of the image should not be trusted.

8.2 AUTHENTICATION WATERMARKS

Authentication watermarks embed a reference signal into the document. The embedded signal is modified during any tampering operations in the same way as the content itself or it disappears entirely. Thus, estimation of the embedded watermark may provide information on the type of distortion a document underwent. An attacker model is used to distinguish incidental distortions from deliberate attacks.

Figure 8.3 illustrates the framework of a watermarking system for document authentication. A reference watermark, which can be a random sequence, a visual binary logo, or certain features derived from the document, is embedded into the original document (also known as the cover or host data) in an imperceptible way.

At the receiver side, the detector can be fine-tuned as to how much distortion should be tolerated. The extracted watermark is compared to the reference watermark in order to verify the integrity of the received document. If any mismatch occurs or no watermark is detectable at all, the document is considered manipulated.

Like the usage of secret key in steganography in Section 1.4.2, to ensure the security of the watermarking system, a secret key is used to control the reference watermark generation, the watermark embedding, and the detection processes.

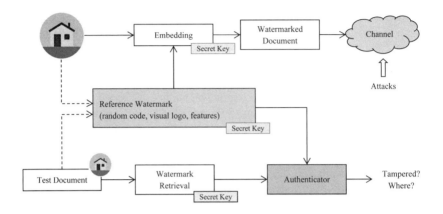

Figure 8.3   General framework of watermarking for document authentication

Thus, the unknown secret key prevents an attacker from changing the embedded watermark or forging a document with a valid reference watermark embedded.

All watermarking-based data authentication algorithms share the following characteristics. First, the watermarking algorithm has to be blind. This is an obvious requirement: if an original is needed to detect an authentication watermark, a direct comparison between the copy and the original can be performed. Second, the embedding procedure needs to be content-preserving. Not only should an authentication watermark be perceptually transparent, but the embedding must not cause a nonreversible quality degradation that could be seen as content-changing. This requirement depends on the application domain. The more important small details of the cover are, the fewer nonreversible changes to it are allowed.

Most authentication watermarks share the following properties:

8.2.1   Tampering Detection

The primary objective of authentication watermarks is to verify the integrity of the data; therefore, the capability of detecting possible tampering is of essential importance. The embedded watermark must be fragile or sensitive to deliberate manipulations of the content. Every kind of authentication watermark may have different levels of tolerance on content alteration, and can subsequently provide different types of authentication. Fragile watermarks have zero tolerance to any change of signal sample value, which therefore provides exact/hard authentication. On the contrary, semifragile watermarks allow moderate signal processing and content-preserving manipulations, providing selective/soft authentication accordingly.

8.2.2 Tampering Localization

Another common characteristic that is also one of the big advantages compared to hash-based authentication is the possibility of localizing tampering. A watermark detector will not only signal that a change to the cover did occur, but will also show where in the cover the change took place. Often it can also indicate how strong the change was (e.g., by giving the area of potentially modified pixels in an image). For multimedia document authentication, the capability of localizing manipulations is a particularly desirable feature in most applications. Knowledge of the tampered regions of a document allows accepting the other untampered parts. Furthermore, knowledge of the exact position where a manipulation occurred helps to infer the motives of an adversary. For example, authentication watermarks providing pixel-wise localization are able to describe the exact contour of the tampered areas or objects.

8.2.3 Tampering Recovery

The possibility of recovering the original content from the tampered version is another big advantage and unique feature provided by some watermarking solutions. When it is enabled by the authentication watermark algorithms, not only can the position of the manipulations be localized by verifying the embedded watermark, the modified content can also be recovered by the information carried by the extracted watermark. Like tampering localization, tampering recovery is also a desirable feature in applications of multimedia authentication. It helps to estimate the extent of the modifications and reveals how the original content looked. However, this feature usually demands high embedding payload, which will inevitably compromise other properties, such as the watermark transparency, and the robustness against incidental signal processing.

8.2.4 Security

Watermark security refers to the ability to resist intentional or hostile attacks. Unlike the attacks to robust watermarks, for authentication watermarks, the goal of the attacks is not to make the watermark undetectable, but to compromise the authentication (i.e., to disguise a modified cover as authentic). To ensure the security of the whole watermarking system, authentication watermarks are usually protected by one or multiple secret keys. The secret key is commonly used to control the generation of the watermark and the embedding process, for example, by randomly selecting positions or components where the watermarks are actually embedded. The secret key is an indispensable input to performing successful watermark detection and authentication. Without the knowledge of the proper secret key, it should be difficult for an adversary to forge or remove an authentication watermark in a document, or copy a valid authentication watermark from one document to another, even if the watermarking algorithm is publicly known. Any attempts to forge or remove a watermark should destroy the data's authenticity.

8.3 FRAGILE WATERMARKS

Fragility is the most representative characteristic of fragile watermarks, which makes them unique and different from other types of watermarks. In contrast to robust watermarks, a fragile watermark is embedded in such a way that the alteration of the cover data will also destroy the underlying watermark. This characteristic makes it suitable for authentication applications.

Fragile watermarks have minimal tolerance to data manipulations. Even one single bit alteration will impair the embedded watermark and render the document inauthentic. From the sensitivity point of view, it resembles a digital signature, except that it does not need separate storage. Nevertheless, in addition to basic integrity verification, fragile watermarks can provide more authentication functions than digital signatures, such as tampering localization and content recovery.

8.3.1 Fragility

Fragility is an essential property of fragile watermarks, which enables authenticating the document by verifying the integrity of the embedded watermark. A fragile watermark should stay complete only when the document remains intact. The probability that a watermark can survive any change of the document should be kept as low as possible.

The fragility of a fragile watermark relies on two aspects. One is the fragility of the embedded watermark; the other is the fragility of the generated reference watermark itself. In a typical fragile watermark scheme, the former is ensured by the embedding location and the embedding mechanism, and the latter is achieved by the construction of the reference watermark.

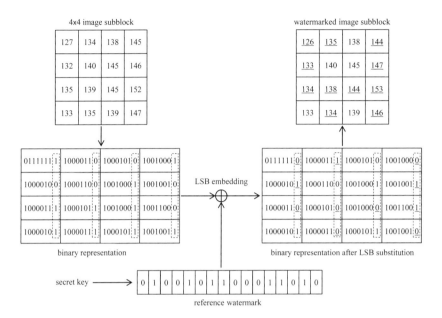

Figure 8.4 An example of LSB fragile watermark.

Since they should be altered along with even slight document changing, fragile watermarks are usually embedded into the parts which are sensible to document alteration. For example, in image watermarking, a typical fragile watermark algorithm modifies the least significant bit (LSB) of pixels to embed the desired reference watermark [3–6]. Figure 8.4 illustrates the basic idea of a typical LSB watermark. The key-dependent reference watermark is embedded into the image block by directly substituting the least significant bits of pixels with the bits of the watermark. At the receiver side, the least significant bits of pixels are extracted to compare with the regenerated watermark. Any mismatch reveals that the corresponding pixels were manipulated. Although an LSB watermark is simple and has many limitations, embedding an LSB watermark into a document is very efficient and therefore it can meet the requirements of some real-time applications.

However, the most sensible parts of a document often correspond to the parts of least significance, like the LSB in an image. Modifying those parts will not bring notable effect on the perceptual quality of the document. On the one hand, this property ensures the imperceptibility of the embedded watermark. On the other hand, it also makes it possible for an attacker to forge a perceptually different document by arbitrarily modifying the most significant parts while keeping the least significant parts intact. In this case, solely verifying the integrity of the extracted watermark is insufficient to authentication.

To invalidate a copied watermark, the significant parts of a document must be involved in the generation of the reference watermark. Therefore, the reference watermark in Figure 8.4 should be defined as content-dependent; for example,

$$w = g\left(I - I_{lsb}, k\right) \tag{8.1}$$

where I is the cover image, I_{lsb} is the part of least significant bits and k is the secret key. In many fragile watermark schemes, cryptographic techniques are used in the watermark generation. For example, the scheme proposed in [3, 7] calculates the cryptographic hash of the pixel values (except the LSB) in every nonoverlapping block. The XOR result of the hash value and the watermark message is then encrypted using a private key. Finally, the encrypted XOR result is embedded as the final reference watermark into the LSB plane of the block. The hashing and encryption process in the watermark generation ensures that the verification will fail if any bit of the pixels gets changed.

8.3.2   Localization

To enable the localization of manipulations, the embedded watermark components should be independent of each other. Failing to verify one watermark component shall have no effect on the extraction and verification of other parts of the watermark.

Most of fragile watermarks are embedded directly in the original signal domain (i.e., spatial domain for image, time domain for audio) where each watermark component is independently embedded in a local way. This establishes a direct positional connection between the watermark and the cover data. The position where the watermark verification fails will correspond to the location of manipulation. Hence, most of fragile watermarks are able to localize the detected tampering.

The resolution of tampering localization depends on the nature of the embedding algorithm, which is determined by the size of the used embedding unit. An embedding unit is referred to a set of signal samples in which one watermark component is embedded. The minimal embedding unit is one single sample, which corresponds to a pixel in an image. When the watermark is embedded in a pixel-based way into an image, like the simple LSB watermark in Figure 8.4, pixel-wise localization accuracy can be achieved. In pixel-based embedding, each pixel is individually watermarked, carrying one watermark symbol (usually one bit), respectively. The extraction of one watermark symbol solely depends on the value of its host pixel:

$$w_i = f_{ext}(p_i) \tag{8.2}$$

where f_{ext} is the extraction function, w_i is the ith watermark bit, and p_i is the corresponding pixel in which w_i is embedded. If the extracted w_i matches the expected bit, p_i is deemed as authentic; otherwise, it is altered. For example, in the Yeung-Mintzer scheme [4] $f_{extract}$ is defined as the output of a set of binary look-up tables, $f_{extract}(p_{i,j}) = LUT(p_{i,j})$. The output of every pixel is forced to match the corresponding bit of a watermark logo by modifying the pixel value. In the verification process, the extracted watermark image is visually examined and the detected artifacts reveal the corresponding positions of image alteration.

For the sake of good fragility and high security, many fragile watermarks use multiple signal samples as an embedding unit where more watermark bits can be embedded. For images, the embedding is often performed in a block-based way [3, 8]. As illustrated in Figure 8.5, each image block is considered as an embedding unit where a watermark message—which is highly dependent of the block content—is embedded. The extraction function becomes:

$$w_i = f_{ext}(b_i), b_i = \{p_1, p_2, ..., p_n\} \tag{8.3}$$

where b_i is the ith image block consisting of a set of pixels. When the verification of the watermark message of a block fails, it is usually not possible to further localize the modified positions inside the block, yet the whole block will be deemed as manipulated. Because the watermark messages between different blocks are independent of each other, each block can be verified separately. Thus, the maximal resolution of tampering localization is bounded to the block size used for watermark embedding. Smaller block sizes usually result in better localization resolution, but will increase the embedding payload accordingly.

Besides fragile watermarks in spatial or time domain, some fragile watermarks are carried out in transform domains, like discrete cosine transform (DCT) [9] or discrete wavelet transform (DWT) domain [10]. The advantages of using the transform domains mainly lie in the following aspects. One of them is that the watermarking system becomes compatible with the popular image compression standards (e.g., JPEG). The embedding can be integrated into the compression process or completed directly in the compressed representation of the data. Another advantage is that the perceptual distortion caused by the watermark can be better controlled in

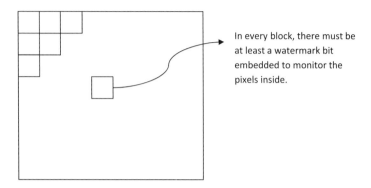

Figure 8.5   Illustration of the block-based watermarking for document authentication.

the frequency domain than in the spatial domain. Therefore, the watermarked image quality could be improved. In addition, since the frequency components are taken into account in the watermarking process, it becomes possible for tamper detection to be localized in both spatial and frequency regions. Nevertheless, because the watermark is embedded in the frequency domain instead of by directly modifying the samples, some slight sample modification may not be detected. Moreover, the tamper localization accuracy is also bounded by the size of the unit used to calculate the frequency components, such as the block size used in the block-based DCT schemes. Subsequently, the sensitivity and accuracy of tamper detection are both decreased. Therefore, the transform domain methods are more often used in the design of the semifragile watermarking schemes, as described in Section 8.4.

8.3.3 Recovery

Recovery capability is a more challenging feature than localization, usually demanding high watermark payload. In order to restore the tampered fragment, an additional *reconstruction reference* that describes the original content needs to be embedded into the host data itself as a part of the watermark payload, which is therefore referred to as *self-embedding* [11]. Thus, the watermark payload consists of two parts: (i) authentication information, and (ii) reconstruction reference information.

Self-embedding schemes have three key factors that determine the performance:

- The embedding payload and the watermarked image quality;

- The maximal allowed tampering rate, corresponding to the maximal tampered region that can be restored;

- The reconstruction fidelity.

Ideally, the total embedding payload should stay as low as possible. A higher payload usually leads to more quality degradation on the cover data. The maximal allowed tampering rate and the reconstruction fidelity should be kept as high as possible, which measures the recovery capability. However, these factors are mutually competitive with each other. Large-area and high-quality recovery will require more embedded reference information.

The reference information used for reconstruction is commonly a quality-reduced version of the original data. In case of images, it can be a low-resolution or downscaled version, a halftone version, or a vector quantization version of the original image [12]. A straightforward approach to achieving the recovery capability is to embed the reference information for one part of the image into another part. If the host image is divided into N blocks, $b_1, b_2, ..., b_N$, the reconstruction reference is generated as follows.

$$r = r_1, r_2, ..., r_N = g(b_1), g(b_2), ..., g(b_N) \qquad (8.4)$$

where $g(.)$ is a reference generation function. The reference information r_i for b_i is embedded into b_j. The block pair (b_i, b_j) is often chosen pseudo-randomly. If b_i is tampered, the embedded r_i in b_j can be used to recover it. This approach is widely used in many watermark schemes, although it does not fulfill the above-mentioned three key factors well because of the following two problems.

First, the recovery success of one block highly depends on the integrity of the block carrying its reference information (i.e., the recovery of b_i is possible only when b_j still remains authentic). In other words, if both b_i and b_j are tampered with, the recovery of b_i will fail. This problem is referred to as the *reconstruction dependency* or the *tampering/missing coincidence* [12, 13], which limits the allowed tampering rate. The second problem is that the embedded reference information in b_j is useful only when b_i is tampered with. In case b_i is authentic, the embedded reference information in b_j becomes useless because no recovery of b_i is necessary, and it does not contribute to the recovery of other tampered blocks, either. This problem is referred to as the *reference waste* or the *watermark-data waste*, which implies that the embedding scheme does not make full use of the available watermark payload.

Some schemes try to alleviate the problem of reference dependency by embedding multiple copies of the reference information [14, 15]. If one copy is destroyed, the tampered blocks can still be restored by other available copies. This strategy, however, only partly solves the problem because the recovery success still depends on the probability that at least one copy survives the tampering. Moreover, it aggravates the problem of reference waste because the useless watermark payload is accordingly increased.

To deal with these two problems, the reference information can be pseudo-randomly permuted r and spread over the whole image instead of embedded in single local blocks [12, 16]. The random distribution of reference information eliminates the reconstruction dependency on the authenticity of local areas. In the recovery process, the reference information for tampered fragments can be collected from the authentic parts. Thus, all the content that remains authentic contributes to the recovery of tampering. The more authentic content remains, the more reference information can be extracted, and vice versa. In other words, the reconstruction quality deteriorates when the tampering rate increases. This feature is referred to as *flexible*, for it provides variable recovery quality.

As the generalization of the idea of distributing r over the whole cover data and making use of all available authentic content for recovery, the self-embedding problem can be modeled as a special erasure channel [13, 17], where the media content is deemed as the communication channel and the reference information is the message to transmit. Thanks to the authentication part in the watermark, the tampering localization information is available after content authentication. Thus, the reference information for tampered fragments is regarded as erased, while the one for the authentic blocks is regarded as successfully transmitted. With the help of the communication model, the trade-off between the above-mentioned three key factors can be quantitatively analyzed.

Erasure coding theory is applied to encode the reference information before embedding (e.g., fountain codes [18]), more specifically, systematic raptor code [19] is used in [17]. The generated reference information r is first rearranged into X, which consists of K symbols, $X_1, X_2, ..., X_K$. X is then encoded using erasure coding into Y containing N symbols, $Y_1, Y_2, ..., Y_N$. Finally, Y_i is embedded into b_i together with the corresponding authentication information of b_i. When b_i is tampered with, the embedded Y_i is regarded as erased. X can be successfully decoded, provided that sufficient symbols in Y are correctly transmitted. Let E denote the number of tampered blocks, the tampering rate is $p = \frac{E}{N}$. Given a code rate λ, the upper bound of maximal allowed tempering rate can be derived as follows:

$$p \le \frac{1}{\lambda + 1} \qquad (8.5)$$

where λ is the code rate, $\lambda = \frac{K}{N}$, which reflects the rate of the effective payload with respect to the available watermark capacity.

Nevertheless, the upper bound in Equation (8.5) can be achieved only when the symbols in r and X are perfectly aligned. In case that they are misaligned, the tampering in one block may invalidate more than one of the symbols in X, which will result in extra decoding demand for Y and subsequently lower the allowed temping rate. This constraint can be eliminated by encoding the reference information twice using erasure codes [17]. In the first coding stage, r is encoded into S using systematic raptor code. Then the *check symbols* in S is rearranged into T that consists of K symbols, $T_1, T_2, ..., T_K$. In the second coding stage, T is encoded into Y containing N symbols. The reconstruction process also consists of two stages. T is first restored from the correctly extracted symbols of Y. Then the tampered blocks are reconstructed by decoding $\hat{S}$, which consists of the regenerated symbols r_i from the authentic blocks and the restored check symbols from T. Figure 8.6 shows an example of tampering recovery using the algorithm in [17]. The original and watermarked images are shown in Figure 8.6(a) and (b), respectively. The embedded watermark is perceptually invisible. Figure 8.6(c) shows the tampered image. To demonstrate the recovery capability, 30% blocks are completely deleted. The recovered image is shown in Figure 8.6(d), in which all deleted blocks are successfully restored with an overall PSNR over 36dB.

8.3.4   Security

As mentioned in Section 8.3.2, in order to achieve the desired feature of localization, the reference watermark is often distributed in different parts of the cover data to monitor the change of every part (e.g., in a block-based way). Each part can be authenticated separately by the watermark embedded in it. Since the embedding is performed locally, it is possible to swap the embedding units inside the same document or across different authenticated documents without invalidating the authentication. Therefore, it is vulnerable to so-called *vector quantization* (VQ) attacks [8, 20, 21]. VQ attacks are also referred to as *collage attacks*, which forge an authentic document through a collage of authenticated blocks out of the same or different documents.

If an attacker has access to a database of documents authenticated with the same key, it is possible to make an arbitrary document authentic. The document

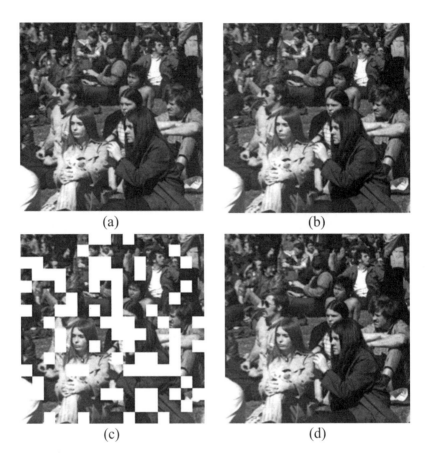

(a)   (b)

(c)   (d)

Figure 8.6 Example of tampering recovery: (a) original image (b) watermarked image (c) tampered image, p=0.3 (d) recovered image, PSNR=36.1dB.

can be first divided into blocks corresponding to embedding units. For each block, a search is performed through all blocks in the database. The original block is replaced with the perceptually closest match. Theoretically, a VQ attack can be mounted on any authentication watermark, provided that the authentication of each embedding unit is independently performed without context. This is not only applicable to watermarking in signal domain, but also to the schemes in transform domain, like DCT- or DWT-based watermarks. It becomes even easier to mount a VQ attack when the watermarking algorithm is known to the adversary.

Possible solutions counteracting VQ attacks include using a larger block, using overlapping blocks [22], introducing neighborhood dependency [5], embedding in hierarchical blocks [6], and binding each block with document index and its position or index [7, 8]. Using a larger block as an embedding unit will alleviate the problem, but it will also worsen the localization accuracy thereby. Using overlapping blocks expands the content dependency of the watermark to the neighborhood around the local area where the watermark is embedded. Swapping an authenticated unit becomes impossible without changing its surrounding samples. Using hierarchical blocks embeds multiple watermarks into blocks of various sizes at different levels of the document. The watermarks in the small blocks at the lowest level provide localization accuracy, while the ones in the large blocks at higher levels enable resistance to local attacks. Another solution is to combine the content-dependent hash value with a unique document-dependent ID, block index, or position and other document information in the construction of the watermark. Thus, each authenticated block carries its unique watermark and can be only be authenticated in its original context.

Essentially, all of these methods try to establish a connection between different blocks and between the local area and the whole document, which can be generalized by modifying the watermark generation function in Equation (8.1) as

$$w = g(b_i, D_{b_i}, D_I, k) \qquad (8.6)$$

where D_{b_i} is the block relevant data, like the block position, and D_I is the data relevant to the document (e.g., the document index, dimension, etc.). Hash functions are often used in the watermark generation. If an authenticated block is swapped, the underlying watermark becomes invalid due to the inconsistency with the new context, subsequently invalidating the authentication. These solutions, however, will all cause a significant loss of localization accuracy due to larger or overlapping blocks.

Basically, the vulnerability to local attacks is mainly attributed to the local embedding way that lacks mutual reference between blocks. Hence, pseudo-randomly spreading the watermark over the whole document can thwart such attacks [23]. Before dividing the document into blocks, all samples in the document are first pseudo-randomly permuted. Each block consists of samples or frequency coefficients coming from random positions in the original document instead of from a local area. In each block, one watermark is embedded. Thus, dependency between these samples in one block is established by the embedded watermark. Alteration of any samples in one block will destroy the watermark embedded in that block, subsequently the authentication of that block will fail. Without knowledge of the secret key used for the permutation, it is very hard for the adversary to reveal the construction of the used blocks, and therefore, swapping or replacing similar blocks can not be performed. Even if the algorithm is publicly known, an adversary cannot modify the embedded data without knowing the secret key. The high security against local attacks is achieved at the cost of extra effort in localization, which will be discussed in Section 8.4.2.

8.4 SEMIFRAGILE WATERMARKS

Due to their extreme fragility, fragile watermarks are easily corrupted by any signal processing procedure failing to distinguish incidental distortions from intentional manipulations. For example, lossy compression is widely used in multimedia applications, and necessary post-processing after watermarking is often an inevitable step. Slight—even imperceptible—distortions caused by lossy compression or post-processing will impair the embedded fragile watermarks and subsequently render the document inauthentic, although they do not change the content semantics. Hence, the pervasive usage of lossy compression limits the practicability of fragile watermarks.

It is highly desired that the authenticator can distinguish incidental and intentional manipulations. To fulfill this requirement, semifragile watermarking techniques have been proposed. In contrast to the exact/hard authentication by fragile watermarks, semifragile watermarks provide selective/soft authentication. Semifragile watermarks monitor the document content instead of its digital representation. They allow slight or moderate modifications caused by common signal processing, like mild lossy compression, filtering, and enhancement, but will detect the content-changing manipulations, like object addition, deletion, and replacement. The extent of robustness of a semifragile watermark against incidental distortions is usually customizable according to the application requirements. Because they are robust to content-preserving processing, yet fragile to content-changing manipulations, many semifragile watermarks are also referred to as "content-fragile" watermarks in the literature.

8.4.1 Fragility and Robustness

The unique characteristic of a semifragile watermark is that it balances the two contradictory properties: fragility and robustness. Fragility is required to detect intentional manipulations, while the robustness is needed to survive incidental distortions. Before a trade-off between the fragility and robustness can be found, a clear definition of intentional and incidental distortions must be given:

1. Incidental distortions refer to the changes or noise introduced by lossy compression, like MP3, JPEG, MPEG, and common signal processing (which includes filtering, enhancement, contrast or brightness adjustment, etc.). Such distortions may change the digital representation of the document, and even become audibly or visually perceptible, but they should not change the underlying semantics of the document.

2. Intentional manipulations refer to changes which modify the semantic content of the document (which includes removing objects, adding additional objects, severe modifications, etc.). Such manipulations usually intend to modify the information that the document carries.

When an incidental distortion becomes severe enough, it will also be deemed as an intentional manipulation. For example with lossy compression, mild JPEG compression reduces the image storage size, but will not affect the image quality significantly. Severe JPEG compression with an extreme low quality factor will blur image details or even make them unrecognizable. Thus, modifications caused by mild JPEG compression are considered as incidental distortions, while severe compression will be deemed as intentional manipulation.

To achieve fragility and robustness at the same time, semifragile watermark combines the techniques of fragile watermarks and robust watermarks. The embedding techniques of robust watermarking (like spread spectrum method introduced in Section 5.3) are also used in semifragile watermarks [24, 25]. However, because a large amount of signal samples are necessary for good performance of the correlation detection, it is difficult for this embedding method to achieve a sufficient watermark payload in order to allow the tamper localization on a fine scale. Therefore, quantization index modulation (QIM), introduced in Section 5.4.2, is more widely used [26, 27]. The watermark information is embedded by quantizing the selected frequency coefficients or some particular feature values to some predetermined scales according to a look-up table or the simple odd-even mapping rule. By the QIM embedding, the embedding strength can be well-controlled by the used quantization step, so that the watermark robustness can be customized quantitatively.

8.4.2   Localization and Recovery

Semifragile watermarks can also localize tamperings. In order to achieve the capability of tampering localization, many semifragile watermarks also perform the embedding in a block-based way as fragile watermarks [9, 27–29]. As illustrated in Figure 8.5, the image is divided into blocks and the watermarks are embedded into every block respectively. The authentication of each block is done by verifying whether the watermark can be successfully extracted from the block. Hence, in the block-based methods, the maximal resolution of tampering detection is again bounded to the block size used for embedding. The often used block sizes vary from 64x64 pixels to 4x4 pixels [9, 24, 27, 28, 30].

Semifragile watermarks are usually embedded in transform domains (such as DCT and DWT) instead of the spatial domain in order to achieve moderate robustness and good imperceptibility. The spatial-frequency property of the wavelet transform also enables good tamper localization capability in the authentication process. Each wavelet coefficient corresponds to a certain locality in the spatial domain. From the localization point of view, local embedding in the wavelet domain is equivalent to a block-based embedding in the spatial domain. Note that the DCT transform does not have such a spatial-frequency property. Therefore, block-based DCT transform instead of a full DCT of the image is usually used in semifragile watermarks.

Moreover, because a block is the minimal unit that can contain at least one watermark bit, the localization resolution is proportional to the watermark payload. Using smaller block sizes can increase the detection resolution, which will subsequently lead to higher watermark payload. For example, when a small block size of 2x2 pixels is used to improve the localization accuracy [29], at least one watermark bit has to be embedded in each 2x2 block. Compared to 8x8 blocks, the total watermark payload is increased by 16 times. Thus, the improvement of localization accuracy is achieved at the cost of significantly increased watermark payload, which in turn causes more artifacts and degrades the image quality.

As high localization accuracy and high image quality are often both desired in practical applications, improving localization accuracy by using smaller block sizes is clearly suboptimal. Classical block-based schemes, where one block consists of a set of local samples, cannot eliminate the mutual constraint between these two competitive factors because the embedded watermark is bound to the local samples carrying it. To break the connection between localization accuracy and block size, it is necessary to embed the watermark into a set of samples coming from different areas, which amounts to spreading every embedded watermark over the entire document. As mentioned in Section 8.3.4, such nonlocal sets can be constructed by applying a pseudo-random permutation to scramble the samples or frequency coefficients before dividing them into embedding groups [23]. Each group corresponds to a block in the classical block-based schemes where one watermark will be embedded. Thus, the watermarks are distributed into samples or coefficients from random positions. Similar to the classical block-based schemes, the authenticity of the members in a group depends on the integrity of the embedded watermark. Manipulating any member of a group will destroy the underlying watermark; subsequently, the group and all members in it will be deemed as unauthenticated.

Suppose a local region l_i of the watermarked document is tampered, the watermarks in all the groups that contain samples from l_i will become undetectable and all samples in these groups will be deemed as unauthenticated. Besides the samples from l_i, these unauthenticated groups also contain samples from other positions, which are referred to *innocent samples*. Hence, when the unauthenticated samples are mapped back to their original positions, they will randomly spread over the whole document. In the tampered area l_i, however, the density of unauthenticated samples will be notably higher than other areas, while the innocent samples will be sparsely distributed. Therefore, localization of actually tampered areas can be identified by finding where the unauthenticated samples converge. Provided that the tampering rate is low, near sample-wise localization accuracy can be achieved.

Since the final tamper localization is based on the distribution of an unauthenticated sample, its accuracy depends on the discernibility of the detected unauthenticated samples in the tampered areas that are not directly related to the used group sizes. With a larger group size, the required watermark payload will be reduced, while the overall localization resolution will not change. Thus, compared to the classical block-based schemes, the same—or even higher—localization accuracy can be achieved with a much lower watermark payload. However, the allowed tampering rate will decrease when the group size increases. Larger group sizes will result in more innocent samples, which subsequently makes it difficult or even impossible to distinguish tampered areas from noise-like innocent samples. Hence, tampering localization is only possible when the tampering rate is below a certain threshold.

Because semifragile watermarks must balance robustness and fragility, the available payload becomes much lower than that in fragile watermarks. Due to the limited available payload, it is very hard to embed the necessary redundancy information for tampering recovery. Therefore, most semifragile watermarks do not have the capability to recover the tampered parts. Nevertheless, some semifragile watermarks do have the option to embed additional watermark bits for recovery [31, 32], which can reconstruct the corrupted blocks approximately. The embedding of additional recovery bits will, however, increase the payload and subsequently degrade the image quality. Compared to fragile watermarks, the achievable reconstruction quality is much lower, and the maximum allowed tampering rate is also very limited. Usually, only the tampering that affects a small area can be restored.

8.4.3   Compatibility

As mentioned in the previous section, semifragile watermarks are often embedded in transform domains like DCT and DWT. Since DCT and DWT are used in the popular image compression standards JPEG and JPEG2000, semifragile watermarks have good compatibility with these compression standards. Embedding techniques in DCT and DWT domains can be easily designed to be resistant to the distortions introduced by JPEG and JPEG2000 compression. The robustness (i.e., the tolerance of compression), can be exactly fine-tuned to a predetermined JPEG quality factor [27, 31]. Furthermore, the previous studies on human visual models in these domains can be directly reused in adaptively controlling the watermark embedding strength to improve watermark imperceptibility.

8.5   REVERSIBLE WATERMARKS

Embedding a watermark into a cover is usually a process that cannot be inverted. The changes made by the watermark cannot be undone by 'subtracting' the watermarking that has been 'added' to the content during embedding. This is at least true for most common watermarking methods, like patchwork watermarking, where the energy level of groups is raised or lowered to a specific threshold, but the original amount of energy is lost in the process or QIM where quantization also causes the loss of original pixel or sample values. Even LSB watermarking cannot be reversed in its basic form; replacing the least significant bits with message bits means the loss of the original LSB sequence. When an application features very high integrity requirements, this can be a significant argument against utilizing digital watermarks. This has been discussed in medical imaging and satellite observation, where tiny changes in the content could have dire consequences. In 1999 Marq and Dewey [33] state '*In the case of medical image, many actors may want to have access to a perfect copy of the original image.*' To counter this, reversible watermarking has been introduced. An early example for medical imaging was proposed by Coatrieux et al. in 2000 [34], stressing the need of acceptance by medical staff when utilizing watermarking. Reversible algorithms allow to revert to the state of the cover before embedding if no further changes have been made to it.

One common approach to achieve this is based on compression and insertion. First, a part of the cover is compressed in a lossless manner. Then, the original part so compressed is overwritten by its compressed version; the difference in memory requirement between the original content and the compressed one represents the space gained for watermark embedding. Now, an embedder writes watermarking information into the gained space. The watermark is usually very fragile and includes a hash of the original content.

At the retrieval stage, the watermark is detected and the message is retrieved. If the original state of the cover is needed, the compressed part is retrieved and decompressed. The decompressed part is written over the compressed part and the watermark message. The hash retrieved is compared to the recreated content. If both are equal, integrity is verified.

Friedrich et al. have introduced the first two invertible watermarking methods for digital image data in [35]. While virtually all previous authentication watermarking schemes introduced some small amount of noninvertible distortion in the data, the new methods are invertible in the sense that—if the data is deemed authentic—the distortion due to authentication can be completely removed to obtain the original data. Their first technique is based on lossless compression of biased bit-streams derived from the quantized JPEG coefficients. The second technique modifies the quantization matrix in order to enable the lossless embedding of one bit per DCT coefficient. Both techniques are fast and can be used for general distortion-free (invertible) data embedding. The two methods provide new information assurance tools for integrity protection of sensitive imagery, such as medical images or high-importance military images viewed under nonstandard conditions when usual criteria for visibility does not apply. Further improvements in [36] generalize the scheme for compressed image and video data.

Dittmann et al. [37] combine an invertible image watermarking scheme with a digital signature in order to provide a public verifiable integrity. Furthermore, the original data can only be reproduced with a secret key. The concept uses the general idea of selecting public key-dependent watermarking positions (here, for example, the blue channel bits) and compressing the original data at these positions lossless to produce space for invertible watermark data embedding. In the retrieval, the watermarking positions are selected again, the watermark is retrieved and the compressed part is decompressed and written back to recover the original data. The scheme is highly fragile and the original can only be reproduced if there is no change. The integrity of the whole data is ensured with two hash functions;

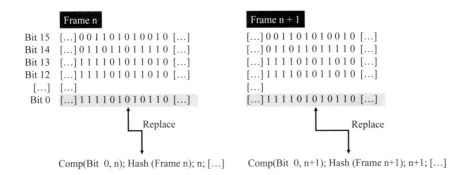

Figure 8.7   A simplified illustration of the reversible audio watermarking algorithm by Steinebach and Dittmann. The least significant bits of a frame n are compressed and together with a hash of frame n and the frame number form the watermark. This watermark then replaces the original least significant bit sequence of the frame. Padding is added if necessary.

the first is built over the remaining image, and the second over the marked data at the watermarking positions by using a message authentication code HMAC. The authenticity is ensured by the use of an RSA digital signature. The reproduction by authorized persons only is granted by the AES symmetric key scheme.

An extension of this concept is introduced in [38], where reversible audio watermarking is discussed. As audio data consists of a stream of samples over time, localization of content changes requires the addition of frames. Sections of the audio data with a fixed duration are defined as one frame. This frame is then watermarked similar to the image scheme. But in addition a frame counter is included into the watermarking message. Figure 8.7 shows a simplified version of the original approach. Thereby an attacker able to identify the individual frames cannot switch frames to modify the meaning of the audio content without being detected. As soon as the sequence of the embedded frame numbers is corrupted, integrity is lost.

Besides compression-based algorithms, various other approaches for reversible watermarking have been introduced by the literature. While the following examples are far from complete, they show that reversibility can be achieved by many different methods. In 2003, Tian [39] suggested to utilize difference expansion (DE) for reversible image watermarking. Here, pixel values are modified in such a way that a pair of pixels can reversibly hold one bit of a watermark message. The histogram bin exchange approach by Chrysochos et al. [40] swaps two image histogram values, A and B, selected pseudo-randomly with the help of a key. The watermarking bit values depend on the comparison of A and B: if A>B then a 0 is embedded, otherwise a 1. Thereby, by swapping A and B, the watermark can be embedded. The changes can be reverted with the help of a 'secret key' generated during the embedding of the message, basically storing the positions where swapping occurred. Hong et al. [41] also used histograms for reversible watermarking in their method based on prediction error expansion (PEE), but in this case, histograms of prediction errors of images are utilized instead of pixel value histograms. Coltuc and Chassery [42] use reversible contrast mapping (RCM) to achieve reversible watermarking. RCM allows the restoration of pixel pairs even if their LSB is lost. The suggested watermarking approach allows the storage of one message bit for each pixel pair.

8.6 APPLICATIONS

Given the multiple examples of image manipulations in the media, one could assume that authentication watermarking is a common application of digital watermarks. But the current situation is different. To our knowledge, only few real-world examples of applications exist. Image forensics (see Chapter 9), seeking to find traces of manipulations within images, is much more common. One reason may be the much lower organizational overhead of the forensic approach: if one does not trust an image, he can apply forensic techniques on it. Authentication watermarking requires a framework where predistribution watermark embedding and post-manipulation detection is offered. Keys must be assigned, kept and protected during the entire life cycle of the media.

Another alternative are hash-based approaches. Robust hashes also have a certain chance of recognizing and localizing modifications [43]. Cryptographic hashes on the other hand used withing digital signature schemes provide a security level sufficient even for legal requirements.

Still, a number of applications are either steadily mentioned in scientific literature or have even found their way to real-world usage. Medical image protection is a common example in the literature [3, 34, 44]. As medical images can be the foundation of significant decisions made by doctors, it is assumed that the importance of authenticity is high. As watermarking always induces a certain level of noise caused by embedding, often watermarking schemes like reversible watermarking [45] or ROI-controlled watermarking [46] are suggested. Other applications for watermarking-based authentication have been mentioned in the literature

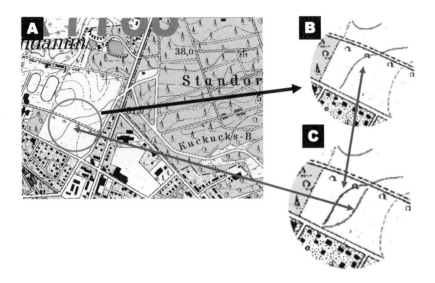

Figure 8.8 Example of application. A: Original map where watermark is embedded, B: An attacker modifies one line within the watermarked map, C: During detection the original line is recovered and both lines are highlighted for evaluation

sporadically. In [47], Zmudzinski et al. discuss protecting audio recordings of interviews (e.g., during police investigation, or telemarketing). Being able to verify the authenticity of the content helps to increase the trust in it if it is used as evidence. Kim and de Queiroz [48] argue that their algorithm can help to increase the trust in documents transmitted via unprotected channels like the Internet or also fax. Also, the example shown in Figure 8.8 comes from a real-world challenge addressed in a research project. Here, the problem was the forgery of maps made available to the public by German agencies. With the help of image authentication watermarking, these maps were to be protected without the need of complex key infrastructures. While it was proven that the watermarking technology was able to provide the necessary level of robustness and security, the protocols and architectures needed to actually run a service allowing protecting and verifying such maps have never been designed.

[1] Seenivasagam, R., V.and Veluman, "A QR Code Based Zero-Watermarking Scheme for Authenti-cation of Medical Images in Teleradiology Cloud," *Computational and Mathematical Methods in Medicine*, Vol. 2013, 2013.

[2] Popescu, A. C., and H. Farid, "Statistical Tools for Digital Forensics," in *In 6th International Workshop on Information Hiding*, Springer-Verlag, Berlin-Heidelberg, 2004, pp. 128–147.

[3] Wong, P. W., "A public key watermark for image verification and authentication," in *Proceedings of the IEEE International Conference on Image Processing*, Vol. 1, Oct 1998, pp. 455–459.

[4] Yeung, M. M., and F. Mintzer, "An invisible watermarking technique for image verification," in *Proceedings of the IEEE International Conference on Image Processing*, Vol. 2, Oct 1997, pp. 680–683.

[5] Fridrich, J., M. Goljan, and A. C. Baldoza, "New fragile authentication watermark for images," in *Proceedings of the IEEE International Conference on Image Processing*, Vol. 1, 2000, pp. 446–449.

[6] Celik, M. U., et al., "A hierarchical image authentication watermark with improved localization and security," in *Proceedings of the IEEE International Conference on Image Processing*, Vol. 2, Oct 2001, pp. 502–505.

[7] Wong, P. W., and N. D. Memon, "Secret and public key authentication watermarking schemes that resist vector quantization attack," in *Proceedings of SPIE*, Vol. 3971, 2000, pp. 417–427.

[8] Fridrich, J., "Security of fragile authentication watermarks with localization," in *Proceedings of SPIE*, Vol. 4675, 2002, pp. 691–700.

[9] Wu, M., and B. Liu, "Watermarking for image authentication," in *Proceedings of the IEEE International Conference on Image Processing*, Vol. 2, Oct 1998, pp. 437–441.

[10] Si, H., and C. T. Li, "Fragile Watermarking Scheme Based on the Block-wise Dependence in the Wavelet Domain," in *Proceedings of the 2004 Workshop on Multimedia and Security*, MM&Sec '04, New York, NY, USA: ACM, 2004, pp. 214–219.

[11] Fridrich, J., and M. Goljan, "Images with self-correcting capabilities," in *Proceedings of the IEEE International Conference on Image Processing*, Vol. 3, 1999, pp. 792–796.

[12] Zhang, X., et al., "Watermarking With Flexible Self-Recovery Quality Based on Compressive Sensing and Compositive Reconstruction," *IEEE Transactions on Information Forensics and Security*, Vol. 6, No. 4, Dec 2011, pp. 1223–1232.

[13] Korus, P., and A. Dziech, "Efficient Method for Content Reconstruction With Self-Embedding," *IEEE Transactions on Image Processing*, Vol. 22, No. 3, March 2013, pp. 1134–1147.

[14] Lee, T. Y., and S. D. Lin, "Dual watermark for image tamper detection and recovery," *Pattern Recognition*, Vol. 41, No. 11, 2008, pp. 3497–3506.

[15] Yang, C. W., and J. J. Shen, "Recover the tampered image based on VQ indexing," *Signal Processing*, Vol. 90, No. 1, 2010, pp. 331–343.

[16] Zhang, X., et al., "Reference Sharing Mechanism for Watermark Self-Embedding," *IEEE Transactions on Image Processing*, Vol. 20, No. 2, 2011, pp. 485–495.

[17] Cai, H., et al., "A new method for image reconstruction using self-embedding," in *Proceedings of the IEEE International Conference on Acoustics, Speech and Signal Processing*, May 2014, pp. 7430–7434.

[18] MacKay, D. J. C., "Fountain codes," *IEE Proceedings of Communications*, Vol. 152, No. 6, Dec 2005, pp. 1062–1068.

[19] Shokrollahi, A., "Raptor codes," *IEEE Transactions on Information Theory*, Vol. 52, No. 6, June 2006, pp. 2551–2567.

[20] Holliman, M., and N. Memon, "Counterfeiting attacks on oblivious block-wise independent invisible watermarking schemes," *IEEE Transactions on Image Processing*, Vol. 9, No. 3, 2000, pp. 432–441.

[21] Ouda, A. H., and M. R. El-Sakka, "Localization and security enhancement of block-based image authentication," in *Proceedings of the IEEE International Conference on Image Processing*, Vol. 1, September 2005, pp. I–673–6.

[22] Coppersmith, D., et al., "Fragile imperceptible digital watermark with privacy control," in *Proceedings of SPIE*, Vol. 3657, 1999, pp. 79–84.

[23] Liu, H., and M. Steinebach, "Digital Watermarking for Image Authentication with Localization," in *Proceedings of the IEEE International Conference on Image Processing*, October 2006, pp. 1973–1976.

[24] Fridrich, J., "Image watermarking for tamper detection," in *Proceedings of the IEEE International Conference on Image Processing*, Vol. 2, October 1998, pp. 404–408.

[25] Lin, E. T., C. I. Podilchuk, and E. J. Delp, "Detection of image alterations using semifragile watermarks," in *Proceedings of SPIE*, Vol. 3971, 2000, pp. 152–163.

[26] Chen, B., and G. W. Wornell, "Quantization index modulation: a class of provably good methods for digital watermarking and information embedding," *IEEE Transactions on Information Theory*, Vol. 47, No. 4, May 2001, pp. 1423–1443.

[27] Lin, C. Y., and S. F. Chang, "Semifragile watermarking for authenticating JPEG visual content," in *Proceedings of SPIE*, Vol. 3971, 2000, pp. 140–151.

[28] Ekici, Ö., et al., "Comparative evaluation of semifragile watermarking algorithms," *Journal Electronic Imaging*, Vol. 13, No. 1, 2004, pp. 209–219.

[29] Winne, D. A., et al., "Digital watermarking in wavelet domain with predistortion for authenticity verification and localization," in *Proceedings of SPIE*, Vol. 4675, 2002, pp. 349–356.

[30] Kundur, D., and D. Hatzinakos, "Digital watermarking for telltale tamper proofing and authentication," *Proceedings of the IEEE*, Vol. 87, No. 7, July 1999, pp. 1167–1180.

[31] Lin, C. Y., and S. F. Chang, "A robust image authentication method distinguishing JPEG compression from malicious manipulation," *IEEE Transactions on Circuits and Systems for Video Technology*, Vol. 11, No. 2, 2001, pp. 153–168.

[32] Wang, H., A. T. S. Ho, and X. Zhao, "A Novel Fast Self-restoration Semi-fragile Watermarking Algorithm for Image Content Authentication Resistant to JPEG Compression," in *Digital Forensics and Watermarking*, Vol. 7128 of *Lecture Notes in Computer Science*, Springer Berlin Heidelberg, pp. 72–85, 2012.

[33] Macq, B., and F. Dewey, "Trusted Headers for Medical Images," in *International Workshop on Digital Watermarking (IWDW)*, 1999.

[34] Coatrieux, G., et al., "Relevance of watermarking in medical imaging," in *Proceedings of the IEEE EMBS International Conference on Information Technology Applications in Biomedicine*, 2000, pp. 250–255.

[35] Fridrich, J., M. Goljan, and R. Du, "Invertible authentication watermark for JPEG images," in *In Proceedings of International Conference on Information Technology: Coding and Computing, 2001.*, April 2001, pp. 223–227.

[36] Fridrich, J., M. Goljan, and R. Du, "Lossless Data Embedding–New Paradigm in Digital Watermarking," *EURASIP Journal on Advances in Signal Processing*, Vol. 2002, No. 2, 2002, pp. 986842.

[37] Dittmann, J., M. Steinebach, and L. Ferri, "Watermarking protocols for authentication and ownership protection based on timestamps and holograms," in *Proceedings of SPIE, Vol. 4675, Electronic Imaging 2002: Multimedia Processing and Applications, Security and Watermarking of Multimedia Contents IV, San Jose, CA, USA.*, Bellingham, Washington, USA, 2002, pp. 240–251.

[38] Steinebach, M., and J. Dittmann, "Watermarking-based Digital Audio Data Authentication," *EURASIP Journal Applied Signal Processing*, New York, NY, United States: Hindawi Publishing Corp., Vol. 2003, Jan. 2003, pp. 1001–1015.

[39] Tian, J., "Reversible data embeddeding using a difference expansion," *IEEE Transactions on Circuits and Systems for Video Technology*, Vol. 13, No. 8, 2003, pp. 890–896.

[40] Chrysochos, E., et al., "Reversible image watermarking based on histogram modification," in *Proceedings of the 11th Panhellenic Conference Informatics*, 2007, pp. 93–104.

[41] Hong, W., T. S. Chen, and C. W. Shiu, "Reversible data hiding for high quality images using modification of prediction errors," *Journal of Systems and Software*, Elsevier, Vol. 82, No. 11, 2009, pp. 1833–1842.

[42] Coltuc, D., and J. Chassery, "Very fast watermarking by reversible contrast mapping," *IEEE Signal Processing Letters*, IEEE, Vol. 14, No. 4, 2007, pp. 255–258.

[43] Zhao, Y., et al., "Robust Hashing for Image Authentication Using Zernike Moments and Local Features," *IEEE Transactions on Information Forensics and Security*, Vol. 8, No. 1, 2013, pp. 55–63.

[44] Rey, C., and J. L. Dugelay, "A Survey of Watermarking Algorithms for Image Authentication," *EURASIP Journal on Applied Signal Processing*, New York, NY, United States: Hindawi Publishing Corp., Vol. 2002, No. 1, Jan. 2002, pp. 613–621.

[45] Coatrieux, G., et al., "Reversible Watermarking for Knowledge Digest Embedding and Reliability Control in Medical Images," *IEEE Transactions on Information Technology in Biomedicine*, Vol. 13, No. 2, March 2009, pp. 158–165.

[46] Fotopoulos, V., M. L. Stavrinou, and A. N. Skodras, "Medical image authentication and self-correction through an adaptive reversible watermarking technique," in *Proceedings of the 8th IEEE International Conference on BioInformatics and BioEngineering*, October 2008, pp. 1–5.

[47] Zmudzinski, S., B. Munir, and M. Steinebach, "Digital audio authentication by robust feature embedding," in *Proceedings of SPIE*, Vol. 8303, 2012, pp. 83030I–83030I–7.

[48] Kim, H. Y., and R. L. de Queiroz, "A public-key authentication watermarking for binary images," in *Proceedings of the IEEE International Conference on Image Processing*, Vol. 5, October 2004, pp. 3459–3462.

Chapter 9

Media Forensics

Rainer Böhme, Matthias Kirchner

9.1 OBJECTIVES

Media forensics is the youngest subfield associated with information hiding and most closely related to the detection techniques discussed in previous chapters of this book. Like all forensic sciences, media forensics concerns the provision of evidence to support decisions, for example in the court of law. Over the past decade, scholars in media forensics have developed and evaluated a growing set of tools to extract information from media objects pertaining to the authenticity of digital media as valid representations of reality, such as the natural scene depicted in a digital image. Media forensics exploits the fact that potentially compromising editing operations (e. g., tampering) leave traces that render forgeries statistically distinguishable from authentic media objects. Forensically useful traces are often imperceptible, which connects to the theme of information *hiding*. However, unlike for the hiding techniques discussed in previous chapters, forensically useful traces are not actively embedded but emerge as side effects of other processing [1].

While ensuring authenticity is closest to the objectives of watermarking and fingerprinting, many known forensic methods are inspired by steganalysis: media forensics at its core is a signal detection problem (see Chapter 3 in this book). The forensic analyst tests if an observed signal X is compatible with the distribution of authentic media objects:

$$H_0 : \quad \mathbf{X} \sim p_a, \qquad\qquad (9.1)$$

$$H_1 : \quad \mathbf{X} \not\sim p_a. \qquad\qquad (9.2)$$

As in the case of covers for steganalysis, the distribution of authentic media objects p_a is generally not known, arguably unknowable [2], and often conditional to the context and the prior knowledge of the analyst. Therefore, most analysis methods approximate the optimal statistical test using heuristics and often also human expertise. The role of the human analyst is to select and parametrize analysis methods as well as to cross-check and interpret the results.

Media forensics also shares similarities with other forensic sciences, such as computer forensics [3]. A common feature of both media forensics and computer forensics is the focus of analysis on *digital evidence*, which is data represented in discrete and perfectly observable symbols stored in computer systems. But media forensics and computer forensics assume different generation processes for the digital data. Computer forensics analyses data structures generated by (in principle) deterministic computer programs, such as file system tables in the case of data recovery. By contrast, the distinctive feature of media data is that it originates from the outside of a computer system. A *sensor* maps parts of reality into imperfect and not fully deterministic digital representations. We will see that sensors and their imperfections play a very important role in many techniques of media forensics.

The notion of media data as data acquired by sensors is very general. It comprises audio, image, and video signals as well as more exotic sensory inputs (e. g., location, acceleration). For a number of reasons, researchers have mainly focussed on forensic techniques for still images. Reflecting this state of the art, we focus our discussion in this chapter on digital *image* forensics. Many of the principles can be adapted to other kinds of media data, and we point to important characteristics for the forensics analysis of other media in Section 9.3.

9.1.1   Digital Image Forensics

A simple system model puts the forensic analysis at the end of a processing chain, which consists of at least one acquisition step with optional subsequent processing (see Figure 9.1). The abstract acquisition function takes as input a natural scene and outputs a digital signal. This involves the analog-to-digital conversion of a sensor. Every processing step assumes digital signals as inputs and outputs. The abstract processing step can be instantiated by the identity function (resulting in authentic images) or any combination of operations used to produce a forgery. The

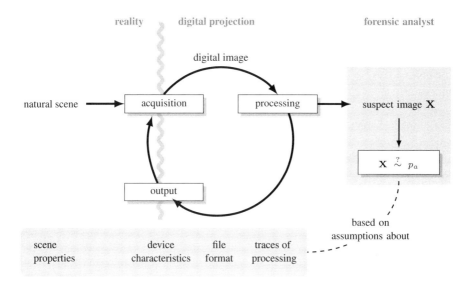

Figure 9.1   Image generation process and forensics.

intended result of a forensic analysis is a decision about unknown properties of the processing chain, for example whether the processing step was the identity function (H_0) or not (H_1). If ground truth is available, then forensic methods can be benchmarked by measuring decision errors with similar metrics, as introduced for steganalysis in Chapter 3. The possibility of repeated transformations between analog and digital representations—for instance by redigitizing a 2 D-print of a digital photograph—is reflected by the loop in Figure 9.1. While the possibility of such complex processing chains must always be on the mindset of forensic practitioners, many methods presented in the literature assume simple processing chains without digital-to-analog conversions. Another difficulty in practice is that the distinction between acquisition and processing is not always as clear-cut as this model suggests. Many acquisition devices do substantial post-processing on the digitized data in order to compensate for mechanical or optical shortcomings, offer image processing operations to their users, or presume some sort of post-processing for instance with specialized software installed on a mobile device (e. g., smartphone) connected to the acquisition device (e. g., body-mount camera).

The notion of *passive* image forensics generally assumes no knowledge of the analyst about the specific instance of the processing chain. However, hypothesis tests for the signal detection problem are not possible without assumptions about typical processing chains. Formally, these assumptions are encoded in the probability distribution of authentic images p_a. As it is hard to deal with the high-dimensional joint distribution p_a in practice, assumptions about different steps of the processing chain are tested independently. Technically, this approach is a projection of the unknown distribution p_a on several low-dimensional subspaces, where for each subspace the distribution of a decision criterium between authentic and forged images can be obtained experimentally. One can organize the assumptions, their corresponding subspaces, and decision criteria along the stages of the system model. As illustrated at the bottom of Figure 9.1, known methods make use of assumptions on scene properties, device characteristics, data structures like the image file format, and traces of processing.

The properties of processing chains of interest to the forensic analyst can be broadly divided into properties indicating the source of an image and properties indicating possible manipulations. For authentic images we expect that

- The signal contains statistical traces of a plausible acquisition function (consistent throughout the entire signal);

- There are no traces of manipulation present in any part of the signal.

In practice, the question of authenticity is often tackled step by step.

9.1.2   Source Identification

Image source identification tries to infer information about the acquisition device from a given signal. Known methods differ in their levels of granularity depending on available information and accessibility of the presumed acquisition device.

The most basic question is to distinguish between natural and computer-generated images [4]. A general approach analyzes the noise characteristics of image pixels, which emerge from imperfections of sensor-based acquisition devices and are generally not modeled or mimicked in rendering software [5]. For specific image contents (e. g., landscapes, faces) approaches based on computer vision have been proposed. They try to identify imperfect modeling of physical or physiological properties in typical rendering software [6].

The next question to ask for natural images is to identify the class of acquisition devices, for example whether an image was digitized with a digital camera or a flatbed scanner. Methods dealing with this question leverage knowledge of fundamental engineering differences between types of sensors. Images acquired with line sensors (e. g., in flatbed scanners) exhibit distinct noise characteristics compared to images acquired with sensor arrays (e. g., in digital still and video cameras). Moreover, many flatbed scanners do not interpolate color information from a filter array. The absence of the characteristic interpolation artifacts of color filter arrays (CFA, see Section 9.2.2.4) can identify scanned images [7, 8].

Each class of acquisition devices can be further divided into different models[1] (or makes). Images acquired with devices of the same model share characteristics introduced by the combination of hardware or software components in this model's processing chain. Emphasis is on the combination because there is no single characteristic known that systematically varies between models and is similar for all devices of a model. Typical methods measure a broad range of features spanning optical aberrations, noise metrics, digital signal processing artifacts, and parameter choices of the primary image compression. They feed the resulting feature vector to machine learning algorithms for classification [9]. To generate the labeled data necessary for supervised learning, example images from at least one (preferably more) devices of each model are needed. As the number of models grows constantly, maintaining a comprehensive training database becomes quite challenging [10].

If the actual acquisition device (possibly among others) or sufficiently many test images from that device are available to the forensic analyst, a digital image can even be linked to its acquisition device with high certainty by leveraging traces of inevitable manufacturing imperfections and wear and tear of the sensor (e. g., defective pixels) in the resulting image signal. (See Section 9.2.2.3 for details.)

9.1.3 Manipulation Detection

Manipulation detection tries to detect and possibly specify content-changing post-processing after the acquisition of a digital image. It broadly takes two approaches. First, if sufficient information about the acquisition device is known (from context or preparatory source identification forensics), then the device-specific characteristics can be checked for consistency. Global or local deviations from the reference values can be interpreted as indications of post-processing. For example, an image acquired with a specific digital camera may exhibit linear dependencies between pixels of different color channels resulting from the CFA interpolation in the acquisition device. If the dependence structure is missing or differs in parts of the image,

---

1   For consistency with the terminology in the literature, we overload the term *model*. It refers to a
     device type in this paragraph and to a set of simplifying assumptions in the rest of the chapter.

it is very likely that this region has been edited locally [11]. Other features of this kind include parameters of measurable aberrations relative to the optical center of the image, inconsistent sensor noise, or linear independence at block boundaries of the primary JPEG compression.

Second, many content-changing processing operations add statistical traces to the signal independent of how it was acquired. For example, geometric transformations, often used to adjust size and orientation of pasted objects to the environment, leave traces that are characteristic for the resampling method and the parameters of the transformation [12, 13]. Other traces of processing include duplicated image regions resulting from attempts to cover up manipulations with local operations like the copy stencil, or artifacts introduced after repeated quantization if intermediate states of a processing chain are stored in a lossy compressed image format.

9.2   METHODS

Traces useful for forensics, whether generated by the acquisition device or processing operations, appear on different layers of analysis. We broadly distinguish between scene level, signal level, and data structure level.

9.2.1   Layers of Analysis

The *data structure level* refers to the syntactical encoding of the data stream, which is defined—albeit loosely—by the file format or communication protocol specification. Forensic evidence emerges from different implementations of the specification as most complex standards include many optional elements and do not support a single canonical form. The multitude of metadata options available in image file formats (e. g., EXIF and custom application headers in JPEG files) has turned out to be a most valuable resource for image forensics on this layer [14]. Also the order of elements in a tagged data structure as well as the parameters of lossless encoding add variability that helps to identify at least the last encoder of the processing chain [15]. While critics argue that forensic analyses based on data structures alone are unreliable because metadata can be changed with relatively little effort, it still requires substantial knowledge, skill, and patience to do this plausibly and consistently. Another strong argument for analyses on more than one layer is that data structures may indicate some processing but do not reveal much about what operation has been applied. It may make a difference whether an image has been recompressed by a social media platform (unavoidable in many cases) or locally edited and then recompressed.

The borderline between *scene level* and signal level is less clear. As a rule of thumb, we speak of scene level if the forensic method tries to analyze macroscopic properties of the image to support a decision based on the extracted semantics. The last qualifier is important because, for instance, a global histogram is also a macroscopic property, but it conveys little information about the scene. Therefore, scene level analysis is more related to computer vision than to signal detection. Most known methods require more human intervention and are more sensitive to the human part than methods operating on the signal level. For example, [16] proposes a computer-aided method to estimate the direction of diffuse light at selected points in a suspect image. This may help to substantiate claims about inconsistent lighting of multiple objects in the same scene, which may indicate a composition from multiple source images. In a similar vein, [17] study light directions at specular reflections and [18] support the analysis of complex shading and shadows. All mentioned approaches fit geometric models of the physical world depicted in a scene to the digital representation.

The *signal level* is by far the best researched and so far the most promising approach to image forensics [19]. It combines many desirable properties such as the independence of the scene content (disregarding pathologic cases of singular scene content), high accuracy of automated decisions for simple processing chains, and sufficient information to carry out in-depth manual investigations of complex processing chains. The signal level carries characteristics of the acquisition device. In addition, characteristic traces of typical processing operations are measurable in the signal level as well. Taken together, all these characteristics offer a wealth of information to the forensic analyst. We will review the most important principles and methods to extract and interpret signal level information in the following sections.

9.2.2 Device Characteristics

Device characteristics refer to image characteristics that can be attributed to the acquisition device. They serve for source identification and as a kind of inherent watermark to track further processing, which may partly erase or transform the device characteristics, thereby unveiling the processing operation and its parameters. Considering the widespread use of digital cameras, our review will follow the literature and will emphasize digital camera characteristics. We refer to [20] for a comprehensive review of scanner characteristics.

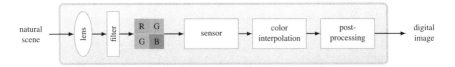

Figure 9.2   Digital image acquisition with a digital camera: stylized pipeline.

9.2.2.1   Digital Camera Pipeline

Figure 9.2 shows a stylized processing pipeline of a digital camera with its most relevant components. Incoming light of the scene is focused on the sensor by a complex system of lenses. An optical filter to reduce undesired light components (e. g., infrared light) sits between these components. Typical camera sensors capture image pixels by individual CCD or CMOS sensor elements, which output an electric charge proportional to the light received at the corresponding position on the two-dimensional sensor plane. These sensor elements are color-blind; they can only measure light intensity. Color information is obtained by arranging the sensor plane in the form of a color filter array (CFA) where each sensor element is sensitive to light of a certain wavelength only—red (R), green (G), and blue (B) in most cases. Missing color information can then be estimated from surrounding pixels of the raw intensity map. This process is also known as CFA interpolation or demosaicing. After CFA interpolation, the image is subject to a number of camera-internal post-processing steps, including for instance color correction, edge enhancement, and finally compression.

9.2.2.2   Lens Distortions

Modern digital cameras are equipped with a complex optical system that projects a scene to a sensor of much smaller dimension. This projection is in general not perfect. As a result, a plethora of lens distortions (also known as aberrations) are present in digital camera images. Forensic source identification assumes that shape and strength of lens distortions depend on the lens(es) in use. Tractable models of aberrations are typically parametrized by the radial distance to the optical center of the image. For the purpose of manipulation detection, these models can be fitted globally and then tested for local consistency throughout an image.

Prevalent types of distortion are lens radial distortion, vignetting, and chromatic aberrations. Lens radial distortion is a nonlinear geometric distortion that lets straight lines appear curved. This effect is generally more pronounced toward image

Figure 9.3 Lateral chromatic aberration in a digital camera image. Red color fringes along edges are marked by arrows in the magnified (and contrast-enhanced) details on the right. The occurrence and strength of color fringes generally varies with the position of edges in the image. This image was acquired with a Nikon 18–200 mm zoom lens at a focal length of 150 mm. (A version of this chapter with color figures is available on the authors' homepages.)

corners, typically modeled by a polynomial of small degree [21]. Some cameras try to correct for it during post-processing, which may leave characteristic traces by itself [22]. Vignetting refers to the radial decrease of light intensity toward the corners of an image. It is best visible and measurable in homogenous images captured with wide apertures [23], for which only a fraction of the light reaches the outer regions of the sensor plane.

Chromatic aberrations are perhaps most relevant for forensics. They describe the effect that polychromatic light is spread over different positions on the sensor plane because the lens' dispersion index varies with the wavelength. Lateral chromatic aberrations often produce visible color fringes along edges. They are particularly well measured by the spatial displacement (i. e., contraction or expansion) of different color channels relative to each other [24]. Let the green channel, G, be the reference. Then the coordinates of the displaced red or blue channel $D \in \{R, B\}$ with optical center (i'_D, j'_D) are modeled as

$$\begin{pmatrix} i_D \\ j_D \end{pmatrix} = \begin{pmatrix} \alpha_D \cdot (i_G - i'_D) + i'_D \\ \alpha_D \cdot (j_G - j'_D) + j'_D \end{pmatrix}. \tag{9.3}$$

The tuple of model parameters, (α_D, i'_D, j'_D), can be estimated efficiently from a single image [25]. Figure 9.3 illustrates how the orientation of these displacements varies across the image. The red channel expands relatively to the other channels

manipulation   correlation map   detector output

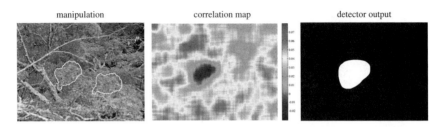

Figure 9.4 Manipulation detection based on sensor noise [26]. Image manipulation (left): part of the image was copied, rotated by $30°$ and then reinserted at a different position. The two regions are marked in the image. Correlation map (center): each intensity value in the map corresponds to the correlation score of a 128×128 pixel block from the image's noise residual with the corresponding fingerprint estimate. The manipulated region lacks the expected sensor noise pattern, yielding low correlation between local sensor noise estimates and the fingerprint of the image's camera (indicated by darker colors in the map). Detector output (right): post-processing and binarization of the correlation map gives a clear indication of the manipulated region. (A version of this chapter with color figures is available on the authors' homepages.)

in this example (i.e., $\alpha_R > 1$). This can be exploited for manipulation detection, for instance if one region of an image is copied to another region with a different expected aberration profile [24].

9.2.2.3   Sensor Imperfections

Sensor imperfections created by inevitable variations in the manufacturing process of sensor elements and sensor wear-out are valuable device characteristics. Sensor outputs are generally noisy: the intensity values fluctuate slightly even if the sensor plane is lit absolutely homogeneously. Sensor noise is composed of temporal and spatial noise. Temporal noise subsumes noise components that are stochastically independent between different images acquired with the same sensor. Shot noise and read-out noise are typical sources of temporal noise. By contrast, spatial noise is relatively stable over time and only varies between individual sensor elements. This makes spatial noise particularly interesting to forensic analysts. It can serve as a camera "fingerprint", and can also be tested for consistent appearance in different regions of an image [27, 28]. This quality is commonly attributed to photo-response nonuniformity (PRNU), a noise source that adds a camera-specific unique multiplicative pattern to the signal. It is caused by inevitable material imperfections and variations in the manufacturing process of individual sensor elements. A sensor fingerprint $\mathbf{K}$ can be estimated by some form of pixel-wise averaging of noise residuals over a number of images $\mathbf{X}^{(n)}$ taken with the same camera,

$$\hat{\mathbf{K}} = \sum_{n=1}^{N} \mathbf{H}^{(n)} \mathbf{W}^{(n)} = \sum_{n=1}^{N} \mathbf{H}^{(n)} \left(\mathbf{X}^{(n)} - F(\mathbf{X}^{(n)}) \right), \qquad (9.4)$$

with $\mathbf{H}^{(n)} = 1/N$ for simple averaging [27], or $\mathbf{H}^{(n)} = \mathbf{X}^{(n)} / \sum_{n=1}^{N} \left(\mathbf{X}^{(n)} \right)^2$ for a maximum likelihood estimator of multiplicative noise [28]. The noise residuals $\mathbf{W}$ are obtained by processing images with a denoising filter $F(\cdot)$. Cameras can be identified by extracting the noise residual from the image under investigation and measuring its similarity to an estimated camera fingerprint. Suitable similarity metrics include Pearson correlation [27], normalized cross-correlation [28], and peak-to-correlation energy (PCE) [29].

For manipulation detection, the similarity between an image's noise residual and the camera fingerprint estimate is evaluated for small (possibly overlapping) blocks. If the processing operations of interest corrupt the local sensor noise pattern as a side effect, then low local similarity scores indicate a forgery. The two leftmost panels of Figure 9.4 illustrate this effect. Modern detectors apply more sophisticated criteria. For instance, the right panel of Figure 9.4 shows the outcome of a state-of-the-art detector that employs a Bayesian Markov random field model to account for local dependencies between blocks in close proximity [26].

Photo-response nonuniformity has also been applied to examine scanned images [30, 31]. Typical line sensors of flatbed scanners repeat spatial noise characteristics along rows. This directional characteristic of the noise pattern allows forensic investigators to distinguish between digital camera images and scanned images [32].

Sensor noise estimates may also contain traces of sensor defects (i. e., sensor elements that constantly output too high or too low intensity values). The occurrence of these defects is characteristic for individual cameras [33] and accumulates over time, enabling temporal forensics [34]. A similar effect is caused by dust particles on the sensor protective glass [35]. Yet many cameras try to correct sensor defects and sensor dust particles with post-processing. In general, their appearance also depends strongly on the image content and on lens settings. All these factors limit the usefulness of sensor defects compared to sensor noise.

9.2.2.4 Color Filter Array Characteristics

To acquire color images with sensors that are physically limited to measure light intensity only, the incoming light has to be split up in several components. Most digital cameras do this by combining a single sensor with an array of color filters

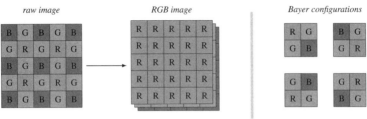

Figure 9.5 Typical digital cameras employ a color filter array (usually one of the four Bayer configurations shown on the right). Each sensor element is sensitive to light of a certain wavelength (here red, green, and blue) only. A color image is produced by interpolating the remaining color information from surrounding pixels of the raw image.

so that different sensor elements capture different color information. The missing information is then interpolated, a procedure that is also known as *demosaicing* (because color filters are arranged like mosaics; see Figure 9.5).

A CFA *configuration* describes how color filters are arranged. As different camera models use different CFA configurations, this parameter is a valuable device characteristic for forensics [36–38]. Although, in principle, a wide variety of CFA configurations is conceivable, the dominant CFA layout repeats a 2×2 Bayer pattern over the entire sensor pane. Bayer patterns exist in four configurations and are characterized by two green elements arranged diagonally with one red and one blue element filling up the remaining space (see Figure 9.5).

Demosaicing a Bayer pattern implies that at most one-third of all pixels in an RGB image contain genuine information from a sensor element. The remaining pixels are interpolated from the local neighborhood of the raw signal. As a side effect, pixels become locally dependent even stronger and more systematically than local correlations in the original signal. The repetition of a fixed pattern over the entire image causes periodic dependency structures in the image [11]. (See Section 9.2.3.3 below for a method to identify periodic dependencies.) The specific form depends not only on the CFA configuration, but also on the demosaicing algorithm. This observation has motivated CFA-based camera model identification approaches [36, 39]. Similar dependencies occur between the color channels of an image. Some forms of post-processing destroy these demosaicing traces. The resulting local inconsistencies have successfully been exploited to localize tampering [40]. Finally, the absence of any CFA traces is an indication that a given image was not acquired with a digital camera [7, 8].

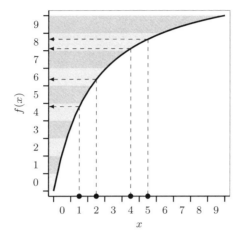

Figure 9.6 Requantization after applying continuous functions on discrete data. Depending on the curvature of the mapping (here: gamma correction) and the quantization step size (here: 1), some output values appear twice as frequently and others not at all. (This holds strictly for uniformly distributed input data and approximately for smooth marginal distributions as in typical media signals.)

9.2.3   Processing Traces

Recall from Section 9.1.1 that processing traces emerge as side effect of the image processing operations used to produce a perceptually convincing forgery (see also Figure 9.1). The presence of processing traces in a suspect image indicates manipulation and their exact realization may reveal information about the parameters of processing operations. Processing traces may permeate an entire image or parts of it. In the latter case, the distribution of traces within an image helps to localize tampering.

9.2.3.1   Requantization

Arguably the most important source of processing traces is requantization: already quantized discrete numbers are used as inputs of functions defined for continuous domains and codomains. The return values are quantized *again* in order to be mapped to the discrete alphabet of typical signal representations.

An introductory example for requantization is a detector of gamma correction. Gamma correction refers to the point operation defined by the continuous function

$$y_{ij} = (x_{ij})^\gamma, \tag{9.5}$$

where parameters $\gamma < 1$ decreases the contrast of a grayscale image $\mathbf{X}$ and $\gamma > 1$ increases the contrast. If $\mathbf{X}$ and $\mathbf{Y}$ are integer arrays interpreted as ℓ-bit fixed-point representations of numbers in the normalized intensity range $[0, 1]$, then the assignment in Equation (9.5) is implemented as discrete function $f : \{0, \ldots, 2^\ell - 1\} \to \{0, \ldots, 2^\ell - 1\}$. Specifically,

$$y_{ij} = f(x_{ij}) = \left[(2^\ell - 1) \left(\frac{x_{ij}}{2^\ell - 1} \right)^\gamma \right], \tag{9.6}$$

where square brackets denote rounding to the nearest integer.

Figure 9.6 shows this mapping for $x \in \{0, \ldots, 9\}$. Observe that for the chosen parameters, f can never take the value 5 because no discrete input maps to it. Likewise, two values in the domain of f, 4 and 5, map to the same value 8. If the input signal's histogram is broadly smooth, this coincidence will add up to a peak in the output histogram. This is exactly what we can observe in gamma-corrected grayscale images as illustrated in Figure 9.7. The contrast-reduced ($\gamma = 0.6$) lower half of the image exhibits gaps in the left tail of the histogram and peaks on the right side. For comparison, the histogram of the unprocessed upper half is locally smooth and does not contain such artifacts.

Gamma correction is a relevant operation in typical image processing chains, in particular for producing visually plausible compositions from parts of images taken under different lighting conditions or exposures. A simple way to automatically detect the resulting processing traces is to analyze the histogram of suspect image in the frequency domain. Gaps and peaks produce strong high-frequency components in the spectrum that do not appear in natural images. If the high-frequency components, after some necessary windowing close to the boundary values 0 and $2^\ell - 1$, exceed a certain threshold, a suspect image (or image region) is flagged as processed with gamma correction [41].

This simple method works best for images in spatial domain representations. Transformations to the frequency domain, like the DCT used in the popular lossy JPEG compression, tend to smooth the histograms of intensity values after back-transformation to the spatial domain. This attenuates peaks and gaps in the histogram and makes gamma correction more difficult to detect.

grayscale image histograms

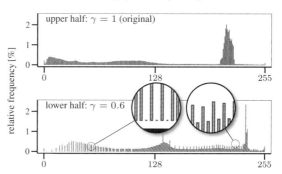

Figure 9.7 Processing traces realized as gaps and peaks in the histogram after gamma correction.

But lossy compression itself involves several requantization steps, which leave forensically useful processing traces. For example, requantization happens at many stages in a JPEG compression–decompression cycle:[2]

- After color transformation from RGB to YCbCr;

- After chrominance channel subsampling;

- During the (fast) 2D-DCT transformation;

- During and after the (fast) inverse 2D-DCT transformation;

- After chrominance channel upsampling (for certain implementations);

- After color back-transformation to RGB;

and, most importantly,

- When DCT coefficients are explicitly quantized with frequency-dependent step sizes taken from the quality-dependent JPEG quantization matrix.

Every stage in the enumeration above can be written as a continuous function f with subsequent rounding (although some implementations reuse intermediate results for efficiency, complicating the analysis). A save-and-open sequence of image editing software goes through all these stages, thereby leaving traces of requantization in the form of perceptible or imperceptible compression artifacts.

2   See Chapters 2 and 3 for more details on JPEG compression.

9.2.3.2   Lossy Compression

The complexity of the popular JPEG compression and the interaction of many factors precludes a formal or even comprehensive treatment in the context of this chapter. What matters is that virtually all traces useful for the forensic exploration of the (potential) JPEG compression history [42] emerge from requantization in one form or another. In this sense, most forensic methods analyzing compression artifacts can be seen as special cases of detectors of requantization. The approaches proposed in the literature differ in how processing traces are extracted, in the supported image formats, and the assumed knowledge of (candidate) quantization matrices and of the specific implementation of the JPEG standard. For instance, methods exists to check spatial domain images for prior JPEG compression and its parameters [43] or to identify local inconsistencies in JPEG errors indicating compositions [44]. Images in JPEG format can be analyzed for double or multiple compressions [45]. The literature is so specialized that it contains already tailored methods to evaluate one form of requantization traces (e. g., JPEG history detection) in the presence of distortion by other forms of requantization (e. g., contrast enhancement) [46].

Technically, many methods rely on (recomputed) JPEG DCT coefficients and apply adapted versions of Benford's law on the distribution of numerical digits to test for singularities resulting from requantization [47]. This approach can draw on solid theory [48] and is surprisingly effective given that only first-order statistics are evaluated [49]. (Part of the reason is that good statistical models are known for histograms of DCT coefficients, unlike for spatial domain intensity histograms.) However, the approach loses precision if multiple compressions use exactly the same parameter and it reaches its limits if the quantization step sizes are very small (i. e., for images compressed with JPEG quality close to 100%).

Under these conditions, another approach is more reliable. It leverages the fact that JPEG compression cuts the image into nonoverlapping blocks of 8×8 pixels and then applies the compression–decompression chain on each block independently. Repeated requantization introduces complicated dependencies between pixels within a block. These effects are not fully modeled yet and do not seem to be measurable with first-order statistics, like histograms. However, a key observation is that blocks converge to a stable state after a small but seemingly random number of iterations. In this context, a block is called *stable* if all its pixel intensity values in the spatial domain representation take exactly the same values after a full compression–decompression cycle.

Empirical evidence from natural images as well as from synthetic data suggests that the distribution of the time until convergence is fairly independent of the

 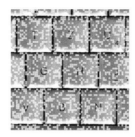 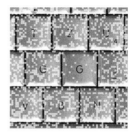

Figure 9.8 Convergence of JPEG blocks after repeated requantization. White marks indicate 8×8 blocks that remain stable between the first and the second JPEG compression (left) and the second and third JPEG compression (center and right). The right image has been locally manipulated after the first JPEG compression and the result was stored as JPEG. All experiments use libjpeg default settings for compression and decompression and quality factor 100 %. The test image size is 512×512 pixels.

image content (disregarding flat blocks, which are always stable after one iteration). By tabulating the steps until convergence for all blocks of an image, the estimated distribution can be matched against ground truth distributions obtained under controlled conditions. This enables a detector for prior JPEG compression up to the highest possible quality of 100% where all scale factors in the quantization matrix are set to one. This detector can also reveal the number of recompressions, which may indicate the depth of the image editing chain [50].

Block convergence can also help to localize tampered regions as illustrated in Figure 9.8. The left image has been compressed with JPEG quality factor 100% once. The white marks superimposed in the figure indicate blocks that remain stable after another compression–decompression cycle with the same parameters. Observe that the number of stable blocks increases substantially if the whole JPEG image is opened and resaved (i. e., recompressed) unaltered with image-editing software (center). Hence, the ratio of stable blocks indicates the compression history. The right image shows the distribution of stable blocks if local editing happened between opening and resaving the image: blocks in the altered region appear like never-compressed content and converge slower on average than the surrounding blocks.

In summary, block convergence analysis complements the analysis of DCT coefficient histograms in situations where the JPEG quality is high and the parameters of multiple compressions remain constant. However, the lack of solid theory and the reliance on more subtle higher-order dependencies observable only by counting steps until convergence makes block convergence more sensitive to the implementation of the JPEG standard, in particular the DCT and inverse DCT algorithms [51].

There also exist forensic methods evaluating artifacts of compression algorithms other than JPEG [52], but these methods are omitted here for their lower practical relevance in still image forensics.

9.2.3.3   Resampling

Realistic manipulations often involve resizing or rotating images or parts thereof. Technically, such geometric transformations can be described as *resampling* of the original image grid. A rather naive approach would be to transform the discrete source coordinates of every pixel with a continuous function and round the resulting coordinates to destination coordinates. This would result in severe visual distortion because the mapping between source and destination pixels is not always bijective. The effect is comparable to the source of requantization artifacts described in Section 9.2.3.1 with the only difference that it affects spatial coordinates rather than intensity values.

Researchers in image processing have recognized this problem for long and use interpolation to produce smooth and visually appealing transformations. Very similar to color filter array interpolation (cf. Section 9.2.2.4), resampling introduces linear dependencies between adjacent pixels. These dependencies vary periodically throughout the image and can be understood as traces of resampling [12, 53]. Figure 9.9 illustrates the formation of periodic linear dependencies for the particularly indicative case of upscaling by factor two using bilinear interpolation. Arbitrary geometric transformations produce similar artifacts (except strong downscaling and rotations by multiples of $90°$). The periodicity and amplitude generally depend on the transformation parameters as well as on the interpolation method [13].

The standard output of resampling detectors is a so-called p-map [12], where "p" stands for the probability that a pixel has been interpolated. P-maps have the same size as the image under investigation and can be computed from a linear predictor of pixel intensities [13],

$$r_{ij} = x_{ij} - \mathrm{Pred}(\mathcal{N}_{ij}) , \qquad (9.7)$$

as known from steganalysis (see Section 3.1.1). Adopting the notation of Equation (3.9), function $\mathrm{Pred}(\cdot)$ is a linear predictor that estimates the intensity of pixel x_{ij} from its local neighborhood $\mathcal{N}_{ij}$. A finite impulse response filter like the one in Equation (3.11) has been confirmed to work well [13]. The predictor residuals contain relevant information because interpolated pixels are more correlated with their neighbors pixels and have a better fit with the linear model. Therefore they

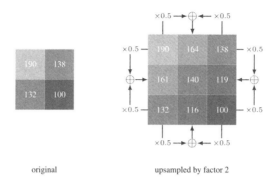

original   upsampled by factor 2

Figure 9.9 Bilinear resampling of a 2×2 pixel block (left) by a factor of two. Every other pixel in the resized block is a linear combination of its direct neighbors (right). Geometrically transformed images are composed of a large number of such blocks (i. e., periodic linear correlations occur).

produce comparably lower absolute prediction residuals than pixels with more genuine signal information. A simple variant of the p-map evaluates for each pixel the likelihood p_{ij} that its predictor residue r_{ij} obeys a suitable global distribution assumption. An i. i .d. zero-mean Gaussian model has been found to work sufficiently well in practice,

$$
p_{ij} = \frac{1}{\sqrt{2\pi\sigma^2}} \exp\left(-\frac{r_{ij}^2}{2\sigma^2} \right) .
\tag{9.8}
$$

The empirical variance σ^2 can be estimated from the residual image. Periodic artifacts in a resampled (part of an) image are particularly well detected after transforming its p-map to the frequency domain, where distinct peaks become visible in the magnitude spectrum. The center panel of Figure 9.10 shows a typical example.

Linear predictor residuals and p-maps computed from them are not only sensitive to resampling artifacts, but naturally capture a much wider range of image characteristics. CFA interpolation, for example, is known to produce high-frequent periodic artifacts similar to upscaling by a factor of two [11]. As well, JPEG compression leaves traces in the p-map. The right panel of Figure 9.10 indicates that increased prediction errors along JPEG block boundaries result in periodic artifacts with a frequency of $1/8$. Forensic analysts need to carefully differentiate between these types of artifacts in practice.

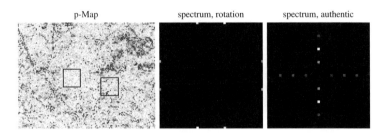

Figure 9.10 Resampling detection for the manipulation depicted in Figure 9.4. Plain p-map (left): brighter shades indicate that pixels are more correlated with their spatial neighbors. JPEG blocking artifacts are visible in authentic image regions. The rotated image region (marked by the left square) exhibits distinct characteristics. Fourier spectra from rotated and authentic regions of the p-map (right panels): rotation yields strong high-frequency peaks, visible at the borders of the left spectrum; JPEG blocking artifacts cause characteristic peaks (at multiples of $1/8$) in the spectrum of the authentic region.

9.2.3.4 Duplicate and Near-Duplicate Regions

Copy–move forgeries are another common class of image manipulations where a region of an image is copied, possibly filtered, and then reinserted at a different position in the *same* image. The copied region will typically undergo some form of post-processing for a more realistic alignment with its surroundings. Copy–move forgeries contain near-duplicate image regions, which can be localized with a suitable matching procedure. A straightforward approach considers (possibly overlapping) blocks of small size and compares local image contents block-wise. A manipulation is declared if a sufficiently large number of near-duplicate blocks share the same spatial relation [54]. To achieve robustness against operations beyond simple copying (e. g., geometric transformations of the reinserted region, image filtering, or lossy compression), image blocks are transformed to a suitable feature space prior to running the matching procedure. The rotation-invariant Zernike moments are among the most promising feature representations for this purpose [55, 56]. Post-processing the correspondence map from the matching procedure helps to remove isolated false positive matches.

A major challenge of block-based matching is computational complexity: an exhaustive search over all block pairs is prohibitive for megapixel-sized images. More efficient approaches restrict the search space by preordering blocks, by the use of structured data representations such as kD-trees, or by means of randomized nearest-neighbor search algorithms like PatchMatch [57]. Figure 9.11 presents a

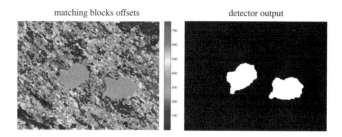

Figure 9.11 Copy–move forgery detection for the manipulation depicted in Figure 9.4. Matching blocks offsets (left): PatchMatch is used to find near-duplicate blocks (in terms of their Zernike moments) in the image [58]. The map visualizes the magnitudes of spatial offsets between matching block pairs. Detector output (right): post-processing and binarization of the offset map gives a clear indication of the duplicated regions. (A version of this chapter with color figures is available on the authors' homepages.)

typical result of a state-of-the-art copy–move detector that combines Zernike moments computed from overlapping blocks of size 16×16 pixels with a PatchMatch-based matching procedure [58]. In terms of computational efficiency, the algorithm is only outperformed by approaches that trade off the high localization accuracy of spatially dense block matching against a search over the much more sparsely populated set of key point descriptors (for instance based on the popular scale-invariant feature transform [59]). We refer to Christlein et al. [55] for a comprehensive benchmark of a variety of different feature representations and matching procedures.

A more general variant of copy–move forgery detectors relax the assumption that the copied region originates from the spurious image under investigation. The literature often refers to this type of forgery, where the image manipulation can be a composition of arbitrary image parts, as *splicing*. Splicing detection is generally a much more difficult problem. In practice, any forensic technique designed to uncover inconsistencies across different parts of image can be used as splicing detector, but we are not aware of a detector that reliably separates all inconsistencies caused by splicing from differences between spatial segments in authentic images.

9.3 LIMITATIONS AND OUTLOOK

Over the past decade, media forensics has developed as a serious research field combining security with signal processing. The resulting toolbox of specialized methods is still growing at an increasing rate. However, the available methods differ in their maturity. As in many fields, there remains a gap between laboratory results and real-world performance. This gap is quite narrow for a few methods where the forensically useful characteristics have been shown to be robust, and where reliable benchmark datasets exist to validate the effectivity of known approaches [60, 61]. The gap is larger for methods that require specific conditions and many assumptions on the exact implementation of the processing chain.

For the case of digital still images, sensor imperfections, specifically PRNU (see Section 9.2.2.3), and metadata are the most reliable source of information for nowadays forensic analyses. Device identification using PRNU has been confirmed in many realistic settings and shown to be robust against various sources of distortion. Among the processing traces, requantization is pretty robust and most indicative in the special case of lossy JPEG compression. However, there are many reasons why images are recompressed. Hence, the compression history does not always answer all questions of the forensic analyst. Traces of resampling interfere with compression, which limits their applicability. Duplicate detection is computationally expensive in large images, sensitive to parameter settings, and still prone to false positives in many natural images. Scene level analyses still suffer from the subjectivity of the human operator and are by principle limited to specific scene contents. Nevertheless, while each method has its specific limitations (hopefully known to the decision maker), the combination of available methods puts forensic analysts in a much better position than imaginable 10 years ago.

A general limitation of forensic detectors is that most of them are designed with a signal processing mindset rather than a security mindset: few methods consider an intelligent adversary who tries to defeat or mislead forensic analyses by erasing traces or deliberately inserting false traces [62]. Technical methods that help the counterfeiter in defeating forensic analysts are typically referred to as *counter forensics* (or *anti forensics*). A simple yet effective approach is to reduce the available information for forensic analyses by downgrading the image quality after performing a manipulation in high resolution. Since most forensic methods are statistical in nature and thus rely on the law of large numbers and increase in precision with the number and precision of observations (samples), this method is effective in situations where low-quality media are plausible (e. g., on the web). More serious advances in counter forensics preserve the image quality and are actively researched in order to assess the limitations of known forensic methods [63, 64], to develop more robust methods [65, 66], and to erase indicative traces in legitimate cases [67], such as to protect the privacy of people sharing media data online. For an overview on digital image counter forensics we refer the reader to our book chapter [68].

As alluded above, forensic detectors can identify processing, but they cannot (and should not) conclude about the authenticity of a media signal in a nontechnical context. So-called *legitimate processing* is common practice: many digital images are resized or recompressed for transmission and almost all art directors adjust exposure and color before reproduction. Therefore, not every form of processing that technically qualifies as editing indicates an attempt of deception or other malicious intentions. There exist approaches to quantify the amount of processing in a metric that tries to respect editing conventions with customizable weights [69]. But the inherent subjectivity and unavoidable measurement errors from failing to recognize the context limits the applicability of this approach to very narrow domains. Our outlook here is reserved because even perfect technical detectors cannot answer the socially relevant questions of authenticity or legitimacy: the very same processing operation can be legitimate in one context and deceptive in another.

While the technical exposition in this chapter focused on digital still images, the most researched subfield of media forensics, many of the approaches presented generalize to other media as well (e. g., analyses on the data structure level, traces of requantization, lossy compression, etc., on the signal level [70]). Yet the detectors need to be adapted to the specific target signal and format. For example, the common practice of motion vector estimation in video compression displaces patches of fixed pattern noise and creates traces similar to copy–move forgeries if predictive-coded frames are analyzed like still images [71]. Temporal editing (e. g., removing frames) of compressed video leaves characteristic traces in the recompressed groups-of-pictures [72]. For audio recordings, the *electrical network frequency* (ENF) criterion deserves special attention [73]. It is a different type of trace that exists in the time domain of many audio recordings and has recently been explored for video as well [74, 75]. The ENF gets interspersed from the electrical network surrounding the recording device at the time of recording. As the frequency of this signal varies slightly around its norm (e. g., 50 Hz in Europe, Africa, and large parts of Asia, and 60 Hz in the United States and parts of Latin America), isolating and analyzing the ENF component in recordings allows the forensic analyst to verify the authenticity by checking the (broad) geolocation and time of recording (provided that a database of ENF time series is available, as in many forensics departments of law enforcement agencies). Moreover, inconsistencies in the ENF frequency or phase can reveal editing operations. A particular challenge is related to testing new forensic methods for more exotic media types, formats, and editing operations. Reliable benchmark datasets often do not exist and are expensive to create, in particular if they should include controlled forgeries that are convincing to human perception. Simply repurposing data generated for other reasons (e. g., for compression or pattern recognition) is prone to fallacies and often not adequate because these sources hardly contain any (known) forgeries.

In the future, undoubtedly the relevance and scope of media forensics is going to grow. What we consider media data today (audio, images, video) continues to become ever more prevalent. In addition, as sensors become smaller, cheaper, and more pervasive, the authenticity of sensor data in general will be of utmost importance for many decisions that affect people's lives. Key questions will remain on what confidence we can put in forensic methods, passive and active alike, to deliver reliable results, automated and without human intervention, in environments with intelligent adversaries. We should embrace that new methods for sensor and signal forensics, in a very general sense, will be developed, critically evaluated, and deployed at large scale. Many of them will draw on principles inspired by information hiding and signal detection, the foundations of which were reviewed in this book.

ACKNOWLEDGMENTS

The authors thank Luisa Verdoliva for providing the materials for Figures 9.4 and 9.11. The work of the first author on this chapter has been supported by Archimedes Privatstiftung, Innsbruck, Austria.

References

[1] Ng, T.-T., et al., "Passive-Blind Image Forensics," in *Multimedia Security Technologies for Digital Rights Management*, Academic Press, pp. 383–412, 1st ed., 2006.

[2] Böhme, R., "An Epistemological Approach to Steganography," in *Information Hiding*, Vol. LNCS 5806 of *LNCS*, Berlin, Heidelberg: Springer Verlag, 2009, pp. 15–30.

[3] Böhme, R., et al., "Multimedia Forensics is not Computer Forensics," in *Computational Forensics, Third International Workshop*, Vol. 5718 of *Lecture Notes in Computer Science*, Springer, 2009, pp. 90–103.

[4] Lyu, S., and H. Farid, "How Realistic is Photorealistic?" *IEEE Transactions on Signal Processing*, Vol. 53, No. 2, 2005, pp. 845–850.

[5] Dehnie, S., H. T. Sencar, and N. Memon, "Digital Image Forensics for Identifying Computer Generated and Digital Camera Images," in *IEEE International Conference on Image Processing (ICIP)*, 2006, pp. 2313–2316.

[6] Ng, T.-T., and S.-F. Chang, "Discrimination of Computer Synthesized or Recaptured Images from Real Images," in *Digital Image Forensics: There is More to a Picture Than Meets the Eye*, Springer-Verlag, pp. 275–309, 2013.

[7] Dirik, A. E., et al., "New Features to Identify Computer Generated Images," in *IEEE International Conference on Image Processing (ICIP)*, Vol. 4, 2007, pp. 433–436.

[8] McKay, C., et al., "Image Acquisition Forensics: Forensic Analysis to Identify Imaging Source," in *IEEE International Conference on Acoustics, Speech, and Signal Processing (ICASSP)*, 2008, pp. 1657–1660.

[9] Kirchner, M., and T. Gloe, "Forensic Camera Model Identification," in *Handbook of Digital Forensics of Multimedia Data and Devices*, John Wiley & Sons Ltd., 9, 2015.

[10] Gloe, T., "Feature-Based Forensic Camera Model Identification," in *LNCS Transactions on Data Hiding and Multimedia Security VIII (DHMMS)*, Vol. 7228 of *Lecture Notes in Computer Science*, 2012, pp. 42–62.

[11] Popescu, A. C., and H. Farid, "Exposing Digital Forgeries in Color Filter Array Interpolated Images," *IEEE Transactions on Signal Processing*, Vol. 53, No. 10, 2005, pp. 3948–3959.

[12] Popescu, A. C., and H. Farid, "Exposing Digital Forgeries by Detecting Traces of Re-sampling," *IEEE Transactions on Signal Processing*, Vol. 53, No. 2, 2005, pp. 758–767.

[13] Kirchner, M., "Fast and Reliable Resampling Detection by Spectral Analysis of Fixed Linear Predictor Residue," in *Proceedings of the Multimedia and Security Workshop*, ACM Press, 2008, pp. 11–20.

[14] Kee, E., M. K. Johnson, and H. Farid, "Digital Image Authentication from JPEG Headers," *IEEE Transactions on Information Forensics and Security*, Vol. 6, No. 3, 2011, pp. 1066–1075.

[15] Gloe, T., "Forensic Analysis of Ordered Data Structures on the Example of JPEG Files," in *IEEE International Workshop on Information Forensics and Security (WIFS)*, 2012, pp. 139–144.

[16] Johnson, M. K., and H. Farid, "Exposing Digital Forgeries in Complex Lighting Environments," *IEEE Transactions on Information Forensics and Security*, Vol. 2, No. 3, 2007, pp. 450–461.

[17] O'brien, J. F., and H. Farid, "Exposing Photo Manipulation with Inconsistent Reflections," *ACM Transactions on Graphics*, Vol. 31, No. 1, 2012, pp. 4:1–4:11.

[18] Kee, E., J. F. O'brien, and H. Farid, "Exposing Photo Manipulation from Shading and Shadows," *ACM Transactions on Graphics*, Vol. 33, No. 5, 2014.

[19] Popescu, A. C., and H. Farid, "Statistical Tools for Digital Forensics," in *Information Hiding. 6th International Workshop, IH 2004, Toronto, Canada, May 2004, Revised Selected Papers*, Vol. LNCS 3200 of *LNCS*, Berlin, Heidelberg: Springer Verlag, 2004, pp. 128–147.

[20] Chiang, P.-J., et al., "Printer and Scanner Forensics: Models and Methods," in *Intelligent Multimedia Analysis for Security Applications*, Springer Verlag, No. 282 in Studies in Computational Intelligence, pp. 145–187, 2010.

[21] Choi, K. S., E. Y. Lam, and K. K. Y. Wong, "Automatic Source Camera Identification Using Intrinsic Lens Radial Distortion," *Optics Express*, Vol. 14, No. 24, 2006, pp. 11551–11565.

[22] Gloe, T., S. Pfennig, and M. Kirchner, "Unexpected Artefacts in PRNU-Based Camera Identification: A 'Dresden Image Database' Case-Study," in *Proceedings of the Multimedia and Security Workshop*, ACM Press, 2012, pp. 109–114.

[23] Lyu, S., "Estimating Vignetting Function from a Single Image for Image Authentication," in *Proceedings of the Multimedia and Security Workshop*, New York: ACM Press, 2010, pp. 3–12.

[24] Johnson, M. K., and H. Farid, "Exposing Digital Forgeries through Chromatic Aberration," in *MM&Sec'06, Proceedings of the Multimedia and Security Workshop 2006*, New York: ACM, 2006, pp. 48–55.

[25] Gloe, T., K. Borowka, and A. Winkler, "Efficient Estimation and Large-Scale Evaluation of Lateral Chromatic Aberration for Digital Image Forensics," in *Proceedings of SPIE: Media Forensics and Security II*, Vol. 7541, 2010, p. 754107.

[26] Chierchia, G., et al., "A Bayesian-MRF Approach for PRNU-Based Image Forgery Detection," *IEEE Transactions on Information Forensics and Security*, Vol. 9, No. 4, 2014, pp. 554–567.

[27] Lukáš, J., J. Fridrich, and M. Goljan, "Digital Camera Identification from Sensor Pattern Noise," *IEEE Transactions on Information Forensics and Security*, Vol. 1, No. 2, 2006, pp. 205–214.

[28] Chen, M., et al., "Determining Image Origin and Integrity Using Sensor Noise," *IEEE Transactions on Information Forensics and Security*, Vol. 3, No. 1, March 2008, pp. 74–90.

[29] Goljan, M., J. Fridrich, and T. Filler, "Large Scale Test of Sensor Fingerprint Camera Identification," in *Proceedings of SPIE: Media Forensics and Security XI*, Vol. 7254, 2009, p. 72540I.

[30] Gloe, T., E. Franz, and A. Winkler, "Forensics for Flatbed Scanners," in *Proceedings of SPIE: Security, Steganography, and Watermarking of Multimedia Contents IX*, Vol. 6505, 2007, p. 65051I.

[31] Khanna, N., et al., "Scanner Identification with Extension to Forgery Detection," in *Proceedings of SPIE: Security, Forensics, Steganography, and Watermarking of Multimedia Contents X*, Vol. 6819, 2008, pp. 6819–16.

[32] Caldelli, R., I. Amerini, and F. Picchioni, "A DFT-Based Analysis to Discern between Camera and Scanned Images," *International Journal of Digital Crime and Forensics*, Vol. 2, No. 1, 2010, pp. 21–29.

[33] Geradts, Z. J., et al., "Methods for Identification of Images Acquired with Digital Cameras," in *Proceedings of SPIE: Enabling Technologies for Law Enforcement and Security*, Vol. 4232, 2001, pp. 505–512.

[34] Fridrich, J., and M. Goljan, "Determining Approximate Age of Digital Images Using Sensor Defects," in *Proceedings of SPIE: Media Forensics and Security III*, Vol. 7880, 2011, p. 788006.

[35] Dirik, A. E., H. T. Sencar, and N. D. Memon, "Digital Single Lens Reflex Camera Identification from Traces of Sensor Dust," *IEEE Transactions on Information Forensics and Security*, Vol. 3, No. 3, September 2008, pp. 539–552.

[36] Swaminathan, A., M. Wu, and K. J. R. Liu, "Nonintrusive Component Forensics of Visual Sensors Using Output Images," *IEEE Transactions on Information Forensics and Security*, Vol. 2, No. 1, 2007, pp. 91–106.

[37] Dirik, A. E., and N. Memon, "Image Tamper Detection Based on Demosaicing Artifacts," in *IEEE International Conference on Image Processing (ICIP)*, 2009, pp. 1497–1500.

[38] Kirchner, M., "Efficient Estimation of CFA Pattern Configuration in Digital Camera Images," in *Proceedings of SPIE: Media Forensics and Security II*, Vol. 7541, 2010, p. 754111.

[39] Cao, H., and A. C. Kot, "Accurate Detection of Demosaicing Regularity for Digital Image Forensics," *IEEE Transactions on Information Forensics and Security*, Vol. 4, No. 4, 2009, pp. 899–910.

[40] Swaminathan, A., M. Wu, and K. J. R. Liu, "Digital Image Forensics via Intrinsic Fingerprints," *IEEE Transactions on Information Forensics and Security*, Vol. 3, No. 1, 2008, pp. 101–117.

[41] Stamm, M. C., and K. J. R. Liu, "Forensic Detection of Image Manipulation Using Statistical Intrinsic Fingerprints," *IEEE Transactions on Information Forensics and Security*, Vol. 5, No. 3, 2010, pp. 492–506.

[42] Neelamani, R., et al., "JPEG Compression History Estimation for Color Images," *IEEE Transactions on Image Processing*, Vol. 15, No. 6, 2006, pp. 1365–1378.

[43] Luo, W., J. Huang, and G. Qiu, "JPEG Error Analysis and Its Applications to Digital Image Forensics," *IEEE Transactions on Information Forensics and Security*, Vol. 5, No. 3, 2010, pp. 480–491.

[44] Bianchi, T., and A. Piva, "Image Forgery Localization via Block-Grained Analysis of JPEG Artifacts," *IEEE Transactions on Information Forensics and Security*, Vol. 7, No. 3, 2012, pp. 1003–1017.

[45] Pevný, T., and J. Fridrich, "Detection of Double-Compression in JPEG Images for Applications in Steganography," *IEEE Transactions on Information Forensics and Security*, Vol. 3, No. 2, 2008, pp. 247–258.

[46] Ferrara, P., et al., "Reverse Engineering of Double Compressed Images in the Presence of Contrast Enhancement," in *IEEE International Workshop on Multimedia Signal Processing (MMSP)*, 2013, pp. 141–146.

[47] Fu, D., Y. Q. Shi, and W. Su, "A Generalized Benford's Law for JPEG Coefficients and its Applications in Image Forensics," in *Security and Watermarking of Multimedia Content IX*, Vol. 6505 of *Proceedings of SPIE*, SPIE, 2007, p. 65051L.

[48] Pérez-González, F., G. L. Heileman, and C. T. Abdallah, "Benford's Law in Image Processing," in *IEEE International Conference on Image Processing (ICIP)*, Vol. 1, IEEE, 2007, pp. 405–408.

[49] Milani, S., M. Tagliasacchi, and S. Tubaro, "Discriminating Multiple JPEG Compressions Using First Digit Features," *APSIPA Transactions on Signal and Information Processing*, Vol. 3, 2014, pp. e19.

[50] Lai, S., and R. Böhme, "Block Convergence in Repeated Transform Coding: JPEG-100 Forensics, Darbon Dating, and Tamper Detection," in *IEEE International Conference on Acoustics, Speech and Signal Processing (ICASSP)*, 2013, pp. 3028–3032.

[51] Carnein, M., P. Schöttle, and R. Böhme, "Forensics of High-Quality JPEG Images with Color Subsampling," in *IEEE International Workshop on Information Forensics and Security (WIFS)*, 2015.

[52] Lin, W. S., et al., "Digital Image Source Coder Forensics Via Intrinsic Fingerprints," *IEEE Transactions on Information Forensics and Security*, Vol. 4, No. 3, 2009, pp. 460–475.

[53] Gallagher, A. C., "Detection of Linear and Cubic Interpolation in JPEG Compressed Images," in *Canadian Conference on Computer and Robot Vision (CRV)*, 2005, pp. 65–72.

[54] Fridrich, J., D. Soukal, and J. Lukáš, "Detection of Copy-Move Forgery in Digital Images," in *Digital Forensic Research Workshop*, 2003.

[55] Christlein, V., et al., "An Evaluation of Popular Copy-Move Forgery Detection Approaches," *IEEE Transactions on Information Forensics and Security*, Vol. 7, No. 6, 2012, pp. 1841–1854.

[56] Ryu, S.-J., et al., "Rotation Invariant Localization of Duplicated Image Regions Based on Zernike Moments," *IEEE Transactions on Information Forensics and Security*, Vol. 8, No. 8, 2013, pp. 1355–1370.

[57] Barnes, C., et al., "PatchMatch: A Randomized Correspondence Algorithm for Structural Image Editing," *ACM Transactions on Graphics*, Vol. 28, No. 3, 2009.

[58] Cozzolino, D., G. Poggi, and L. Verdoliva, "Efficient Dense-Field Copy-Move Forgery Detection," *IEEE Transactions on Information Forensics and Security*, Vol. 10, No. 11, 2015, pp. 2284–2297.

[59] Amerini, I., et al., "A SIFT–based Forensic Method for Copy-Move Attack Detection and Transformation Recovery," *IEEE Transactions on Information Forensics and Security*, Vol. 6, No. 3, 2011, pp. 1099–1110.

[60] Gloe, T., and R. Böhme, "The Dresden Image Database for Benchmarking Digital Image Forensics," *Journal of Digital Forensic Practice*, Vol. 3, 2010, pp. 150–159.

[61] Dang-Nguyen, D.-T., et al., "RAISE — A Raw Images Dataset for Digital Image Forensics," in *Proceedings of the 6th ACM Multimedia Systems Conference*, ACM, 2015, pp. 219–224.

[62] Barni, M., and F. Pérez-González, "Coping With the Enemy: Advances in Adversary-Aware Signal Processing," in *IEEE International Conference on Acoustics, Speech and Signal Processing (ICASSP)*, 2013, pp. 8682–8686.

[63] Gloe, T., et al., "Can We Trust Digital Image Forensics?" in *15th International Conference on Multimedia*, ACM Press, 2007, pp. 78–86.

[64] Kirchner, M., and R. Böhme, "Hiding Traces of Resampling in Digital Images," *IEEE Transactions on Information Forensics and Security*, Vol. 3, No. 4, 2008, pp. 582–592.

[65] Goljan, M., J. Fridrich, and M. Chen, "Defending Against Fingerprint-Copy Attack in Sensor-Based Camera Identification," *IEEE Transactions on Information Forensics and Security*, Vol. 6, No. 1, 2011, pp. 227–236.

[66] Lai, S., and R. Böhme, "Countering Counter-Forensics: The Case of JPEG Compression," in *Information Hiding, 13th International Conference*, Vol. 6958 of *Lecture Notes in Computer Science*, Springer Verlag, 2011, pp. 285–298.

[67] Dirik, A. E., H. T. Sencar, and N. Memon, "Analysis of Seam-Carving-Based Anonymization of Images Against PRNU Noise Pattern-Based Source Attribution," *IEEE Transactions on Information Forensics and Security*, Vol. 9, No. 12, 2014, pp. 2277–2290.

[68] Böhme, R., and M. Kirchner, "Counter-Forensics: Attacking Image Forensics," in *Digital Image Forensics: There is More to a Picture Than Meets the Eye*, Springer-Verlag, pp. 327–366, 2013.

[69] Kee, E., and H. Farid, "A Perceptual Metric for Photo Retouching," *Proceedings of the National Academy of Sciences*, Vol. 108, No. 50, 2011, pp. 19907–19912.

[70] Böhme, R., and A. Westfeld, "Feature-based Encoder Classification of Compressed Audio Streams," *Multimedia Systems*, Vol. 11, No. 2, 2005, pp. 108–120.

[71] Milani, S., et al., "An Overview on Video Forensics," *APSIPA Transactions on Signal and Information Processing*, Vol. 1, 2012.

[72] Stamm, M. C., W. S. Lin, and K. J. R. Liu, "Temporal Forensics and Anti-Forensics for Motion Compensated Video," *IEEE Transactions on Information Forensics and Security*, Vol. 7, No. 4, 2012, pp. 1315–1329.

[73] Grigoras, C., "Digital Audio Recording Analysis: the Electric Network Frequency (ENF) Criterion," *Speech, Language and the Law*, Vol. 12, No. 1, 2005, pp. 63–76.

[74] Garg, R., A. L. Varna, and M. Wu, "Seeing ENF: Natural Time Stamp for Digital Video via Optical Sensing and Signal Processing," in *ACM International Conference on Multimedia*, ACM Press, 2011, pp. 23–32.

[75] Su, H., et al., "Exploiting Rolling Shutter for ENF Signal Extraction from Video," in *IEEE International Conference on Image Processing (ICIP)*, IEEE, 2014, pp. 5367–5371.

Chapter 10

Watermarking in the Encrypted Domain

Mauro Barni, Alessandro Piva, Tiziano Bianchi

Multimedia content protection is with no doubt one of the most important application scenarios for watermarking technology within those mentioned in Section 1.3. In a content protection scenario, information about the creator, the distributor, the customer, or the licensing terms between these players is embedded into the content itself by means of watermarking. The hidden information can be used later to demonstrate content ownership, content misappropriation or as a proof of purchase [1, 2]. The adoption of digital watermarking for multimedia content protection in realistic scenarios raises a set of important problems, including the possible collusion of malicious customers, the fact that the distribution mechanism may leak sensible information about the customers, and the scalability to large-scale scenarios. The collusion problem has already been addressed in Chapter 7. In this chapter, we will illustrate possible solutions to the remaining problems. All of the described solutions are based on the possibility of processing encrypted data [3], which permits to efficiently combine watermarking and cryptographic techniques.

10.1 INTRODUCTION

Let us suppose that a content owner, commonly referred to as the seller, provides an image to a customer, referred to as the buyer, through a server. Let us also assume that the owner is supposed to receive a royalty for the image's use. The owner is concerned about the possibility that the publisher will not pay the royalties. To discourage such misbehavior, the owner could embed into the image a watermark containing information about either the owner or the user of the image. In the first case, the watermark is used for *ownership assertion*: here the owner is interested to control the published content by detecting if the owner's watermark is embedded in the content in such a way that its presence can be used as evidence of ownership. In the second case, the watermark is used for *fingerprinting* or *forensic tracing*: to avoid unauthorised duplication and distribution of the image, the owner can embed specific information, called a *fingerprint*, linking each copy to a particular user in such a way that if a nonauthorized copy of the image is found, the owner can identify the original recipient who has redistributed the content without permission. In this chapter, we are mainly interested in the second case.

In classical distribution models, the watermark embedding process is carried out by a server before releasing the content to the user; the server is assumed to be trustworthy, in that it would never distribute content illegally and always embed the watermark honestly. However, in practice, such assumptions cannot be granted with certainty. This problem was first identified by Qian and Nahrstedt [4] as the *customer's rights problem*. When the watermark is generated and embedded solely by the content provider (or the seller), a customer, whose watermark has been found in nonauthorized copies, can claim that the pirated copy was created by a malicious seller interested in framing the buyer or by a reselling agent who could benefit from the distribution of nonauthorized copies. Finally, there is always the possibility that a nonauthorized copy containing the buyer's fingerprint could have originated from a security breach in the seller's system rather than from the buyer. The owner-customer watermarking protocol proposed by Qian and Nahrstedt [4] tried to solve this issue by letting the customer provide the owner with an encrypted predetermined bit-string and letting the owner embed this encrypted value by means of watermarking. Upon receiving the watermarked content delivered from the owner, the customer is able to prove to a third party the legitimate ownership of the copy in his possession, since only the buyer knows the decryption key. The drawback of this protocol is that it does not solve the problem of binding the buyer and the specific copy sold to him or her, and thus does not allow to accuse the customer when a nonauthorized copy is found by the owner. The mere existence of this problem may discredit the trustability of the whole forensic tracing architecture. A possible solution consists in resorting to a trusted third party (TTP), who takes care of watermark embedding and decoding. However, TTPs are difficult to implement in real scenarios and may easily become the bottleneck of the whole system.

An elegant solution to the aforementioned problems is represented by *asymmetric fingerprinting*; that is, fingerprinting schemes where, unlike the traditional symmetric schemes, in which both buyer and seller know the copy that the buyer gets, only the buyer receives the data with the fingerprint. However, if the seller later finds this fingerprinted copy somewhere, he or she can identify the buyer and prove to third parties that this buyer bought this copy [5]. In practice, an asymmetric fingerprinting scheme is built as a set of protocols. During the *registration protocol* the buyer first commits to a secret that only he or she knows obtaining the fingerprint data. Then the buyer and the seller follow a *fingerprinting protocol* that allows them to jointly embed the watermark in such a way that the original content is a private input of the seller, the fingerprint data is a private input of the buyer, and at the end of which the buyer obtains a watermarked content containing the buyer's secret while the seller does not get any information. Finally, in the case of an unauthorized distribution of the copy, the seller can identify the buyer from whom the copy originated and prove it to a judge by using a proper *dispute resolution protocol*. The main watermarking techniques used in asymmetric fingeprinting protocols will be illustrated and discussed in Section 10.3.

Another problem with the use of watermarking for fingerprinting-based applications is the limited *scalability* of the classical distribution models: in large-scale systems, the server may be overloaded, since the computational burden due to watermark embedding grows linearly with the number of buyers. In addition, since the distribution of individually watermarked copies requires the use of point-to-point communication channels, the required bandwidth can become unacceptably large. A different architecture, proposed in [6], is based on a federation of web entities constituting a distributed protection center that relieves the content provider of the direct implementation of the watermarking procedure. This model is designed for applications where the client is required to be as light as possible, but has the drawback of requiring the setup of services based on complex technologies and ad hoc web architectures. In addition, bandwidth requirements can still be prohibitive in presence of many users, due to the distribution of individually watermarked copies.

An interesting solution to the scalability problem is represented by client-side watermark embedding: the server broadcasts an unique copy of the content to all the interested users, without the need to generate different watermarked copies (thus removing the bottlenecks present in the server-side watermark embedding approach). Instead, each client is in charge of embedding a personal watermark identifying the received copy. Since the clients cannot be trusted, proper solutions are devised to avoid that malevolent users have access to the original content or to the watermark to be inserted. A new approach, defined as *secure client-side watermark embedding*, has been proposed to face the lack of trust of the clients. In this approach, the server transmits the same encrypted version of the original work to all the clients, but a client-specific secret, previously distributed to each customer, allows to decrypt the content and at the same time implicitly embeds a personalized watermark, obtaining a uniquely watermarked copy of the content. An extensive survey of client-side watermarking techniques is provided in Section 10.4.

Recently, some authors have started to address another issue, which is that in some scenarios a third party can embed a watermark into an already encrypted content without having access to the decryption key, possibly in an noninteractive way. An example of a possible application is a scenario where a data center collects large amounts of encrypted data and wants to embed annotations within them for the purpose of redistribution. The main requirement of these techniques is that the watermark should be readable from both the encrypted and the decrypted content. In addition, in some cases, for example when dealing with medical images used for for medical diagnosis, the distortion introduced during watermark embedding is not acceptable. In these circumstances, reversible watermarking techniques may be used, where a watermark is said to be invertible if the original content can be recovered from the watermarked document together with the hidden watermark. In this way, the watermarking process has no impact on the image quality while still allowing the transmission of an informative message. By coupling the quest for reversible watermarking with the security concerns raised before, the need for reversible data hiding methods working in the encrypted domain is evident. In Sections 10.5, we illustrate the main techniques for reversible watermarking of encrypted data, and provide the reader with a clear understanding of their merits and main limitations.

10.2   A FEW PRELIMINARIES

In this section, we briefly review some basic concepts that will help to understand the solutions described in the next sections: the watermarking model [7], homomorphic encryption [8], and the adversary model [3].

10.2.1   Watermarking Model

In the following sections, we will refer to a simplified watermarking model, defined according to the generic watermarking architecture illustrated in Figure 5.1. Given a vector $\mathbf{x} = (x_0, x_1, \ldots, x_{M-1})$, representing the output of a content adaptation layer that maps the input signal to the watermarking space (e.g., they can be either a subset of the host signal samples or, more generally, a set of features of the host signal), and the to-be-hidden information, represented as a binary vector $\mathbf{b} = (b_0, b_1, \ldots, b_{L-1})$, the watermark *embedder* inserts the watermark code $\mathbf{b}$ into the signal $\mathbf{x}$ to produce a watermarked signal $\mathbf{y}$, usually making use of a secret key sk to control some parameters of the embedding process and allow the watermark recovery only to authorized users. It is often useful to describe the embedding function by introducing a watermark signal $\mathbf{w}$, so that the watermarked signal can be expressed as $\mathbf{y} = \mathbf{x} + \mathbf{w}$.

10.2.2 Homomorphic Cryptosystems

A cryptosystem is said to be *homomorphic* with respect to an operation $\star$ if there exists an operator $\phi(\cdot, \cdot)$ such that for any two plain messages m_1 and m_2, we have:

$$\mathcal{D}\big(\phi(\mathcal{E}(m_1), \mathcal{E}(m_2))\big) = m_1 \star m_2, \tag{10.1}$$

where $\mathcal{E}(\cdot)$ and $\mathcal{D}(\cdot)$ denote, respectively, the encryption and decryption operators. Homomorphic encryption allows to perform a set of operations by working on encrypted data. In particular, an additively homomorphic cryptosystem maps an addition in the plaintext domain to an operation in the ciphertext domain (usually a multiplication). Given two plaintexts m_1 and m_2, the following equalities are then satisfied:

$$\mathcal{E}(m_1) \cdot \mathcal{E}(m_2) = \mathcal{E}(m_1 + m_2) \tag{10.2}$$

and, as a consequence,

$$\mathcal{E}(m)^a = \mathcal{E}(am), \tag{10.3}$$

where a is a public integer. Additively homomorphic cryptosystems allow to perform additions, subtractions and multiplications with a known (nonencrypted) value in the encrypted domain, thus providing a way to apply any linear operator in the encrypted domain. Note that division can not be carried out by relying on homomorphic encryption since it could lead to non integer values.

Another desirable property of a homomorphic cryptosystem is *semantic security*. A cryptosystem is said to be semantically secure if given two encrypted values it is not computationally feasible to decide whether they conceal the same value or not. This property guarantees the confidentiality of the cryptosystem when encrypting data with a restricted set of possible values (for example bits), or when a set of data exhibiting a peculiar correlation structure (for example consecutive signal

samples) is encrypted as separate encryptions. A well known additively homomorphic and semantically secure asymmetric encryption scheme is the one proposed by
Paillier [8] and later extended by Damgård and Jurik [9].

10.2.3   Adversary Model

The security of the protocols that we will describe in the next sections critically
rely on assumptions about the behavior of adversaries. In the following, we will
always assume that the participants in the computation are honest-but-curious or
semi-honest [10]. According to this adversary model, each party follows all protocol
steps correctly, but collects all input, intermediate, and output data in an attempt to
learn every possible information about the other parties.

In practical settings, the honest-but-curious model can be too optimist in
modeling the behavior of realistic adversaries. A much more aggressive adversary
model considers a malicious adversary that intentionally deviates from the protocol,
for example providing wrong inputs or aborting the execution of the protocol at
some point.

Achieving security against malicious adversary is much more challenging and
usually requires some modifications to the involved protocols. It can be shown
that any protocol that is secure against a honest-but-curious adversary can be
transformed into one that is secure against malicious adversaries by proving the
correctness of all intermediate computation steps. This can be obtained by using
cryptographic techniques known as commitment schemes [11] and zero-knowledge
proofs [12] that, however, are computationally demanding and significantly increase
the complexity of the protocol.

10.3   ASYMMETRIC FINGERPRINTING PROTOCOLS

In an early solution proposed by Pfitzmann and Schunter [5], both the original
content and the watermark signal were modeled as bit strings, with the latter being
equal to the buyer's code. Hence, a simple privacy homomorphism allowing the
server to compute the exclusive or (XOR) of encrypted bits was sufficient. However,
the above technique is not adequate in the case of realistic multimedia contents,
since it guarantees neither the robustness nor the perceptual fidelity required in this
scenario.

The first combination of encryption methods with effective digital watermarking algorithms was proposed by Memon and Wong [13], who introduced the definition of a buyer-seller Watermarking Protocol (BSWP): an asymmetric fingerprinting protocol where the fingerprint is embedded by means of watermarking in the encrypted domain.

Following the work by Memon and Wong [13], more secure and less complex implementations of the buyer seller protocol have been proposed in [14–18], but the actual implementation of such protocols in a realistic multimedia protection scenario has been investigated only recently [19]. Another issue we are faced with is represented by the fact that the fingerprint depends on private inputs from the buyer, so that it is not easy to enforce the use of specific anticollusion codes. A recently proposed solution consists of letting the buyer pick up the fingerprint elements from a list controlled by the seller in such a way that the seller does not know the chosen elements [20].

We now describe the protocol by Memon and Wong [13] in more detail. Let Alice be the seller, Bob the buyer, and WCA a trusted watermark certification authority in charge of generating valid watermarks and sending them to any buyer upon request. The protocol uses a public key cryptosystem that is homomorphic with respect to the operation used in the watermark embedding equation; moreover, Alice and Bob possess a pair of public/private keys denoted by pk_A, pk_B (public keys) and sk_A, sk_B (private keys).

In the first part of the protocol, on request of Bob, the WCA generates a valid watermark signal $\mathbf{w}$ and sends back to Bob its version encrypted with Bob's public key $\mathcal{E}_{pk_B}(\mathbf{w})$, along with its digital signature $S_{WCA}(\mathcal{E}_{pk_B}(\mathbf{w}))$, to prove that the watermark is valid.

Then, Bob sends to Alice the received values $\mathcal{E}_{pk_B}(\mathbf{w})$ and $S_{WCA}(\mathcal{E}_{pk_B}(\mathbf{w}))$, so that Alice can verify that the encrypted watermark has been generated by the WCA. Alice performs two watermark embedding operations. First, she embeds (with any watermarking scheme) a watermark $\mathbf{v}$ into the original content $\mathbf{x}$. The watermark conveys a distinct ID that is used by Alice to univocally identifying the transaction. Let us indicate the watermarked content as $\mathbf{x}'$. At this point a second watermark is built by using $\mathcal{E}_{pk_B}(\mathbf{w})$: Alice permutes the watermark components through a secret permutation σ:

$$\sigma(\mathcal{E}_{pk_B}(\mathbf{w})) = \mathcal{E}_{pk_B}(\sigma(\mathbf{w})), \tag{10.4}$$

and inserts $\mathcal{E}_{pk_B}(\sigma(\mathbf{w}))$ in $\mathbf{x}'$ directly in the encrypted domain, obtaining the final watermarked content $\mathbf{y}$ in encrypted form due to the homomorphic property of

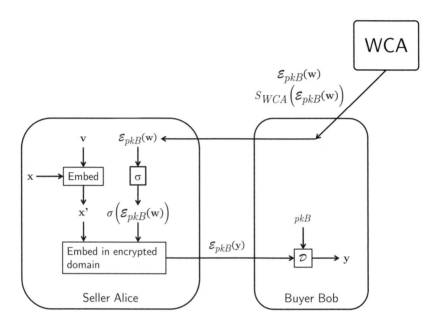

Figure 10.1   The scheme of the buyer seller protocol proposed in [13].

the cipher. In Section 10.3.1, we will describe how this step can be implemented according to different watermarking techniques.

When Bob receives $\mathcal{E}_{pk_B}(\mathbf{y})$, he decrypts it by using his private key sk_B, thus obtaining $\mathbf{y}$, with the embedded watermarks $\mathbf{v}$ and $\sigma(\mathbf{w})$. Note that Bob cannot read the watermark $\sigma(\mathbf{w})$, since he does not know the permutation σ. The scheme is represented in Figure 10.1.

In order to recover the identity of potential copyright violators, Alice first looks for the presence of $\mathbf{v}$. Upon detection of an unauthorized copy $\mathbf{y}$ of the content, she can use the second watermark to effectively prove that the copy originated from Bob. To do so, Alice must reveal to a judge the permutation σ, the encrypted watermark $\mathcal{E}_{pk_B}(\mathbf{w})$ and the digital signature $S_{WCA}(\mathcal{E}_{pk_B}(\mathbf{w}))$. After verifying the validity of the digital signature, the judge asks Bob to use his private key sk_B to compute and reveal $\mathbf{w}$. Now it is possible to check the presence of $\sigma(\mathbf{w})$ within $\mathbf{y}$: if such a presence is verified, then Bob is judged guilty, otherwise Bob's innocence is proven. Note that if $\sigma(\mathbf{w})$ is found in $\mathbf{y}$, Bob can not state that this content originated from Alice, since to do so Alice should have known either the watermark $\mathbf{w}$ to insert it within the plain asset $\mathbf{x}$, or sk_B to decrypt the content $\mathcal{E}_{pk_B}(\mathbf{y})$ after the watermark was embedded in the encrypted domain.

10.3.1 Secure Watermark Embedding by Means of Homomorphic Encryption

In the protocol described in the previous section it is assumed that the server Alice is able to embed Bob's watermark in the encrypted domain. In the following, we will describe in detail how this can be obtained by means of different secure watermark embedding techniques based on homomorphic encryption. Let us assume that the buyer holds a public/private key pair (puk, prk) of an additively homomorphic cryptosystem, like the Paillier cipher. If the seller and the buyer can share an encryption of the watermark signal $\mathbf{w}$, encrypted with the buyer's public key puk, then watermark embedding can be performed by the seller in the encrypted domain as follows:

$$\mathcal{E}_{puk}(y_i) = \mathcal{E}_{puk}(x_i) \cdot \mathcal{E}_{puk}(w_i), \tag{10.5}$$

where the operation is applied componentwise on the data vector. Indeed, the seller, knowing the plaintext values of x_i, can compute the encryptions $\mathcal{E}_{puk}(x_i)$ by relying on buyer's public key puk. However, the computed value $\mathcal{E}_{puk}(y_i)$ is meaningless for the seller, since the private key for decrypting belongs to the buyer, the only one having access to the watermarked content.

In the following we show how homomorphic encryption can be used to implement the two main classes of watermarking techniques on encrypted data.

One of the most known watermarking algorithms for multimedia content is the spread-spectrum technique [7]. The transmission of a single bit with the above technique can be achieved using the following embedding rule

$$y_i = x_i + \gamma(2b - 1)s_i, \tag{10.6}$$

where $b \in \{0, 1\}$ is the embedded bit, s_i is the ith component of a spreading sequence and γ is a scaling factor controlling the watermark strength (see Section 5.3 for more details on spread-spectrum watermarking). Multiple bits can be encoded by partitioning the host features into several chunks and by using the above technique to embed a bit in every chunk.

A secure version of spread-spectrum watermarking can be obtained in a very simple way by relying on an additively homomorphic and semantically secure cryptosystem. If we assume that the seller receives the encrypted bit $\mathcal{E}(b)$ as the output of the registration protocol of the fingerprinting scheme, then the encrypted watermarked signal can be computed as

$$\mathcal{E}(y_i) = \mathcal{E}(x_i) \cdot \mathcal{E}(b)^{2\gamma s_i} \cdot \mathcal{E}(\gamma s_i)^{-1}. \tag{10.7}$$

The seller can easily compute the above expression, since he/she knows the plaintext values of both x_i and s_i. Similar schemes based on Cox's spread spectrum watermarking technique [7] are also possible based either on multiplicatively [13] or additively [21] homomorphic cryptosystems.

Dither modulation (DM) techniques, belonging to the class of informed data hiding schemes, hide a signal-dependent watermark by using as embedding rule the quantization of some content features. The simplest example of such techniques is binary dither modulation with uniform scalar quantizers (see Section 5.4 for a more detailed survey on informed data hiding and dither modulation techniques). In this realization, we assume that each bit of **b**, say b_i, determines which quantizer, chosen between two uniform scalar quantizers, is used to quantize a single scalar host feature x_i. Two codebooks $\mathcal{U}_0$ and $\mathcal{U}_1$ associated respectively to $b = 0$ and $b = 1$ are built as:

$$\begin{aligned}
\mathcal{U}_{\delta,0}^{\Delta} &= \{u_{0,k}\} = \{k\Delta + \delta, k \in \mathbb{Z}\}, \\
\mathcal{U}_{\delta,1}^{\Delta} &= \{u_{1,k}\} = \{k\Delta + \Delta/2 + \delta, k \in \mathbb{Z}\},
\end{aligned} \tag{10.8}$$

where Δ is the quantization step and δ is the dithering value.

A watermark is embedded by applying to the feature x either the quantizer $\mathcal{Q}_0$ associated to $\mathcal{U}_0$, or the quantizer $\mathcal{Q}_1$ associated to $\mathcal{U}_1$, depending on the value assumed by b:

$$\mathcal{Q}_{\delta,b}^{\Delta}(x) = \arg \min_{u_{b,k} \in \mathcal{U}_{\delta,b}^{\Delta}} |u_{b,k} - x| \tag{10.9}$$

where $u_{b,k}$ are the elements of $\mathcal{U}_{\delta,b}^{\Delta}$. By letting x_w indicate the marked feature, we have $x_w = \mathcal{Q}_{\delta,b}^{\Delta}(x)$.

Secure watermark embedding schemes based on dither modulation techniques can be efficiently implemented by relying on homomorphic cryptosystems [16, 22]. Let us assume that a vector of host features **x** has been extracted from the original content and denote a generic feature as x_i. The corresponding watermarked features using a scalar binary dither modulation can be expressed as

$$y_i = f(\mathbf{x}, i) + b_i \cdot \Delta(\mathbf{x}, i), \tag{10.10}$$

where $f(\mathbf{x}, i)$ and $\Delta(\mathbf{x}, i)$, denoting, respectively, a suitable function of the original features and a signal dependent quantization step, depend on the specific embedding technique. For example, quantization index modulation (QIM) [23] can be obtained by choosing

$$f(\mathbf{x}, i) = \mathcal{Q}_{\delta_i,0}^{2\Delta}(x_i)$$
$$\Delta(\mathbf{x}, i) = \Delta \cdot \mathrm{sgn}(x_i - \mathcal{Q}_{\delta_i,0}^{2\Delta}(x_i)),$$

whereas rational dither modulation (RDM) [24] can be obtained as:

$$f(\mathbf{x}, i) = \mathcal{Q}_{\delta_i,0}^{2\Delta}\left(\frac{x_i}{\mu(\mathbf{x})}\right)\mu(\mathbf{x}, i)$$
$$\Delta(\mathbf{x}, i) = \Delta \cdot \mathrm{sgn}\left(\frac{x_i}{\mu(\mathbf{x}, i)} - \mathcal{Q}_{\delta_i,0}^{2\Delta}\left(\frac{x_i}{\mu(\mathbf{x}, i)}\right)\right)\mu(\mathbf{x}, i),$$

where $\mathrm{sgn}(x) = x/|x|$ and $\mu(\mathbf{x}, i)$ is a suitable function of the features around x_i [22, 24, 25].

By assuming an additively homomorphic cryptosystem, (10.10) can be translated into the encrypted domain as

$$\mathcal{E}(y_i) = \mathcal{E}(f(\mathbf{x}, i)) \cdot \mathcal{E}(b_i)^{\Delta(\mathbf{x}, i)}. \qquad (10.11)$$

Note that, being the content owner, the seller knows the plaintext version of $\mathbf{x}$ and can compute both $f(\mathbf{x}, i)$ and $\Delta(\mathbf{x}, i)$ in the plain domain. Hence, (10.11) can be implemented by the seller relying only on the homomorphic properties of the underlying cryptosystem.

10.3.2 Data Expansion and Signal Representation

One of the main problems of the secure embedding approach defined by (10.7) and (10.11) is that each sample of $\mathbf{x}$ must be encrypted separately.

In traditional watermarking applications, the number of bits required to correctly represent each feature is usually quite small, typically ranging from 8 to 16 bits. On the contrary, the security of the underlying cryptosystem requires the use of very large algebraic structures (e.g., a secure implementation of Paillier requires that each encrypted value is represented at least as a 2048-bit integer). The combination of these conditions results in a high data expansion from the plaintext to the encrypted representation of signals, so that the bandwidth requirements may soon become very demanding. In addition, since the number of features can be very large, the computational cost of encrypting such data may become prohibitive, so current solutions based on homomorphic encryption offer provable security, but at the price of a very high complexity [19].

A possibility to mitigate the above problem consists in resorting to a composite representation of the signals [26]. This representation permits to group several signal samples into a single encrypted message and to perform basic linear operations on them in parallel, thus speeding up linear operations on encrypted signals and reducing the size of the whole encrypted signal.

Let us consider a signal a_n. Given a pair of positive integers β, R, the *composite* representation of a_n of order R and base β is defined as

$$a_{C,k} = \sum_{i=0}^{R-1} a_{i,k}\beta^i, \quad k = 0, 1, \ldots, M - 1, \tag{10.12}$$

where $a_{i,k}$, $i = 0, 1, \ldots, R - 1$ indicate R disjoint subsequences of the signal a_n. Under suitable hypotheses [26], the composite representation $a_{C,k}$ can be processed through modular arithmetic without losing information, and several kinds of linear processing can be directly applied to the composite representation of the signal, allowing the parallel processing of the original signal samples. As an example, a much more efficient secure embedding algorithm can be obtained [25]. Let us define the signals $\tilde{x}_i = f(\mathbf{x}, i)$ and $\tilde{w}_i = b_i \cdot \Delta(\mathbf{x}, i)$. By dividing the feature vector into blocks of M samples, the composite representations of the above signals can be expressed as $\tilde{x}_{C,k} = \sum_{j=0}^{R-1} \tilde{x}_{jM+k}\beta^j$ and $\tilde{w}_{C,k} = \sum_{j=0}^{R-1} \tilde{w}_{jM+k}\beta^j$, and composite embedding can be defined as

$$y_{C,k} = \tilde{x}_{C,k} + \tilde{w}_{C,k} = \sum_{j=0}^{R-1} \{\tilde{x}_{jM+k} + \tilde{w}_{jM+k}\} \beta^j = \sum_{j=0}^{R-1} y_{jM+k}\beta^j, \tag{10.13}$$

where the result is the composite representation of the watermarked features y_i.

The watermarked features in the previous example are not suitable for direct processing through a homomorphic cryptosystem, since they are represented as real values. An integer valued watermarked feature is usually obtained as

$$\begin{aligned} z_i &= \lceil f(\mathbf{x}, i) \cdot Q \rfloor + b_i \cdot \lceil \Delta(\mathbf{x}, i) \cdot Q \rfloor \\ &= f_Q(\mathbf{x}, i) + b_i \cdot \Delta_Q(\mathbf{x}, i), \end{aligned} \tag{10.14}$$

where $\lceil \cdot \rfloor$ is the rounding function and Q is a scale factor that can be adjusted according to the required precision. It is worth noting that computing with the above representation is somewhat different than traditional fixed point arithmetic. Since secure division of encrypted values requires an interactive protocol, in computations relying only on the privacy homomorphism the scale factor Q accumulates after each multiplication, and particular care must be taken to chose the correct number of bits to represent the scale factor. Nevertheless, for the schemes presented in the previous section, experimental results show that in most cases 11-15 bits are sufficient to obtain the same watermarking performance of a floating point implementation [25].

An alternative approach is to use integer valued features that can be obtained by using integer transforms [27]. In this case, however, the watermarking algorithm must be modified to satisfy the integer constraint.

10.3.3 Applications to Peer-to-Peer Networks

In peer-to-peer networks, the classical buyer-seller watermarking protocols cannot be applied directly: the decentralized structure of these systems, where most of the downloads come from other users, does not allow that clients receive their watermarked copy of the content directly from the vendor. It is then required to design proper peer-to-peer (P2P) content distribution systems, satisfying security and privacy requirements and at the same time avoiding high computational costs at the vendor's and/or at the client's end.

In [28] a buyer-seller watermarking system is extended to allow the controlled redistribution of content directly between buyers while maintaining a watermark that uniquely identifies each recipient. This is obtained by introducing the concept of watermark transferability. A proof-of-concept protocol is proposed that requires only limited interaction with the original seller to exchange the watermark and satisfies the requested security requirements assuming that there is no collusion between the players.

In [29], the authors propose a P2P content distribution system where the content to be distributed is split by the merchant into a base and a supplementary part. The base file, much smaller than the original file and containing the most important information, is sent by the vendor to the client. The supplementary file, unusable in the absence of the base file, is distributed in a P2P fashion. The base file is sent through an asymmetric fingerprinting protocol performed by the merchant and the buyer in the presence of a trusted party, allowing to embed a collusion-resistant fingerprinting code while preserving the anonymity of the buyers. To ensure anonymous communication between buyers, onion-routing is used for an anonymous data transfer. Moreover, to provide accountability, a key agreement protocol is adopted.

10.4   CLIENT-SIDE WATERMARK EMBEDDING

In client-side watermarking systems, the server transmits the same encrypted version of the original content to all the clients but a client-specific decryption key allows to decrypt the content and at the same time to implicitly embed a watermark. When the client uses his/her key to decrypt the content, he/she obtains a uniquely watermarked version of the content. The security properties of the embedding scheme usually guarantee that obtaining either the watermark or an unencrypted version of the original content is of comparable difficulty as removing the watermark from the personalized copy.

Several approaches for secure client-side embedding have been proposed. In [30] a pseudorandom mask is blended over each frame of a video. Each client is given a different mask, which, when subtracted from the masked broadcast video, leaves an additive watermark in the content. The scheme is not very secure because the same mask is used for all the frames of a video and can therefore be estimated by averaging attacks.

In broadcast environments, stream switching [31, 32] can be performed. Two differently watermarked signals are chopped up into small chunks. Each chunk is encrypted by a different key. Clients are given a different set of decryption keys that allow them to selectively decrypt chunks of the two broadcast streams such that each client obtains the full stream decrypted. The way the full stream is composed out of the two broadcasted versions encodes the watermark. This solution consumes considerable bandwidth, since the data broadcasted to the clients is twice as large as the content itself.

Another solution involves partial encryption, for instance encrypting the signs of DCT coefficients of a signal [33]. Since the sign bits of DCT coefficients are perceptually significant, the partially encrypted version of the signal is heavily distorted. During decryption, each user has a different key that decrypts only a subset of these coefficients, so that some signs are left unchanged. This leaves a detectable fingerprint in the signal. A similar approach was used in [34] to obtain partial encryption-based secure embedding solutions for audiovisual content.

A particularly interesting approach is represented by methods using a stream-cipher that allows the use of multiple decryption keys, which decrypt the same cipher-text into slightly different plaintexts. The difference between the original and the decrypted content represents the embedded watermark. The first scheme following this approach was proposed by Anderson et al. [35], who designed a special stream cipher, called Chameleon, which allows to decrypt Chameleon-encrypted content in slightly different ways. During encryption, a secure number generator, driven by a secret key, produces a sequence of indices used to select four entries from a *lookup table* (LUT). These entries are XORed with the plaintext to form a word of the ciphertext. The decryption process is identical to encryption except for the use of a decryption LUT, obtained by properly inserting bit errors in some entries of the encryption LUT. Decryption superimposes these errors onto the content, thus leaving a unique watermark.

Celik et al. [36] have proposed a generalization of Chameleon that operates on lookup tables composed of real numbers and replaces the XOR operation by an addition. The scheme, shown in the following, is suitable for embedding robust spread spectrum watermarks. In addition, perceptual requirements can be taken into account, as demonstrated by a recent extension to audio watermarking. In particular, the method proposed in [37, 38], choses an optimal embedding key from numerous available keys for the encryption, and joint decryption and watermarking. The key determines not only the client-specific watermark to be inserted, but also the embedding position, in such a way that the imperceptibility requirement can be taken into account. In [39], the LUTs are replaced by matrices generated according to pseudo random number generators and modified Lagrange polynomial interpolation. The LUT-based scheme has also been modified to handle joint decryption and watermarking on vector quantized data [40]. In [41], a solution based on selective encryption is proposed, in which encoding results in the generation of a partially encrypted content while decoding produces a slightly different version of the original content; in particular, selective encryption of JPEG images is achieved by randomly selecting Huffman codewords in such a way that image size is preserved.

A common problem of fingerprinting is that several clients may collude and try to remove the fingerprint by comparing the respective watermarked copies. Collusion resistance can be achieved by using specific anticollusion codes in the design of the fingerprint, as explained in Chapter 7. In the case of client-side embedding, a first proposed solution has been to design the watermarking LUTs so that they produce a specific anticollusion code for each client [42]. Nevertheless, the above strategy suffers from the fact that watermarking LUTs has to be managed by a trusted third party. In the following, the LUT-based approach is described in more detail.

10.4.1 LUT-Based Client-Side Spread Spectrum

A distribution server generates a long-term master encryption lookup table $\mathbf{E}$ of size T, whose entries, denoted by $\mathbf{E}(0), \mathbf{E}(1), \dots, \mathbf{E}(T-1)$, are i.i.d. random variables following a Gaussian distribution $\mathcal{N}(0, \sigma_E)$. The LUT $\mathbf{E}$ will be used to encrypt the content to be distributed to the K_U clients. Next, for the kth client, the server generates a personalized watermark LUT $\mathbf{W}_k$ whose entries follow a Gaussian distribution $\mathcal{N}(0, \sigma_W)$, and builds a personalized decryption LUT $\mathbf{D}_k$ by combining componentwise the master encryption LUT $\mathbf{E}$ and the watermark LUT $\mathbf{W}_k$:

$$\mathbf{D}_k(t) \quad = \quad -\mathbf{E}(t) + \mathbf{W}_k(t), \tag{10.15}$$

for $t = 0, 1, \ldots, T - 1$. The personalized decryption LUTs are then transmitted once to each client over a secure channel. It is worth noting that the generation of the LUTs is carried out only once during the setup phase.

A content, represented as a vector $\mathbf{x}$ of size M, is encrypted by adding to each element R entries of the LUT $\mathbf{E}$ pseudo randomly selected according to a content-dependent key sk. We assume that each content is linked to a unique key sk that could be retrieved from a particular content by using, for example, a robust hashing technique, like those described in [43, 44].

The encrypted content $\mathbf{c}$ is sent to all the authorized clients along with the key sk. The k-th client can decrypt $\mathbf{c}$ by using his/her personalized decryption LUT $\mathbf{D}_k$, with the final effect that a spread-spectrum watermark sequence is embedded into the decrypted content $\mathbf{y}_k$, through an additive rule (i.e., each content feature is modified according to the rule $y_{k,i} = x_i + w_{k,i}$). The full process is summarized in Figure 10.2.

In more detail, driven by the content-dependent key sk, a set of $M \times R$ values t_{ih} in the range $[0, T - 1]$ is generated, where $0 \leq i \leq M - 1, 0 \leq h \leq R - 1$. Each of the M content features x_i is encrypted by adding R entries of the encryption LUT identified by the indexes $(t_{i0}, \ldots, t_{i(R-1)})$, obtaining the encrypted feature c_i as follows:

$$c_i \quad = \quad x_i + \sum_{h=0}^{R-1} \mathbf{E}(t_{ih}). \tag{10.16}$$

Joint decryption and watermarking is accomplished by reconstructing the same sequence of indexes t_{ih} using the content dependent key sk and by adding R entries of the decryption LUT $\mathbf{D}_k$ to each encrypted feature c_i:

$$y_{k,i} = c_i + \sum_{h=0}^{R-1} \mathbf{D}_k(t_{ih}) = x_i + \sum_{h=0}^{R-1} \mathbf{W}_k(t_{ih}) = x_i + w_{k,i}, \tag{10.17}$$

where the ith watermark component is given as the sum of R entries of the LUT $\mathbf{W}_k$. The result of this operation is the watermarked content $\mathbf{y}_k = \mathbf{x} + \mathbf{w}_k$,

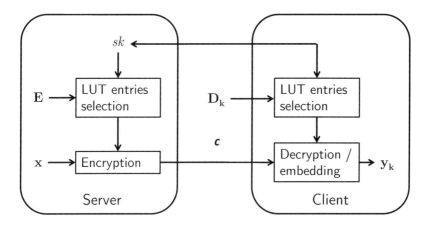

Figure 10.2 Encryption and following joint decryption and watermarking procedure proposed in [36].

identifying the kth user. As explained in [36], the parameter R influences the security of the encryption and should be set to $R > 1$ in order to provide resilience against known-plaintext attacks.

During watermark detection, the same sequence of indexes t_{ih} used for encryption and embedding is reconstructed by means of the key sk. For each client, identified by the corresponding watermark LUT $\mathbf{W}_k$, a watermark sequence $\mathbf{w}_k$ is generated and correlated with an estimated watermark $\mathbf{z}$ extracted from the possibly watermarked content. The obtained correlation is then compared with a properly chosen threshold to decide if the watermark of that particular client is present in the content or not.

10.4.2 LUT-Based Client-Side Dither Modulation

LUT-based client-side embedding can be also extended to dither modulation techniques. The key observation is that these algorithms can be also viewed as watermarking schemes using *syndrome coding* (i.e., systems in which the information is coded in the residual error after quantization). Namely, the marked feature of a QIM watermarking system can be modeled as:

$$y = \mathcal{Q}_0(x) + \theta_b, \tag{10.18}$$

where $\theta_b = b\Delta/2$ is a shift encoding the information bit b and can be considered as the error introduced by quantizing y with the quantizer $\mathcal{Q}_0$ (i.e., the information is encoded in the *syndrome* obtained after decoding y as an element of the codebook $\mathcal{U}_0$). The syndrome coding approach is useful for client-side embedding, since it permits to separate the watermarked feature into a server-dependent part $\mathcal{Q}_0(x)$, which depends on the cover content, and a client-dependent part θ_b, which depends on the information to be embedded.

Syndrome coding can be also used to generalize conventional dither modulation by allowing arbitrary syndrome codewords θ_b, so as to provide an additional degree of freedom in the generation of the client-dependent part. For example, if a generic syndrome codeword can be expressed as the sum of S entries of a LUT, client-side QIM embedding can be obtained by encrypting the original content as

$$\mathcal{E}(x_i) \quad = \quad \mathcal{Q}_0(x_i) + \sum_{j=0}^{S-1} \mathbf{E}[t_{ij}] \qquad (10.19)$$

and the client can compute the watermarked features as

$$y_i = \mathcal{E}(x_i) + \sum_{j=0}^{S-1} \mathbf{D}[t_{ij}] = \mathcal{Q}_0(x_i) + \sum_{j=0}^{S-1} \mathbf{W}[t_{ij}] = \mathcal{Q}_0(x_i) + \theta_{b,i}. \quad (10.20)$$

More sophisticated client-side embedding algorithms can be devised by applying the above principle along random projections of the original content, so as to increase the security, like in spread-transform dither modulation [45].

10.4.3   Client-Side Asymmetric Fingerprinting

Although client-side embedding provides an elegant solution to the system scalability problem, the incorporation of the aforementioned technique in an asymmetric fingerprinting protocol is not an easy task. The main problem is that the watermarking LUT should not be revealed to the server. At the same time, the client should not have access to the watermarking LUT, since the knowledge of both decryption and watermarking LUTs would immediately disclose the encryption LUT as $\mathbf{E}[i] = \mathbf{W}_k[i] - \mathbf{D}_k[i]$.

Early solutions proposed to use a TTP to manage both encryption and watermarking LUTs [46, 47], however such a TTP can become quickly overloaded. In [48], a TTP-free solution is proposed, where existing buyer-seller watermarking protocols are used to securely distribute personalized decryption LUTs in such a way that the server does not have access to plaintext versions of those decryption LUTs. However, since existing TTP-free protocols require the buyer to be identified by a unique binary fingerprint vector $\mathbf{b}_k$, the watermarking LUT must be properly modified so as to embed a binary message into the content and guarantee that the embedded message can be reliably decoded from a possibly modified watermarked content.

In the system described in [48], the L-bit fingerprint $\mathbf{b}_k$ is encoded using a binary antipodal modulation, yielding the to-be-transmitted message $\mathbf{m}_k$. Hence, the watermarking LUT of the kth user can be obtained as:

$$\mathbf{W}_k = \mathbb{G}\mathbf{m}_k, \tag{10.21}$$

where $\mathbb{G}$ is an encoding matrix. Several choices are possible for $\mathbb{G}$: a really simple solution is to use a repetition code. In this case, $\mathbb{G}$ has only one entry equal to one for each row and approximately T/L entries equal to one for each column, otherwise it is possible to generate the elements of $\mathbb{G}$ as i.i.d. Gaussian variables with zero mean and variance $1/L$.

Since encoding is a linear operation, the personalized decryption LUT $\mathbf{D}_k$ can be implemented in a secure way by using a secure buyer-seller protocol like the one described in [19], where the server obtains an encryption of the client's fingerprint $\mathcal{E}(\mathbf{b}_k) = [\mathcal{E}(b_{k,0}), \mathcal{E}(b_{k,1}), \ldots, \mathcal{E}(b_{k,L-1})]$, encrypted with the client's public key, together with a proper identity proof. Thanks to the homomorphic properties of the cryptosystem, the Server can compute a rescaled encrypted message as

$$\mathcal{E}(\tilde{m}_{k,l}) = \mathcal{E}(b_{k,l})^2 \mathcal{E}(1)^{-1} = \mathcal{E}(2b_{k,l} - 1). \tag{10.22}$$

In a similar way, each entry of the Client's personalized LUT can be directly computed in the encrypted domain as

$$\mathcal{E}(\mathbf{D}_k(j)) = \mathcal{E}(\mathbf{E}(j))^{-1} \prod_{l=0}^{L-1} \mathcal{E}(\tilde{m}_{k,l})^{\sigma_W \mathbb{G}(j,l)}. \tag{10.23}$$

Finally, the server can send the encrypted LUT $\mathcal{E}(\mathbf{D}_k)$ to the client, who decrypts it with his/her private key obtaining

$$\mathbf{D}_k = -\mathbf{E} + \mathbb{G}\mathbf{m}_k. \tag{10.24}$$

In practice, Equation (10.23) requires that both $\mathbf{E}(j)$ and $\sigma_W \mathbb{G}(j,l)$ are expressed as integer values to be used with an additively homomorphic cryptosystem defined on modular arithmetic, like Paillier's cryptosystem. This can be achieved by representing such values according to a fixed point representation.

To embed the fingerprint encoded as in (10.21) in a multimedia content, two client-side embedding techniques are introduced in [48]: the first one relies on standard spread-spectrum like client-side embedding, while the second one implements an innovative client-side informed embedding technique. Simulation results show that the fingerprint can be reliably recovered by using either nonblind decoding with standard embedding or blind decoding with informed embedding. In both cases the fingerprint is robust with respect to common attacks.

10.5   REVERSIBLE WATERMARKING OF ENCRYPTED CONTENT

By means of reversible watermarking on encrypted data, we denote a set of techniques in which a message is directly embedded into an encrypted host signal and can be extracted at the receiver side from the decrypted data. Some techniques address message extraction from the decrypted data only; in other techniques the embedded message can be read from both the decrypted data and the encrypted data. In such techniques, the message is typically embedded by a third party who does not have access to the encryption key and does not interact with the entity owning the encryption key. Moreover, an important requirement of these techniques is that the original content should be recovered without any error after decryption.

A basic reversible watermarking technique for encrypted images has been proposed in [49]. It requires that the content be encrypted with a stream cipher and that the plaintext satisfy some local smoothness constraints. Let us assume that an image is encrypted as

$$\mathcal{E}(x_i) = x_i \oplus r_i,$$

where r_i is a keystream and $\oplus$ denotes a bitwise XOR operation. The encrypted image is first partitioned into equal size blocks, then, for each block, two sets of pixel S_0 and S_1 are pseudorandomly selected according to a watermarking key. A single bit b is embedded in each block by simply flipping k least significant bits (LSBs) of the encrypted pixels belonging to S_b. At the receiver side, the decrypted watermarked image is partitioned in the same way, then for each block the receiver computes two versions B_0 and B_1 of the block by flipping the k LSBs of the pixels belonging to S_0 and S_1, respectively. Thanks to the properties of the stream cipher, when the same k LSBs that were flipped in the encrypted content are flipped again, the original LSBs are recovered. Hence, either B_0 or B_1 will be equal to the original image block. The receiver can decode the embedded bit by choosing the block version that yields the smoothest recovered content; that is,

$$\hat{b} = \arg\max_b s(B_b), \tag{10.25}$$

where $s(B_b)$ denotes a suitable smoothness metric computed over B_b [49, 50].

With the above basic technique, the watermark can be recovered in a blind way from the decrypted content only. In [51], blind decoding in the encrypted domain is enabled by compressing the encrypted LSBs using the syndrome of a random linear code. Compression maps the encrypted LSBs into a reduced number of compressed bits, leaving some unused LSBs that can be used for embedding the message bits. Let us denote by $\mathbf{v}$ the vector obtained by concatenating the k LSBs of the encrypted pixels in a block and with $\mathbf{b}$ the message to be embedded. Let us also assume that they have size M and L, respectively. The encrypted and watermarked LSBs are obtained as

$$\mathbf{v}_w = \mathbf{H}\mathbf{v}|\mathbf{b}, \tag{10.26}$$

where $\mathbf{H}$ is the $M - L \times M$ parity check matrix of a random linear code and | denotes concatenation of vectors. At the decoder, reversibility can be obtained by extracting the first $M - L$ bits of $\mathbf{v}_w$, which correspond to the syndrome $\mathbf{H}\mathbf{v}$, and choosing, among all LSB vectors $\mathbf{v}$ that generate the same syndrome, the vector that yields the best smoothness metric after decryption. It can be noted that there are 2^L candidate vectors, which can be computed by using the generator matrix of the same random code.

All the above techniques are reversible with high probability, depending on the smoothness of the content, the block size, and the choice of parameter k. Results in [51] show that an embedding rate of about 0.01 bit per pixel can be obtained when applying the technique to natural images. In order to increase the embedding rate, the image can be preprocessed before encryption using standard histogram shifting techniques so as to reserve some space for embedding [52]. However, this approach is not as flexible as the original technique, since it cannot be applied without the cooperation of the party which encrypts the data.

Although initially devised for images, watermarking in the encrypted domain can be applied to any other content as well [53]. Interesting extensions of the techniques we have described thus far, include both reversible watermarking [54] and format compliant watermarking [55] of selectively encrypted H.264/AVC video sequences.

10.6 SUMMARY

Digital watermarking has been proposed as a possible primitive of multimedia content protection systems, but its application in realistic scenarios raises several issues. In this chapter, we have illustrated some well established approaches, combining secure signal processing and watermarking, which have been proposed to solve those issues.

Asymmetric fingerprinting protocols based on secure watermark embedding at the server's side are an effective solution for solving the customer's rights problem. In this solution, independent encrypted and watermarked copies of the content can be securely distributed to each customer in such a way that only the customer has access to the actual watermarked content in the plaintext domain. Different watermarking techniques can be securely implemented by relying on homomorphic encryption. Moreover, the efficiency of encrypted domain watermarking can be greatly improved by employing suitable representation techniques that group several signal samples in a single encryption. Server side solutions can be also extended to address the requirements of decentralized distribution systems, like peer-to-peer networks. An important drawback of server side watermark embedding is that the generation of independent encrypted and watermarked copies may limit the scalability to large scale scenarios.

Client-side watermark embedding is an effective solution to the scalability problem. In client-side embedding, a unique encrypted copy of the content is broadcasted. Independent decryption keys allow each client to decrypt a slightly different copy bearing a personalized watermark. Both spread spectrum and dither modulation techniques can be applied at the client's side by relying on lookup table based encryption. Moreover, a client side distribution framework can be integrated into existing asymmetric fingerprinting protocols, avoiding the need of a dedicated trusted third party for the distribution of decryption keys.

Finally, reversible watermarking of encrypted content is an effective way of managing the redistribution of already encrypted content without affecting the integrity of sensitive data. Existing solutions allow a third party to embed a watermark in encrypted data without knowing the encryption key and without requiring the cooperation of the data owner in such a way that the watermark can be extracted from the decrypted content. In the simpler solutions, reversibility is usually achieved with high probability, provided that the content satisfies some smoothness constraints. Perfect reversibility can be achieved by preprocessing the content before encryption, at the cost of reduced flexibility.

References

[1] Erkin, Z., et al., "Protection and Retrieval of Encrypted Multimedia Content: When Cryptography Meets Signal Processing," *EURASIP Journal on Information Security*, Vol. 2007, No. 1, 2007, pp. 078943.

[2] Bianchi, T., and A. Piva, "Secure Watermarking for Multimedia Content Protection: A Review of its Benefits and Open Issues," *IEEE Signal Processing Magazine*, Vol. 30, No. 2, Mar. 2013, pp. 87–96.

[3] Lagendijk, R. L., Z. Erkin, and M. Barni, "Encrypted Signal Processing for Privacy Protection," *IEEE Signal Processing Magazine*, Vol. 30, No. 1, Jan. 2013, pp. 82–105.

[4] Qiao, L., and K. Nahrstedt, "Watermarking Schemes and Protocols for Protecting Rightful Ownership and Customer's Rights," *Journal of Visual Communication and Image Representation*, Vol. 9, No. 3, 1998, pp. 194–210.

[5] Pfitzmann, B., and M. Schunter, "Asymmetric fingerprinting," in *Advances in Cryptology — EUROCRYPT'96*, LNCS 1070, 1996, pp. 84–95.

[6] Frattolillo, F., "Watermarking Protocol for Web Context," *IEEE Transactions on Information Forensics and Security*, Vol. 2, No. 3, Sept. 2007, pp. 350–363.

[7] Barni, M., and F. Bartolini, *Watermarking Systems Engineering: Enabling Digital Assets Security and Other Applications*, Marcel Dekker, 2004.

[8] Paillier, P., "Public-Key Cryptosystems Based on Composite Degree Residuosity Classes," in *Advances in Cryptology — EUROCRYPT 1999*, No. 1592 in Lecture Notes in Computer Science, Springer Verlag, 1999, pp. 223–238.

[9] Damgård, I., and M. Jurik, "A Generalisation, a Simplification and Some Applications of Paillier's Probabilistic Public-Key System," in *4th International Workshop on Practice and Theory in Public-Key Cryptography*, LNCS 1992, 2001, pp. 119–136.

[10] Goldreich, O., *Foundations of Cryptography I*, Cambridge University Press, 2001.

[11] Brassard, G., D. Chaum, and C. Crépeau, "Minimum Disclosure Proofs of Knowledge," *J. Comput. Syst. Sci.*, Orlando, FL: Academic Press, Inc., Vol. 37, No. 2, Oct. 1988, pp. 156–189.

[12] Goldreich, O., S. Micali, and A. Wigderson, "Proofs That Yield Nothing but Their Validity or All Languages in NP Have Zero-knowledge Proof Systems," *J. ACM*, New York, NY: ACM, Vol. 38, No. 3, Jul. 1991, pp. 690–728.

[13] Memon, N., and P. Wong, "A Buyer-Seller Watermarking Protocol," *IEEE Transactions on Image Processing*, Vol. 10, No. 4, Apr. 2001, pp. 643–649.

[14] Lei, C.-L., et al., "An Efficient and Anonymous Buyer-Seller Watermarking Protocol," *IEEE Transactions on Image Processing*, Vol. 13, No. 12, Dec. 2004, pp. 1618–1626.

[15] Zhang, J., W. Kou, and K. Fan, "Secure Buyer-Seller Watermarking Protocol," *IEE Proceedings on Information Security*, Vol. 153, No. 1, Mar. 2006, pp. 15–18.

[16] Kuribayashi, M., and H. Tanaka, "Fingerprinting Protocol for Images Based on Additive Homomorphic Property," *IEEE Transactions on Image Processing*, Vol. 14, No. 12, Dec. 2005, pp. 2129–2139.

[17] Ahmed, F., et al., "A Secure Watermarking Scheme for Buyer-Seller Identification and Copyright Protection," *EURASIP Journal on Applied Signal Processing*, Vol. 2006, 2006, pp. Article ID 56904, 15 pages.

[18] Katzenbeisser, S., et al., "A Buyer-Seller Watermarking Protocol Based on Secure Embedding," *IEEE Transactions on Information Forensics and Security*, Vol. 3, No. 4, Dec 2008, pp. 783–786.

[19] Rial, A., et al., "A Provably Secure Anonymous Buyer-Seller Watermarking Protocol," *IEEE Transactions on Information Forensics and Security*, Vol. 5, No. 4, Dec. 2010, pp. 920–931.

[20] Charpentier, A., et al., "An Asymmetric Fingerprinting Scheme Based on Tardos Codes," in *Proceedings of the 13th International Conference on Information hiding*, IH'11, Berlin, Heidelberg: Springer-Verlag, 2011, pp. 43–58.

[21] Kuribayashi, M., "On the Implementation of Spread Spectrum Fingerprinting in Asymmetric Cryptographic Protocol," *EURASIP Journal on Information Security*, New York, NY: Hindawi Publishing Corp., Vol. 2010, 2010, pp. 1:1–1:11.

[22] Prins, J. P., Z. Erkin, and R. L. Lagendijk, "Anonymous Fingerprinting with Robust QIM Watermarking Techniques," *EURASIP Journal on Information Security*, Vol. 2007, Article ID 31340, 13 pages, 2007.

[23] Chen, B., and G. Wornell, "Quantization Index Modulation: a Class of Provably Good Methods for Digital Watermarking and Information Embedding," *IEEE Transactions on Information Theory*, Vol. 47, No. 4, May 2001, pp. 1423–1443.

[24] Perez-Gonzalez, F., et al., "Rational Dither Modulation: A High-Rate Data-Hiding Method Invariant to Gain Attacks," *IEEE Transactions on Signal Processing*, Vol. 53, No. 10, Oct. 2005, pp. 3960–3975.

[25] Deng, M., et al., "An Efficient Buyer-Seller Watermarking Protocol Based on Composite Signal Representation," in *Proceedings of the 11th ACM workshop on Multimedia and security*, New York, NY: ACM, 2009, pp. 9–18.

[26] Bianchi, T., A. Piva, and M. Barni, "Composite Signal Representation for Fast and Storage-Efficient Processing of Encrypted Signals," *IEEE Transactions on Information Forensics and Security*, Vol. 5, No. 1, Mar. 2010, pp. 180–187.

[27] Zheng, P., and J. Huang, "Walsh-Hadamard Transform in the Homomorphic Encrypted Domain and Its Application in Image Watermarking," in *Information Hiding*, Lecture Notes in Computer Science, Springer Berlin Heidelberg, 2013, pp. 240–254.

[28] Terelius, B., "Towards Transferable Watermarks in Buyer-Seller Watermarking Protocols," in *2013 IEEE International Workshop on Information Forensics and Security (WIFS)*, Nov. 2013, pp. 197–202.

[29] Qureshi, A., D. Megías, and H. Rifá-Pous, "Framework for Preserving Security and Privacy in Peer-to-Peer Content Distribution Systems," *Expert Systems with Applications*, Vol. 42, No. 3, 2015, pp. 1391–1408.

[30] Emmanuel, S., and M. Kankanhalli, "Copyright Protection for MPEG-2 Compressed Broadcast Video," in *IEEE International Conference on Multimedia and Expo (ICME 2001)*, 2001, pp. 206–209.

[31] Crowcroft, J., C. Perkins, and I. Brown, "A Method and Apparatus for Generating Multiple Watermarked Copies of an Information Signal," WO Patent No. 00/56059, 2000.

[32] Parviainen, R., and P. Parnes, "Large Scale Distributed Watermarking of Multicast Media Through Encryption," in *Proceedings of the International Federation for Information Processing, Communications and Multimedia Security Joint Working Conference IFIP TC6 and TC11*, 2001, pp. 149–158.

[33] Kundur, D., "Video Fingerprinting and Encryption Principles for Digital Rights Management," *Proceedings of the IEEE*, Vol. 92, No. 6, June 2004, pp. 918–932.

[34] Lemma, A., et al., "Secure Watermark Embedding through Partial Encryption," in *International Workshop on Digital Watermarking (IWDW)*, Vol. 4283 of *Springer Lecture Notes in Computer Science*, 2006, pp. 433–445.

[35] Anderson, R. J., and C. Manifavas, "Chameleon—A New Kind of Stream Cipher," in *Proceedings of the 4th International Workshop on Fast Software Encryption (FSE'97)*, London: Springer-Verlag, 1997, pp. 107–113.

[36] Celik, M., et al., "Look-up Table based Secure Client-Side Embedding for Spread-Spectrum Watermarks," *IEEE Transactions on Information Forensics and Security*, Vol. 3, No. 3, Sept. 2008, pp. 475–487.

[37] Jiang, J.-J., and C.-M. Pun, "Secure Client-Side Digital Watermarking Using Optimal Key Selection," in *Communication and Networking*, Vol. 266 of *Communications in Computer and Information Science*, Berlin, Heidelberg: Springer, pp. 162–168, 2011.

[38] Pun, C.-M., and J.-J. Jiang, "Secure Client-Side LUT-Based Audio Watermarking Using Adaptive Embedding Strength," *Journal of Convergence Information Technology*, Vol. 8, No. 11, 2013, pp. 696–706.

[39] Sun, J.-H., Y.-H. Lin, and J.-L. Wu, "Secure Client Side Watermarking with Limited Key Size," in *MultiMedia Modeling*, Vol. 8935 of *Lecture Notes in Computer Science*, Springer International Publishing, pp. 13–24, 2015.

[40] Lin, C.-Y., et al., "Joint Fingerprinting and Decryption With Noise-Resistant for Vector Quantization Images," *Signal Processing*, Vol. 92, No. 9, Sept. 2012, pp. 2159–2171.

[41] Thanh, T., and M. Iwakiri, "A proposal of Digital Rights Management Based on Incomplete Cryptography Using Invariant Huffman Code Length Feature," *Multimedia Systems*, Berlin, Heidelberg: Springer, Vol. 20, No. 2, Mar. 2014, pp. 127–142.

[42] Katzenbeisser, S., et al., "Combining Tardos Fingerprinting Codes and Fingercasting," in *Information Hiding*, Vol. 4567 of *Lecture Notes in Computer Science*, Springer Berlin / Heidelberg, pp. 294–310, 2007.

[43] Venkatesan, R., et al., "Robust Image Hashing," in *Proceedings of the IEEE Internationak Conference on Image Processing (ICIP'00)*, Vol. 3, Vancouver, BC, Canada, Sept. 2000, pp. 664–666.

[44] Swaminathan, A., M. Yinian, and M. Wu, "Robust and Secure Image Hashing," *IEEE Transactions on Information Forensics and Security*, Vol. 1, No. 2, June 2006, pp. 215–230.

[45] Piva, A., T. Bianchi, and A. De Rosa, "Secure Client-Side ST-DM Watermark Embedding," *IEEE Transactions on Information Forensics and Security*, Vol. 5, No. 1, Mar. 2010, pp. 13–26.

[46] Katzenbeisser, S., et al., "A Buyer–Seller Watermarking Protocol Based on Secure Embedding," *IEEE Transactions on Information Forensics and Security*, Vol. 3, No. 4, Dec. 2008, pp. 783–786.

[47] Poh, G., and K. Martin, "An Efficient Buyer-Seller Watermarking Protocol Based on Chameleon Encryption," in *Digital Watermarking*, Vol. 5450 of *Lecture Notes in Computer Science*, Berlin, Heidelberg: Springer, pp. 433–447, 2009.

[48] Bianchi, T., and A. Piva, "TTP-Free Asymmetric Fingerprinting Based on Client Side Embedding," *IEEE Transactions on Information Forensics and Security*, Vol. 9, No. 10, Oct. 2014, pp. 1557–1568.

[49] Zhang, X., "Reversible Data Hiding in Encrypted Image," *IEEE Signal Processing Letters*, Vol. 18, No. 4, Apr. 2011, pp. 255–258.

[50] Hong, W., T.-S. Chen, and H.-Y. Wu, "An Improved Reversible Data Hiding in Encrypted Images Using Side Match," *IEEE Signal Processing Letters*, Vol. 19, No. 4, Apr. 2012, pp. 199–202.

[51] Zhang, X., "Separable Reversible Data Hiding in Encrypted Image," *IEEE Transactions on Information Forensics and Security*, Vol. 7, No. 2, Apr. 2012, pp. 826–832.

[52] Ma, K., et al., "Reversible Data Hiding in Encrypted Images by Reserving Room Before Encryption," *IEEE Transactions on Information Forensics and Security*, Vol. 8, No. 3, Mar. 2013, pp. 553–562.

[53] Karim, M. S. A., and K.-S. Wong, "Universal Data Embedding in Encrypted Domain," *Signal Processing*, Vol. 94, Jan. 2014, pp. 174–182.

[54] Xu, D., and R. Wang, "Efficient Reversible Data Hiding in Encrypted H.264/AVC Videos," *Journal of Electronic Imaging*, Vol. 23, No. 5, Oct. 2014, pp. 053022.

[55] Xu, D., R. Wang, and Y. Shi, "Data Hiding in Encrypted H.264/AVC Video Streams by Codeword Substitution," *IEEE Transactions on Information Forensics and Security*, Vol. 9, No. 4, Apr. 2014, pp. 596–606.

About the Authors

Stefan Katzenbeisser is a full professor at Technische Universität Darmstadt, where he heads the Security Engineering Group in the Department of Computer Science. His main research interests include information hiding, applied cryptography, and privacy. Before joining TU Darmstadt, he worked as senior scientist at Philips Research on watermarking and Digital Rights Management.

Stefan graduated from the Vienna University of Technology in 2001 and obtained a Doctorate degree in 2004.

Fabien Petitcolas is research manager at Vasco Data Security, where he's contributing to grow and lead a newly established research center. Before joining Vasco, Fabien spent fifteen years at Microsoft where he took on various roles. Starting as a security researcher at Microsoft Research, he later became head of Microsoft Research's Intellectual Capital Development programs, before becoming Director for Innovation at Microsoft Europe, supporting the company's presence in EU policy and political dialogue for and around innovation and R&D.

Fabien graduated in 1996 from École Centrale, Lyon. He then studied at the University of Cambridge under the guidance of Professor Ross Anderson FRS FREng for a doctorate, which was partly funded by the Intel Corporation and was awarded in 1999 when he joined Microsoft Research.

Index

Recent Titles in the Artech House Computer Security Series

Rolf Oppliger, Series Editor